The Welfare State in Post-Industrial Society

Jason Powell · Jon (Joe) Hendricks

The Welfare State in Post-Industrial Society

A Global Perspective

 Springer

Jason Powell
School of Sociology & Social Policy
University of Liverpool
Bedford Street South, Liverpool
Eleanor Rathbone Bldg.
United Kingdom L69 7ZA
j.l.powell@liv.ac.uk

Jon (Joe) Hendricks
Oregon State University
Corvallis OR 97331-2302
USA
hendricj@onid.orst.edu

ISBN 978-1-4419-0065-4   e-ISBN 978-1-4419-0066-1
DOI 10.1007/978-1-4419-0066-1
Springer Dordrecht Heidelberg London New York

Library of Congress Control Number: 2009928458

Printed on acid-free paper

Springer is part of Springer Science+Business Media (www.springer.com)

Contents

Contributors

Kylie Agllias School of Social Work, University of Newcastle, New South Wales, Australia

Anneli Anttonen Department of Social Research, University of Tampere, Tampere, Finland

Yitzhak Berman European Center for Social Welfare Policy and Research, Vienna

Ingo Bode Institute for social policy and the organisation of social services, Department of Social Work, University of Kassel, Germany

Patricia M. Daenzer Department of Social Work, McMaster University, Hamilton, Ontario. Canada

Alex Dumas Faculty of Health Sciences, University of Ottawa, Ontario, Canada

Robin Gauld Department of Preventive and Social Medicine, University of Otago, Dunedin, New Zealand

Mel Gray Institute of Social Wellbeing, University of Newcastle, New South Wales, Australia

Anton Hemerijck (Eramus) Dean Faculty of Social Sciences, Free University, Amsterdam, Netherlands

Jon (Joe) Hendricks Office of Provost, Oregon State University, Oregon, USA

Hyunsook Yoon Department of Social Welfare, Hallym University, South Korea

Joseph Katan School of Social Work, Tel-Aviv University, Tel-Aviv, Israel

Teppo Kröger Department of Social Sciences and Philosophy, University of Jyväskylä, Jyväskylä, Finland

Cynthia Leedham Department of Sociology, University of Kentucky, Kentucky, USA

Antoinette Lombard School of Social Work, University of Pretoria, Pretoria, South Africa

Ariela Lowenstein Center for Research & Study of Aging, Faculty of Welfare & Health Sciences, The University of Haifa, Haifa, Israel

David Phillips Department of Sociological Studies, University of Sheffield, UK

Chris Phillipson Centre for Social Gerontology, Keele University, Keele, Staffordshire, UK

Jason L. Powell School of Sociology and Social Policy, University of Liverpool, Liverpool, UK

Tim Owen Centre for Criminology and Criminal Justice, University of Central Lancashire, Preston, UK

Michael Reisch School of Social Work, University of Maryland, Baltimore, MD, USA

Ryan Sheppard Faculty of Sociology, St Olaf College, University of Thailand, Thailand

Jorma Sipilä Department of Social Work Research, University of Tampere (until July 31, 2009); Institute for social research, University of Tampere, Tampere, Finland (from August 1, 2009)

Bryan S. Turner Department of Sociology, Wellesley College, Wellesley, MA, USA

A Wagner The New School for Management and Urban Policy, New York City, USA

Part I
Rethinking Social Welfare
in a Post-industrial World

Chapter 1
The Welfare State in Post-industrial Society: The Lay of the Land

Jon (Joe) Hendricks and Jason L. Powell

Introduction

To say that the world is a far different place than it was just a few short decades ago sounds a trifle banal. Has that not been the case throughout history? Well, yes, this is indeed true, but it is our contention that the dynamics of change underwent a qualitative transformation in the latter half of the twentieth century. As we move into what can be called the global century, many aspects of life are changing, and post-industrial shifts are unparalleled by virtue of the interconnectedness that brings together the far corners of the globe. New technologies, new economic relationships, new social processes, and new political processes are all characteristics of globalization (Hudson & Lowe, 2004: 22). As the world has contracted, people's quality of life has changed regardless of where they live. In fact, the propagation of free market mind-sets in emerging economies has created collective network connections with considerable good but pervasive inequalities as well. A principal goal of this volume is to explicate how these changes are of historical scale, how they are part of what post-industrial welfare is all about, and how they play out in terms of risks and inequalities shaping human experience.

The Shape of Well-Being and Inequality

On the upside, life expectancy, health status, and per capita income are at an all-time high and many feudal practices have been relegated to the past. On the downside, vast numbers of people struggle with poverty and significant pockets of poverty portend more than lack of income. Those living on the bottom of the socioeconomic ladder labor under the burden of avoidable, lifestyle diseases, hunger and related maladies, not to mention myriad social risks. Those on the upper reaches of the same ladder garner disproportionate shares of the

J. Hendricks (⊠)
Office of Provost, Oregon State University, Oregon, USA

J. Powell, J. Hendricks, *The Welfare State in Post-Industrial Society*,
DOI 10.1007/978-1-4419-0066-1_1, © Springer Science+Business Media, LLC 2009

resources and are able to support comfortable lifestyles. Around the globe, there are bona fide challenges facing nation-states as they attempt to adapt to the impact of modifications in morbidity, mortality, and need gradients among diverse segments of their populations. In the face of rapid demographic trans-formations resulting in fewer casualties from acute diseases, aging populations, and tumultuous economies, there are widening disparities between the "haves" and the "have-nots" and considerable quality-of-life inequalities within and between populations. In developing countries, China being one of the most striking cases in point – but with parallels in a number of other developing countries – the difference in the per capita income of the urban and rural people is at least a factor of three, with virtually no top quartile wage earners residing in rural areas. Not surprisingly, there is a tangible rural to urban migration for economic gain, thereby creating even greater disparities, as those left behind barely eke out subsistence livings, and then too only under the most favorable circumstances.

It is impossible to overstate the risks of planetary poverty. The evening news routinely offers warnings before showing footage of wide-eyed and emaciated children in relocation camps made necessary by man-made or natural disasters. As extreme as that example may seem, it is also just the tip of the iceberg, as more than 2.5 billion of the planet's population live on less than US $2 a day and a billion-plus have less than US $1 daily. As might be apparent, in this day and age, poverty creates conditions in which rationality is redefined, nation-states struggle to control circumstances, not to mention criminality, low birth weights are ubiquitous, ill-health a fact of life, illiteracy rampant, malnutrition commonplace, environmental degradation seen as the cost of doing business, and notions of social justice are brought face-to-face with priorities said to have greater standing (Beck, 1999). Focusing on the extent of the disparities just for a moment: there is not only asymmetry but real immiseration as well – only about 5 percent of the world's income is earned by the poorest 40 percent of its people.

The chasm between the rich and the poor is becoming even wider. According to the 12th Annual World Wealth Report (2008), the wealth of people around the world with more than US $1 million in assets grew faster in 2007 than the world's economy. The world's economy exhibited a 5 percent gain in 2007 compared with a growth rate of over 9 percent among those with at least US $1 million in assets. Furthermore, the average wealth of these high net worth individuals (HNWIs) climbed to over US $4 million, exclusive of their residence. Interestingly, the greatest growth among HNWIs occurred in Eastern Europe, Latin America, and the Middle East, led by Brazil, Russia, India, and China. When the "mass affluent" population (those with less than US $1 million but with substantial assets nonetheless) is added to the picture, the result is that the richest 20 percent of the world's population controls more than 75 percent of its wealth. In the past few decades, there have been some astonishing gains among a relatively small percentage of the world's population (approximately 10 million out of 6.7 billion people can be classified as HNWIs) who are tapped into robust gains and wealth generation strategies (Annual World Wealth Report, 2008). As should be apparent, the ascendancy of those forces concentrating high net worth wealth and capital accumulation among a narrow upper crust is also capable of producing abject poverty among other segments of the population (Arias & Logan, 2002: 197; Jessop, 2002). While the richest 1 percent of wealthy outliers are benefiting from speculation and the deregulation of commerce and free trade, those on the other end of the economic ladder are gaining little, if at all, as the wealth gap widens.

Some estimates conservatively place the gap between the richest and poorest nations at an all time high of more than 50 to 1 (Clark, 2007). Even with the stalling of mature economies, the gulf between the most advantaged and the most disadvantaged in developed countries is no less dramatic; factor in the impact of gender, ethnicity, or other social impediments and the complexity intensifies as formidable inequalities shape well-being. The disparities play out in a number of ways, extending well beyond vital income differentials to quality of life issues, education, structured dependencies, or social exclusions resulting from policy decisions (Townsend, 2007). Navarro (2007) and others add their voice to Townsend's assertion by noting that escalating differentials can be attributed in no small part to interventionist strategies adopted and endorsed by national governments. Not surprisingly, as a consequence, the richest segments of the population having far greater assets and control over their lives, they feel they have more in common with their counterparts in other regions than they do with their less affluent opposite number in their own regions (Hoogvelt, 1997). These trends are becoming increasingly vivid, and no government is evading the prospect of having to reshuffle what they provide to their citizens.

Globalization and Jurisdiction

The proliferation of adjuvant ideologies evolving out of the marketplace of ideas associated with burgeoning free-market economies along with an accompanying diffusion of instrumental rationality, standardization, commoditization, or secularism have become embedded in our thinking, challenging all other relational metrics of daily life. In the process, modes of interaction and standards of assessing relational status or personal worth are recast. In both developed and emerging economies, the nature of work and the meaning of careers are also undergoing major reformulations. There is a global softening of labor markets linked to downsizing of local employment opportunities, redundancies, a spate of subcontracting arrangements, and an economic volatility abetted by technological innovations that chip away at employment security, wage, or benefit packages bringing a degree of economic and existential uncertainty to a greater number of people. Of course, such changes are not distributed evenly across all forms of employment, further exacerbating inequalities.

It should also be stressed that adversity does not appear to strike women and men equally – and it is certainly reasonable to say that disadvantage begets disadvantage when downturns occur. Women are disproportionately among the most disadvantaged, and, with age, even greater hardships accrue to them. Adding to the intricacies of these unparalleled changes is the velocity with which they are taking place and the fact that they are accompanied by a deepening division between those whose principal pursuits are in subsistence or service sector markets and their counterparts who are primarily involved in large-scale export, international sectors, or equity markets. Together these forces are bringing about a profound imbalance within and between populations as one group shares the generation of wealth while the other becomes increasingly dependent and is being subordinated to decisions made in the other sector, by a cartel half a world away (Bauman, 1998).

Without suggesting or trying to make it sound as though national governments or their policies are anything less than all-encompassing in their reach, it is also the case that national governments no longer set their own course independently of economic currents sweeping around the globe, felt in every country and affecting virtually every policy a government might implement. This is not to say that states are mere minions of transnational interests, but it is no longer the case that the nation-state sovereignty can be taken-for-granted in the policy realm. Nor is it necessarily the case that state policies are as all-powerful as they once were in shaping daily life (Dallmayer, 2005; Fraser, 2005). As Cerny and Evans (2004) so cogently assert, the welfare state of the last century has been replaced by a competitive state of the twenty-first century, always mindful of its global positioning (see also, Hudson & Lowe, 2004). Foucault (1978) coined the phrase "nonsovereign power" when he was discussing issues of bodily control. By drawing a nice analogy, Yapa (2002: 15) proposes that a parallel concept may provide insights into the vagaries of post-industrial public-sector decision-making. To make sense of domestic versus international priorities and their effect on daily life, scholars would do well to come to terms with the notion of "nonsovereign power," as it applies to social justice, autonomy, monetary policies and capital mobility, and other forms of extra-national pressures emending local policies. We would assert that, to date, there has been a real lag between transnational developments and the way analysts think of social policies. Appadurai (2002) attributes the stumbling blocks in conceptualization to " . . . the disjunctures between various vectors characterizing this world-in-motion that produce fundamental problems of livelihood, equity, suffering, justice, and governance" (Appadurai, 2002: 6). In his characterization, proximate social issues have causes that are hardly local and call for nonparochial perspectives if they are to be addressed.

As Giddens maintains, one of the most significant impacts of globalization is that it has brought an "intensification of worldwide social relations which link distant localities in such a way that local happenings are shaped by events occurring many miles away and vice versa" (Giddens, 1990: 64). As a consequence, few governments are eager to make decisions separately from their reliance on global enterprise; it is as though they are in a situation of shared sovereignty, having to negotiate between domestic, international, corporatist, and transnational interests (Esping-Andersen, 1990; Hill, 2006; Kennett, 2001; Navarro, 2007). NGOs such as the World Bank and the International Monetary Fund have also become architectural partners in local policy deliberations by sanctioning preferred welfare policies as a condition of their support of monetization (Deacon et al., 1997; Dembele, 2007; Hart, 2002). Even so, nation-states nonetheless serve important administrative functions in a world dominated by transnational corporate interests, and it is unlikely that governmental responsibilities are either going to be usurped or allowed to wither in light of their functionality (Hill, 2006; Navarro, 2007). It is not too far-fetched to say that certain transnational interests see themselves as having universal jurisdiction, assertions of state autonomy notwithstanding.

With the spreading of these transformations has come a reshuffling of local priorities, with governmental emoluments directed or redirected to areas defined as having the greatest public importance and bringing the greatest returns. Of course, the realities behind that assertion deserve close scrutiny, as the policy process is unquestionably political and the state must mediate rival claims, as it serves as the principal mechanism by which revenues are collected and resources distributed. Meanwhile, social entitlements, expenditures, and daily experiences for people who may not fully grasp the *raison d'être* behind their situations reflect these same priorities. Hill (2006) suggests that social policy regimes are regularly structured to be consistent with other forms of social stratification within a country. To the extent there is a convergence in social welfare policies around the globe, it might not be mere coincidence that social stratification and social class divisions are growing more pronounced in the face of globalization. In the light of global economic flows, the salience and permeability of national borders, whether in Europe, the western hemisphere, or in the east, are a different matter than they were even half a century ago (Kearney, 1995).

In terms of both economics and domestic social policies, the impact of international economic relations has recontoured the landscape, so to speak, all the way to the regionalization and appropriation of economic relations. What were once bold lines of demarcation are now dotted lines more suggestive of administrative spheres than jingoistic borders. In the global century, deregulated markets are tightly integrated with political and social transformations, affecting local circumstances and communality (Geertz, 1973; Hendricks, 2005). All in all, the globalizing influences of the early twenty-first century are producing a distinctive era in social history linked to the emergence of transnational actors as well as economics and technologies that are helping fuel the shifts. Global economic change portends more than alterations in per capita income, the nature of financial products and currency markets, or the rapid circulation of goods, communication, or technologies, it is precursor to broad cultural and political shifts that challenge precontact arrangements, notions of social justice and solidarity as well as local interaction patterns. In the postmodern world, globalization is creating interlocking dependencies linked to the ways in which priorities are ordained by transnational interests. As Chen and

Turner (2006) point out in a discussion focused on the welfare of the elderly but equally applicable to all social welfare, the accrual of public benefits reflects the invisible hand of market forces, the invisible handshake of tradition, and the invisible foot of political decisions. Despite avowals about the secularity of modern life, economic thinking, what might be termed spreadsheet logic, is accorded near theological status, its canons seen as universally applicable and providing appropriate precepts for adjudicating what is considered fair and just. These tendencies are abetted by what is sometimes called the cyber infrastructure, or more simply, informatics, reinforcing these shifts and creating a digital divide, separating those on either edge of the diffusion of innovations. Of course, there is more to this technological transformation than the appearance of new ways to communicate, it has also paved the way to a post-Fordist formulation that Castells (2000) labels network capitalism.

Globalization and the Social Contract

We do not mean to imply that globalization comes as a unified package; it is, nonetheless, true that major changes have resulted from an ability to move capital around as summarily as desired to gain leverage, possibly destabilizing local financial and labor markets in the process. Real questions have emerged about the autonomy of nation-states and the balancing of altruistic social expenditure with economic participation on the world stage. The tensions between social protection and global connection are contributing to what can aptly be called "social deficits," in which people are left to fend for themselves to the extent they are able. In the face of inflation and other economic adversities, slashing social spending is routinely offered as a fitting resolution preferable to raising taxes for wealthy individuals or corporations (Mishra, 1999). The global span of information technologies and the advent of the global compass held by transnational corporations means that they are able to shift extraction, manu-facturing, fabrication, and many service functions to whatever locale offers the most favorable economic returns, including tax structures. These and other consequences of globalization are fraught with new risks and ambiguities in daily experience and in the way matters of worth are defined along with the many positive aspects that are undeniably part of the process associated with privatization.

In a synopsis of a few of the more evident effects of globalization, Navarro (2007) points to the privatization of services, public assets, and other public provisions in asymmetrical fashion; deregulation of labor and currency markets as well as other forms of commerce; free trade; escalation of an accompanying anti-interventionist rhetoric; and encouragement of individualism and consu-merism. A number of commentators have noted that a corollary of globaliza-tion results in an unprecedented pattern of social risk. As Townsend (2007) so elegantly points out, globalization of the marketplace is changing the face of dependency. It is as though the configuration of risks has shifted from settling on just those poor, down and out individuals living along society's margins to those derailed by restructuring of labor markets, the dramatic spread of employment in service sector jobs, shifts in the types of career patterns that so characterized the twentieth century, and the role of informatics affecting employability of middle-class workers.

These risks are not grounded merely in the absence of resources, but in an absence of personal autonomy and by people's position relative to others. Add to these factors, the fact that as they wrestle with the issues, national and local governments are assailed from multiple fronts; pressed by transnational interests to provide open trade liberalization for private enterprises; and pressed by the growing need for social protection and labor policies to sustain the working populace and those whose lives have fallen through the proverbial social safety net. Evermore inclusive protections call for targeted expenditures at exactly the time when expenditures are hemmed in by capacity to levy taxes of any type, but especially, progressive taxes and by powerful interested constituencies. The neoliberal globalizing drive has disenfranchised workers and their representatives in ways that have eroded their ability to bargain for benefits. Many commentators have noted that governments have generally adopted a laissez faire stance when for one reason or another they have chosen not to intervene in the disempowerment of the citizenry (Navarro, 2007).

As a facet of a much broader movement toward privatization, governmental social services are adopting a market-based management model and relying on nongovernmental organizations (NGOs) to take up the slack. There is a wide array of subtypes and expenditure patterns associated with every form, but an underlying logic in nearly all instances is a push toward commodification or cost-effectiveness of the programs (couched in terms of return on investment measured by market-driven stipulations), in contrast to their ability to genuinely affect lives. Policy recipients not likely to provide economic returns on governmental investments in them tend to be defined as burdensome charity cases. As they might say in China, there are extensive changes afoot, all with Chinese characteristics – meaning whatever changes may come will be adapted to local contextual factors reflecting long-standing norms, values, religions, policies, existing social metrics, and institutionalized arrangements even as they embody overtones imposed by international priorities (Dallmayer, 2005; Fraser, 2005). Unraveling the relative importance of domestic arrangements and transnational influences can be a tricky task, to say the least. It involves both an in-depth grasp of domestic issues and an international perspective, an awareness of transnational forces impinging on local decisions and sophisticated methodological and theoretical frameworks.

The commodification of social services, as it is sometimes called, is abetted by a transfer of issues of citizenship to a forum which is no longer native in its scope but transnational, marked by intergovernmental structures, multinational corporate influence, and population changes (Ascoli & Ranci, 2002; Phillipson, 2006: 202). There is another layer of complexity added by a worldwide tendency to view a number of social issues through medical lens, and the insecurities experienced by the citizenry in general are without parallel in world history. What might be described as apodictic, self-evident truths of tradition tend to lose their currency and help demarcate generational and participatory categories from one another.

In the face of an unswerving drive to be players on the world's stage, enhance market share, and survive economic riptides, nation-states must balance the demands of competing claimants – leaving them with fewer options, but to make hard choices. Not only do they have to adjudicate where to put scarce resources and which groups deserve protection or support, but few actions are indemnified against the next economic shortfall – meaning they will have to review their priorities anew each time the economic tides turn. It has always been true that, in times of plenty, making promises about solutions to societal woes is an easy pledge to make; during times of scarcity it is a different story, and keeping even the best intentioned promises oftentimes creates real conflicts. Societal-level redefinitions of what is fair and just are a common means to solutions that do not always do well for citizens in need of assistance, under-mining personal sense of security and identity as well as social solidarity.

An illustration of a macro-level problem may be helpful for thinking about the type of quandary involved. As nation-states undergo economic development via participation in global commerce, per capita incomes generally increase, never mind for the moment internal disparities, life expectancies increase, and demands for health care mount. Continued changes and desires to remain viable in a global economy mean a country will face enduring challenges in providing social safety nets, medical interventions, or financing health care protections. To focus on just the health care issue for a moment: despite subsidized provisions for indigent citizens, most health care coverage around the world is linked to employment and economic productivity (workfare), and as employment is desta-bilized, so, too, is health care. Needless to say, employment-based systems are costly, leading to cost shifting, which also serves to grant license to employers to cut jobs and move production around to minimize the expense of doing business. For those not covered by employment-based plans, subsidized coverage is often-times available but financed by taxes and premiums or by government mandated insurance groups saddled with high expectations and expenditures but social policies supportive of indigent care for those not involved in economically productive activities are often singled out as a cost sink and are among the first issues put on cost-cutting agenda (Jessop, 2002).

To comprehend the underpinning of certain forms of inequalities, it is also important to examine some of the transformations that are altering people's lives. One postmodernist reality of the twenty-first century is the existence of a digital divide between those who have always known how to navigate in key-stroke technologies and those "ancients" who learned it later or not at all. Those who are comfortable with the technology have the world at their finger tips and no longer depend on local relationships or role models for solace or validation. The result is an indisputable social segmentation. Whatever norms of reciprocity had existed before are likely to falter and fray under the impact of interdicting worldviews, in which the deep grammar of sociability is no longer meaningful to those versed in the newer modes of activity. At the same time, there is an erosion of like-minded communities with shared representations cutting across society at large and fostering social solidarity. Instead, they are replaced by segmented, smaller communities and a blurring of ways of knowing the world. Beck et al. (2003:6) characterize the effects of technological innovation as "revolution through side effects" and suggest that a deep-seeded societal segmentation is a likely upshot and should not be surprising. Addressing comparable consequences, Dasgupta (2006: 159) phrased it succinctly: "globalization has thus created an identity crisis, since many are neither local nor global and are overloaded with changing stimuli ... resulting in a 'don't care' attitude, commercial interactions among family members, a rise of individualism and a disequilibrium ...."

Transnational private enterprises cannot be ignored, as they are altering the landscape but not doing so single-handedly. It is fair to say there are both private and semipublic but non-governmental organizations (NGOs) involved. Multilateral NGOs are playing an especially crucial role and certainly a role that is influencing developing countries as they sort out their welfare regimes. For example, since the issuance of the Berg Report in 1981, the World Bank and the International Monetary Fund (IMF) have become major players on the world's stage oftentimes stipulating structural adjustments and preferred policies nation-states should adopt as a condition of support and to attract direct capital investments or other fiscal cooperation, including monetization. One illustration is that the World Bank began urging diminutions in pay-as-you-go (PAYG) pension provisions in favor of means-tested pension and private provisions in the mid-1990s. The World Bank and the IMF have been staunch advocates for over three decades for broadly defined market-led welfare policies as a preferred alternative to un- or under-funded public welfare (Dembele, 2007; Wade, 2007). Encapsulating both the criticisms and the confluence of forces fueling such a movement, McMichael (2000) asserts that the drive for economic integration pays little attention to nation-building, national interests, or public sector regulatory control.

Corollaries of Public Policy

Although there is a remarkable absence of consensus, social welfare is customarily taken to mean statutory governmental intervention designed to provide supportive services and resources to those in need. Right away one question that has to be addressed revolves around eligibility requirements and stipulations of entitlement. Issues such as gender are very much a part of the state as are discussions on family responsibilities and welfare policies. At the risk of extreme simplification, whether women are eligible for social benefits and services in their own rights or as members of a male breadwinner family is an abiding question whenever welfare regimes are examined. By the same token, gender ideologies are very much an aspect of poverty, labor markets, and other market experiences, or the myriad inequalities that cut across the life course and through virtually every facet of experience (Calasanti, 2001; Hatch, 2000; Sainsbury, 1994, 1996).

These forces also affect lives in even more subtle ways beyond the realm of income, access, or protection. Just one case in point out of scores of similar situations should suffice to illustrate our contention. It is fair to say that institutional arrangements and structural realignments have altered time and temporality, as they have altered space and other normative aspects of life. Containing our focus to the issues discussed thus far: the ebb and flow of transnational capital markets operate round the clock and penetrate virtually every aspect of governmental policy and, accordingly, daily life. Analysts generally concur that there has been a compression of time in many corners of the world, as they are pulled into global market flows (Hendricks, 2008; Steger, 1997). As should be fairly obvious, any attenuation of earlier subjective temporal reckoning requires recalibration and reintegration, as new templates are incorporated into mental models of what life is about. Analysts have asserted that globalization brings a dilation, fragmentation, and acceleration of the sense of time unsettling many (Lestienne, 2000). But, as with so many other aspects of globalization, the results do not settle on all people in equal fashion. For those who live along the margins of such change, feelings of being in control and the clarity of their proleptic future may be challenged, as the tempo, pace, and types of engagements in their lives are restructured. Considered in a broader sense, temporal reorganization is also impacting event timing and thereby the shape of life, views of dependency, and definitions of personal worth. As normative perspectives on the shape of life are reformulated and/or personal functionality wanes, the chances increase that some subgroups within the population will lose track of their referential guidelines (Hendricks, 2008).

In her insightful analysis of German pension provisions, Scheiwe (1994) brings a fresh perspective to discussion a fresh perspective of how institutionalized welfare rules also structure temporality. She broadens the focus considerably in her examination of time politics and gendered times in legislation that grants standing to many market-related definitions of time and discounts others associated most frequently with women's roles outside the market or which result from discontinuous market-related activities deemed to be below time thresholds written into public welfare provisions. The gendered differentials in recognizing life's events, their timing, and related circumstances serve to create essential inequalities in financial and other types of well-being. Time and temporality, sense of the future, and eligibility for entitlements impose structure on lives in ways that may not have been intended but are highly salient, nonetheless.

Making Sense of Welfare Policies

For the most part, a definition derived from the legendary Beveridge Report published in the midst of World War II in Britain has been utilized to identify and operationalize major features of the welfare state (Finer, 1999). Yet that formulation begs the question of whether that world and those circumstances still exist and how they may have been modified by post-industrial or globalizing influences. We would assert that a definition of social welfare must extend beyond questions of delivery to include its financing and function. Almost certainly the provision of nongovernmental services through NGOs or volunteer agencies and programs should be included as well. Ambiguities notwithstanding, it is hardly surprising that scholars looking at social welfare in a comparative focus have noted that there is a fairly direct correlation between national prosperity and percentage of GDP directed at supportive programs (Hill, 2006). However, within groups of nations (such as OECD, G-7, G-8, or G-77 countries), there are differences based on governmental types or economic developments, and, we assert, in terms of underlying principles of moral economy that have shaped the formulation of welfare, whether that be public or private. Although the parameters of social welfare may at first appear obvious, there is by no means consensus on its measure or analysis.

Scholars studying social policies and social welfare have expended considerable energy to outline typologies and methodologies for comparative analysis across nation-states. Mabbett and Bolderson (1999) offer an insightful précis of the issues involved and problems encountered in setting forth what "data" should be compared. As they ask: just what governmental or nongovernmental programs should be included in the data? or the purpose of comparison must each country have comparable programs? Do only formal provisions count, or do informal familial, communal, or religion-based care form part of the calculation? And lest it be overlooked, there is the question of whether welfare is confined to what is generally called charitable support or are other tax exemptions and provisions to be included? Undoubtedly, there are many other forms of support as well, and depending on cultural practices, there may be variations of support available in some places that are far from normative elsewhere.

Despite quandaries of operationalization, comparative analyses have become quite methodologically sophisticated in an effort to examine particulars, convergences, or divergences characterizing diverse economies and political systems. In the end, the question is: what do such analyses contribute to an understanding of current or emergent welfare systems (Mabbett & Bolderson, 1999:43)? Case studies are oftentimes offered as alternatives to broad-based comparative approaches, yet in spite of the richness of their in-depth insights, it is harder to draw generalizations that might provide templates for comparison. Here we hasten to add that, to date, relatively few examinations of the welfare state in the twenty-first century have taken into account emergent global currents, opting instead to look at nationalistic patterns with an overlay of either convergence or divergence among them. There is no discounting these later analyses, as they have yielded great insights frequently couched in terms of social rights espoused by the types of welfare regimes characterizing various countries (Esping-Andersen, 1990, 2002; Hill, 2006).

Gaining Perspective

As a way to stimulate discussion on social welfare under the aegis of a new century, this volume takes a bit of a unique tact both in terms of methodologies and conceptualizations. The contributors are primarily concerned with the human impact of what is often termed neoliberal globalization. As an ideological or motivating principle, neoliberal globalization emphasizes the spread of capital markets without undue impediments imposed by national borders, privatization of public policies previously thought to be the purview of national governments, deregulation of both labor and financial affairs to spur economic growth, fostering a worldwide economy operating quasi-independently of national governments (Navarro, 2007). As noted above, this is not to say that the state may not formulate welfare policies, but to assert that these policies are synchronized with broader goals of market-based international positions. Our intention is to survey the human impact of these changes. Specifically, this volume provides an overview of welfare policies in the context of a global milieu and provides interpretative scaffolding for making sense of how they are changing in the twenty-first century. Looked at serially or in isolation, recent changes have created new vulnerabilities as new priorities have emerged. We assert that these shifts have altered the definitions of citizenship, social protection, and notions of what is fair and just.

Cross-cultural comparisons are extraordinarily valuable in helping layout causal connections and for double-checking inferences. For example, the Organization for Economic Co-operation and Development (OECD) has a reliable cross-national comparative database of indicators of social policy expenditures in 30 member nations and their state-sponsored social welfare provisions, entitled Social Expenditures (SocX), in the period 1980–2003. It covers public expenditures for typical forms of welfare, including old age, survivors, incapacity-related benefits, health, family, active labor market programs, unemployment, housing, and other social policy areas (education excepted). Shalev (2007) points out that if health and pension benefits are combined as a share of GDP, countries like Sweden rank at the top by devoting some 14 percent of its GDP to health and pension protections. Data for the period 1980–2001, the latest available on the OCED web site, suggests that Germany expends about 8 percent and the United States and Japan about 4 percent. Overall, however, the English-speaking countries are among the most conservative spenders for health and old-age provisions, while Japan is a high spender when all provisions are considered.

In the chapters to follow it is our hope that in the aggregate the chapters cut across what Hudson and Lowe (2004) term the micro-, meso-, and macro-level examinations of social welfare. Still, there is the need to provide a comparative framework regardless of particular foci. Once we identified probable contributors to this volume, we launched an iterative process, in which each of the contributors was invited to participate in a consensus process to identify a small number of themes an international effort of this sort ought to include. The editors compiled a list of the suggestions received, winnowed out duplicates or overlapping suggestions, and resent the compilation to the authors. In a process of condensing and iteration, the authors identified the following as principal cross-cutting themes to be included in each of the chapters to the extent the focus of that chapter would permit.

Principal Themes

1. Impact of globalization (economic and social changes)
    a. New sites of vulnerabilities
    b. Changing or new priorities for state investment
    c. Shifts in the nature of citizenship
    d. Issues of global aging

2. Post-industrialism and the nation state
    a. Relationship of work and welfare
    b. Issues of equality
    c. Contested identity
    d. Erosion of citizenship
    e. Issues of aging and post-industrialism

3. Changes to the welfare state
    a. Changing ideologies
    b. Multi-culturalism
    c. Importance of technological change
    d. Marketization and the Welfare State
    e. Public-sector and for-profit sector welfare delivery

4. New forms of solidarity
    a. Intergenerational linkages
    b. Cross-border ties
    c. Possibilities of a global constituency

In reading the following chapters, the issues outlined above will appear as recurring themes, allowing for variability based on the particular focus of the chapter. The chapters are divided into two major subsections: the first focuses on rethinking conceptual and critical cross-cutting issues with which social welfare analysis must deal; the second provides a series of international case studies drawn from an array of post-industrial societies. Obviously, not all countries are represented; rather a number of types of regimes influenced the selection of case studies to be provided. In all instances, another objective has been to prompt critical thinking, and the best indicator of our success is whether readers come up with questions and suggestions of their own. The emerging post-industrial societies in the global world are shaped by inward forces of social welfare policies as well as outward forces of economic globalization; each conspiring to make welfare states uncertain in modern times. The chapters examine the driving forces of economic transformations in post-industrial societies. Macroscopic global trends are highlighted as undoubtedly powerful, yet their influence will be traced and rivaled by domestic institutional traditions in nation-states. Hence, to grasp better what drives today's social welfare systems in the world economy, it is necessary to both highlight how social foundations within nation-states are shaped and with equal coverage of how global forces on the outside shape social welfare practices of all nation-states. The following chapters meet this challenge head on with rich variety of topics and case studies of nation states' social welfare practices as well as teasing out the implications for comparative social welfare drawn from debates framed within a triumvirate of national, international, and global analyses.

References

Annual World Wealth Report (2008). *12th Annual World Wealth Report*. New York: Merrill Lynch/Capgemini.

Appadurai, A. (2002). Grassroots globalization and the research imagination. In A. Appadurai (Ed.), *Globalization* (pp. 1–21). Durham, NC: Duke University Press.

Arias, A. O., & Logan, B. I. (2002). Conclusion: From globalization towards universalization in the twenty-first century. In B. I. Logan (Ed.), *Globalization, the third world state and poverty-alleviation in the twenty-first century* (pp. 197–202). Aldershot, UK: Ashgate.

Ascoli, U., & Ranci, C. (2002). The context of new social policies in Europe. In U. Ascoli & C. Ranci (Eds.), *Dilemmas of the welfare mix: The new structure of welfare in an era of privatization* (pp. 1–24). New York: Kluwer Academic/Plenum Publishers.

Bauman, Z. (1998). *Globalization: The human consequences*. New York: Columbia University Press.

Beck, U. (1999). *World risk society*. Cambridge: Polity Press.

Beck, U., Bonss, W., & Lau, C. (2003). The theory of reflexive modernization: Problematic, hypotheses and research programme. *Theory, Culture & Society, 20*, 1–33.

Calasanti, T. M. (2001). *Gender, social inequalities and aging*. Walnut Creek, CA: AltaMira.

Castells, M. (2000). *The rise of the network society: The information age: Economy, society and culture, Volume 1* (2nd ed.). Oxford, UK: Blackwell.

Chen, Y.-P., & Turner, J. (2006). Economic resources: Implications for aging policy in Asia. In H. Yoon & J. Hendricks (Eds.), *Handbook of Asian Aging* (pp. 67–90). Amityville, NY: Baywood.

Cerny, P. G., & Evans, M. (2004). Globalisation and public policy under new labour. *Policy Studies, 25*, 51–65.

Clark, G. (2007). *A farewell to alms: A brief economic history of the world*. Princeton, NJ: Princeton University Press.

Dallmayer, F. (2005). *Small wonder: Global power and its discontents*. Lanham, MD: Rowman & Littlefield.

Dasgupta, S. (2006). Globalization and its future shock. In S. Dasgupta & R. Kiely (Eds.), *Globalization and after* (pp. 143–183). Thousand Oaks, CA: Sage.

Deacon, B., Hulse, M., & Stubbs, P. (1997). *Global social policy: International organizations and the future of welfare*. Thousand Oaks, CA: Sage.

Dembele, D. M. (2007). The International Monetary Fund and the World Bank in Africa: A disastrous record. In V. Navarro (Ed.), *Neoliberalism, globalization and inequalities: Consequences for health and quality of life* (pp. 369–377). Amityville, NY: Baywood.

Esping-Andersen, G. (2002). *Why we need a new welfare state*. Oxford: Oxford University Press.

Esping-Andersen, G. (1990). *Three worlds of welfare capitalism*. Cambridge: Polity Press.

Finer, C. (1999). Trends and developments in welfare states. In J. Clasen (Ed.), *Comparative social policy: Concepts, theories and methods* (pp. 15–33). Oxford: Blackwell.

Foucault, M. (1978). *The history of sexuality*. New York: Pantheon Books.

Fraser, N. (2005). Transnationalizing the public sphere. In M. Pensky (Ed.), *Globalizing critical theory* (pp. 37–47). Lanham, MD: Rowman & Littlefield.

Geertz, C. (1973). *The interpretation of cultures*. New York: Basic Books.

Giddens A. (1990). *The consequences of modernity*. Cambridge: Polity Press.

Hart, G. (2002). *Disabling globalization: Places of power in post-apartheid South Africa*. Berkeley, CA: University of California Press.

Hatch, L. R. (2000). *Beyond gender differences*. Amityville, NY: Baywood.

Hendricks, J. (2008). Age, self and identity in the global century. In D. Dannefer & C. Phillipson (Eds.), *International handbook of social gerontology* (pp. xx–xx). Thousand Oaks, CA: Sage.

Hendricks, J. (2005). Moral economy and aging. In M. L. Johnson (Ed.), *Cambridge handbook of age and ageing* (pp. 510–517). Cambridge: Cambridge University Press.

Hill, M. (2006). *Social policy in the modern world*. Oxford: Blackwell.

Hoogvelt, A. (1997). *Globalization and the postcolonial world: The new political economy of development*. Baltimore, MD: Johns Hopkins University Press.

Hudson, J., & Lowe, S. (2004). *Understanding the policy process: Analysing welfare policy and practice*. Bristol, UK: Polity Press.

Jessop, B. (2002). *The future of the capitalist state*. Bristol, UK: Polity Press.

Kearney, M. (1995). The local and the global: The anthropology of globalization and transnationalism. *Annual Review of Anthropology, 24*, 547–565.

Kennett, P. (2001). *Comparative social policy*. Buckingham: Open University Press.

Lestienne, R. (2000). Time and globalization: does the emergence of a global identity entail a loss of individualities. *Time and Society, 9*, 289–291.

Mabbett, D., & Bolderson, H. (1999). Theories and methods in comparative social policy. In J. Clasen (Ed.), *Comparative social policy: Concepts, theories and methods* (pp. 34–56). Oxford: Blackwell.

McMichael, P. (2000). *Development and social change*. Thousand Oaks, CA: Pine Forge Press.

Mishra, R. (1999). *Globalization and the welfare state*. Cheltenham, UK: Edward Elgar.

Navarro, V. (2007). Neoliberalism as a class ideology; or, the political causes of the growth of inequalities. In V. Navarro (Ed.), *Neoliberalism, globalization and inequalities: Consequences for health and quality of life* (pp. 9–23). Amityville, NY: Baywood.

Phillipson, C. (2006). Ageing and globalization. In J. Vincent, C. Phillipson, & M. Downs (Eds.), *The futures of old age* (pp. 201–207). Thousand Oaks, CA: Sage.

Sainsbury, D. (1996). *Gender equality and welfare states*. Cambridge: Cambridge University Press.

Sainsbury D. (Ed.). (1994). *Gendering welfare states*. Thousand Oaks, CA: Sage.

Scheiwe, K. (1994). German pension insurance, gendered times and stratification. In D. Sainsbury (Ed.), *Gendering welfare states* (pp. 132–149). Thousand Oaks, CA: Sage.

Shalev, M. (2007). Book review of G. J. Kasza *One world of welfare: Japan in comparative perspective. American Journal of Sociology, 112,* 905–907.

Steger, M. B. (1997). The future of globalization. In A. D. King (Ed.), *Culture, globalization and the World-System* (pp. 116–129). Minneapolis, MN: University of Minnesota Press.

Townsend, P. (2007). Using human rights to defeat ageism: Dealing with policy-induced 'structured dependency.' In M. Bernard & T. Scharf (Eds.), *Critical perspectives on ageing societies* (pp. 27–44). Bristol, UK: Polity Press.

Wade, R. H. (2007). The causes of increasing world poverty and inequality; or, what the Matthew effect prevails. In V. Navarro (Ed.), *Neoliberalism, globalization and inequalities: Consequences for health and quality of life* (pp. 119–141). Amityville, NY: Baywood.

Yapa, L. (2002). Globalization and poverty: From a poststructural perspective. In B. I. Logan (Ed.), *Globalization, the third world state and poverty-alleviation in the twenty-first century* (pp.15–29). Aldershot, UK: Ashgate.

Chapter 2
Social Quality in Post-industrial Societies: The Growth of Migrant Remittances in International Social Welfare

Yitzhak Berman and David Phillips

Introduction: Impact of Globalization

One of the main aims of this book is to put the spotlight on global welfare systems in post-industrial societies. The most obvious of these systems accrue to formal global, international, and national bodies, either governments, nongovernmental organizations, or multinational corporations, and it is these formal systems which are the focus of most scholarly publications on international welfare and 'the welfare state' (Clasen and Siegel, 2007; Deacon, 2007). The emphasis in this chapter is different: it is on informal systems of international support at individual and family level, specifically exemplified by remittances made by migrants to families in their country of origin. In spite of the fact that these are informal systems, their consequences are by no means negligible, with remittances being the second highest source of external funding for developing countries and even accounting for over 20 percent of the GDP in some countries (de Haas and Plug, 2006). Crucially for this book, they are a central – and rapidly growing – phenomenon of the post-industrial world.

The importance of remittances is not only at the financial level; they affect all major aspects of individual, family, and community quality of life. One of the most frustrating aspects of discussions of welfare is that it is all too easy to slip into the error of treating it only in financial terms, particularly of income (be this family income or national GDP). A major challenge in discussing and measuring welfare is to find a holistic approach which is both theoretically sound and capable of being operationalized. Many of the welfare and quality of life measures in present use are ad hoc lists of disparate unconnected elements (Hagerty et al., 2001; Fahey et al., 2002) or are rather narrowly based on needs without taking into account other elements of the 'good life' (Stewart, 1996), whereas others are more conceptually robust, based on, for example, capabilities or prudential values (Sen, 1993; Griffin, 1986), but which do not have definitive measures, relying instead on a process of deliberation to arrive at consensual measures in specific settings (Phillips, 2008b).

Y. Berman (✉)
European Centre for Social Welfare Policy and Research, Vienna
e-mail: yberman@netvision.net.il

J. Powell, J. Hendricks, *The Welfare State in Post-Industrial Society*,
DOI 10.1007/978-1-4419-0066-1_2, © Springer Science+Business Media, LLC 2009

Welfare here is addressed in the context of the emergent theory of *social quality*, a multidisciplinary theoretical construct on the quality of societies and individuals which has been operationalized into an integrated system of domains and indicators and has been tested out in 13 European countries and is, at present, being implemented in five Asian countries (Gasper et al., 2009).

Social Quality

Social quality was developed by European scholars in the mid-1990s as an antidote and counterbalance to the predominance of economic measures of quality of life (particularly GDP) over social measures. Its influence in both academic and policy circles has grown rapidly. The declaration at its launch in 1997 was signed by 74 academics from the fields of social policy, sociology, political science, law, and economics. Within two years, it had been signed by 800 European social science academics, and the European Union has since actively embraced the concept and incorporated it into its social reporting: in 2001, the primary EU annual social statistical report, *The Social Situation of the European Union*, was themed around social quality. In addition, the European Commission's Directorate General for Employment and Social Affairs chose social quality as one of its three priority areas for action in 2000. Three books have been devoted to the exposition and theoretical development of social quality (Beck et al., 1997, 2001, forthcoming), and an international journal devoted to the topic was inaugurated in 1999 as *The European Journal of Social Quality* and has now been rebadged as *The International Journal of Social Quality* because of its recent international academic and policy implementation, particularly in Asia. Social quality is now probably the most thoroughly theorized and operationalized holistic societal quality of life constructs (Phillips, 2006: 176).

The Architecture of Social Quality

Social quality is defined as 'the extent to which people are able to participate in social relationships under conditions which enhance their well-being, capacity and individual potential' (Beck et al., 2007: 25).

Social quality focuses on the social as well as the individual level. The social quality of a collectivity is not just the accumulation of the life quality of each of its individual members; it incorporates collective as well as individual attributes and is holistic in its orientation. Its epitome is a society that not only is economically successful but also promotes social participation and social justice. A society with high social quality is envisaged by its promulgators as one where:

Citizens would be able and required to participate in the social and economic life of their communities and to do so under conditions which enhance their well-being, their individual potential and the welfare of their communities. To be able to participate, citizens must have access to an acceptable level of economic security and of social inclusion, live in cohesive communities, and be empowered to develop their full potential. In other words, social quality depends on the extent to which economic, social and political citizenship is enjoyed by all residents (Walker, 1998: 109).

Social quality is intended to be comprehensive and to encompass both objective and subjective interpretations. Beck et al. (1997) identified four conditional factors of social quality:

Socioeconomic security is the extent to which people have sufficient resources over time: It concerns the outcomes of the provision of protection by collective entities (communities as well as systems and institutions) as conditions for processes of self-realization. Socioeconomic security has two aspects: (i) all welfare provisions which guarantee the primary existential security of citizens (income, social protection, health), basic security of daily life (food safety, environmental issues, safety at work), and internal freedom, security, and justice; and (ii) enhancing people's life chances: 'Its mission is to enlarge the realm of options between which people can choose' (Beck et al., 2001: 341).

Social inclusion is the extent to which people have access to institutions and social relations: It refers to participation and to processes of being included in collective identities and the realities that determine self-realization. Social inclusion is connected with the principles of equality and equity and their structural causes. Its subject matter is citizenship, which 'refers to the possibility of participation in economic, political, social and cultural systems and institutions' (Beck et al., 2006: 346). This participation has three dimensions: material, via articulating and defending special interests; procedural, via guaranteeing citizens' public and private autonomy; and personal, via voluntary participation.

Social cohesion is the nature of social relations based on shared identities, values, and norms: Social cohesion refers to solidarity as the basis for collective identities and concerns the processes that create, defend, or demolish social networks and the social infrastructures underpinning these networks. An adequate level of social cohesion is one which enables citizens 'to exist as real human subjects, as social beings' (Beck et al., 1997: 284).

Social empowerment is the extent to which the personal capabilities of individual people and their ability to act are enhanced by social relations: Social empowerment is the realization of human competencies and capabilities to fully participate in social, economic, political, and cultural processes. It refers to being enabled to engage in collective identities as essential preconditions for self-realization and primarily concerns enabling people, as citizens, to develop their full potential. Three types of empowerment are identified: (i) personal: knowledge, skills, and experiences that lead to self-respect and self-development; (ii) social: interpersonal, intermediary, and formalized relationships; and (iii) political: access to processes of decision making, information, and resources.

These conditional factors have been operationalized via a series of domains and subdomains into 95 indicators, which have been trialed in 13 EU countries (Gordon, 2004). Full reports are available in a double issue of the *European Journal of Social Quality* (2004: 5/1-2). At present, the indicator set is being reviewed for an Asian context and the revised set is being piloted during 2009 in Taiwan, Hong Kong, Thailand, and Japan (Phillips, 2008a).

Social quality theory draws upon the critical realism of Bhaskar and is based on four assumptions as follows:

(i) people are essentially social beings
(ii) there is *constitutive interdependency*: a dialectic between the self-realization of individuals as social beings and processes leading to the formation of collective identities. This dialectic is the realization of 'the social'
(iii) two sets of tensions: (a) between societal development and biographical development (originally characterized as being between the macro and the micro); and (b) between the formal world of systems, institutions, and organizations and the informal life-worlds of families, groups, and communities
(iv) social change relating to the interactions between the second and third assumptions (Beck et al., 2007: 17)

Beck et al. (2007: 17) claim that this ontological position leads to three types of factors relating to objective, subjective, and normative aspects of daily life. The objective conditional factors are delineated above. The four subjective (constitutional) factors are:

- *Personal security* including environmental security, the institutionalization of the rule of law and human rights. It results from the collectivization of human norms, primarily in the setting of societal development.
- *Social recognition* including respect and human dignity, primarily in the setting of societal development. This implies interpersonal respect between members of families and communities and the formal world of systems.
- *Social responsiveness* and openness of groups, communities and systems, primarily in the interactive setting of biographical development.
- *Personal capacity,* particularly with regard to relationships with other people. This helps to determine the scope for individual activation and is primarily in the interactive setting of the world of daily life and biographical development (Beck et al., 2007: 13).

The four normative factors are claimed to be intrinsically linked to the four conditional and constitutional factors, as follows:

- Social justice based on socioeconomic security via personal security.
- Solidarity based on social cohesion via social recognition.

- Equal value based on social inclusion via social responsiveness.
- Human dignity based on social empowerment via personal capacity (Beck et al., 2007: 22).

Thus, according to the proponents of social quality, there is a tight, necessary, logical link, derived from critical realism, between each conditional (objective) factor and its corresponding constitutional (subjective) factor and normative factor. Beck et al. use the notion of *inscription* as a sort of connective tissue between these sets of individual factors as follows:

> The normative factors are inscribed in the consequences of the constitutional factors (subjective dimension) and the conditional factors (objective dimensions). As a result of this inscription, the normative factors are logically connected with the constitutional and the conditional factors (although it is possible that there will be more than four normative factors) (Beck et al., 2007: 23).

The work on fleshing out the substance and operationalizing the subjective and normative factors is still in its early stages, so the remainder of this chapter deals only with the objective, conditional factors, where domains, subdomains, and indicators have been constructed.

Social Quality and Migration: Ethnos Community Social Quality: New Forms of Solidarity

Phillips and Berman (2003) initiated social quality analysis of communities within societies. They introduced the notion of *community social quality* in the context of what Delanty (1998) calls *ethnos* communities, including immigrant communities or minority communities with a high proportion of immigrants or their descendants. The main focus of Phillips and Berman (2003) was on the relationships between the ethnos communities and national agencies and institutions in their destination country. According to Phillips and Berman, there are three facets to the social quality of community members: individually as *citizens* in relation to their dealings with the nation and society in which they live; individually as *community members* (derived from the support provided by community institutions and from the strength of community identity); and collectively via the social quality of the community itself depending on its strength as a collective entity in its own right and on its relationship to the nation-state. (These are discussed respectively in Berman and Phillips, 2000; Phillips and Berman, 2001, 2003).

However, Phillips and Berman (2003) did not take into account the interactions between members of the migrant ethnos community and their families and communities in their country of origin. Their analysis is further developed here in an international framework to include interactions and relationships between communities in the destination countries and their countries of origin. In principle, international community social quality can include three geographical facets, two of which are specific locations: in the destination country; in the country of origin; and between the two as a transnational community, or perhaps more precisely as a community whose members have a transnational identity (Ong, 1999). Often the destination country site is the most important on a day-to-day basis: this is where the ethnos migrant community resides, either on a permanent, temporary, or intermittent basis. The country of origin site is often a major long-term focus of attention, particularly for those who are temporary migrants and also for many who perhaps see themselves as temporary migrants, but end up living permanently in the destination country under the 'myth of return' (Anwar, 1979). Indeed, given their ethnos identity, many migrants – even those who settle for life and bring up children and grandchildren who ultimately might be incorporated into the mainstream destination society – will often feel intensely socially included in, and with a strong sense of identification with, their community and society of origin.

The more cosmopolitan, post-industrial transnational identity incorporates aspects of the previous two facets and is increasingly important, particularly among members of second generation migrant families who are born and brought up in one country as members of a minority community but who have their roots and relatives in their country of origin, which they often visit and where some feel equally at home (Bains, 2005). And the notion of a transnational community at the social level as well as transnational identity at the individual level is one with considerable promise for furthering the theoretical dimension of social quality into an international and ultimately global framework.

But that is for the future; for the present, let us explore the potential consequences for the four social quality conditional factors – socioeconomic security, social inclusion, social cohesion, and social empowerment. To begin with, Table 1 gives an indication of examples of the potential consequences of migration upon the four conditional factors of social quality in each of the three types of community.

Table 1 Social quality and ethnos communities

	Consequences for		
	Community in destination country	Community of origin	Transnational community
Socioeconomic security (normally a positive sum game although risky, particularly in times of recession)	Initial stages on migration supported by family at home	Receipt of remittances once migrants are settled; also provides financial support for further migration	Potential for long-term mutual support and sociogeographical flexibility

Table 1 (continued)

| | Consequences for | | |
	Community in destination country	Community of origin	Transnational community
Social inclusion (high risk of loss of network-based resources in all three settings but enhanced 'virtual inclusion' a possibility through mobile phone, Internet, and Skype technology)	Strong risk of isolation, discrimination, and exclusion from mainstream destination society, particularly in early days of migration or in socially fractured societies. See Phillips and Berman (2003)	Potentially problematic in terms of loss of face-to-face network and other social resources if a high proportion of economically active population migrates	Goal of strong inclusion in both communities; danger of dilution of inclusion or of exclusion for one or both
Social cohesion (high levels of trust, altruism, and reciprocity needed in linkages between all three sectors)	Strong bonding and reciprocal norms essential for community survival. High levels of trust required for community of origin to make investment	Danger of reduction of social cohesion through increased inequality between families receiving and not receiving remittances	Potential for development of strong nonspatial community identity
Social empowerment (depends upon strong personal relationships within and between communities)	Transformative if community thrives	Double-edged in that extra material and financial resources become available through remittances, but at the cost of reduction in on-site human capital	Potentially highly empowering in terms of realization of capabilities in both settings and globally, but danger of disempowerment though loss of identity if transnational community is weak

Because the most readily available data is on remittances, the empirical discussion in the remainder of this chapter concentrates mostly on the socio-economic security aspects of migrant community's social quality with particular reference to the community of origin. This discussion is preceded by a review of the extent and impact of remittances.

International Welfare – Migrant Remittance Funds: Changes to the Welfare State

Migration itself is a substantial contemporary demographic factor. The United Nations Population Division estimated that, in the year 2000, 175 million people, one in 40 worldwide, were living outside their country of birth or citizenship (Hagen, 2006). Foreign-born residents in developed countries have increased in recent years. In 2000, 50 million migrants resided in Europe, Asia and 41 million in North America. The United States has more migrants than any other country (35 million in 2000, a 50 percent increase from 1990). Wealthy countries have about 60 percent of the world's recorded migrants (Hagen, 2006). Some migrants tend to cluster in a limited number of countries; for example, the number of resident Turkish citizens in Germany is 2,053,600 or 58.3 percentof Turkish residents living outside Germany (Koksal, 2006).

Salomone (2006) reports that the majority of migrants maintain a strong long-term link with their country of origin. The most tangible evidence of this link is in the form of remittances, defined by Bascom (1990) as 'transfers made from earnings and/or accumulated stock of wealth by individuals who are residents in a foreign country on a temporary or permanent basis to their countries of origin for dependent support, investment or any other purpose.' Given that they are the second-largest source of external funding for developing countries after foreign direct investments, it is clear that they form an extremely important element of international welfare (de Haas, 2007).

Additionally, the increasing amounts of money migrants send back home in the form of remittances establishes a broad transnational economic diaspora. Indeed, remittances more than doubled between 2002 and 2007 (see Table 2)

Table 2 Remittance flows to developing countries selected years ($ billions)

	2002	2004	2006	2007	Increase 2002–07 (%)
South Asia	24	29	40	44	81
Middle East and North Africa	15	23	27	28	86
East Asia and the Pacific	29	39	53	58	97
Latin America and the Caribbean	28	41	57	60	115
Sub-Saharan Africa	5	8	10	11	116
Europe and Central Asia	14	21	35	39	175
Developing countries total	**116**	**161**	**221**	**240**	**107**

Based on: Ratha et al. (2007)

The International Monetary Fund reported in 2005 that 16 countries gained more than 10 percent of their GDP from remittances. the highest being Lesotho (39.5 percent), with Tonga, Lebanon, and Samoa all having more than 20 percent with Jordan, Albania, the West Bank and Gaza, Yemen, El Salvador, Granada, and Jamaica among those with more than 10 percent (see Appendix A(i)).

In money terms, India and Mexico are the largest beneficiaries, both receiving over six billion dollars in 2005, followed by the Philippines, Egypt, Turkey, Morocco, Lebanon, and (perhaps surprisingly) Russia, all with over two billion dollars (Page and Plaza, 2006: see Appendix A(ii)).

Social Quality, Migration, and Remittances: Post-industrialism and the Nation-State

Two of the three types of migration communities, noted in Table 1 above, are addressed in this section; first, the community of origin, with particular reference to socioeconomic security, and second, transnational identity and community, with particular reference to social cohesion and inclusion. Social quality in the destination country community is not addressed in detail here because it has been discussed elsewhere (Phillips and Berman, 2003). Briefly, Phillips and Berman (2003) conclude that community social quality has two dimensions: internal and external to the community. *Internal* community social quality – that is the social quality of community members within the community itself – in the destination country depends crucially upon community inclusion, via strong networks, and community cohesion, where a strong sense of identity, along with trust and other integrative norms and values, is essential. High levels of community socioeconomic security are beneficial, but not essential, to internal community social quality. *External* community social quality – that is the social quality of the community within the destination society – is primarily dependent on the nature of societal social cohesion: a society which has homogeneous social cohesion will exclude minority groups unless they assimilate, whereas one with pluralistic social cohesion provides opportunities for enhanced community empowerment. An example of the latter is the British education system, which provided state finances for the establishment of Jewish schools (Phillips, 2002).

Kapur (2004) reports that remittances are used differently in different countries and communities: they can finance consumption, land and housing purchases, and philanthropy. de Haas (2007) states that migration and remittances can improve well-being, stimulate economic growth, and reduce poverty both directly and indirectly. Koc and Onan (2001) conclude from their study in Turkey that households receiving remittances were better off than nonremitting households and spent more on basic necessities, housing, education, land, cattle, and consumer goods, such as washing machines and televisions.

But migration is very much a two-edged sword in overall social quality terms. On the negative side, it is often the most highly educated, qualified, and resourceful people who migrate. This deprives the country of human capital: for example doctors and nurses trained partly at state expense often migrate to developed countries (in effect subsidizing their already well-endowed health provision) and leave their country of origin even further underresourced and socially disempowered. Remittances can also have a negative impact on social cohesion in communities by increasing inequality between families and communities with migrant members and those without migrant members. A recent overview of case studies on migration and inequality across Central America, Eastern Europe, West Africa, and South Asia demonstrates how the mutual causality between migration and inequality varies both between and within regions (de Haas and Plug, 2006). For example, in Zimbabwe, there is evidence that remittances underpin preexisting class locations and exacerbate inequalities (Bracking, 2003). Thus, it is important to weigh these disadvantages against the more obvious benefits of remittances.

Most of the literature on remittances relates specifically to their financial consequences, so this survey of the social quality implications of remittances begins with a discussion of the social quality conditional factor of socioeconomic security.

Socioeconomic Security: Relationship of Work and Welfare

This section deals with the effect that migration and remittances have on the country of origin, both at the macro level, affecting the nation and society as a whole, and the micro level, in relation to families, neighborhoods, and communities. Socioeconomic security – the extent to which people have sufficient resources over time – has five domains: financial resources; housing and environment; health and care; work; and education. The financial resources domain is of overriding importance to remittances and is dealt with first.

Financial Resources

The financial resources domain has two subdomains: income sufficiency and income security.

Macro-level Consequences

(i) **Income sufficiency**: International remittances have reduced the level, depth, and severity of poverty in the developing world and thus have ameliorated problems relating to income sufficiency. Adams and Page (2005) conclude that a 10 percent increase in per capita international remittances will lead to a 3.5 percent decline in the share of people living in poverty (using the dollar per day definition). More specifically, de Haas and Plug (2006) estimates that 1.17 million out of 30 million Moroccans would fall back into absolute poverty without international remittances and that the proportion living below the poverty line would increase from 19.0 to 23.2 percent. Similarly, Gustafsson and Makonnen (1993) claim that without remittances from its migrant mine workers in South Africa the incidence of poverty in Lesotho would be 15 percent higher. Other studies have concluded that global remittances improve welfare and reduce abject poverty among the 'poorest of poor households' (Siddiqi, 2008; Puri and Ritzema, 1999).

(ii) **Income security**: In a longer term perspective, Jones (1998) argues that remittances act as a safety net for relatively poor areas, and Hagen-Zanker and Siegel (2007) found that the level of remittances responds dynamically to the poverty situation in the home country, thus providing at least a small measure of income security. Kapur (2004) concludes that remittances have emerged as the most stable and important source of external development finance for developing countries in general and play a critical social insurance role in many countries afflicted by economic and political crises. Lucas (2006) identifies a wider indirect multiplier effect of remittances stimulating the local economy. This effect is enhanced when remittances are used to start or expand local businesses and employment opportunities and often has long-term implications for economic development (Kapur, 2004).

Micro-level Consequences

As with the macro level, at the micro level, too, it is income sufficiency which is most often the initial primary objective in sending remittances, and issues of income security often emerge only later. It is important to bear in mind that, initially, there are usually some negative consequences for financial security both before migration takes place, when families often have to reduce consumption of necessities to finance migrants, and in the early days of migration when migrants are finding their feet in the destination country and are unable to send much money at a time when the loss of their labor in the community of origin is being keenly felt (de Haas, 2007).

Once the migrant is in the process of settling down at the destination and has found relatively secure employment, remittances can be sent home on a regular basis to help fulfill the most basic household needs, such as food, clothing, basic household amenities, paying off debts. Subsequently, there will be more room for investments and other activities oriented to income security. Page and Plaza (2006) and Roberts and Morris (2003) identify three basic motives for remittances: family obligations, including assistance and inheritance; family insurance against income shocks; and investment (asset accumulation back home as a part of migration life-cycle planning). de Haas (2007) identifies three stages in the consumption and investment pattern in the community of origin, as can be seen from Table 3.

Table 3 Relationship between household migration stage, consumption, and investments in the community of origin

Migration stage	Consumption and investment patterns by migration households
Migrant is in the process of settling	Most urgent needs are filled if possible: food, health, debt repayment, education of children
Migrant is settled and has more or less stable work	Housing construction, land purchase, basic household amenities, continued education
Ongoing stay	(Higher) education of children. Diverse long-term investments

Based on: de Haas 2007, Table 2, p. 16.

Income Sufficiency

Income sufficiency is the primary, and sometimes the only, use to which remittances are put by families in poorer developing countries once migration loans have been repaid (Hagen-Zanker and Siegel, 2007). Remittances are usually made in small amounts to families struggling to meet their requirements for daily life, and they make up a significant portion of household income. They are most commonly used to buy necessities, including food, clothing, housing, and basic health care (Hagen, 2006; Puri and Ritzema, 1999). An example of this is given in Appendix B, which gives details of differential expenditure on necessities between migrant and nonmigrant households in Turkey (Koc and Onan, 2001).

Income Security

Conway and Cohen (1998) provide a classification of strategies by recipients of migrant remittances once income sufficiency has been achieved. They identify five sets of activities: savings; fixed location-specific capital; flexible capital for human resources; diversified microeconomic investments; and community support systems (often funded by migrant associations in the destination country). These activities give some medium-term economic security and provide an economic cushion to migrants' families and to the migrants themselves should they return to their home community. de Haas (2007) reports that households receiving international remittances have a higher propensity to invest than nonmigrant households when controlling for income and other relevant household variables, and Kapur (2004) identifies remittances as an important source of social insurance in lower income countries. Nevertheless, in Turkey, for example, only a small percentage of remittances are spent on savings and investment on income-generating activities, such as buying land or tools or starting a business (Koc & Onan, 2001).

Housing and Environment

There is a heavy concentration on investment of migrant remittances in building, real estate and in improving existing housing (de Haas, 2007; Hagen, 2006; Koc & Onan, 2001). Kapur (2004) and Puri and Ritzema (1999) report remittances being used for land and housing purchases. In Conway and Cohen's (1998) classification, migrant remittances have an impact on location-specific capital, manifested in purchasing land and housing, home improvements and utility upgrades. In a wider environmental context Puri and Ritzema (1999) report remittances being used for the purchase of cattle, fulfilling the double function of providing both sustenance and wealth in pastoral communities.

Health and Care

Several commentators identify paying for basic health care items as a centrally important use of remittances (de Haas, 2007, Hagen, 2006; Puri and Ritzema, 1999;). Additionally, health status is enhanced through the better nutritional levels achieved through using remittances to purchase food. For example, Frank and Hummer (2002) report a positive correlation between remittances and health profiles of Mexican households receiving remittances. There are also longer-term benefits for pregnant women: Frank and Hummer (2002) concluded that children born in remittance-receiving migrant households are less likely to be exposed to health risks at birth. Similarly, Page and Plaza (2006) report improved developmental outcomes, including reduced infant mortality, as remittances rise in a community. Siddiqi (2008) reported similar long-term health multiplier effects of remittances in sub-Saharan Africa through increased household consumption, better nutrition, and investment in healthcare.

Work

Kapur (2004) states that remittances can provide liquidity for small enterprises as well as capital investments in agricultural works. This is in addition to investment in cattle noted above and in improvements to market gardens through investment in fencing and irrigation (Schroeder, 1999). de Haas (2007) points to the importance of the indirect multiplier effect here, where even nonmigrant families benefit indirectly from consumption and investments by remittance-receiving migrant households through increased expenditure and employment creation in the local economy. Conway and Cohen (1998) provide an excellent example of this – in their diversified microeconomic investments category – in relation to remittances sent by a migrant Mexican community in the United States. Between 1993 and 1996, several businesses were opened in the Mexican village: three new stores, two cafes, two barbershops, and – in response to the home building boom begun in the late 1980s – a glass shop, two door shops, and at least three local contractors. Many of these initiatives made extensive use of household labor power.

Education

There is also a strong positive link between migrant remittances and education (de Haas, 2007; Rapoport and Docquier, 2005). Conway and Cohen (1998) found that migrant remittance funding for education led to increased levels of technological skill, resulting in increased diversified microeconomic investments. Page and Plaza (2006) cite a study from the Philippines showing that remittances lead to an increase in both educational expenditure and children's school attendance, along with a drop in illiteracy. In El Salvador, remittances tend to reduce the likelihood of children leaving school (Cox Edwards and Ureta, 2003). In a case study in Nepal, Thieme and Wyss (2005) similarly conclude that international migration and remittances have a positive effect on the education of children.

Social Cohesion, Social Inclusion, and Social Empowerment: Shifts in the Nature of Citizenship

Remittances have a less direct effect on these three conditional factors of social quality than on socioeconomic security, and their effects are often interactive among the factors. Social empowerment is the most straightforward and is dealt with first. Social empowerment – the extent to which people's personal capabilities are enhanced by social relations – is primarily about enabling people to develop their full potential. Four of its five domains are of limited relevance here (knowledge base, labor market, openness of institutions, and public space). But the fifth domain, that of personal relationships, is centrally important. Its subdomains are supporting physical and social independence, personal support services, and support for social interaction. A wide range of uses of remittances cover these areas, but it is clear that spending remittances on children's health, education, and welfare expand capabilities and develop human potential (Conway and Cohen, 1998).

Social cohesion and social inclusion interact with each other and are to some extent interdependent. Social cohesion is the nature of social relations based on shared identities, values, and norms and its domains are trust; other integrative norms and values (including altruism and reciprocity); social networks; and identity. Social inclusion is the extent to which people have access to institutions and social relations. It refers specifically to participation, and the social inclusion domain of most relevance to remittances is that of social networks, including neighborhood participation, friendships, and family life. Social cohesion operates more at the societal, macro level; and social inclusion operates more at the biographical, micro level. So, although they each have a domain relating to social networks, for social cohesion this relates more to the cohesive effects of networks on society and for social inclusion it relates more to the levels and extent of community members' inclusion in, or exclusion from, networks. Whereas the brief discussion above on empowerment focused mostly on the impact of remittances on the community of origin, the following discussion on social cohesion and social inclusion concentrates upon transnational cohesion and inclusion.

Cross-Border Ties

Migration in developing countries takes place from within well-defined village and community networks (Roberts, 1994). The resulting transnational community comprises migrant networks connecting origins and destinations which are 'woven together so tightly that, in an important sense, they have come to form a single community spanning the various locales...a transnational migrant circuit' (Rouse, 1992: 45, cited in Roberts, 1994). Migrants usually maintain close contact with their communities of origin through visits, remittances, and gifts to their family and donations to community projects. The social cohesion domains of identity, trust, and other integrative norms and values (particularly reciprocity and altruism) are important for transactions that extend over long periods of time and about which information on the quality of what is being exchanged is imperfect, such as insurance. From a social inclusion perspective, migrants might want to retain ties with their rural households after having gone to work elsewhere, because they are insuring themselves against unemployment, sickness, and old age, in situations where good markets for these services are not available (Roberts, 1994). Therefore, it is important for them to continue to participate in networks which reinforce their transnational community membership and inclusion.

The social network domain of social inclusion has a subdomain associated with neighborhood participation, friendships, and family life. Remittances are of major importance here in enhancing family standing in the local community in the country of origin. This heightened status can be acquired through the symbolic demonstration of affluence via gift-giving, organizing large and ostentatious parties, and making extravagant donations to community projects, including the church, mosque, or temple. Using migrant remittances to establish, maintain, and develop community support systems enhances community and local identity and thus social cohesion in the country of origin. It also strengthens links between the migrant and the home community, thus enhancing transnational social inclusion, and becomes embedded through the development of associations in the destination country (Conway and Cohen, 1998).

Investment in community support explicitly demonstrates the loyalty and continuing community identity of overseas members as well as provides a public display of the financial success of the migrants, thus increasing the status of their families in the community of origin. There is growing evidence that local community systems are receiving valuable and essential inputs of remittances and goods in kind, as overseas community organizations actively invest in local community development and infrastructure improvement projects (Conway and Cohen, 1998).

There are also different patterns of consequences of remittance giving for community social quality in the country of origin. de Haas and Plug (2006) reports on the strength and durability of intergenerational transnational links between Morocco and the migrant communities settled in northwest Europe, and although second and third generations might be less inclined to remit, integration in the destination country does not automatically imply less involvement in the country of origin. Hagen-Zanker and Siegel (2007) compared remittance behavior in Albania and Moldova. In Albania, there was an emphasis on self-provided insurance and a bequest motive and altruism, all leading to enhanced transnational social cohesion and social inclusion whereas in Moldova there was a strong motive to repay migration loans, thus focusing more on socioeconomic security in the country of origin.

Conclusion

International migration has taken on a particular characteristic in the post-industrial society. The link between origin and destination countries is manifested in increasing migrant remittances that enhance welfare levels in communities in the developing countries. The main impact of these remittances on the social quality of the population of remittances-receiving communities relates to the conditional factors of socioeconomic security and, to a lesser extent, social empowerment, relating specifically to the domains of financial resources, housing, education, health (socioeconomic security), and personal relationships (social empowerment). The main impact on the social quality of the transnational community is on social cohesion and social inclusion, relating specifically to the domains of identity, altruism and networks (social cohesion), and the neighborhood participation, friendships, and family life subdomain of the network domain in social inclusion.

Our analysis of international welfare using social quality theory demonstrates that the characteristics of the post-industrial society facilitate social change in the sources of welfare. Social quality as an analytic tool enables us to identify changes in 'the welfare state' in the post-industrial society. Using the social quality theory, we demonstrate how ethnic communities have taken on a more prominent role in the post-industrial society by becoming facilitators of international social welfare. International migration has brought about a shift in the roles of collective identities as the core of social welfare from the nation-state to the ethnic community. Our analysis emphasizes the role of remittances in this process. Earlier studies (Phillips and Berman, 2003, 2001; Berman and Phillips, 2000) have demonstrated how ethnic communities have enhanced social quality in the ethnic communities in industrialized European countries. Our theme of remittances demonstrates an adaptation by ethnic communities to globalization, which has brought about vulnerabilities in the welfare state. The post-industrial nation-state has brought about a redefinition of sources of social cohesion. The impact of globalization as a result of economic and social changes has led to contested identity, issues of equality and inequality within nation-states, and an erosion of national citizenship. Multiculturalism as a result of mass migration has facilitated the development of new forms of solidarity in the form of cross-border ties and international intergenerational linkages. As a result, ethnic communities on a global scale are taking up the slack and are playing a more prominent role in providing social welfare.

Analyzing the post-industrial society within the context of social quality enables us to understand how ethnic groups have adapted to changes in the welfare state. International transfer of remittances is an example of an international social welfare process. The inability of the welfare state to provide services under conditions of globalization established the need for alternative ways of providing social welfare. Changes in the welfare state as a result of changing ideologies, multiculturalism, and marketization mandated alternate means of social welfare transfer. What is found analyzing the welfare state in the post-industrial society is that economic change, changing ideologies, and increasing multiculturalism have facilitated a shift in the source of social quality from the nation-state to the community. Large ethnic communities brought about new forms of solidarity, which has facilitated cross-border ties. Based on ethnic community and family ties, the post-industrial society has seen a globalization of social welfare outside the ambit of the nation-state.

Appendix 1 Largest Recipients of Remittance in Developing Countries in Dollars and Percent of GDP

(i) Countries % of GDP	
Lesotho	39.5
Tonga	24.4
Lebanon	23.9
Samoa	21.4
Jordan	19.9
Bosnia & Herzegovina	18.6
Kiribati	17.9
Cape Verde	16.8
Albania	16.5
West Bank & Gaza	15.0
Yemen, Rep. of	13.3
El Salvador	13.0
Moldova	11.7
Grenada	10.9
Jamaica	10.6
Serbia & Montenegro	10.3
Vanuatu	8.7
Haiti	8.5
Georgia	8.4
St. Kitts & Nevis	7.9

(ii) Countries	US $ Billions
India	6.91
Mexico	6.37
Philippines	4.90
Egypt	3.72
Turkey	3.26
Morocco	2.28
Lebanon	2.13
Russia	2.08
Brazil	1.92
Pakistan	1.80
Bangladesh	1.59
Jordan	1.46
Thailand	1.34
Serbia & Montenegro	1.27
China	1.25
Colombia	1.22
El Salvador	1.22
Yemen, Rep. of	1.18
Iran	1.16
Dominican Rep.	1.12

Source: World Economic Outlook: Globalization and External Imbalances. IMF, 2005.

Appendix B: Ways of Spending Remittances (Percent) by Household Migration Status in Turkey

Migration status/remittances	Total
Current migration household	
Daily expenses	75.0
Land/house	2.6
Medical expenses	9.2
Marriage expenses	3.9
Other items	9.2
Non-migrant households	
Daily expenses	84.9
Land/house	3.8
Medical expenses	7.5
Marriage expenses	1.9
Other items	1.9

Derived from Koc and Onan, 2001, p. 42.

References

Adams, R.H., Jr., & Page, J. (2005). Do international migration and remittances reduce poverty in developing countries? *World Development, 33*(10), 1645–1669.

Anwar, M. (1979). *The Myth of Return: Pakistanis in Britain.* London: Heinemann.

Bains, H. (2005) *Individual and family expectations among first and second generation Sikh women in the UK: Aspirations, constraints and patriarchal practices.* University of Sheffield, PhD.

Bascom, W. (1990). Remittances inflows and economic development in selected anglophone Caribbean countries. (Working Paper No. 58) Commission for the Study of International Migration and Cooperative Economic Development, Washington, DC.

Beck, W., van der Maesen, L., & Walker, A. (Eds.). (1997). *The social quality of Europe.* The Hague: Kluwer Law International.

Beck, W., van der Maesen, L., Thomése, G., & Walker, A. (Eds.). (2001). *Social quality: A vision for Europe.* The Hague: Kluwer Law International.

Beck, W., van der Maesen, L., & Walker, A. (Eds.). (2007). Chapter 3: Theoretical foundations for forthcoming third book on social quality. European Foundation for Social Quality.

Beck, W., van der Maesen, L., & Walker, A. (Eds.). (forthcoming). Third book on social quality. European Foundation for Social Quality.

Berman, Y., & Phillips, D. (2000). Indicators of social quality and social exclusion at national and community level. *Social Indicators Research, 50*(3), 329–350.

Bracking, S. (2003). Sending money home: Are remittances always beneficial to those who stay behind? *Journal of International Development, 15*(5), 633–644.

Clasen, J., & Siegel, N. (Eds.). (2007). *Investigating welfare state change.* London: Edward Elgar.

Conway, D., & Cohen, J. H. (1998). Consequences of migration and remittances for Mexican transnational communities. *Economic Geography, 74*(1), 26–44.

Cox Edwards, A., & Ureta, M. (2003). International migration, remittances, and schooling: Evidence from El Salvador. *Journal of Development Economics, 72*(2), 429–461.

Deacon, B. (2007). *Global social policy and governance.* London: Sage.

de Haas, H. (2007). Remittances, migration and social development: A conceptual review of the literature. (Social Policy and Development Programme Paper No. 34). United Nations Research Institute for Social Development, Geneva.

de Haas H., & Plug, R. (2006). Cherishing the goose with the golden eggs: Trends in migrant remittances from Europe to Morocco 1970–2004. *The International Migration Review, 40*(3), 603–634.

Delanty, G. (1998). Reinventing community and citizenship in the global era: A critique of the communitarian concept of community. In E. Christodoulidis (Ed.), *Communitarianism and citizenship.* Aldershot: Avebury.

Fahey, T., Nolan, B., & Whelan, C. (2002). *Monitoring living conditions and quality of life in Europe: Developing the conceptual framework – Final report.* Dublin: European Foundation for the Improvement of Living and Working Conditions.

Frank, R., & Hummer, R. (2002). The other side of the paradox: The risk of low birth weight among infants of migrant and non-migrant households within Mexico. *International Migration Review, 36*(fall), 746–765.

Gasper, D., van der Maesen, L. Truong, T., & Walker, A. (2009). Human security and social quality: Contrasts and complementarities. *International Journal of Social Quality, 1*(1) forthcoming.

Gordon, D. (2004). Editorial. *European Journal of Social Quality, 5*, 1–2.

Griffin, J. (1986). *Well Being: Its Meaning, Measurement and Moral Importance.* Oxford: Oxford University Press.

Gustafsson, B., & Makonnen, N. (1993). Poverty and remittances in Lesotho. *Journal of African Economies, 2*(1), 49–73.

Hagen, J. (2006). Migration and remittances. *UN Chronicle, 42*(4), 12.

Hagen-Zanker, J., & Siegel, M. (2007). The determinants of remittances: A comparison between Albania and Moldova. http://www.governance.unimaas.nl/home/staff/research_fellows/jessica_hagen_zanker/Hagenzanker_Siegel_2007_short.pdf. Accessed 20 August 2008.

Hagerty, M., Cummins, R., Ferriss, A., Land, K., Michalos, A., Peterson, M., et al. (2001). Quality of life indexes for national policy: Review and agenda for research. *Social Indicators Research, 55*, 1–96.

International Monetary Fund. (2005). Workers remittances and economic development in World economic outlook: Globalization and external imbalances (pp. 69–70), http://www.imf.org/external/pubs/ft/weo/2005/01/pdf/chapter2.pdf. Accessed 20 August 2008, Washington, DC.

Jones, R. C. (1998). Introduction: The renewed role of remittances in the new world order. *Economic Geography, 74*(1), 1–7.

Kapur, D. (2004, April). Remittances: The new development mantra? Harvard University and Center for Global Development. (G-24 Discussion Paper No. 29), http://casi.ssc.upenn.edu//about/Remittances.pdf

Koc, I., & Onan, I. (2001). The impact of remittances of international migrants on the standard of living of left-behind families in Turkey. http://www.iussp.org/Brazil2001/s20/S26_03_Koc.pdf. Accessed 20 August 2008.

Koksal, N. E. (2006). Determinants and impact on the Turkish economy of remittances. Université Paris I Panthéon – Sorbonne Ecole Doctorale d'Economie, http://www.luc.edu/orgs/meea/volume8/PDFS/koksal.pdf. Accessed 20 August 2008.

Lucas, R. E. B. (2006). Migration and economic development in Africa: A review of evidence. *Journal of African Economies, 15*(Suppl.), 337–395.

Ong, A. (1999) *Flexible citizenship: The cultural logics of transnationality*. Durham, NC: Duke University Press.

Page, J., & Plaza, S. (2006). Migration remittances and development: A review of global evidence. *Journal of African Economies, 15*(Suppl. 2), 245–336.

Phillips, D. (2002). Community citizenship and community social quality: The British Jewish community at the turn of the twentieth century. *European Journal of Social Quality, 3*(1/2), 26–47.

Phillips, D. (2006). *Quality of life: Concept, policy and practice*. New York: Routledge.

Phillips, D. (2008a, April). *Social quality: Indicators from Europe and their implications for Asia*. Paper presented at National Taiwan University Workshop on Social Quality. Taipei: National Taiwan University.

Phillips, D. (2008b). *A comparative study of quality of life and development approaches, including social quality and human development*. Paper presented at Conference of the Human Development and Capability Association. New Delhi, India.

Phillips, D., & Berman, Y. (2001). Social quality and community citizenship. *European Journal of Social Work, 4*(1), 17–28.

Phillips, D., & Berman Y. (2003). Social quality and ethnos communities: Concepts and indicators. *Community Development Journal, 38*(4), 344–357.

Phillips, D., & Berman, Y. (2001). Social quality and community citizenship. *European Journal of Social Work, 4*(1), 17–28.

Puri, S., & Ritzema, T. (1999). Migrant worker remittances, micro-finance and the informal economy: Prospects and issues. (Working Paper No. 21). Enterprise and Cooperative Development Department, Social Finance Unit. International Labour Office Geneva, Geneva. http://www.ilo.org/public/english/employment/ent/papers/wpap21.htm. Accessed 20 August 2008.

Rapoport, H., & Docquier, F. (2005). *The economics of migrants remittances*. Institute for the Study of Labor (IZA), Bonn. http://ftp.iza.org/dp1531.pdf. Accessed 20 August 2008.

Ratha, D., Mahapatra, S., Vijayalakshmi, K. M., & Xu, Z. (2007, November). Remittance trends 2007. *Migration and Development Brief 3*. http://siteresources.worldbank.org/EXTDECPROSPECTS/Resources/476882-1157133580628/BriefingNote3.pdf. Accessed 20 August 2008.

Roberts, B. R. (1994). Urbanization, development, and the household. In Kincaid, D. & Portes A. (Eds.), *Comparative national development: Society and economy in the new global order* (pp. 199–236). Chapel Hill: University of North Carolina Press.

Roberts, K. D. & Morris, M. D. S. (2003). Fortune, risk, and remittances: An application of option theory to participation in village-based migration networks. *The International Migration Review, 37*(4), 1252–1281.

Rouse, R. (1992). Making sense of settlement: Class transformation, cultural struggle, and transnationalism among Mexican migrants in the United States. *Annals of the New York Academy of Sciences, 645*, 25–52.

Salomone, S. (2006). Remittances, overview of existing literature. http://www.iue.it/RSCAS/ Research/SchoolOnEuro-MedMigration/2006pdfs/Paper%20Salomone.pdf. Accessed 20 August 2008.

Schroeder, R. (1999). *Shady practices: Agroforestry and gender politics in the Gambia.* Berkeley: University of California Press.

Sen, A. (1993). Capability and well-being. In M. Nussbaum & A. Sen (Eds.), *The quality of life.* Oxford: Clarendon.

Siddiqi, M. (2008). The global remittances boom. *African Business, 338*, S12–S16.

Stewart, F. (1996). Basic needs, capabilities, and human development. In A. Offer (Ed.), *In pursuit of the quality of life.* Oxford: Oxford University Press.

Thieme, S., & Wyss, S. (2005). Migration patterns and remittance transfer in Nepal: A case study of Sainik Basti in western Nepal. *International Migration, 43*(5), 59–98.

Walker, A. (1998). The Amsterdam declaration on the social quality of Europe. *European Journal of Social Work, 1*, 109–111.

Chapter 3
Aging in Post-industrial Societies: Intergenerational Conflict and Solidarity

Alex Dumas and Bryan S. Turner

> To reject the old and young and to condemn them to an inferior
> status is incompatible with democracy, for a democracy is sick
> when a society hides an important part of its own reality from
> itself.
>
> Touraine (2000: 14)

Introduction

Alain Touraine and Manuel Castell have contributed extensively to the understanding of profound societal changes occurring in post-industrial societies. It comes as no surprise that both signed the preface of Anne-Marie Guillemard's (2000) important piece *Aging and the Welfare-State Crisis,* originally published in France in the 1980s. This sociohistorical study of policies for old age highlighted many of the challenges that faced the welfare state in postwar France. Although Guillemard's work deals primarily with the welfare of the elderly globally, it points to the need for political sensitivity in promoting changes to the welfare state and new forms of intergenerational solidarity that will cater to the needs of all generations despite emergent social and demographic transformations that threaten all forms of collective social welfare.

Most industrialized societies have witnessed a number of popular protests over the social welfare of specific generations. Public forums are repeatedly reporting the angst of various generational groups toward the public expenses derived from age-based policies. For example, issues surrounding the pension crisis, sustainable health care systems, and inequitable working conditions are attracting considerable attention in the political arena. In France, the vigorous

A. Dumas (✉)
Faculty of Health Sciences, University of Ottawa, Ontario, Canada
e-mail: adumas@uottawa.ca

J. Powell, J. Hendricks, *The Welfare State in Post-Industrial Society,*
DOI 10.1007/978-1-4419-0066-1_3, © Springer Science+Business Media, LLC 2009

mobilization surrounding the First Employment Contract (*contrat de première embauche*), which increased job insecurity of young workers, exemplified youth's reaction toward unequal working conditions in comparison to their elders. In academic circles, Laurence Kotlikoff (1992) model of generational accounting, vouching for a reduction of fiscal contribution of Baby Boomers, has been extensively criticized because of its narrow understanding of generational imbalances and its inability to offer social protection for preceding generations. In light of these concerns, some social theorists have evoked fears of a gerontocracy, whilst others are alarmed by the prospect of youth rebellions (Fukuyama, 2002).

This chapter argues that many of these conflicts are expressions of generational struggles to achieve a form of social equity and that further discussion is needed on the forms of solidarity which promote the rights and duties required to secure the current and future welfare needs of each generation. Sociological research has suggested that post-industrial society and its demographic changes are reshaping the welfare state and eroding the solidarity between generations. We aim to pursue this discussion by presenting a conceptualization of generations and generational struggles by identifying the demographic shift in post-industrial societies as capable of enhancing intergenerational division, by discussing the economic rationalization that is threatening the welfare state and its connection with generational solidarity, and by highlighting the reciprocal feature of institutions as an essential feature of intergenerational solidarity.

Mannheim, Bourdieu, and Generations: Issues of Equality and Identity

Unlike the analytical categories of social class, gender, and ethnicity, the study of generations and intergenerational conflict has been underdeveloped in sociology. This shortcoming can be partly explained by the lack of a consensual definition of the concept of generation and the criticism regarding the extent of significant generational conflict. Recent publications in the sociology of generations draw from the legacies of Karl Mannheim and Pierre Bourdieu by developing an analytical framework based on some of their key ideas (Dumas and Turner, 2006; Eyerman and Turner, 1998; Gilleard and Higgs, 2005; Mauger, 1990; Edmunds and Turner, 2002). In his pivotal essay 'The problem of generations,' Mannheim established the foundations for a research program on generations distinct from demographical approaches to generations (as predetermined age cohorts), which he believed are unable to explain the sociohistorical conditions involved in shaping generational groups. In this perspective, new generations are not determined by the succession of equivalent time frames, that is 30 or 40 years, but rather by dramatic sociopolitical events. By being distinct from previous generations, each new generation generates a renewal effect which serves as a fundamental factor of historical change.

Mannheim's framework is complemented by Bourdieu's social class model to propose a more complete theory of generational relations and inequalities. Gérard Mauger (1990) provides an example of this integration through the concept of generational habitus, which refers to sets of embodied schemes of perceptions, appreciations, and dispositions that are harmonized with the conditions of existence of one's historical period. In other words, this concept mediates new generational experiences (the embodiment of generational living conditions) and new forms of expression (sociocultural practices), in which generations differ to the extent that each holds its own legitimate view of the world and distinctive cultural practices, because each has adapted to the condition of its generational location. For the sake of this chapter, we will draw from both theoretical approaches and define a generation as a class of social agents of similar ages (age groups who relate similarly to a social phenomenon) that have witnessed similar historical events; that share similar experiences, aspirations, feelings, and ideas; and that face similar constraints and opportunities. This approach is not meant to replace or minimize the importance of social classes, but to offer an additional tool for analyzing social inequities.

This combined approach also forms the basis for a theory of power between generations by emphasizing their struggles for legitimacy and their competition over access to scarce resources.[1] Generally speaking, there are two distinct but related perspectives for understanding intergenerational conflict that are applicable to study the welfare of generations. The first emphasizes the importance of the struggle over scarce resources between generations and suggests that this will be at the forefront of political debates in the years to come. The second perspective has more to do with confrontations that occur because of conflicting world views. In this case, the focus is placed primarily on generational thoughts, dispositions, and aspirations fashioned by the constraints and opportunities generated by sociohistorical events (for example wars, natural disasters, and economic instability).

A significant difficulty in obtaining a clear picture of generational injustices arises because of their synchronic and diachronic characteristics. Both Mannheim and Bourdieu provide some conceptual clarity regarding this issue. Mannheim's concepts of *generational location* and *generation as actuality* refer, respectively, to groups that share a sociohistorical destiny and are subject to similar possibilities and constraints. By focusing on the distinctive sociohistorical realities that shape age groups and their interrelations, his approach differs from those who solely use 'age' as an analytical unit. It inquires less about youth and old age per se, but rather about what it is to be young or old today within a specific society and in relation to previous generations. For Bourdieu (1993), such conflicts are illustrated as antagonism between age groups competing within a particular field of cultural production. This approach provides a more relativistic comprehension of

---

[1] This approach has been previously exposed in an on-line forum by Dumas and Laforest (2008) in a study of intergenerational conflict in the context of sport and skateboarding.

the experiences of inequality. The generational habitus fashioned in different contexts translates into clashes between generations which have different reference points, systems of aspiration, and sets of anxieties linked to their social position (Bourdieu, 1993; Chauvel, 2002).

This combined approach helps to decipher the sense of entitlement of generations to fulfill their needs and the resulting conflict that may appear when a generation believes it is receiving inequitable returns from public wealth or inequitable treatment due to a decrease in social status. Youth may believe they should have access to free education as did their parents, and elders may believe they deserve decent pensions because of previous contributions to society. In periods of scarcity, it can be assumed that what one generation has struggled to achieve may be regarded by another as irrelevant and unimportant (Eyerman & Turner, 1998). The dilemma over the value of experience in comparison to formal educational qualifications is a classic example of the opposition between older and younger workers. Such conflict is not new; however, there is increasing proof that governing structures, political systems, and social trends are eroding the solidarity between generations that has traditionally had the role of ensuring equitable treatment and protecting individuals from the rapid social changes to the post-industrial society.

Post-industrialism, Aging, and Economic Pressures on the Welfare State

The changes occurring in post-industrial society, particularly when considering its socioeconomic and demographic components, have become key transformations for understanding the social conditions which make up intergenerational struggles and conflict. These tensions are explained as conflicting attitudes toward social change, including the struggle over scarce resources and legitimacy (including social status). Daniel Bell's classic piece, *The Coming of Post-industrial Society,* can be seen as a theory of social change which has identified transformations in the spheres of economics, work, politics, and social relations. He argued that the rise of the service sector was the main characteristic of post-industrial economies. This transition had significant consequences on the nature and character of work. Whereas earlier, to employ Bell's (1999: 30) terminology, workers were mostly involved in a *game against nature,* in which constraints were predominantly environmental (within the primary and secondary sectors of the economy), they now are involved in a *game between persons,* in which individual actions are fashioned by reciprocal judgments of other's intentions. Bell also noted the growing importance of the quinary sector of the economy (for instance healthcare and postsecondary education) and the increasing value of human capital as a strategic resource for maintaining the productivity of societies. The sectors of higher education and health care, two main sources of contemporary human capital, are already provoking age-related tensions and generational divisions, both at the macro level of politics and the micro level of individual relations. In facing these changes, the welfare state plays an important role in the solidarity between generations. Guillemard (2007), for instance, argues that social policies must prioritize access to human capital (continuing education and professional development) of individuals of all ages to provide them with a sense of security in the face of the professional and economic uncertainties that are accompanying the post-industrial society.

These changes are transforming the social structure, changing the nature of class struggles, and creating new forms of social hierarchy (Bell, 1999; Touraine, 1971). Bell refers at length to the 1960s social scientist, Rodocan Richta, who was commissioned to respond to the changes facing East European countries, brought about by the technological revolution. Bell agreed with Richta and challenged the singularity of class conflict by claiming: '...new society itself will generate new conflicts and new struggles not necessarily along the old lines of class and power, but of attitudes to change...' (p. 111). For Richta (1969), this period of change was likely to increase the misunderstanding between generations: 'The signs are that society will undergo a repeated and ever stronger polarization between progressive and conservative attitudes' (p. 258). Bell's (1999) forward to the second edition extends this issue to the resistance of changes brought about by Americanizaton:

> For what we can anticipate is the widening of the arena geographically and socially . . . , the multiplication of interaction between the individuals through the creation of affinity groups along the Internet and the like, the increased mingling of cultures, and the resistance to these new onslaughts of change by the older and traditional elites. What has already begun to happen is a *kulturkampf*, a set of "cultural wars" between generations and the efforts of many countries to resist "Americanization" . . . (p. lxxvi).

Another important aspect of post-industrial societies is a demographic shift toward an older population. Statistics show that between 1960 and 2004, the proportion of population over 65 years old in the G7 and EU15 has increased respectively from 9.0 to 15.6 percent and from 10.1 to 17.3 percent (OECD, 2005). The majority of demographic projections indicate that these trends will continue at least for the next three decades. In the United States, it is projected that 20 percent of the population will be over 65 in 2050. In Japan, female life expectancy is now 85 years. The aging of the post-second world war generation, low fertility rates, and rising life expectancy participate in restructuring the welfare state and resource allocation between age groups. The fiscal consequences of an aging society are unique to contemporary times. Because the welfare state is at the center of the redistribution of wealth measures, it involves a number of sectors that influence generational relations, such as caring within families, healthcare, and provision of public pensions and post-secondary education (Walker, 1996). According to Pierson's (1998) economic study on the OECD countries, the demographic shift underway is profound and its effects are precisely in the most expensive areas of the welfare state: healthcare and pensions. By 2050, both health and long-term care of the elderly will, on their own, increase public spending by between 3.5 and 6.0 percentage points of the GDP (OECD, 2007). Changing demography is also associated with the forecast increase in the old age dependency ratio (those aged 65 and over: those aged between 20 and 64). This factor is problematic because for the first time in history those with the capacity to contribute to the fiscal reserves will need to cover public expenses for more than one group of retirees: the large cohort of Baby Boomers and their parents. Current OECD projections indicate that, by 2050, this ratio will at least double in the OECD countries (OECD, 2007: 42). At the heart of the question of generational conflict is the contrasting perception of generations regarding the distribution of resources in periods of scarcity. The welfare state crisis represents precisely this strain on social provision in a context of diminishing sources of national income in relation to the increasing demand on social welfare spending (Masson, 1995).

Historical demographer Peter Laslett (1989) argued, two decades ago, that the equitable distribution of wealth between age groups was one of the most urgent issues in this state of affairs. However, specific policies directly related to intergenerational solidarity seem to be lagging behind social change, and the political risk in pitting one generation against another is high. The challenge for contemporary governments will be to avoid this confrontation and understand that sociopolitical upheavals between generations erupt when there is an authoritative structure that imposes its agenda or when demographic imbalances exacerbate the vulnerability of social groups (Attias-Donfut, 1991). The challenge, thus, lies in the management of social change and the conservation of socially valued resources.

New Sites of Vulnerability

In his influential publication, *Children and the Elderly: Divergent Paths for America's Dependents,* Samuel Preston (1984) argued that economic resources were not distributed evenly across age groups, and consequently, following the demographic shift to the elderly, the social conditions for children deteriorated while those of the elderly greatly improved. This assumed responsibility of older generations toward youth remains, but is strongly criticized; it proves to be difficult, at least scientifically, to make members of one generation accountable for the (mis)fortunes of others. With the advent of new problems that affect the elderly, we are far from the existence of an opulent old age and underprivileged youth (Attias-Donfut, 1991). In the area of health, social trends reflecting the epidemiological transition indicate that the quality of life at both ends of the life course is compromised. For instance, the increasing privatization of state health services is decreasing access to quality care for the elderly, and changes in the social structure and lifestyle are increasing chronic diseases (obesity and diabetes) and suicides among the youth.

The social status and well-being of both the youth and the elderly are being challenged in this context. Louis Chauvel's (2002) study on the inequality of the destinies of generations in France has provided a thorough account of the economic decline of youth, their weakened social mobility, and their lower social status in comparison to their parents. His analysis concludes that the collective fate of birth cohorts varies considerably and that generations benefit unequally from society's wealth. He argues that this time in history marks the first period during peace time where youth entering the workforce are worse-off than their parents. One major contribution of his study was that conditions, such as unemployment and poverty, have scarring effects that have lasting consequences, which contribute to generational fractures and resentment of the disadvantaged generations. Moreover, the problems facing older adults are quite different from youth: increased life expectancy has produced a new realm of experience for populations within which social institutions have yet to adapt satisfactorily. Their social security involves mainly shorter term issues, like economic security, provided by public pension and health care. The social and physical vulnerability of older adults has been exemplified in Klinenberg's (2002) analysis of social capital. For Klinenberg, the consequences of the demographic shift to an older society increased poverty, while the cultural changes (individualism and increase crime) and the spatial transformation of cities (such as concentration of poverty and low quality housing) have isolated older men from friends and relatives, making them more vulnerable to morbidity and mortality when facing harsh living conditions. In the spirit of social rights, the state faces increasing responsibility in reshaping the economic and political structures involved in the management of solidarity to face such social contingencies (Cheal, 1995).

A generational approach is useful for increasing our awareness and diagnosis of the sources of social inequities and conflict in the context of an aging population. The conservative 'wind,' which is said to restructure the welfare state, has contributed to the perception of old age and youth as burdens on society's economic health (Phillipson, 1996). Not only did this 'wind' not respond to the development of new sites of vulnerability in some of the most important sectors of society, that is, health, education, work, and pensions, it positively contributed to the erosion of the most prominent social institutions that are responsible for generational solidarity.

Threats to the Welfare State and Intergenerational Linkages

We can view intergenerational solidarity as a result of citizenship, which is a collection of rights and obligations, that regulates access to scarce resources and protects social groups from the negative consequences of the market (Turner, 2005: 399). The study of citizenship can be usefully formulated in terms of the contradiction between two forces: scarcity, the state of resources which are produced and are the result of exclusionary structures (such as age or generational classes), and solidarity, the social measures resulting from the management of social conflict produced by scarcity (Turner, 2005). Although traditional models of citizenship (based on the Marshallian model) focused on social classes as the main social division in society, it is possible to extend this approach to the solidarity between generations. As we have noted that this approach, which extends collective rights to generational factions of society, is underdeveloped.

Ralf Dahrendorf (1959) argued that industrial societies had avoided the crisis of capitalism predicted by Karl Marx because there had been an 'institutionalization of class conflict' and that citizenship had ameliorated the antagonistic interests between social classes. The societies of Western Europe were relatively successful in the post-war period because they were able to combine three important ingredients to sustain social solidarity and citizenship: the production of resources to sustain a welfare state, the safeguarding of national identities, and the protection of fundamental rights. An institutionalization of generations is more difficult, partly because of its difficult conceptualization and partly because of the specificity of biographical life courses and the historical context of generational inequities. Nonetheless, it proves to be useful in identifying inequities and determining their causes.

The concerns over the threats to social solidarity between generations have been globally understood through the generational contract (Cheal, 1995). Alan Walker (1996) and Chris Phillipson (1996) in the United Kingdom have claimed that the demographic threat is being used as an ideological platform for a more general neoliberal attack on the welfare state in favor of both private insurance and greater personal responsibility for our own future. What Walker calls the ideology of 'familism' played an important role in the Thatcher government's emphasis on personal responsibility for our families and their futures. As state support for welfare has been systematically eroded, there is a greater potential burden on family members to provide familial care, but in reality it is difficult for family members to undertake responsibility of the elderly because the notion of 'family' itself has been changing dramatically. With high levels of divorce, increasing longevity, and greater geographical mobility, families are often too fragmented and diverse to provide the care that occurred between children and parents in the traditional (extended) family. As life expectancy increases, families may often contain two generations of pensioners who need support. Walker (1996: 35) concludes by noting that although 'age-group conflicts have the potential for greater prominence in the decades to come,' whether or not such conflicts will be significant depends on how the state functions to enhance or undermine the capacity of individuals to provide care and support to family members.

As an important contribution to universal citizenship, the welfare state is central to the establishment of values of solidarity and norms of reciprocity in society (Schultheis, 1995). For generational solidarity to function there must be a balance between both its private (family) and public spheres. In fact, each type of welfare state, notwithstanding a political regime of social protection, is involved to varying degrees in this dual investment. Because of state investment in both forms of solidarity, we can say that it is increasingly significant in enhancing intergenerational linkages. By managing the interplay between ascendant and descendant transfers within both spheres, the state should act as an arbitrator for the welfare of generations (Masson, 1995). Hespanha's (1995) study of intergenerational solidarity in Portugal discussed the need for maintaining both these levels of state intervention on solidarity. Although solidarity within families acts as a buffer in the context of rapid social change or disengagement of state responsibilities, public forms of social protection function to distribute scarce resources between citizens to protect vulnerable populations, such as the elderly. This balance between the public and private involvement of the state does not function by the law of communicating vessels; disengagement from one form of solidarity is not necessarily compensated by another (Hespanha, 1995). For example, Thatcher's policy of privatization of social and health care resulted in a shift of social responsibility for the dependant elderly from the formal to informal sector of care (Phillipson, 1996). While the private sphere of the family has an important role to play, this should not be used to justify the passivity of the state in its public and formal role (Hespanha, 1995). Furthermore, the burden of care tends to fall unequally on female members of the family, thereby reinforcing gender inequalities.

Erosion of Solidarity: A Case Study on the Relationship of Work and Welfare

In traditional societies with high fertility and low life expectancy, the survival of human beings into old age was a relatively unusual occurrence. There was no significant problem of dependency. In Europe, the Black Death created a significant labor shortage, and without pestilence famine and warfare were sufficient to retain a balance between arable land and population. Old age and retirement are products of the demographic transition (from high to low fertility and increased life expectancy) and industrialization. Citizenship and social welfare were, in part, responses to a new situation – how to provide adequate cover for the elderly unemployed where relatives and kinfolk could not be relied upon. The social rights of citizenship were then closely tied to compulsory retirement, and these were contributory rights since citizens were expected to make investments through social security payments to provide themselves with a modicum of protection in old age. These schemes have never been entirely satisfactory – with the possible exception of some Scandinavian societies – because the contributions have not kept the elderly out of poverty or at least out of considerable economic hardship.

National surveys are consistent, as they express positive sentiments of the state's involvement in decent pension schemes. It is the moral capital that binds these linkages that are at stake in intergenerational conflict (Kohli, 1995). Pensions and social security schemes are important components of social solidarity in industrial societies, which would otherwise typically experience higher levels of industrial unrest, civil disturbance, and class conflict. Universal social welfare benefits provide citizens with a sense of membership in society and a responsibility for its continuing well-being. Pensions imply a social contract between the individual and society. Starting with the governments of Mrs. Thatcher, the decline of union membership, the deindustrialization of the economy, and the privatization of many public utilities, such as transport, gas, and water, are economic changes that have brought the social contract into question. With the growth of global economies, one general response to what is seen as a crisis of dependency resulting from aging populations, declining profitability because of heavy taxation for welfare benefits, and declining productivity because of rigidities in labor laws has been to attack existing pension rights mainly by attempting to encourage individuals to invest in private retirement schemes and to weaken the state's involvement in universal social security.

As discussed earlier, we need to see the issue of pensions against the more general issues of social solidarity and social security. These questions point to the fact that we should look at pensions from the perspective of intergenerational exchanges and the question of generational equity. It is well recognized that the welfare states of Europe have rested on an explicit social contract between generations. This contractual welfare state is based on intergenerational transfers of resources through taxation and social expenditure. In addition to this public or formal contract, there is an informal and domestic contract between generations within households. Generally speaking, the state works to reinforce and sustain the informal contractual arrangements within households. With the aging of Western populations, declining fertility, and compulsory retirement, there has been, as we have seen, increasing pressure to modify the generational contract. Critics of the existing arrangements have argued that the Baby Boomers or the 'welfare generation' has captured the welfare state and its resources, ensuring that social funding is directed away from the young to the elderly (Thomson, 1996). The social construction of a 'demographic imperative' is based on the economic assumption that welfare is a 'public burden.' Lobby groups in the United States have campaigned against public expenditure on the elderly and promoted the idea of personal responsibility and obligation within the family. We have already drawn attention to similar developments in Thatcher's Britain.

There has been considerable discussion on the nature of norms of reciprocity (Goudlner, 1960) and their significance for 'age integration' that is intergenerational solidarity. It has been claimed that modern societies are less tightly organized around age boundaries, and as a result, there is more 'age heterogeneity' in public institutions such as universities and work places (Riley White and Riley, 2000). This view of the breakdown of age stratification along ascribed criteria creates greater opportunities for age integration, and this process would improve age integration. In these debates, however, it is important to treat generational relations among kin as distinct but not separate from generational relations within society more generally. While one might take an optimistic view of familial affection and reciprocity, can we still anticipate a decisive conflict on generational interests and cultures in the public domain? We must not confuse affection between immediate kin with the absence of generational conflict in society more broadly.

The debate about intergenerational reciprocity can be usefully divided into two broad camps (Williamson et al., 2003). There is the generational equity (GE) argument that each generation should take care of itself rather than relying on other generations or the state. Privatization of resources is one logical outcome of this position. The alternative is generational interdependence (GI), which emphasizes the diversity of emotional, cultural, and economic exchanges between generations, and in criticizing the emphasis on economic exchange, the GI draws attention to the social importance of reciprocity norms.

The GE framework arose, as we have noted earlier, in the 1980s as a response to the perception of a looming economic crisis attendant upon radical demographic changes. This framework was associated with a number of conservative institutions, such as the Cato Institute and the Olin Foundation. It also had an advocacy wing characterized by AGE (Americans for Generational Equity). Their argument was based on the findings of empirical research, which suggested that while the economic status of the elderly had been improving, that of their children had been declining. This framework argued both that existing provisions were unfair and more importantly unaffordable (Marmor et al., 1999). Dependency ratios, it was claimed, between workers and pensioners showed that current welfare arrangements could not be sustained in the twenty-first century and immediate action was required to provide for these demographic changes. It was in this context that economists like Lester Thurow (1996) predicted that age wars would replace class wars as the elderly use their political influence through interest groups, such as AARP, to steer resources toward pensions and health care and away from educational investments for younger generations. As age conflict increases, the possibilities for age integration decline.

The GI framework arose essentially as a critique of these pessimistic predictions about generational conflict. The GI position notes that the elderly do not function as an integrated and coherent category but are divided, like the rest of the population, by class, gender, and ethnicity. The interests of rich and poor elderly do not necessarily coincide. Furthermore, there is little evidence that they vote as a block and often the interests of different age groups coincide. For example, in the early 1980s, young and old opposed cuts to education and health programmes (Minkler, 1991). A recent analysis of data from the British Retirement Plans Survey, undertaken by the Office for National Statistics on behalf of the Department of Social Security, found that parents who help their children are more likely to receive support, children respond to parents in need, and that divorced fathers are the least likely to be involved in exchanges with children (Grundy, 2005). These findings also suggested that parents are giving more than they receive, and therefore, they are not a burden on the young. Finally, it is unrealistic to expect each generation to be responsible for itself, because this ignores historical contingency. The generation of the Depression faced unusually hard circumstances, which shaped its entire future (Elder, 1974). Similarly, we may speculate that the current credit crisis and the turmoil in the American housing market will have a significant impact on young families who are struggling with a global financial meltdown, which is not of their making. Research on generations clearly demonstrates that historical contingency means that we cannot assume a level playing field between generations, and hence, the idea of fairness is not easily applied in these circumstances. The problem with the GE perspective is that it makes little allowance for vulnerable groups who do not have the resources to cope with exceptional circumstances, such as natural disasters, economic recession, or civil conflict. In all of these responses to aging populations and resources, it is very difficult to see how social justice between generations can be achieved. Any significant prolongation of life certainly intensifies conflicts over resources even where these public conflicts may be absent within the family and the domestic household. Despite the cogency of the GI criticism, it is nevertheless the case that the GE lobby has been successful because the simple logic of its appeal to individualism resonates with the neoliberal climate that was sustained after the departure of political leaders like President Reagan and Prime Minister Thatcher. The appeal to responsibility and personal choice against mandatory measures remains a potent aspect of the view that generational interests are on a collision course.

Concluding Thoughts on Intergenerational Solidarity

There is an ongoing debate in sociology over the tendency of social scientists to overemphasize generational conflict at the risk of pitting one generation against the other. In the analysis of social classes, sociologists have faced a similar issue when discussing the conflict between 'real' or 'theoretical' classes (Bourdieu, 1998). In historical terms, the existence of generational conflict appears to depend on the real or assumed scarcity of resources available to sustain a reasonable level of generational equity. Scarcity of arable land in much of Northern Europe during the Middle Ages was a contributing factor in such generational disputes. By contrast, an abundance of land in colonial New England contributed to generational harmony (Cole, 1992). By focusing on the concept of generational habitus, it is suggested here that generational groups, which are unequally equipped with power, are continuously involved in struggles for scarce resources and legitimacy. It is also argued that the sociopolitical space defines the nature of these struggles and that their intensity may vary according to different social fields. We can imagine, for instance, harmonious relationships between father and son in the family setting, but a discordant one over pension schemes allocated by the collective agreement of their trade union. We agree with John Vincent (2005: 582) that such relations are not stable and constitute a set of continuing relationships between the groups through time.

From the perspective of social citizenship, we can assume that intergenerational solidarity has two main functions. First, at the individual level, it contributes to well-being or more technically to our ontological security in periods of uncertainty. With continuous threats to the welfare state, employment, income security, and the collective provision of care, it is likely that the most dependant groups will suffer hardship from lack of control over their future. This claim follows from our more foundational argument that human beings are characterized by their vulnerability and by the precarious character of their social and political arrangements (Turner, 2001: 206). If we consider that generations embody the conditions of existence of their time, then this issue of ontological security becomes relevant for their present and future situation. How will a generation react when facing such an urgent crisis? Will they tend toward an individualistic or solidaristic response? If there is no generational contract or no solidarity, who will determine the type of social protection required to reduce social suffering or to prevent it from reoccurring? The globalization of strategies to privatize pensions suggests that individualistic solutions are being adopted despite significant opposition from trade unions in continental Europe.

Second, from a societal level, intergenerational solidarity can be perceived through the lens of social capital. We can speculate that the continuous fracturing and fragmentation of society in general will lead to increasing alienation, reduction in trust, and generation gaps, which will have some profound societal consequences. The GI framework's focus on reciprocal relations is essentially a reaction against the decline of social capital in society. Implicit in this problem is the erosion of social citizenship and the weakness of institutions to promote the entitlements and obligations between members of society to strengthen social ties through mutual reciprocity. Because many of the sources of conflict emerge from issues which are endogenous to the welfare state (education, health care, work, and pensions), this erosion signifies a strong control of internal politics. Although all nation-states privilege a particular form of solidarity with regard to pensions – given the clear success of Japan and North European countries – some types of solidarity function better than others. This solidarity can take multiple forms, such as transmission of knowledge between generations, later retirements, and better access to continuing education. These policy arrangements would likely increase cohesion in the workforce and reduce the negative consequence of the pension crisis on the welfare state and shortage of qualified workforce (Guillemard, 2000, 2007).

Younger generations have often been portrayed as the creators of new models attenuating the problems of their generation. However, with regard to intergenerational politics, the social, economic, and demographic context appears to be incompatible with such political developments. Drawing on Mannheim, these agents of social change participate in the historical transformation of a field by contributing to the birth of fundamental intentions of a generation; they meet through social exchanges, mentally stimulate each other, and ultimately work together to concretize their intentions (Mannheim, 1972). With the struggles over scarce resources between generations, social groups may feel overwhelmed to attempt to change the dynamic between generations. Perhaps, the debates on intergenerational justice will, as Touraine (2000) would argue, be sufficient to raise social awareness on new social demands and on the new forms of social and cultural participation that face the demographic challenges of our times.

There is a trend for new regimes of postnational rights that aim to protect social groups against the negative effects of globalization and to protect future generations from global environmental crises. It is clear that globalization has generated new conditions of vulnerability, particularly among the emergent generations in underdeveloped countries. The HIV/AIDS epidemic, the peculiarities of modern warfare, and sex trafficking are likely to afflict areas of the world with increased crime, inappropriate education, and demographic imbalance. Just as social class or gender analysis have offered valuable insights into social stratification, the sociology of generations will certainly be useful in understanding the generational divides, the reproduction of inequality, and the pauperization of the working force within these areas of the world. In this chapter, we have attempted to demonstrate the advantages of combining the sociological study of generations and citizenship as a framework for understanding the contemporary transformations of the welfare state.

References

Attias-Donfut, C. (1991). *Générations et âges de la vie*. Paris: Presses Universitaires de France.
Bell, D. (1999). *The coming of post-industrial society. A venture in social forecasting* (new edition). New York, NY: Basic Books.
Bourdieu, P. (1993). Youth is just a word. In P. Bourdieu (Ed.), *Sociology in Question* (pp. 94–102). London: Sage.
Bourdieu, P. (1998). *Practical reason: On the theory of action*. Polity: Cambridge.
Chauvel, L. (2002). *Le destin des générations. Structure sociale et cohortes en France au XXe siècle*. Paris: Presses Universitaires de France.
Cheal, D. (1995). Repenser les transferts intergénérationnels. Axes de recherche sur les relations temporelles dans les pays anglo-saxons. In C. Attias-Donfut (Ed.), *Les solidarités entre les générations. Vieillesse, familles, État* (pp. 259–268). Paris: Natan.
Cole, T. R. (1992) *The journey of life. A cultural history of aging in America*. Cambridge: Cambridge University Press.
Dahrendorf, R. (1959). *Class and class conflict in an industrial society*. London: Routledge and Kegan Paul.
Dumas., A., & Turner, B. S. (2006). Age and ageing: The social world of Foucault and Bourdieu. In J. L. Powell & A. Wahidin (Eds.), *Foucault and ageing* (pp. 145–155). New York, NY: Nova Science Publishers.

Dumas, A., & Laforest, S. (2008). Intergenerational conflict: What can skateboarding tell us about the struggles for legitimacy in the field of sports? *Idrottsforum*. idrottsforum.org. Accessed 1 June 2008.

Edmunds, J. T., & Turner, B. S. (2002). *Generation, culture and society*. Philadelphia: Open University Press.

Elder, G. H., Jr. (1974). *Children of the great depression: Social change in life experience*. Chicago: Chicago University Press.

Eyerman, R., & Turner, B. S. (1998). Outline of a theory of generations. *European Journal of Social Theory, 1*(1), 91–106.

Fukuyama, F. (2002). *Our posthuman futures: Consequences of biotechnology revolutions*. New York, NY: Picador.

Gilleard, C., & Higgs, P. (2005). *Contexts of ageing. Class, cohort and community*. Cambridge: Polity.

Goudlner, A. (1960). The norm of reciprocity: A preliminary statement. *American Sociological Review, 25*(2), 161–178.

Grundy, E. (2005). Reciprocity in relationships: Socioeconomic and health influences on intergenerational exchanges between Third Age parents and their adult children in Great Britain. *British Journal of Sociology, 56*(2), 233–255.

Guillemard, A.-M. (2000). *Aging and the welfare state crisis*. Newark, NJ: University of Delaware Press.

Guillemard, A.-M. (2007). Une nouvelle solidarité entre les âges et les générations dans une société de longévité. In S. Paugam (Ed.), *Repenser la solidarité. L'apport des sciences sociales* (pp. 335–375). Paris: Presses Universitaires de France.

Hespanha, P. (1995). Vers une société providence simultanément pré- et post-moderne. L'état des solidarités intergénérationnelles au Portugal. In C. Attias-Donfut (Ed.), *Les solidarités entre générations. Vieillesse, familles, État* (pp. 209–221). Paris: Nathan.

Klinenberg, E. (2002). *Heat wave: A social autopsy of a disaster in Chicago*. Chicago, IL: University of Chicago press.

Kohli, M. (1995). La présence de l'histoire. In C. Attias-Donfut (Ed.), *Les solidarités entre générations. Vieillesse, familles, État* (pp. 245–258). Paris: Nathan.

Kotlikoff, L. J. (1992). *Generational accounting: Knowing who pays, and when, for what we spend*. Toronto: Maxwell Macmillan.

Laslett, P. (1989). *A fresh map of life. The emergence of the third age*. London: Weidenfeld and Nicolson.

Mannheim, K. (1972). *Essays on the sociology of knowledge*. London: Routledge and Kegan Paul Ltd.

Masson, A. (1995). L'héritage au sein des transferts entre générations: théorie, constat, perspectives. In C. Attias-Donfut (Ed.), *Les solidarités entre générations. Vieillesse, familles, État* (pp. 279–325). Paris: Nathan.

Mauger, G. (1990). Postface. In K. Mannheim (Ed.), *Le problème des générations* (pp. 85–115). Paris: Nathan.

Marmor, T. R., Cook, F. L., & Scher, S. (1999). Social security and the politics of generational conflict. In J. B. Williamson, E. R. Kingson & D. M. Watts-Roy (Eds.), *The Generational Equity Debate* (pp. 185–203). New York, NY: Columbia University Press.

Minkler, M. (1991). 'Generational equity' and the new victim blaming. In M. Minkler & C. Estes (Eds.), *Critical perspectives in aging* (pp. 67–79). Amityville, NY: Baywood Press.

OECD (2005). Labour force statistics: 1984–2004, Trends in international migration. http://ocde. p4.siteinternet.com/publications/doifiles/012005061T001.xls. Accessed 10 August 2008.

OECD (2007). Society at a glance: OECD social indicators – 2006 edition. OECD. www.oecd. org/els/social/indicators/SAG. Accessed 1 August 2008.

Phillipson, C. (1996). Intergenerational conflict and the welfare state: American and British perspectives. In A. Walker (Ed.), *The new generational contract. Intergenerational relations, old age and welfare* (pp. 206–220). London: UCL Press.

Pierson, P. (1998). Irresistible forces, immovable objects: post-industrial welfare states confront permanent austerity. *Journal of European Public Policy, 5*(4), 539–560.

Preston, S. (1984). Children and the elderly: Divergent paths for America's dependents. *Demography, 21*(4), 435–457.

Richta, R. (1969). *Civilization at the crossroads. Social and human implications of the scientific and technological revolution.* New York, NY: White Plains.

Riley White, M., & Riley, J.W. (2000). Age integration: Conceptual and historical background. *The Gerontologist, 40*(3), 266–270.

Schultheis, F. (1995). Trois modèles de solidarité dans les systèmes de protection sociale. In C. Attias-Donfut (Ed.), *Les solidarités entre générations. Vieillesse, familles, État* (pp. 269–278). Paris: Nathan.

Thurow, L. C. (1996). The birth of a revolutionary class. *The New York Times Magazine,* May 19, 46–47.

Thomson, D. (1996). *Selfish generations? How welfare states grow old.* Cambridge: White Horse Press.

Touraine, A. (1971). The post-industrial society. *Tomorrow's social history: classes, conflicts and culture in the programmed society.* New York, NY: Random House.

Touraine, A. (2000). Forward to the original French edition. In A.-M. Guillemard (Ed.), *Aging and the welfare state crisis* (pp. 9–14). Newark, NJ: University of Delaware Press.

Turner, B. S. (2001). The erosion of citizenship. *British Journal of Sociology, 2*(52), 189–209.

Turner, B. S. (2005). Citizenship, rights and health care. In J. Germov (Ed.), *Second opinion 3rd edition* (pp. 399–413). Oxford: Oxford University Press

Turner, B. S. (2006). Citizenship and the crisis of multiculturalism. *Citizenship Studies, 10*(5), 607–618.

Vincent, J. A. (2005). Understanding generations: political economy and culture in an ageing society. *British Journal of Sociology, 56*(4), 579–599.

Walker, A. (1996). Intergenerational relations and the provision of welfare. In A. Walker (Ed.), *The new generational contract. Intergenerational relations, old age and welfare* (pp. 10–36). London: UCL Press.

Williamson, J. B., McNamara, T. K., & Howling, S. A. (2003). Generational equity, generational interdependence and the framing of the debate over social security reform. *Journal of Sociology and Social Welfare, 30*(3), 3–14.

Chapter 4
Social Welfare, Aging, and Globalization in a Post-industrial Society

Chris Phillipson

Introduction

The purpose of this chapter is to provide an interpretation of some of the key social and economic changes affecting older people, relating these to the major developments affecting many organizations and relationships with which they are closely identified. Social welfare, or the welfare state, is one of the most important, but this institution must itself be related to the broader changes now influencing the lives of different groups of older people. Making sense of these developments, especially in the context of aging, raises complex issues, requiring linkages – as the approach taken by this book implies – between a range of concepts and ideas.

This chapter will assess the main issues under a number of headings and themes. First, 'post-industrialism' will itself be defined and its implications for understanding the lives of older people assessed. Second, the chapter will consider the impact of the 'unravelling' of industrialism and the main features associated with this development. Third, the discussion will move to new questions posed by the advent of globalization, with the influence of international governmental organizations (IGOs), and the evolution of transnational communities. Finally, the chapter will conclude with a summary of the main themes and issues examined in the different sections, along with a consideration of the main implications for social policy.

Post-Industrialism and the Nation-State

The first task is to say something about the meaning of 'post-industrial' in the context of aging. The idea of post-industrial societies has been a contested theme within the social sciences (Giddens, 1987), although its shortcomings as a concept have been at least equally matched by the importance of the questions

C. Phillipson (✉)
Centre for Social Gerontology, Keele University, Keele, Staffordshire, United Kingdom
e-mail: spa05@keele.ac.uk

J. Powell, J. Hendricks, *The Welfare State in Post-Industrial Society*,
DOI 10.1007/978-1-4419-0066-1_4, © Springer Science+Business Media, LLC 2009

raised (Kumar, 1995). Essentially, the idea is associated with the work of Daniel Bell (1974), who in his book, *The Coming of Post-Industrial Society*, identified a number of major shifts in the structure of Western societies, notably the move from a manufacturing to a service economy, the apparent decline of the working class (a theme developed in more detail by André Gorz, 1982), and the rise of professional and technical groups (reflected in the expansion – from the 1960s onward – of the university system). These changes were seen as presenting a fundamental challenge to the basis of industrialism, with the creation of a different kind of society – one soon to be dominated by technology and automation (see, for example, Toffler, 1970).

Many analysts of the 'post-industrial' theme have, in fact, preferred to stress the continuities with previous epochs, suggesting that the driving forces appear little different from those associated with industrialism itself (Kumar, 2006). Against this, debates around post-industrialization were to spawn a number of linked ideas, many of which do point to social changes relevant to understanding the issues affecting older people. Lash & Urry (1987), for example, drew a distinction between what they defined as 'organized' and 'disorganized' capitalism. The former characterized by the spread of manufacturing industry alongside an increasingly urbanized society; the latter associated with more flexible forms of work, the growth of the service sector, and the movement of people and jobs from the older industrial cities. Such developments reflected, Lash & Urry (1987) argued, a heightened degree of instability running through capitalist social relations:

> The world of 'disorganized capitalism' is one in which the 'fixed, fast-frozen relations' of organized capitalist relations have been swept away. Societies are being transformed from above, from below, and from within. All that is solid about organized capitalism, class, industry, cities, collectivity, nation state, even the world, melts into air (Lash & Urry, cited in Kumar, 1995: 49).

What is the relevance of such changes for understanding the lives of older people? One argument is that the transformation associated with the 'disorganized' stage of capitalism illustrates important alterations to modernity itself, notably those institutions which characterised its mature phase of development. For our purposes, it might be argued that institutions such as retirement and the welfare state represent some of the 'big ideas' associated with modernity: the latter viewed as a phase of societal development linked to the rise of capitalism and the nation-state (Phillipson, 1998). Retirement policies were closely identified with the mass production institutions characteristic of organized capitalism (Graebner, 1980). And the welfare state can itself be seen in terms of a 'coming of age' of this type of capitalism, although the combination of the economic depression of the 1930s followed by the Second World War were key contributing factors. But the acceptance of 'new deals' for American and European workers signified recognition that (in the words of Maynard Keynes) 'the cravings for personal and social security' needed a response (cited in Judt, 2005: 73). This eventually comes through both new institutions (expressed in different ways across Europe and the USA) and a new form of citizenship, with social rights complementing those associated with the legal system and politics (Marshall, 1950).

The period of the 1950s and 1960s also coincided with the recognition of the importance of long-term demographic change, with a range of associated issues now placed within the framework of what came to be viewed as a 'welfare state for older people' (Myles, 1984). In the postwar period or up until the economic crisis of the early-1970s, old age was constructed through the pathways provided by organized capitalism. Modernity created the conditions, through social reforms, for the creation of a 'standardized' old age, the end phase of a structured life course divided into periods of education, work, and leisure (Cole, 1992).

But the story of aging, over the past decade or so, has unquestionably been the unraveling of the institutions closely associated with modernity and not the least, those intimately connected with the lives of older people. The next section of this chapter examines the main features of these changes and the impact they have had on older people.

Issues of Aging and Post-Industrialism

One way of understanding social changes since the early-1970s has been presented by Young (1999: 6) in the following way: 'The transition from modernity to late modernity can be seen as a movement from an *inclusive* to an *exclusive* society. That is from a society whose accent was on assimilation and incorporation to one that separates and excludes. This erosion of the inclusive world . . . involved processes of disaggregation both in the sphere of community (the rise of individualism) and the sphere of work (transformation of . . . labour markets). Both processes are the result of market forces and their transformation by the human actors involved.' This type of argument was explored in the work of Beck (1992) and Giddens (1991), both pointing to new forms of uncertainty and insecurity affecting daily life: a bewildering range of personal choice at one level and anxiety and awareness of risk at another. Such elements are further illustrated by the move from the prescribed roles, characteristic of post-industrial society, to the mobile and indeterminate positions, characteristic of mass or industrial society. Beck (2000: 168–69) summarizes these developments in terms of the detraditionalization of everyday life or more accurately the 'individualization of tradition..' He goes on to argue that:

> This does not mean that tradition no longer plays any role – often the opposite is the case. But traditions must be chosen and often invented, and they have force only through the decisions and experiences of individuals. The sources of collective and group identity and of meaning which are characteristic of industrial society (ethnic identity, class consciousness, faith in progress), whose lifestyles and notions of security underpinned Western democracy and economies into the 1960s, here lose their mystique and break up exhausted. Those who live in this post-national, global society are constantly engaged in discarding old classifications and formulating new ones. The

hybrid identities and cultures that ensue are precisely the individuality which determines social integration.

One response to these changes within social gerontology has been to argue that 'post-industrialism' or 'late modernity' creates new opportunities for older people, freed from the limitations or 'structured dependency' (Townsend, 1981) fostered by the welfare state. This argument has been advanced, for example, by Gilleard & Higgs (2005: 153) in their development of ideas about a 'third age' where people have the 'freedom to spend time and money in pursuit of individualized lifestyle goals.' They point to the emergence of a new cultural space, formed by the symbolic and material importance attached to consumption, which is now adding 'value to a longer life.' Aging now has a degree of 'agency,' a feature previously submerged by the restrictions imposed by social welfare.

But this line of argument can be challenged from a number of perspectives. In the first place, the approach taken by Gilleard and Higgs (2005) emphasizes 'choice,' but misses the 'risks' highlighted by Beck. Choice is one thing, but with it comes the potential for 'failure,' whereby 'social crisis phenomena, such as structural unemployment, can be shifted as a burden of risk onto the shoulders of individuals' (Beck, 2000: 166). Indeed, this is precisely what has happened with financial support for older people, with areas such as pension provision – notably the move from defined benefit (DB) to defined contribution (DC) schemes – shifting financial responsibility squarely onto the individual worker (Hacker, 2008; Phillipson, 2009; see, further, below).

Second, the movement from 'inclusion' to 'exclusion' from the early-1970s posed a major challenge to different social groups – older people were one but others were also affected – who had moved out of the labor force and who became vulnerable to the charge of being a 'burden' on society. This partly explains the rise of ageism during the 1970s and 1980s, but more general tensions were illustrated in debates, which presented older people as a 'selfish welfare generation,' with the resulting possibility of 'intergenerational conflict' or 'workers' in potential conflict with 'pensioners' (Thomson, 1989).

Finally, there is the problem of the way in which post-industrial organizations have changed and the wider consequences for workers and their families. This issue has been most clearly addressed by Richard Sennett (1998, 2006), who has highlighted a 'new culture of capitalism,' creating forms of social and economic insecurity within and beyond the workplace. Problems of underemployment, together with feelings of 'uselessness,' appear to be widespread in society. Sennett (1998: 146) argues that capitalism in its post-industrial phase 'radiates indifference' to the well-being of individuals: 'It does so in terms of the outcomes of human striving, as in winner-take-all markets, where there is little connection between risk and reward. It radiates indifference in the organization of absence of trust, where there is no reason to be needed. And it does so through reengineering of institutions in which people are treated as disposable. Such practices obviously and brutally diminish the sense of mattering as a person, of being necessary to others.'

The issues summarized above are best located in the consequences arising from the movement of modernity from its 'organized' (industrial) to 'disorganized' (post-industrial) phase. The distinction is important at a structural level and also in respect of the rewards and opportunities available to individuals. Modernity, from the late-1940s to the early-1970s, appeared to be reconstructing old age around mass retirement (supported by the expansion of defined benefit pensions) underpinned by systems (varying in scope from country) of public welfare. In the United Kingdom, employers used pensions (especially in the 1950s and 1960s) to cultivate a loyal workforce in the context of widespread shortages of skilled labor (Phillipson, 1982). Whiteside (2006) notes how some European countries, faced with the social and economic devastation arising from the Second World War, introduced citizenship pensions (illustrated by Sweden and the Netherlands) to prevent the spread of destitution. In the United States, economic prosperity fostered the expansion of employer-based pensions, but with labor unions such as the United Mine Workers also influencing the adoption of pensions as a key item in collective bargaining (Sass, 1989).

How does the above contrast with capitalism in its present 'disorganized' phase? The key issue here is the undertow of instability and crisis running through the system and the resulting consequences for older workers and the elderly people. A 'disorganized' system is one with job insecurity and a deterioration in the quality of work (Sennett, 2006); where incomes at work become subject to larger fluctuations 'so that both poor and moderately affluent people are increasingly exposed to the risk of a large – like 50 percent – drop in income from one year to the next' (Solow, 2008: 79); where companies close their pension plans to new employees, wishing to withdraw from the 'responsibility of providing pensions' (Munnell, cited in Greenhouse, 2008; see, further, below); and where governments press to 'extend working life' even while drastically reducing the employment options available to the older people (Blackburn, 2006; Phillipson, 2009).

But the insecurities arising from a 'disorganized' system – together with the development of a 'disorganized' old age – have themselves been reinforced by the changes associated with economic and social globalization – a key theme of this book. The next part of this chapter turns toward a more detailed consideration of this development.

Globalization and Changes to the Welfare State

Debates around the impact of globalization on aging are now extensive both within the social gerontology literature (see for example Baars et al., 2006; Estes & Phillipson, 2002) and in studies of social welfare (Mishra, 1999; George & Wilding, 2002; Yeates, 2001). The argument here is that globalization, as an economic, social and cultural force, has become an influential factor in the construction of old age, notably in the design of policies aimed at regulating and managing population aging (Estes et al., 2003). Social policy has itself been affected by globalization in a variety of ways. Yeates (2001: 2), for example, argues that the relationship between globalization and social policy is best conceived as 'dialectical' or 'reciprocal' and that: '...far from states, welfare states and populations passively "receiving" [and] adapting to globalization...they are active participants in its development.'

In general terms, globalization has produced a distinctive phase in the history of aging and the welfare state, with tensions between nation-state-based policies concerning demographic changes and those formulated by global actors and institutions. Three examples will be used to illustrate this argument: first, issues relating to the ideological terrain around which late life is constructed; second, the impact of global forces in the field of pensions; third, the role of globalization in the development of transnational communities.

Globalization and the New Social Welfare: The Role of Ideology

The impact of globalization on ideologies relating to aging has been a highly significant development. A key aspect of this has been the move from debates that focused on aging as a burden for national economies to perspectives that view population aging as a worldwide social problem. The report of the World Bank (1994), *Averting the Old Age Crisis*, was a crucial document in this regard, but more recent contributions have included those from the Central Intelligence Agency (2001) and documents such as *The global retirement crisis*, produced by the Washington-based Center for Strategic and International Studies (Jackson, 2002). There is insufficient space in this chapter to deal with the particular arguments raised by these papers (see, however, the discussion in Vincent, 2006), but the general point raised concerns about what amounts to the *politicization of aging* generated by the intensification of global ties.

The above development has been driven by a number of factors: the growth of neoliberalism is one obvious dimension, this propagating hostility toward collective provision by the state or at the very least a view that private provision is inherently superior to that provided by the public sector (Yeates, 2001; Walker & Deacon, 2003). Politicization has also arisen from the way in which globalization fosters awareness about the relative economic position of one nation-state compared to another. George and Wilding (2002: 58) make the point here: 'Globalization has created an economic and political climate in which national states become more conscious of the taxes they levy and their potential economic implications. Neoliberal ideology feeds and justifies these concerns.' Finally, the ideological debate has been promoted through key supranational bodies, such as the Organization of Economic Cooperation and Development (OECD) and the World Trade Organization (WTO), along with transnational corporations (notably pharmaceutical companies), all of which contributed to a distinctive world view about the framing of policies for old age.

Globalization and Welfare: The Role of Pensions

The ideological terrain has been especially influential in the field of pension provision (Phillipson, 2009; Vincent, 2006). A key dimension in this regard has been the way in which intergovernmental organizations (IGOs) contributed to what has been termed the 'crisis construction and crisis management' of policies for older people (Estes & Associates, 2001). Deacon (2000) suggests that globalization generates a global discourse within and among global actors on the future of social policy, with pension provision being a major area of concern. Yeates (2001) observes that 'Both the World Bank and International Monetary Fund have been at the forefront of attempts to foster a political climate conducive to [limiting the scope of] state welfare . . . promoting [instead] . . . private and voluntary initiatives..' This position has influenced both national governments and transnational bodies, such as the International Labour Organisation (ILO) and the OECD, with an emerging consensus supporting minimal public pension provision, an extended role for individualized and capitalized private pensions, and the raising of the age of retirement.

In Deacon's (2000) terms, this debate amounts to a significant global discourse about pension provision and retirement ages, but one which has largely excluded perspectives which might suggest an enlarged role for the state and those which might question the stability and cost effectiveness of private schemes. The ILO (2002: 1) has concluded that: 'Investing in financial markets is an uncertain and volatile business: under present pension plans people may save up to 30 per cent more than they need - which would reduce their spending during their working life; or they may save 30 per cent too little - which would severely cut their spending in retirement.' Add in as well the crippling administrative charges associated with the running of private schemes, and the advocacy of market-based provision hardly seems as persuasive as most IGOs have been keen to present (Blackburn, 2006).

Globalization, in fact, provided fresh impetus to transforming the financing of old age from a social to an individual responsibility. On the one side, growing old has come to be viewed as a global problem and concern; on the other side, has come the individualizing of risks through the life course (O'Rand, 2000). These are no longer seen as requiring the collective solutions of a mature welfare state. Indeed, as Blackburn (2006: 4) suggests, individuals and institutions have now to be "weaned from the teat of public finance and learn how to be 'responsible risk takers' . . . rejecting the old forms of dependence of which the old age pension was a prime example." Globalization has, in fact, introduced a new paradox to the experience of aging. Growing older seems to have become *more* secure, with longer life expectancy and enhanced life styles in old age. Set against this, the pressures associated with the achievement of security are themselves generating fresh anxieties among cohorts of all ages. The language of social insurance, established during the 1940s, appears to have been displaced in the twenty-first century by the 'mantra of personal responsibility' and risk-taking (Hacker, 2008).

In the United States, Hacker (2008) notes that the share of working-age households at risk of being financially unprepared for retirement at 65 years has increased from 31 percent in 1983 to more than 43 percent in 2006. He highlights the fact that: 'Younger Americans, who have borne the brunt of the transformation of retirement protection, are far more likely to be at risk than older Americans. Roughly *half* (author's emphasis) of those born from the mid-1960s through the early 1970s are at risk of being financially unprepared, compared with around 35 per cent of those born in the decade after the war' (Hacker, 2008).

Despite ambitious claims for the virtues of market as opposed to collective provision, the proportion of working-age people in the United Kingdom saving for their retirement actually *declined* over the period from 1999/2000 to 2005/2006 (Department for Work and Pensions (DWP), 2007). This reflects the long-term fall in occupational pension provision, yet to be offset by the growth of personal (DC) pensions (DWP, 2008). There has been a substantial (and – in terms of rapidity – largely unforeseen) decline in the United Kingdom in membership of defined benefit (DB) schemes: in 2000, active members – i.e. current employees accruing new benefits – in nongovernment (private sector) DB schemes totalled *4.1 million*; this figure had dropped to *1.3 million* by 2007 (Office for National Statistics (ONS), 2008). This figure was actually below the modeling assumptions used in the United Kingdom Pension Commission's (2004) *First Report* which suggested a long-term floor of around 1.6–1.8 million members. Seventy percent of final salary DB schemes in the United Kingdom are now (2008) closed to new employees, compared with just 17 percent in 2001. Robert Peston's (2008: 255) summary of the pension crisis bears the hallmarks of the characteristics of 'disorganized capitalism' in its post-industrial phase:

> What has happened to corporate pensions funds reflects a change in the culture of the U.K., the abandonment of the notion that companies have a moral obligation to promote the welfare of their employees after a lifetime of service. It is part and parcel of the death of paternalism and the rise of individualism. Company directors are no longer asking what it cost them to provide a comfortable retirement for staff. Instead, the majority of big companies are investigating the price of ridding themselves of any responsibility for their retired workforce. This is a less conspicuous but hugely important example of how the wealth of the many is being eroded, while that of the super-rich has soared.

Globalization and Welfare: The Role of Transnational Communities

Globalization has also played a significant role in reshaping relationships and communities which give meaning to life in old age. This arises to a considerable extent from what Urry (2007) refers to as the 'mobilities' generated through globalization – the constant movement and interconnectedness of people and ideas. Urry (2000: 13) notes, in this context, Mann's description of the contemporary world: 'Today we live in a global society. It is not a unitary society, nor is it an ideological community or a state, but it is a single power network. Shock waves reverberate around it, casting down empires, transporting massive quantities of people, materials and messages . . . .' Older people sit uneasily in this powerful circulatory system. They are an important migratory group – both within and across different countries (Longino & Warnes, 2005). Warnes (2009) notes the scale of international movement among UK retirees, as recorded in the payment of State Pensions to addresses outside the United Kingdom. These quadrupled from 252,000 in March 1981, through 679,800 in 1995, to over one million in January 2006, an average annual growth rate during 1981–2005 of 5.9 percent. The number of residents in foreign countries is a rising percentage of all UK State Pensioners – 6.6 percent in 1995 and 8.6 percent in 2005.

Just as important are the transnational communities of which older people – whether as migrants or relatives of migrants – are a significant part. For societies in the twenty-first century, communities of families and relations sustained across wide geographical distances are likely to play an increasingly influential role in daily life. The American demographer Douglas Massey (2000: 134) argues that, barring some calamity or radical shift in family-planning trends, 'migration will play a greater role than reproduction in determining the strength and tenor of our societies.' One consequence of this is that what has been termed 'transnational communities' will be increasingly influential in reshaping family life. Transnational communities may be said to arise from a context in which those who leave a country and those who stay may remain connected through social and symbolic ties maintained over time and across space in complex patterns of exchange and support.

Transnational communities themselves create 'global families,' arising through the process of international migration. Arlie Hochschild (2000) argues that most writing about globalization focuses on money, markets, and flow of labor, with limited attention to women, children, and the support from one to the other. But older people need to be added to this list. Elderly people are part of the global flow: they grow old as migrants and are part of the care chain in giving and receiving care. In this context, globalization is producing a new kind of aging, one in which the dynamics of family life may be stretched across a number of continents.

This development produces greater diversity in respect of the social networks within which growing old is shaped and managed. Typically, older people's networks have been examined within national borders, and their need for care and support assessed within this context. But migrants show important varia- tions in social ties with responsibilities and resources that may stretch across considerable physical distances.

King and Vullnetari (2006) explored the impact of the mass migration of young people from Albania, notably on those older people living in rural parts of the country. They report feelings of separation and abandonment among the older generation, heightened by the realization that their children are unlikely to return (Vullnetari & King, 2008). The Albanian case illustrates problems of maintaining ties with relatives who may have entered a destination country without having any legal position, with their 'undocumented status making it difficult for them to return' to their homeland country (Vullnetari & King, 2008: 788).

In contrast to the above, there are numerous examples in the literature of migrants moving 'backwards and forwards' between their 'first' and 'second' homeland, subject to financial and domestic constraints. Goulborne (1999) (see also Bauer & Thompson, 2006) highlights the 'back and forth' movement of his Caribbean families living in Britain. Similar descriptions have been linked to first generation Bangladeshi migrants in the United Kingdom (Gardner, 2002; Phillipson et al., 2003); to Italian migrants in Perth, Western Australia (Baldassar et al., 2007); and to members of the Turkish community living in Germany (Naegele, 2008). This movement reflects what Christine Ho (1991) has described, in her research on Anglo-Trinidadians living in Los Angeles, as 'the concerted effort [of migrants] to sustain connections across time and geography.'

Bauer & Thompson (2006: 210–211) make the point in their study of Jamaican migrants that the possibilities for keeping in touch have greatly increased over the past decade: 'Cheaper flights have encouraged more frequent visits to distant kin. Some older women have become regular fliers visiting children and grandchildren [and] another interesting and apparently growing phenomenon is the transnational family reunion.' Wilding (2006: 132) highlights the role of different forms of Information and Communication Technology (ICT) – notably e-mail – in maintaining contact across national boundaries.

An unspoken assumption in the gerontological literature is that 'proper care' is that which is available 'close by' or within the immediate vicinity of the older person. In contrast, research on transnational communities highlights the possibilities of sustaining support across considerable geographical distances. Baldassar (2007: 276), for example, provides: ' . . . a critique of the preoccupation and assumption in the gerontology literature that care-giving requires proximity.' She notes: 'Empirically, the general preoccupation with geographic proximity means that very little research has been done on the relationships between ageing parents and adult children who live at a distance . . . , with the result that transnational practices of care have remained largely invisible or assumed to be unfeasible.' Against this, if we recognize the different dimensions associated with care and support – practical, financial, personal, emotional, and moral – then distinctive possibilities emerge for maintaining a caring relationship of one kind or another across national boundaries. These will almost certainly introduce new forms of social welfare into the lives of older people, with significant implications for social policy (Warnes et al., 2004). This point is developed further in the final section, which reviews some of the wider implications of the issues raised in this chapter.

Conclusion: Transforming Social Welfare in a Global Context

This chapter has considered a range of issues arising from changes associated with the move from industrial to post-industrial societies. On the one hand, these appear to have introduced greater volatility or 'disorganisation' (to use

Lash and Urry's phrase) into the lives of the older people: retirement, to take one illustration, is more difficult to prepare for when incomes are uncertain or when job tenure is less secure. At the same time, adding to the experience of a less organized world are the forces associated with globalization, we have suggested these as introducing significant ideological, financial, and relational changes into experiences in later life. On the other hand, it is important to recognize arguments which suggest a greater degree of 'agency' is possible as individuals move through the life course. 'Choice' must be balanced against the downsides which can accompany 'risks,' with a more stratified old age one inevitable consequence.

Responding to the above analysis, at the level of social policy, three observations might be made. First, tackling globalization at an *ideological level* will require active interventions on the part of older people, either as individuals or through organizations working on their behalf. The record here, despite the importance of bodies such as the American Association of Retired Persons (AARP) in the USA, is distinctly patchy, especially when viewed in terms of influencing the policies of key IGOs. At the same time, a new basis for a 'politics of aging' may be emerging, one in which issues relevant to old age may be followed throughout the life course. Interest groups of older people could begin to form new alliances with younger workers concerned about their prospects for old age. Moreover, in contrast to the generational equity perspective that attempts to pit older and younger generations against one another, these coalitions are just as likely to be based upon a view of a shared interest across generations in ensuring that rights to state and public pension are maintained.

Second, based on the problems highlighted in this chapter, a new *global discourse on pensions* will need to be developed, one which challenges the view that government provision should be reduced and reliance on the market increased. The experience thus far indicates that market provision has led to a deepening of inequalities among different groups of workers and pensioners, that significant groups are likely to remain without the support of a viable additional pension, and that the volatility of the market is in direct contradiction to the need for security and certainty in old age (Phillipson, 2009; Krugman, 2007). This discourse will need to challenge the neoliberal consensus around pensions, adopted in IGOs, such as the World Bank, the International Monetary Fund, and the OECD (Estes & Phillipson, 2002). These bodies have been able to exert a considerable influence on the pension debate, but one which has marginalized views regarding the necessity of substantial public sector provision.

Third, *transnational communities bring major issues for social policy* with the development of groups holding together care tasks or financial responsibilities that may be strung across continents. Cross-cultural social networks will continue to thrive, sustained through the expanded possibilities introduced by new technology. The key issue, however, is the extent to which these additional elements of citizenship are given due acknowledgement in the countries to which people migrate (Ackers & Dwyer, 2002). The argument here is that, without such recognition, new forms of social exclusion may appear and full participation in society may be compromised. Transnational communities do, in fact, promote social inclusion in a variety of ways – through generating new forms of social capital; through remittances; through paid and unpaid labor; and through the maintenance of strong social ties. All of these aspects may be highly positive for older migrants, especially in a context where the welfare state is withdrawing from significant areas of responsibility. Greater understanding of the meaning of new forms of community is both an important challenge for social policy and a major issue for research on aging to address.

In general terms, social welfare is set to evolve in new and distinctive ways, with policies for older people among those targeted for radical change. The stakes are likely to be high in respect of the implications for the well-being and quality of life of existing and future cohorts. This chapter has identified some of the major issues that are emerging, along with some of the implications for social policy. The post-industrial society brings opportunities for improving the lives of the older people, along with dilemmas and risks. At the same time, ensuring recognition of the different challenges faced will be crucial in the years ahead and will pose a major set of research questions for social gerontology to address.

References

Ackers, L., & Dwyer, P. (2002). *Senior citizenship: Retirement, migration and welfare*. Bristol: Policy Press.

Baars, J., Dannefer, D., Phillipson, C., & Walker, A. (Eds.) (2006). *Aging, globalization and inequality: The new critical gerontology*. Amityville, NY: Baywood.

Baldassar, L. (2007). Transnational families and aged care: The mobility of care and migrancy of ageing'. *Journal of Ethnic and Migration Studies, 33*(2), 275–297.

Baldassar, L., Baldock, C. V., & Wilding, R. (2007). *Families caring across borders*. London: Palgrave.

Bauer, E., & Thompson, P. (2006). *Jamaican hands across the Atlantic*. Kingston: Ian Randle Publishers.

Beck, U. (1992). *The risk society*. London: Sage Books.

Beck, U. (2000). Living your own life in a runaway world: Individualisation, globalisation and politics. In W. Hutton, & A. Giddens, (Eds.). *On the edge* (pp. 164–175). London: Jonathan Cape.

Bell, D. (1974). *The coming of post-industrial society*. London: Heinemann.

Blackburn, R. (2006). *Age shock: How finance is failing us*. London: Verso.

Central Intelligence Agency. (2001). *Long term global demographic trends: re-shaping the geopolitical landscape*. http://www.odci.gov/cia/reports/index/html. Accessed December 1st, 2008.

Cole, T. (1992). *The journey of life*. Cambridge: Cambridge University Press.

Deacon, B. (2000). *Globalisation and social policy: The threat to equitable welfare*. Occasional Paper no.5, Globalism and Social Policy Programme (GASPP), UNRIS3.

Department for Work and Pensions. (2007). *Family resources survey 2005–06*. London: DWP.

Department for Work and Pensions. (2008). *Pensions bill – impact assessment*. London: DWP.

Estes, C., & Associates. (2001). *Social policy and aging*. Thousand Oaks: Sage Books.

Estes, C., & Phillipson, C. (2002). The globalisation of capital, the welfare state and old age policy. *International Journal of Health Services, 32*(2), 279–297.

Estes, C., Biggs, S., & Phillipson, C. (2003). *Social theory, social policy and ageing: A critical introduction*. Buckingham: Open University Press.

Gardner, K. (2002). *Age, narrative and migration*. Oxford: Berg.

George, V., & Wilding, P. (2002). *Globalization and human welfare*. London: Palgrave.

Giddens, A. (1987). *Social theory and modern sociology*. Cambridge: Polity Press.

Giddens, A. (1991) *Modernity & self-identity*. Cambridge: Polity Press.

Gilleard, C., & Higgs, P. (2005). *Contexts of ageing*. Cambridge: Polity Press.

Gorz, A. (1982). *Farewell to the working class*. London: Pluto.

Goulborne, H. (1999). The transnational character of Caribbean kinship. Britain. (pp. 176–199). In S. McRae, (Ed.). *Changing Britain: Families and households in the 1990s*. Oxford: Oxford University Press.

Graebner, W. (1980). *A history of retirement*. Yale: Yale University Press.

Greenhouse, S. (2008). *The big squeeze: Tough times for the American worker*. New York: Knopf.

Hacker, J. (2008). *The great risk shift*. New York: Oxford University Press.

Ho, C. (1991). *Salt-water trinnies: Afro-Trinidadian immigrant networks and non-assimilation in Los Angeles*. New York: AMS Press.

Hochschild, A. (2000). Global care chains and emotional surplus value. In W. Hutton, & A. Giddens, (Eds.), *On the edge: Living with global capitalism*. London: Jonathan Cape.

International Labour Organisation. (2002). *Press Release*. Geneva: ILO.

Jackson, R. (2002). *The global retirement crisis*. Center for Strategic and International Studies. Washington: Citigroup/CSIS.

Johnson, P., Conrad, C., & Thomson, D., (Eds.). (1989). *Workers versus pensioners: Intergenerational justice in an ageing world*. Manchester: University of Manchester Press.

Judt, T. (2005). *Postwar: A history of Europe since 1945*. London: Heinemann.

King, R., & Vullnetari, J. (2006). Orphan pensioners and migrating grandparents: The impact of mass migration on older people. *Ageing and Society, 26*, 783–816.

Kumar, K. (1995). *From post-industrial to post-modern society*. Oxford: Basil Blackwell.

Kumar, K. (2006). Post industrial Society. In B. Turner, (Ed.). *The Cambridge dictionary of sociology* (pp. 457–8). Cambridge: Cambridge University Press.

Krugman, P. (2007). *The conscience of a Liberal*. New York: W. W. Norton.

Lash, S., & Urry, J. (1987). *The end of organised capitalism*. Cambridge: Polity Press.

Longino, C. F., Jr., & Warnes, A. M. (2005). Migration and older people. In M.L. Johnson, (Ed.), *Cambridge Encyclopedia of ageing* (pp. 538–45). Cambridge: Cambridge University Press.

Marshall, T. H. (1950). *Citizenship and social class and other essays*. Cambridge: Cambridge University Press.

Massey, D. (2000). To study migration today, look to a parallel era. *The chronicle of higher education*, August 18th, B4–B5.

Mishra, R. (1999). *Globalization and the welfare state*. Cheltenham: Edward Elgar.

Myles, J. (1984). *Old age in the welfare state: The political economy of public pensions*. Lawrence, KS: University Press of Kansas.

Naegele, G. (2008). *Age and migration in Germany – an overview with a special consideration of the Turkish population*. Paper to the 61st Annual Scientific Meeting of the Gerontological Society of America, Washington, D.C.

O'Rand, A. M. (2000). Risk, rationality, and modernity: social policy and the aging self (pp. 225–249), In K.W. Schaie, (Ed.), *Social structures and aging*. New York: Springer.

Office for National Statistics. (2008) *Occupational pensions schemes Survey* 2007. London: ONS.

Pensions Commission. (2004). *Pensions: Challenges and choices. The first report of the pensions commission*. London: The Stationery Office (TSO).

Peston, R. (2008). *Who runs Britain?* London: Hodder.

Phillipson, C. (1982). *Capitalism and the construction of old age*. London Macmillan.

Phillipson, C. (1998). *Reconstructing old age*. Sage, London.

Phillipson, C. (2009). Pensions in crisis: Aging and inequality in a global age. In L. Rogne, C. Estes, B. Grossman, B. Hollister, & E. Solway, (Eds.), *Social Insurance and Social Justice (Eds.)*, (pp 319–340). New York: Springer Publishing Company.

Phillipson, C., Ahmed, N., & Latimer, J. (2003). *Women in transition: A study of the experiences of Bangladeshi women living in Tower Hamlets*. Bristol: Policy Press.

Sass, S. (1989). Pension bargaining: The heyday of US collectively bargained pension arrangements. In P. Johnson, C. Conrad, & D. Thomson, (Eds.), *Workers versus pensioners: Intergenerational justice in an ageing world* (pp. 92–112). Manchester: Manchester University Press.

Sennett, R. (1998). *The corrosion of character*. New York: W W Norton.

Sennett, T. (2006). *The culture of the new capitalism*. New Haven: Yale University Press.

Solow, R. (2008). Trapped in the new 'You're on Your Own' world. *The New York Review of Books LV, 18*, 79-81.

Thomson, D. (1989). The welfare state and generational conflict: Winners and losers. In P. Johnson, C. Conrad, & D. Thomson, (Eds.), *Workers versus pensioners: Intergenerational justice in an ageing world*. University of Manchester Press, Manchester.

Toffler, A. (1970). *Future shock*. London: Pan Books.

Townsend, P. (1981). The structured dependency of the elderly: the creation of policy in the twentieth century. *Ageing and Society, 1*(1): 5–28.

Urry, J. (2000). *Sociology beyond Societies*. London: Routledge

Urry, J. (2007). *Mobilities*. Cambridge: Polity Press

Vincent, J. (2006). Globalization and critical theory: Political economy of world population issues. In J. Baars, D. Dannefer, C. Phillipson, & A. Walker, (Eds.), *Aging, globalization and inequality: The new critical gerontology* (pp. 245–272). Amityville, NY: Baywood.

Vullnetari, J., & King, R. (2008). 'Does your granny eat grass?' On mass migration, care drain and the fate of older people in rural Albania. *Global Networks, 8*(2), 139–171.

Walker, A., & Deacon, B. (2003). Economic globalization and policies on aging. In *Journal of Societal and Social Policy, 2*(2): 1–18.

Warnes, A. M., Freidrich, K., Kellaher, L., & Torres, S. (2004). The diversity and welfare of older migrants in Europe. *Ageing and Society, 24*(3), 307–326.

Warnes, A. M. (2009). Migration and age. In D. Dannefer, & C. Phillipson, (Ed.), *Handbook of social gerontology*. London: Sage Books

Whiteside, N. (2006). Occupational pensions and the search for security. In H. Pemberton, P. Thane, & N. Whiteside, (Eds.), *Britain's pensions crisis* (pp.125–140). Oxford: Oxford University Press.

Wilding, R. (2006). 'Virtual' intimacies: Families communicating across transnational contexts. *Global Networks, 6*(2), 125–142.

World Bank (1994). *Averting the old age crisis*. Oxford University Press, Oxford.

Yeates, N. (2001). *Globalisation and social policy*. Sage, London.

Young, J. (1999). *The exclusive society*. London: Sage Publications.

Chapter 5
In Search of a New Welfare State in Europe: An International Perspective

Anton Hemerijck

We are still the children of the liberal reformers, patching the mechanisms haphazardly bequeathed to postwar societies proud of their supposed uniqueness.

Hugh Heclo

Introduction: In Search of a New Welfare State in Europe

Modern social policy represents a key component in Europe's advanced political economies. The European welfare state in the shape and form in which it developed in the second half of the twentieth century represents a unique historical achievement. Never before in history, as Fritz Scharpf puts it, 'has democratic politics been so effectively used to promote civil liberty, economic growth, social solidarity, and public well-being' (Scharpf, 2003). The defining feature of the postwar welfare state is that social protection came to be firmly anchored on the explicit normative commitment to grant social rights to citizens in areas of human need (Esping-Andersen, 1994: 712). This implied the expansion of mass education as an instrument for equal opportunities, access to high quality health care for everyone, together with the introduction of a universal right to real income, in T. H. Marshall's seminal work, *Citizenship and Social Class* (1950), 'not proportionate to the market value of the claimant' (Marshall, 1950: 110). Social citizenship held out a promise of the enlargement, enrichment, and equalization of people's 'life chances' (Marshall, 1950: 107). Thus Marshall defined social policy as the use of democratic 'political power to supersede, supplement, or modify operations of the economic system in order to achieve results which the economic system would not achieve of his own'

A. Hemerijck (✉)
Dean Faculty of Social Sciences, Free University, Amsterdam, Netherlands
e-mail: ac.hemerijck@fsw.vu.nl

J. Powell, J. Hendricks, *The Welfare State in Post-Industrial Society*,
DOI 10.1007/978-1-4419-0066-1_5, © Springer Science+Business Media, LLC 2009

(Marshall, 1975: 15). In his first report, *Social Insurance and Allied Services*, Lord Beveridge saw "freedom from want" to be the pivotal objective of the welfare state (Beveridge, 1942). In his 1945 *Full Employment in a Free Society*, however, Beveridge came to view employment, active participation, or inclusion in productive work as a key function of being an accepted part of a larger collective identity (Beveridge, 1945). In Beveridge's participatory view on full employment, social citizenship went beyond the right to a decent income, to include right to live from labor, to combine their income with the recognition of a social function. Jobs benefit people by giving them enhanced opportunities for self-actualization, personal identity, self-esteem, and the feeling of belonging to a community. Inclusion through the labor market remains a cornerstone of every policy strategy of social inclusion. Participating in the labor market is today the most important form of social interaction and, as such, is an indispensable element in achieving social cohesion. In the words of Guenther Schmid: "Not being wanted is worse than being poor" (Schmid, 2008: 3).

From the 1970s onward, the postwar triumph of the welfare state was thrown into question. The final quarter of the twentieth century has often been captured as the epoch of the crisis of the welfare state. The guarantees of the welfare state, long-term growth, and affluence, it was argued, had led to a permissive, overburdened democracy, and inflationary tendencies associated with Keynesian demand management. Since the 1980s, 'vulnerability,' 'fiscal overload,' 'ungovernability,' and 'unsustainability' became keywords in political debates. In the 1990s, with levels of unemployment hovering around 10 percent in a majority of European political economies, the 'prospect for survival' of the welfare state was recognized as poor.

Is the European welfare state fit for the twenty-first century global capitalism? This question has haunted European policymakers for over a decade. Slow economic growth and elusive job creation in the early 2000s culminated in a fierce ideological battle between different socioeconomic "models." The 2005 French referendum campaign over the new Constitutional Treaty of the European Union revealed two polarized positions. The 'French' social model was pitted against a false stereotype of the 'Anglo-Saxon' model of capitalism, allegedly a "free market without a safety net," producing high levels of poverty and inequality. In turn, Tony Blair, in his address to the European Parliament on June 23, posed the rhetorical question: "What type of social model is it that has 20 million unemployed?" Modern social policy, Blair contended, could no longer be based on "regulation and job protection that may save some jobs for a time at the expense of many jobs in the future." With the EU economy falling further behind its US counterpart, the image that *America works*, leading economists, like Andre Sapir, quickly jumped to the negative conclusion that the European social model, due to its overriding emphasis on centralized collective bargaining, overprotective job security, high minimum wages, and generous social insurance, was unable to produce levels of employment and job mobility on a par with the United States . Moreover, the accumulation of perverse labor-market rigidities, produced by the welfare state, has impeded flexible adjustment, blocked technological innovation, and hampered economic growth in an integrating world economy (OECD, 1981, 1994). The fundamental dilemma of the so-called European social model hereby came to be portrayed as a trade-off between welfare and employment, feeding a popular view that efficiency and equality, growth and redistribution, competitiveness and solidarity can only thrive at each other's expense.

Today, amidst the turmoil of the international credit crisis, the policy debate about competing "models," ranging from Anglo-Saxon, Rhineland, and new statist Chinese capitalism, is experiencing something of a revival. It is my contention, however, that couching policy responses to current crisis conditions in terms of a battle between warring alternatives easily triggers ideological strife, separating antagonistic advocacy coalitions, rather than moving the policy discussion, political debate, and comparative analysis toward a better understanding of the current crisis. Although European welfare states share a number of features that set them apart from other geopolitical regions in the world, like North America and South-East Asia, it is important at the outset to qualify reservations against forceful conjectures of the "war of the models," in general, and the underspecified use of the notion of "European social model," in particular.

Notably, the notion of a distinct European social model suggests a large degree of *uniformity* transcending national boundaries, which surely cannot be sustained empirically in the 27-member EU. There are immense differences in development, policy design, eligibility criteria, modes of financing, and institutional makeup across Europe (Esping-Andersen, 1990, 1999; Ferrera et al., 2000). Hence, it would be a mistake to overgeneralize the nature of welfare state change in such a way that obscured these national distinctions and their diverse trajectories. If Europe does have models, they are definitely plural rather than singular. For a number of key socioeconomic longitudinal indicators, Jens Alber has observed that the range of variation within the European Union is even bigger than the gap between Europe and the United States.

Moreover, the notion of a European social "model" is inherently *static*. While the architects of the postwar welfare state, John Maynard Keynes and William Beveridge, could assume stable male breadwinner families and expanding industrial labor markets, this picture of economy and society no longer holds. Since the late 1970s, consecutive changes in the world economy, European politics (most spectacularly the demise of communism in Eastern Europe), labor markets, and family structures, have disturbed the once sovereign and stable social and economic policy repertoires. As a consequence, most member states of the European Union have been recasting the basic policy mix upon which their national systems of social protection were built after 1945 (Hemerijck and Schludi, 2000).

Yet much of the academic literature on the welfare state continues to portray a "frozen welfare landscape." Despite the 'irresistible forces' urging for reform, ranging from the new rules of global competition, intensified European economic integration, the new shape of working life, the predicament of demographic aging, and changing family structures, the European welfare state proved to be, as one leading scholar put it, an 'unmovable object' (Pierson, 2001). To be sure, and notwithstanding the dire predictions of breakdown, the welfare state survived the recession-prone 1970s and 1980s. But does this suggest that social security and employment protection legislation are unsusceptible to reforms? Are European welfare states really that ossified and resilient, unable to improve their employment record, and to address current demands for social protection? I think not. As such, the key objective of this contribution is to correct the prevailing view that nation-states are increasingly impotent to deal with the range of challenges that confront them.

My argument is built up in three steps. First, the section 'A Sequence of Profound Reforms' renders an empirical inventory of a number of substantive changes in the makeup of Europe's mature welfare states over the final quarter of the twentieth century. Second, the section 'Post-industrial Social Change and Economic Internationalization' draws a synthesis of four sets of social, economic, and political challenges impending on European welfare states: (1) economic globalization; (2) post-industrial social change; (3) fiscal austerity; and (4) intensified European integration. Third, the section 'Understanding Welfare Recalibration' tries to capture the recent efforts to recast the welfare state in terms of the multidimensional concept of welfare recalibration, which allows us to analyze change in contemporary welfare state along four (functional, distributive, normative, and institutional) key dimensions (Ferrera et al., 2000; Ferrera and Hemerijck, 2003). More than ever, the welfare state has to be analyzed as evolutionary systems entangled in the dynamic process of institutional transformation in response to inside and outside economic, social, and political challenges. In conclusion, the section 'A New Welfare Edifice' articulates key elements of a 'social investment centered' welfare agenda for the twenty-first century Europe.

A Sequence of Profound Reforms

At first sight, mature European welfare states indeed seem remarkably stable. From the early 1990s to 2003, total social spending as a proportion of the GDP has generally hovered between 27 and 28 percent (Begg et al., 2008). However, if we interpret the welfare state more broadly than aggregate social spending, a finer grained qualitative analysis of long-term policy evolution allows us to paint a broad process of profound, yet gradual, transformation of European welfare states across at least six closely related policy shifts in macroeconomic policy, wage bargaining, labor market policy, social security, pensions, and social services (Hemerijck and Schludi, 2000).

In *macroeconomic policy*, up to the late 1970s, Keynesian macroeconomic policy priorities, geared toward full employment as a principal goal of economic management, prevailed. In the face of stagflation – i.e. the combination of high inflation and rising unemployment – the Keynesian order gave way to a stricter macroeconomic policy framework centered on economic stability, hard currencies, low inflation, and sound budgets, culminating in the introduction of the European Monetary Union (EMU). Building on two decades of monetary integration, the EMU has transferred monetary policy, a core function of the modern welfare state, to an independent central bank (ECB), and it has significantly constrained member states' fiscal policy discretion (Dyson and Featherstone, 1999; Martin and Ross, 2004).

With the supply side revolution in macroeconomic policy in the 1980s, the responsibility for employment shifted away from macroeconomic policy toward adjacent areas of social and economic regulation. In the field of *wage policy*, a reorientation took place in favor of market-based wage restraint in the face of intensified economic internationalization and structural unemployment. Since the early 1980s, wage restraint resumed importance as a requirement for successful adjustment by facilitating competitiveness, profitability, and – as a second-order effect – employment. Strategies of wage moderation have been pursued in many countries through a new generation of social pacts in Europe, linked with wider packages of negotiated reform, including labor market regulation and social protection. The rediscovery of a job-intensive growth path in Denmark, Finland, Ireland, and the Netherlands, by way of a first generation of new social pacts, has also allowed the social partners to strike deals over productivity, training, and job opportunities for less productive workers. In the 1990s, the EMU entrance exam played a critical role for a second generation of national social pacts in Southern Europe. Policymakers and social partners in the so-called hard currency latecomer countries, like Greece, Italy, and Portugal were stimulated to rekindle cooperative, positive sum solutions to the predicament of economic adjustment, i.e. by making taxation, social protection, pension, and labor market regulation more 'employment friendly,' in part, at the expense of privileged groups (Levy, 1999; Fajertag and Pochet, 2000).

In the area of *labor market policy*, in the 1990s, the new objective became maximizing employment rather than inducing labor market exit. The main policy trend here is a shift from passive financial transfers for those participating in the labor market toward activating measures to reduce dependency rates and increase the tax base. In the process, we witness notable increase in spending on active labor market policies, mobilizing women, youths, older workers, less productive workers, based on early intervention, case management, and conditional benefits. Furthermore, public employment services (PES) in many countries have been pushed toward "modern service provision," capable of effectively and efficiently delivering specialized services to an ever-growing clientele in outward-looking fashion. The most important elements of the new PES "service model" include the following: the use of management by objectives and advances toward decentralization; rigorous, independent, and comprehensive labor market policy evaluations and the merging of – or at least closer collaboration between – regimes for social assistance and unemployment benefits; active promotion of new local partnerships; competitive tendering for service provision; and removal of restrictions of private employment service agencies (Weishaupt, 2008).

With respect to *labor market regulation*, more narrowly understood, empirical evidence from Denmark and the Netherlands suggests that these countries have moved toward greater acceptance of flexible labor markets on the condition of strong matching social guarantees. The objective of "flexicurity" implies the development of a new balance between flexibility and security so as to provide an alternative to a deregulation-only policy perspective, as well as an alternative to the continuation of rigid regulation in the areas of labor law and social policy. While systems combining restrictive dismissal protection with meagre unemployment benefits essentially cater to the interests of insiders, so called "flexicure" systems based on minimal job protection but offering decent standards of social protection for the unemployed are best able to bridge the gap between insiders and outsiders in mature welfare states. Flexible hiring and firing and generous social security do not automatically lead to low unemployment, as the Danish case reveals. In the 1990s, the Danes critically strengthened the job search and creation with a series of active labor market policy measures. Central to "flexicurity" policies is that they not only take the conditions under which companies operate into consideration but also bring a life course perspective of workers into the equation. From this, it follows that "flexicurity" is a topic not only of labor market policy and regulation but also of family policy, insofar as family policy interacts with labor market conditions, allowing for more flexible family models and individual life courses.

Within the sphere of *social insurance*, we can observe how benefit generosity has been curtailed; eligibility has become more conditional and increasingly targeted at lower income groups in the majority of European welfare states (Van Gerven, 2008). Like in the case of labor market policy, perhaps most profound was the shift from passive policy priorities aimed at income maintenance toward a greater emphasis on activation and reintegration of vulnerable groups. In the process, the function of social security changed from passive compensation of social risks to corrective attempts to change behavioral incentives of claimants and employers together with a strong emphasis on weeding out adverse selection and moral hazard. This is also captured by the shift from out-of-work benefits to in-work-benefits. Different policy strategies materialized in different welfare states. In Great Britain, where income guarantees and unemployment benefits are modest, individual tax credits to support low-wage workers and their families are very popular. In Continental Europe, the main problem is that heavy social contributions price less productive workers out of the market. In the face of the relative weakening of traditional male breadwinner social insurance programs, policymakers in these countries have turned toward strengthening minimum income protection functions of the welfare state, coupled with strong activation and reintegration measures. Many European welfare states seem to be evolving toward a dual social protection model, combining both Bismarckian social insurance and Beveridgian minimum income protection tiers. In this respect, the French and Belgian welfare states have increased social assistance protection for the neediest, using targeted benefits instead of universal benefits, financed through taxation and general revenues. The 2005 Hartz IV reforms in Germany stand out as a case in point. The most controversial elements of the Hartz IV reform involved a drastic shortening duration of benefits, tighter requirements to accept suitable jobs, simplification of insurance regulations, wage insurance for elderly unemployed, and the merger of unemployment assistance and social assistance.

In the area of *old age pensions*, the most important trend is the development of multipillar systems, combining PAYG and fully funded methods with a tight (actuarial) link between pension benefits and contributions. Virtually all other European countries have also introduced fiscal incentives to encourage people to take up private pension insurance. In the 1990s, a number of countries, notably Belgium, France, Ireland, the Netherlands, and Portugal, started to build up reserve funds to maintain adequate pension provision when the baby boom generation retires. Also changes in indexation rules have helped to reduce future pension reliabilities. In Austria, Germany, Italy, and Spain, restrictions have gone hand in hand with attempts to upgrade minimum pension benefits. Measures to combine work and retirement via partial pension benefits have been introduced in Austria, Belgium, Denmark, and Germany. In Western Europe, one of the most profound reforms has been undertaken by Sweden in the mid-1990s, which introduced a small mandatory funded element and transferred an important part of the risk associated with aging to retirees. The latter was done by indexing future benefits to the life expectancy of the retiring cohort and by linking future benefits to net wages. Benefits will be lower if life expectancy continues to increase and net wages continue to grow slow. But there was also a strong element of redistribution within generations as the reform ensured a universal guaranteed pension for low-income pensioners. (Palme, 2005). The Swedish legislation has also heavily influenced reforms in other countries, like Italy, Latvia, and Poland (Fox and Palmer, 1999; Ferrera and Gualmini, 2000). Finland has developed policy approaches to improve occupational health, work ability, and well-being of aging workers to keep older workers in the workforce as long as possible (Clark and Whiteside, 2003; Immergut et al., 2007).

Social services have experienced a comeback lately. Spending on child care, education, health, and elderly care, next to training and employment services, has increased practically everywhere in Western Europe over the past decade. Almost a fifth of all jobs created in the EU between 1995 and 2001 occurred in the health and social services sector. In particular, aging and longevity make demands on professional care that working families can no longer meet. In the process, all European welfare states are moving away from the breadwinner/caregiver model, under which mothers are enabled to stay at home with children, to a dual-earner norm, under which mothers are enabled to enter the labor force. In Scandinavia, the expansion of services to families began in the 1970s in tandem with the rise in female labor supply. It was in large part this policy of 'defamilialization' of caring responsibilities that catalyzed the dual-earner norm. In most other European countries, female employment growth came much later (Daly, 2000). In Southern Europe, it was only during the past decade that we saw a sharp rise. Throughout the EU, leave arrangements for working parents have also been expanded, both in terms of time and coverage, to include care for the frail elderly and sick children. Last but not least, since the early 1990s, child care has been expanded in countries with a strong breadwinner/ caregiver tradition, like Austria, Germany, Great Britain, and the Netherlands. Here, governments have pushed for increased spending and more flexible opening hours to spur the number of available and affordable child care places.

Over the past two decades, as the above inventory of reform shows, many European welfare states have – with varying success, but also failure – taken measures to redirect economic restructuring and structural social by pushing through adjustments in macroeconomic policy, industrial relations, social security, labor market policy, employment protection legislation, pensions, and social services. In the process, these policy areas have been brought into a new relationship with each other. The character of the relationship changed from loosely coupled policy responsibilities in the shadow of Keynesian macroeconomic policy to one of tightly coupled interdependencies between employment and social policy repertoires under more austere macroeconomic conditions. In terms of performance, it became evident that active service-oriented welfare states were in a stronger position than passive transfer-oriented systems to achieve employment growth. In the process toward activation, the avoidance of early retirement, the promotion of part-time work, lifelong learning, gender mainstreaming, balancing flexibility with security, and reconciling work and family life, practically all European welfare states are moving away from the breadwinner/caregiver model to a dual-earner norm. Moreover, most welfare reform endeavors have remained deeply embedded in normative notions of equity and solidarity, shared cognitive understandings of the efficiency-enhancing effects of well-designed social and labor market policies. And while many reforms were unpopular, it is very important to highlight that a fair amount occurred with the consent of parties in opposition, trade unions, and employer organizations.

Post-industrial Social Change and Economic Internationalization

Until the mid-1970s, the expansion of the European welfare states took place under highly favorable circumstances of high levels of economic growth, stable nuclear families, large industrial sectors, and with the support of broad coalitions of working and middle-class groups in otherwise fairly homogenous societies (Taylor-Gooby, 2004). At the level of international political economy, the objectives of full employment and social protection were supported by the regime of "embedded liberalism" (Ruggie, 1982). Embedded liberalism was thus tailored to a world in which international competition was limited and foreign investment was regulated. The Bretton Woods monetary system of stable exchange rates was central to the regime of embedded liberalism, as it gave national policymakers a substantial degree of freedom to pursue relatively independent social and employment policies without undermining (social and political) and international (economic) stability.

This gave national policymakers in most countries a substantial degree of freedom to pursue relatively independent economic and social policies without undermining domestic and international stability (Scharpf and Schmidt, 2000). During the Golden Age of economic growth between 1945 and the early-1970s, most advanced industrial societies developed their country-specific brands of welfare capitalism. The various models of welfare capitalism were built upon relatively coherent policy mixes of macroeconomic policy, wage policy, taxation, industrial policy, social policy, and labor market regulation. For much of the second half of the twentieth century, the main concern of public policy in Western economies was containment of the inflationary tendencies of Keynesian demand management. Wider social policy played a subsidiary role. Industrial relations and social policy came together again in a limited way during the inflationary crises of the 1970s. Governments' turn to monetary as opposed to demand management policies in response created new environments in both policy areas. Beyond inflation management, European welfare states with their low levels of job turnover and strong job protections, were a source of competitive strength as they enhanced the economy's capacity to deliver high-quality manufactured goods, stable employment, incremental innovation, and an equitable distribution of income.

The steady expansion of *large stable industrial sectors* allowed full employment to become the central social policy objective of the postwar era. Full employment, or 'freedom from idleness' in the words of Beveridge, came to be defined in terms of the achievement of full-time jobs for male workers only; 48 hours a week, with 48 working weeks in a year, for a period of 48 years. Beveridge's conception of full employment assumed women, as housewives, to care for young children, frail elderly, and other dependent groups. As a result, the policy menu of the postwar welfare state remained relatively simple. Modern social policy came to be founded on the idea of guaranteeing security to working population, as well as those outside the labor force on grounds of old age, disability, inability to find work, or motherhood. As such, postwar welfare state innovation very much consolidated traditional gender relationship of male breadwinners and female housewives. Professional social services only came into play at the beginning (education) of individual life cycles, with only rare and brief intermittent periods of dependence on social security and state-sponsored assistance. While social services indeed were no longer the exclusive domain of the church, the neighborhood, or the extended family, male breadwinner job security with dedicated housewives at home allowed welfare state responsibilities to be kept at bay (Esping-Andersen, 1996).

Cohesive *coalitions of working and middle-class groups* pressed for the provision and universalization of comprehensive social insurance, particularly those related to old age, sickness, disability, and unemployment. One of the most prominent perspectives on the expansion of the postwar welfare state is based on the notion that modern social policy is the outcome of, and arena for, conflicts between class-related socioeconomic interest groups and political parties (Korpi, 1983; Esping-Andersen, 1985; Van Kersbergen, 1995). The hegemony of social democracy in the Scandinavian countries provided a propitious ideological base for corporatist governance and welfare expansion. The predominance of Christian democracy in Austria, Belgium, Germany, and the Netherlands was also favorable to stable corporatist political exchange and welfare expansion across the mainland Western Europe. Trade union strategies all over Europe were largely defined in terms of industrial employment for (semi-) skilled, full-time, and male employment in the industrial sector, very much excluding women.

The postwar welfare state was founded on the idea of job security and income guarantees supported by government demand management directed toward male full employment. The basic form, modern social policy assumed was one of *social insurance*, the universal pooling of modern social risks of unemployment, sickness, old age, and motherhood. Social risk management was conceived as a kind of mutual insurance for the risk of loss of income for families closely linked to the employment situation of male breadwinners. A relatively homogenous society presupposed the equality of individuals with regard to various social risks, hinging on John Rawls's concept of a 'veil of ignorance,' from which common rules and arrangements for vast numbers in a common position seemed fair and efficient. In Rawls's theory of justice, the 'principle of difference' (inequalities are acceptable only if they are beneficial to the most disadvantaged) seemed particularly fair because it correctly assumed that male breadwinner and other nuclear family members conjectured that they could potentially among the most disadvantaged.

Today, this picture of economy, politics, and society no longer holds. Four sets of challenges confront policymakers with the imperative to redirect the welfare effort. First, *from outside*, international competition is challenging the redistributive scope of the national welfare state (Scharpf and Schmidt, 2000). The virtuous Keynesian interplay between social and economic regulations was suddenly brought to an end by the breakup of the Bretton Woods system in 1971 and the OPEC oil price increase of 1973. In the wake of the multifold recessions that followed, it became increasingly more difficult for advanced welfare states to deliver on their Keynesian core commitments of full employment and social protection. Three important changes in the international political economy have been held accountable for employment and social policy adjustment (Huber and Stephens, 2001; Begg et al., 2008; Scharpf, 2000). First, the increase in cross-border competition in the markets for labor, goods, and services has substantially reduced the room for maneuver of national welfare states. Greater trade openness exposes generous welfare states to competition and permits capital to move to countries with the lowest payroll taxes for social security. Second, internationalization of production, most notably the creation of a single European market, is held to increase dangers of lower tax revenue, since countries need to compete for investment by making concessions on taxes, payrolls, and corporate profits. Finally, since the mid-1980s, the liberalization of capital markets, in general, and the EMU, in particular, undermined the capacity of national policymakers to use macroeconomic policy instruments to achieve full employment. This further extended the need for austerity in social and employment policy.

There are, however, good reasons for believing that the overall impact of globalization has been exaggerated, as have its potentially adverse consequences for employment and social standards. There is no compelling evidence that economic globalization is necessarily leading to a 'race to the bottom' in social policy. Though income inequalities have been rising somewhat in many European countries since the mid-1980s, there is no (or only weak) evidence that this development has been spurred by globalization. Neither did intensified economic internationalization put a lid on aggregate social spending. Where inequality is rising, it can be attributed, beyond globalization, to explicit political choices or inappropriate responses to more fundamental endogenous process of social change (Begg et al., 2008). Various types of institutional settings and forms of social security and labor market policy are equally compatible with competitiveness. In fact, since the pressures of economic internationalization affect different welfare states in varying ways and to differing degrees at different points of time, a blunt juxtaposition of a 'race to the bottom' versus a generous welfare state is not particularly useful. It fails to capture the full complexities of the economics and politics of national processes of policy adjustment and provides little basis for genuine comparative analysis or policy prescriptions.

From within, aging populations, declining birth rates, changing gender roles, individualization, the shift from an industrial to a service economy, increased migration, and new technologies in the organization of work present new endogenous challenges to the welfare state. Perhaps the most important reason why the existing systems of social care have become overstretched stems from the weakening of labor markets and traditional family units as the default providers of welfare (Esping-Andersen, 1999). In most European countries, the reduction of employment in industry and the rise of the service sector began in the 1960s. The move toward a knowledge-based society is likely to exacerbate and increase the risks of social exclusion. This affects low skilled groups in particular who have not or cannot acquire the skills to succeed in the knowledge-based economy. Highly educated workers, on the other hand, are the winners; their jobs have become more secure and/or better rewarded as a consequence of increased international trade and the advancement of information technology. Job losses continue to be concentrated among people who have not completed at least secondary education or who lack formal vocational qualifications, including some ethnic minorities, young adults, women, and elderly workers. The average unemployment rate of low skilled groups is two to three times as high as that of skilled workers. Spells of unemployment for the low skilled have increased in frequency and duration. Long-term unemployment leads to a further erosion of skill levels. Moreover, the long-term unemployed are stigmatized by employers; once they have been out of the labor market for more than a year, they are perceived to be 'unfit' for work. Whereas the primary risk of widespread poverty in the postwar era was in old age, child poverty is now the bigger problem, together with early school leaving. The first choice of a college, career, or job may not work out. Jobs may be lost in mid-career with the consequence of permanent inactivity and growing inequality, with the steady erosion of semi-skilled jobs. These are all so-called "new" social risks (Bonoli, 2006).

With the steady increase in women's labor force, traditional breadwinner social insurance is gradually becoming dysfunctional. The immediate impact of the growing number of dual-earner families is the combined pressure of paid and unpaid working time, especially among women. Women have entered the labor market in great numbers since the late 1960s, exactly at the moment when male employment in industry was falling. Apart from emancipatory reasons, it has virtually become an economic necessity for women to seek paid work, as two earners are most likely to maintain a decent family income. At the same time, women continue to provide most domestic care. This responsibility limits the number of hours available for paid work. Accordingly, poverty rates are particularly high among lone mothers (Taylor-Gooby, 2004). Moreover, traditional care patterns also impact on fertility rates. Women seeking paid work generate a demand for provision from men, the private sector, and the state. The lack of such provisions has been argued to be an important reason why fertility rates in Scandinavia are among the highest in Europe (Esping-Andersen and Sarasa, 2002). Gøsta Esping-Andersen has even posed that population aging is primarily an issue of drops in fertility (1999: 3). There is a potential mismatch between labor supply and care demand in the social service sector. Demand is rising. Aging societies raise the number of "oldest of the old." Demand for early childhood education will also rise as more mothers taking up paid employment seek high quality nonparental child care. Supply is shrinking, reduced both by rising female employment rates that limit the supply of informal care and because formal care work typically offers poor working conditions, little security, and low pay.

However, as policymakers must find new ways to manage the new social risks associated with changing gender roles, deindustrialization, demographic aging, and economic internationalization, their endeavor to recast the welfare state is constrained, *from the past*, by long-standing social policy commitments in the areas of the "old social risks" of unemployment insurance, disability benefits, and especially pensions. In a period of *relative austerity* and lower economic growth, policies addressing the social risks associated with the postwar industrial era now seem to crowd out the space for new social policy initiatives. In comparison to welfare's golden age, economic growth has slowed down while unemployment has risen. This has seriously reduced the room for maneuver in a variety of ways. Whereas an upsurge of unemployment spurs demands on the welfare state and reduces people's contributions, the overall decline in economic growth reduces tax income and makes it more difficult to raise taxes for welfare state expenditures. Furthermore, advanced welfare states have "grown to limits" (Flora, 1986). Rising health care costs and pension provisions have contributed massively to welfare budgets and fiscal strains (Pierson, 1998).

The spectre of economic austerity is likely to intensify in the face of population aging. Despite the uncertainty involved in assessing aging (due to the difficulties in predicting fertility rates), virtually all policymakers and academics agree that action is needed to mitigate the potentially devastating consequences of aging societies. To a considerable extent, the aging predicament has been reinforced by generous early exit schemes and employment crises in the 1990s and early 2000s. Fiscal sustainability surely requires new ways to finance health and pensions amidst growing cost pressures, as well to change the incidence of the cost burden via changes to taxation or social insurance systems. The maturation of governmental commitments and population aging demand reforms to health care provision and old age pensions (in 1992, these accounted for 80 percent of all social protection outlays in the European Union) if costs are not to escalate and employment creation stymied by higher direct taxation and/ or payroll taxes. Yet such policies are constrained by the popularity of generous welfare programs and the commitment of a range of political and vested interests and beneficiaries to defending them.

As an intervening variable in the process, issues of work and welfare have become ever more entwined with processes of European integration, especially since the 1980s. It is fair to say that in the EU we have entered an era of *semisovereign welfare states* (Leibfried and Pierson, 2000). European (economic) integration is fundamentally recasting the boundaries of national systems of social protection, both constraining the autonomy for domestic policy options and also opening opportunities for the EU social policy agenda setting (Ferrera, 2005; Zeitlin et al., 2005). Since the 1980s, the division of labor between the EU economic and social policy coordination and national welfare states has become increasingly untenable: advances in economic integration prompted the introduction of direct or indirect constraints on national social policy. The Maastricht Treaty of 1992 made such constraints very explicit by agreeing upon the establishment of the EMU and the Stability and Growth Pact (SGP), constraining governments' macroeconomic room for maneuver. Even those member states not committed to becoming EMU members and those outside the EU were constrained by global capital markets to adhere to the austerity policies of the (future) EMU members (Huber and Stephens, 2001:234).

Europeanization has unleashed a restructuring of domestic social citizenship regimes along two dimensions of social and economic policy coordination. First, there is the relevance of cross-border risk pooling through binding legislation against unruly competition through the well-known "Community

Method." Examples include directives and rulings of the European Court of Justice (ECJ). The role of Europe in this regard has obviously increased over time due to the combined effect of earlier and recently legislated European laws, serving to open up national welfare states to competition. This trend is intensified by the shift from public schemes toward multipillar systems in the field of pensions and health care in particular, since private and voluntary arrangements are subject to legislation on the internal market. By contrast, however, many of the ECJ's rulings have also been devoted to employment protection, gender equality, and to the extension of rights to social assistance and other noncontributory benefits to EU citizens.

Second, and equally important, the EU can serve as an external agenda setter, catalyst, and facilitator of domestic reform, rather than a law maker. For instance, the European Employment Strategy, launched in 1997, was deliberately designed to favor a gradual reorientation toward activation, the avoidance of early retirement, the promotion of part-time work, lifelong learning, gender mainstreaming, balancing flexibility with security, and reconciling work and family life. Such a reorientation perhaps is of a similar magnitude as the macroeconomic paradigm shift from Keynesianism to monetarism of the early 1980s. As EU economic regulation has ushered in a period of regime competition, this has opened a window for agenda setting and policy transfer of experience and institutional "borrowing" taking place from outside domestic policy systems via the intermediation of other boundary spanning international organizations, like the OECD, IMF, the World Bank, and the ILO, encouraging domestic redirection of social and employment policy. Rather than requiring strict adherence, these forms of governance are aimed at promoting a certain degree of cognitive and normative harmonization in the areas of employment policy, pension, health care, and social inclusion policies.

In short, four sets of socioeconomic challenges – economic internationalization, post-industrial social change, fiscal austerity, and intensified European integration – invalidate the family and labor market assumptions on which the postwar welfare state was based. Moreover, these challenges have major implications for the structure of coalitions behind or against profound welfare reform. As the distribution of new social risks varies by skills, gender, age, and sector, just to mention a few, this sharply contrasts with the less diversified coalitions of working and middle-class groups behind the postwar expansion of the welfare state during the golden age. Today, cleavage conflicts over issues like childcare and leave arrangements, employment protection legislation, and active aging are being fought out within mainstream social democratic and Christian democratic parties, rather than between left and right (Stiller, 2007; Korthouwer, forthcoming). While the support for the welfare state remains high amongst European public practically everywhere, social anxiety with respect to feelings of job insecurity as a consequence of globalization, is now turning against the European Union, which is increasingly perceived of an agent of market liberalization, threatening to undermine long-standing and deeply held European Christian Democratic and Social Democratic values.

The current predicament suggests that the tension arising out of the unbalanced economic and social development of the European project is not likely to be resolved anytime soon.

Understanding Welfare Recalibration

The future of welfare state is not preordained. We have seen that neither the doomsday scenario of the demise of the European welfare state, predicted by economists in the 1980s, nor the prevalent image of a 'frozen welfare status quo,' pictured by comparative scholarship in the 1990s, can be corroborated by the European welfare reform experience since the late 1970s. In the 1980s, welfare provisions became more austere. The previous decade in particular has shown that the 'newest' politics of the welfare state is distinctly no longer the politics of status quo. Challenges like globalization, aging societies, fiscal austerity, and intensified European integration are forces which many observers see as fundamentally altering the conditions under which different European welfare states operate. To be sure, these challenges do not instruct policymakers under conditions of high levels of uncertainty over their relative weights intensity and scope. Rather, they inform purposive and deliberate policy responses, which are shaped by the normative predispositions of reflexive policy actors and their cognitive interpretations of evolving social and economic conditions.

In an attempt to understand the evolution of the profound, yet gradual, social and economic policy transformation, Maurizio Ferrera, Martin Rhodes, and I have introduced the multidimensional concept of welfare recalibration (Ferrera et al., 2000; Ferrera and Hemerijck, 2003). Our notion of welfare recalibration is based on an explicit recognition that welfare states are multidimensional and made up out of institutionally interdependent social and economic policy repertoires. Multidimensionality implies that welfare reform is likely to take place along several lines of political conflict, compromise, and consensus building, varying from contestation over separate and/or interlinked social policy provisions, their distributive consequences, their normative appropriateness, and their institutional viability and financial sustainability. In accordance with the welfare regime literature, institutional interdependence denotes how specialized socioeconomic policy domain programs have historically developed into functionally differentiated, but institutionally complementary policy domains. As repertoires of interdependent policy areas, it is difficult to change or replace one policy program without indirectly touching on the functioning of others (Hemerijck and Schludi, 2000). Processes of welfare reform, transformation, and institutional change are typically the product of a long chain of interconnected sequences of policy change across different areas of social and economic regulation, in which one policy change conditions another in neighboring policy areas. Only a detailed 'systematic process analysis' of welfare recalibration over a lengthy period of time is able to trace how old welfare settlements are undone and new functions of social risk management are suggested, politically enacted, normatively accepted, and implemented through the policy process.

From a recalibration perspective, reform decisions in different policy areas pass through, and are based on, cognitive and normative judgment, distributive bargaining, and institutional (re-)design as to how improve policy performance under conditions of fundamental environmental change. The notion of welfare recalibration thus highlights four key dimensions: functional, distributive, normative, and institutional. Together they make up for a heuristic to diachronically analyze the complex ways in which the postwar social contract is being redrafted, without abandoning the key insights of path dependency and the political bias toward inertia rooted in mature social policy provisions. Processes of welfare recalibration surely do not involve a search for a "blank slate" new model, a radically novel blueprint to replace existing national social and economic policy repertoires. We live in a world of path-dependent solutions. Each of the four dimensions of welfare recalibration requires elaboration.

Functional recalibration has to do with the changing cognitive diagnosis of the social risks against which the welfare state aspires to protect. Roughly until the early 1970s, social insurance displayed a good degree of congruence with the population, family, and labor market structures of European societies. The traditional catalog of social risks of loss of income tended to reflect quite closely the prevailing pattern of social needs, as shaped by high fertility, a shorter life expectancy than today, industrial employment, and traditional gender relations. But, to varying degrees in Europe's different welfare families, the postwar 'goodness of fit' between the welfare state and an evolving socioeconomic reality has been torn. As we have seen, the transition toward a post-industrial, knowledge-based economy is producing a mismatch between the supply and demand for social policy provision.

Many experts share in the diagnosis that the current imperative of recasting the welfare state is very much rooted in the incongruence between new "post-industrial" social risks and diverse family and labor market needs, on the one hand, and institutional resilience of male breadwinner social policy provisions, on the other (Esping-Andersen et al., 2002; Esping-Andersen, 2005; Jenson and Saint-Martin, 2003; Taylor-Gooby, 2004). The need for functional recalibration is often described in terms of the shift from "old" to "new" social risks confronting people as a result of the transition from a 'male breadwinner' industrial to a 'dual earner' post-industrial society (Taylor-Gooby, 2004; Bonoli, 2005, 2006).

Since the mid-1970s, domestic and international organizations and think tanks have come to provide vital data and new sources of intelligence for the social policy process. New evidence on accumulated problems of unemployment hysteresis, the deficiencies of demand management under globalization, moral hazard, and adverse selection problems in comprehensive social insurance, adverse old age dependency, rising rates of early school dropout, unsatisfactory work-life balance for many working mothers, these and many other pieces of intelligence are today cited in attempts to advocate an alternative new welfare edifice. In response to the emerging post-industrial new social risk profile, we can observe a cognitive shift in many expert policy advices, ranging from reports of national think tanks (NESC, 2005; IFFS, 2006; WRR, 2006) to important OECD publications, like *A Caring World: The New Social Policy Agenda* (1999) and *Babies and Bosses* (2007). The agenda setting volume, *Why We Need a New Welfare State,* by Esping-Andersen et al. (2002), commissioned by the Belgian presidency of the EU in 2001, calls for a paradigm shift from a static perspective of the welfare state, focused on social protection, from income support for social disadvantaged groups to a dynamic concern with social promotion social investment in human capital. Crucial is to adopt a life course perspective, to identify the interconnectedness of social risks and needs across time, from early childhood, education, career, family life, and old age.

Another key idea is to go beyond an emphasis on *protection from the market,* providing people with a replacement income of traditional male breadwinner families in the case of old age, unemployment, illness, and disability. Instead, most scholars promote an emphasis on *labor market (re)integration* for both men and women in an open, knowledge-intensive economy, from a life course perspective, with a strong emphasis on enabling choice and encouraging behavioral patterns rather than providing benefits. In this respect, the Dutch and Danish moves toward 'flexicurity,' a greater acceptance of flexible labor markets and a limited duration of income replacements on the condition of high benefit levels and investments in active labor market policies, are cases in point.

Normative recalibration concerns changing normative and moral orientations regarding social policy. In many countries, lively debates take place on the subject of the "moral foundations" of welfare state and on the need to rethink notions of fairness in the face of economic internationalization and post-industrial social change. Given the political salience of welfare policy in most European countries, policy proposals amending the welfare status quo only have a chance of being enacted through the democratic process if they can be seen as normatively fair. In the case of reform, it is therefore extremely important to reflect upon basic normative principles and objectives of social policy reform. Moreover, as values and attitudes change, the expectations with respect to what constitutes an acceptable standard of social policy provision, given economic and institutional constraints, are also up for grabs.

Also, in academia, there is a revival in the interest of theories of social justice, not only under political philosophers but also among more empirically oriented social policy scholars. In this respect, as Esping-Andersen (2002) observes, the debate at the EU level is close to the normative benchmark of John Rawls, stipulating that substantial changes in the social status of citizens must be to the greatest advantage of the worst-off. In agreement with Rawls's "difference principle," the European social ethos prioritizes social inclusion, the welfare of the least advantaged, and the reduction of inequalities as essential ingredients in any strategy to boost competitiveness. Against the backdrop of economic internationalization and post-industrial differentiation, a number of policy analysts today advocate 'dynamizing' Rawls' theory of social justice (Ferrera et al., 2000; Esping-Andersen et al., 2002; Schmid, 2008). Equality and compensation will certainly remain key value orientations. However, a more demanding view is emerging. This pertains to a view of equality which is able to take account of other differences between men and women, generational data, natural handicaps, across the life course, adjusted to the multiplicity of social risks condition, and aimed at supplying citizens with adequate means for social and economic engagement. Hereby, the old idea of equality is being enriched with notions of generational equity and a new equity of opportunities, like employability, over time.

At the heart of the new normative framework lies a reorientation in social citizenship, away from *freedom from want* toward *freedom to act*, prioritizing high levels of employment for both men and women as the key policy objective, while combining elements of flexibility and security, under the proviso of accommodating work and family life and a guaranteed *rich social minimum* serving citizens to pursue fuller and more satisfying lives (Diamond, 2006). This suggests the need to enrich Rawls' theory with ethical theory and capability perspective. As Rawls' theory of justice is not build on the basic distinction between the causal effects of external circumstances and individual choice, Dworkin maintains that it neglects individual responsibility for outcomes under given differences in talent or differences in the exposure to economic change. According to Dworkin, an ethically acceptable balance of individual rights and obligations is required. Taking heed from Dworkin, we observe how the majority of labor market reforms today combine the right to income support with the obligation to actively search for work or to take up vocational training. For Sen, material equality is at best a necessary, but not sufficient, condition for a fair distribution of life chances. What is more decisive is the ability of individuals to convert the resources available to them into a flexible endowment of resources, which may be quite unevenly distributed but enables all individuals to realize their own life plans. With the correction of Dworkin and Sen, we are able to transcend Rawls' static notion of distributive justice, focused on greater equality in the here-and-now, toward a dynamic notion of responsibility-sensitive equality of opportunity, emphasizing equality of life chances, while advocating modern social policies as societal investments in capabilities rather than as income-replacing consumption.

The elaboration of a new normative framework is particularly urgent in the field of old age policy. The demographic predicament calls for a normative benchmark for reforming pension systems in a financially sustainable and socially adequate manner, touching on norms of intergenerational equity and intragenerational justice. Intergenerational equity implies that the transition costs associated with population aging are shared proportionately by both young and old (Myles, 2002). In Sweden, for instance, the 1994–98 pension reform was explicitly aimed at achieving more generational equity by transferring an important part of the risk associated with aging to retirees. This was done by introducing a calculation method that decreases benefits if life expectancy continues to increase. Yet, there was also a strong emphasis on intragenerational material equality as the reform ensured a universal guaranteed pension for low-income pensioners. Moreover, in an attempt to depoliticize the issue and minimize potential veto points, all parties in parliament agreed to compromise at an early stage. This brings to the dimension of institutional recalibration.

Institutional recalibration concerns reforms in the design of institutions, levels of decision-making and social and economic policy governance, and the responsibilities of individuals, states, markets, and families. Institutional recalibration also involves experimentation with alternative means of social policy delivery and public and private administration. One of the most distinctive institutional features of the European welfare state has been its public legalistic nature: the responsibility of ensuring social solidarity and cohesion ultimately relied on national (i.e. central) government in terms of policy formation, funding, administration, and implementation. For the most part, national governments have not kept pace with changes in the economy and society and the new social risks they come with. Various developments have been challenging this state-centric edifice of the welfare state in recent years – a challenge often summarized in the emergence of new forms of "governance" beyond the traditional territorial nation-state.

The ongoing redefinition of the role of the state with respect to welfare provisions is apparent in three ways (Schmid, 2008). First, national governments no longer hierarchically monopolize welfare provision. Many countries (especially the larger ones) have been experimenting with decentralization of competencies to subnational (regional and local) governments. Markets and families have gained greater responsibility and community-based 'third sector' associations have been called on to deliver new services. Second, from a horizontal perspective, there is an increasing recognition that effective social policy formation and implementation today requires 'joined up' governance across government departments, public agencies, private sector organizations, and community association, together with more effective form of policy coordination across various functionally differentiated policy areas – horizontally across government department and vertically from the national to the local level. The double-edged concern with social policy effectiveness and economic efficiency has led to forms of governance in the areas of work and welfare. These are captured by decentralized self-regulation and coordinated through common normative objectives and quality standards, promoting prevention and empowerment through private delivery.

Finally, in the third place, it is important to emphasize that the EU regulation is becoming increasingly more important in laying the international ground rules and social principles shaping the scope of multilevel governance in social and economic regulation. The EU has in recent years emerged as an autonomous supranational body of social regulation and to some extent redistribution (through the structural funds), creating a complex web of multilevel interactions that has turned national welfare states from fully sovereign to semisovereign institutions. Open coordination processes, in particular, with their strong focus on "new" rather than "old" social risk categories – most notably active aging/ avoiding early retirement, part-time work, lifelong learning, parental leave, gender mainstreaming, flexicurity (balancing flexibility with security), reconciling work and family life, and social exclusion – already play key roles in the ongoing welfare recalibration (Zeitlin et al., 2005).

The politics of institutional recalibration very much requires a 'policy-seeking' style of political management in contrast to a 'power-seeking' or 'office-seeking' political style, because institutional recalibration is driven by ideas of a better 'goodness fit' between policy solutions and the institutional format that is best to deliver on the substantive problems at hand (Stiller, 2007). This requires policy reformers to principally think problem and goal-oriented, but to have very clear ideas about the institutional feasibility and the administrative capabilities of different forms and levels of policy making, whether central, local, functional, or intergovernmental and supranational. For instance, when governments in continental Europe and Scandinavia intend to stimulate advances toward more decentralized employment services, they cannot ignore the interests of social partners who are anxious to preserve their roles in management structures (Weishaupt, 2008).

Distributive recalibration concerns the rebalancing of social protection provisions across organized interests and policy clientele. The majority of Europe's mature welfare states are confronted with a syndrome of labor market segmentation and the insider/outsider cleavage. The postwar welfare state is often seen as the outcome of a democratic class struggle, in the context of broadly Keynesian macroeconomic management. New risk welfare initiatives, under the shadow of more stringent macroeconomic preferences, are likely to be obstructed by the institutional outcomes of that struggle, protecting insiders rather than weakly unionized women, part-timers, and atypical workers. The predicament of aging, if unresolved, moreover, could provoke a "generational clash" – with pension expenditures originated by the increasing number of elderly crowding out resources for the younger generations.

In terms of distributive recalibration, policy reformers will request policy stakeholders to subordinate their short-term distributive interests in favor of long-term societal interests. There is an inherent tension here between, on the one hand, exposing stakeholders abuse of their vested interest positions, and, on the other hand, to appeal to stakeholders to rethink reform resistance to forge a more productive political and societal consensus. To a large extent, distributive recalibration boils down to consensus building to muster support behind reform. After all, welfare recalibration is a political process, a matter of "powering" alongside "puzzling." Electoral incentives, 'institutional stickiness,' and the veto points created by powerful vested interests devoted to defending transfer-heavy welfare states and their redistributive outcomes make anything other than incremental and negotiated reform, based on complex bargains and linkages between policy areas, very difficult. Reforms to health care systems, pensions, and labor markets all require a careful process of adjustment if social cohesion as a governing principle of these systems is not to be sacrificed and if core constituencies and their representatives (welfare professions, the labor movement, citizens) are not to erect insuperable impediments to change.

A New Welfare Edifice

Neither the doomsday scenario of the demise of the welfare state nor the prevailing image of a 'frozen welfare status quo' can be corroborated by the European welfare reform experience highlighted in this chapter. Over the past two decades, many European welfare states have – with varying degrees of success – taken measures to redirect economic and social restructuring by pushing through adjustments in macroeconomic policy, industrial relations, social security, labor market policy, employment protection legislation, pensions, social services, and welfare financing. The result has been a highly dynamic process of self-transformation of the majority of European welfare states (Hemerijck, 2002), marked not by half-hearted retrenchment efforts but by more comprehensive trajectories of "recalibration," ranging from redesigning welfare programs to the elaboration of new principles of social justice (Ferrera et al., 2000; Ferrera and Hemerijck, 2003).

Welfare recalibration is not a tidy technocratic learning process in piecemeal engineering. Surely not: welfare recalibration is a political process, as much a matter of "powering" than of "puzzling," to use Heclo's famous phrase. This involves the strategic framing of policy problems and solutions by political actors and interests. Reforms are the products of lengthy processes of (re)negotiation between political parties, governments, and frequently social partners. Reconciling deep-seated norms and values and routines of behavior with the new challenges of intensified economic internationalization, aging, and post-industrial change, relative austerity and important advancement in European integration has surely not been easy. As European policymakers have not been given a clear political mandate to simply retrench social protection and deregulate labor markets to improve economic performance, they have had to carve out, in a process of learning by doing, the contours of a new welfare state for Europe. To gain political legitimacy for promising new policy formulas, political entrepreneurs wishing to put novel policy alternatives on the political agenda are pressed to elaborate new normative priorities (or, to redefine old ones) and communicate their (novel) cognitive insights on the challenges ahead in a publicly compelling manner, so as to convert current anxieties over economic internationalization, post-industrial differentiation, and conditions of permanent austerity into a pursuit of mobilizing policy priorities and political ambitions. And the more reform proposals alter the distributive balance between groups and vested interests, the more important it is to put forward and elaborate new normative frameworks and discourses capable of advocating welfare recalibration as a "win-win" project, i.e. justifying reform in terms of underlying "normative foundations."

What seems to be emerging, as the result of ongoing reform dynamics, is welfare edifice based on consistent normative principles, coherent causal understandings, (re)distributive concerns, and institutional practices, comparable in scope and reach to that of the male breadwinner Keynesian welfare state of the post-1945 decades. Most importantly, a new welfare edifice should be able to address social disadvantages throughout the life course, alongside maximizing labor force participation to reduce dependency rates, and to increase the tax base and work flexibility among those within and outside the existing workforce. Esping-Andersen calls for a paradigm change from a static perspective on social policies to a dynamic one, from a welfare state being a supporter of disadvantaged categories to a welfare state being an investor in human capital addressing today's inequalities. The normative focus of social policy hereby shifts from *ex post social insurance compensation* to preventive or *ex ante social investment*, hinging on the deployment of resources to improve and equalize citizens' individual abilities to compete in the knowledge economy. To connect social policy more fully with a more dynamic economy and society, citizens have to be endowed with capabilities, through active policies that intervene early in the life cycle rather than later with more expensive passive and reactive policies (Esping-Andersen et al., 2002). In the shadow of intensified economic internationalization and post-industrial societal change, a relative shift from the social protection function of the welfare state to more of an emphasis on the social promotion function of the welfare state seems imperative. Only by adopting a life course perspective, we are best able to identify the social promotion character of the emerging new European welfare edifice.

Child-Centered Social Investment Strategy

Since life chances are so over-determined by what happens in childhood, a comprehensive child investment strategy with a strong emphasis on early childhood development is imperative. Access to affordable quality child care is sine qua non for any workable future equilibrium (Daly, 2000). Public child care provision is no longer seen merely as a facilitator of female employment or as a means to reconcile family and work. It is increasingly perceived as the first pillar of life-long learning. As investments at early stages of the lifecycle provide the basis for further success in education and training, they are seen as an effective and efficient tool to ensure skill acquisition also at later stages of general education or vocational training. The demand for child care cannot be adequately met via commercial care markets. In a purely commercial regime, low-income parents will probably not be able to afford quality care. They may respond by placing children in cheap low quality care or by withdrawing the mother from employment. Inaccessible child care will provoke low fertility; low quality care is harmful to children; and low female employment raises child poverty. The emphasis on early childhood development goes *beyond* the idea that child care is necessary to allow mother and father to reconcile work and family life. A 'child-centered social investment strategy' is needed to ensure that children will be life-long learners and strong contributors to their societies. More children, educated to perform in a knowledge economy, are needed to keep the economies of the continental welfare states going for a retiring baby boom generation with high caring needs.

Human Capital Investment Push

If Europe wishes to be competitive in the new knowledge-based society, there is an urgent need to invest in human capital throughout the life course. Considering the looming demographic imbalances we face, we surely cannot afford large skill deficits and high school dropout rates. While inequalities are widening in the knowledge economy, this also implies that parents' ability to invest in their children's fortunes is becoming more unequal. Everyone's favorite solution is of course education. If social and employment policies are increasingly aimed at developing the quality of human resources for a high-skill equilibrium, they surely assume the role of a 'productive factor.' The revitalization of both Irish and Finnish economies is in part based on increased investments in education, preventing early departure from formal education and training, and facilitating the transition from school to work, in particular school leavers with low qualifications. Here the majority of continental welfare states continue to lag behind significantly.

Flexicure Labor Markets for All

The interaction between economic performance and the welfare state is largely mediated through the labor market. The majority of Europe's continental welfare states are confronted with a syndrome of labor market segmentation between "insiders" and "outsiders" (Schmid, 2008). As family and gender issues were considered subsidiary during the early stages of postwar welfare state development, post-industrial social and economic changes seem to reinforce, this has invoked an overaccumulation of insurance benefits on the side of 'guaranteed' breadwinner workers with quasi-tenured jobs, alongside inadequate protection for those employed in the weaker sectors of the labor market, particularly youngsters, women, immigrants, and older low skilled workers. Most likely, labor markets will become ever more flexible. While the boundaries between being "in" and "out" of work have been blurred by increases in atypical work, low-wages, subsidized jobs, and training programs, one job is no longer enough to keep low-income families out of poverty. Post-industrial job growth is highly biased in favor of high skill jobs. However, increased labor market flexibility, together with the continuous rise in female employment will, in addition, also encourage the growth of a sizeable amount of low skill and semi-skilled jobs in the social sector and in personal services. The policy challenge is how to mitigate the emergence of new forms of labor market segmentation through what could be called "preventive employability," combining increase in flexibility in labor relations by way of relaxing dismissal protection, while generating a higher level of security for employees in flexible jobs. Flexible working conditions are often part and parcel of family friendly employment policy provisions. There is a clear relation between the ratio of part-time jobs and female employment growth. But the ability of part-time employment to harmonize careers with family depends very much on employment regulation, whether part-time work is recognized as a regular job with basic social insurance participation, and whether it offers possibilities for career mobility.

Later and Flexible Retirement

Many of the so-called 'new social risks,' like family formation, divorce, the elderly becoming dependent on care, declining fertility, and accelerating population aging, bear primarily on young people and young families, signifying a shift in social risks from the elderly to the young. Late entry into the labor market of youngsters, early exit of older workers, together with higher life expectancy confront the continental welfare state with a looming financing deficit. Two trends justify an adjustment in our thinking about retirement: (a) the health status of each elderly cohort is better than that of the last; at present, a man aged 65 can look forward to a further 10 healthy years; (b) the gap between old age and education is rapidly narrowing, so that old people in the future will be much better placed than now to adapt in the coming decades with the aid of retraining and lifelong learning. The education gap between the old and the young will begin to disappear when the baby boomers approach retirement. Beyond the development of multipillar, including both PAYGO (pay-as-you-go) and funded schemes, in the area of *pension policy*, the challenge lies in how to allocate the additional expenditures that inevitably accompany population aging (Myles, 2002). Of crucial importance remains a general revenue financed first-tier pension guarantee with a price index guarantee for the next generation of flexible labor market cohorts. Sustainable pensions will be difficult to achieve unless we raise employment rates of older workers and raise the retirement age to at least 67 years. Delaying retirement is both effective and equitable. It is efficient because it operates simultaneously on the nominator and denominator: more revenue intake and less spending at the same time. It is intergenerational equitable because retirees and workers both sacrifice in equal proportions. We are all getting healthier and more educated with each age cohort. Flexible retirement and the introduction of incentives to postpone retirement can greatly alleviate the pension burden. Although there has been a slight increase in part-time work among the elderly, it has been shown that part-time work and participation rates among older people are positively related, there is still little systematic and comprehensive policy activity to enhance the variable opportunity set for older workers. If older workers remain employed 10 years longer than what is now typically the norm, household incomes will increase substantially. This means less poverty and need for social assistance and greater tax revenue to the exchequer.

Migration and Integration Through Participation

More than before priority should be given to problems of participation and integration of migrants and non-EU nationals, whose rates of unemployment are, on average, twice that of EU nationals. Integration and immigration policy should have a central place in our discussion about the future of the continental welfare state, something we failed to do in the past. In our ethnically and culturally diversified societies, the welfare state faces a major challenge of ensuring that immigrants and their children do not fall behind. The recent outbreak of violence in the *ban lieus* of the metropolitan cities of France reveals how economic exclusion and physical concentration reinforces educational underperformance, excessive segregation, and a self-destructive spiral of marginalization.

Strong Safety Nets

We cannot assume that early childhood development, human capital push, together with high quality training and activation measures, will remedy current and future welfare deficiencies.

To confront successfully the problem of poverty requires broad action against social exclusion, which is linked to employment opportunities, education, housing, and living conditions across the life cycle. Hence, in the medium terms, it is impossible to avoid some form of passive minimum income support unless we are willing to accept the rising household welfare inequalities. An unchecked rise in income inequality will worsen citizens' life chances and opportunities. Greater flexibility and widespread low-wage employment suggest a scenario of overall insecurity for a sizeable group. It is, therefore, necessary to have an even more tightly woven net below the welfare net for the truly needy to meet the minimum standard of self-reliance. The overriding policy lesson is that, in the face demographic aging and in the light of a declining work force, nobody can be left inactive (for long)!

European Social Narrative

What role can the EU play in this era of welfare recalibration? Since the 1990s, the dynamics of European integration have been playing an increasingly important role in shaping social policy developments within the member states. Slowly but surely, the EU has been carving out a distinct 'policy space' for social policy agenda setting, especially in the areas of gender policy and employment. As an effective agent of welfare reform with an eye on economic competitiveness, the EU needs to further strengthen this role as an external catalyst and facilitator of the social face of reform agendas. But it needs to do this on a basis of a more visible caring dimension or new social narrative. This is a matter of urgency as significant numbers of EU citizens increasingly perceive Europe as a threat rather than a driver of economic dynamism and social justice, compatible with democratic stability and social cohesion.

References

Begg, I., Draxler, J., & Mortensen, J. (2008). Is social Europe fir for globalisation? A study of the social impact of globalization in the European Union, CEPS, European Commission, Brussels

Bonoli, G. (2005). The politics of the new social policies: Providing coverage against new social risks in mature welfare states. *Policy & Politics*, *33*(3), 431–449

Bonoli, G. (2006). New social risks and the politics of post-industrial social policies. In: K. Armingeon & G. Bonoli (Eds.), *The politics of post-industrial welfare states: Adapting post-war social policies to New social Risks* (pp. 3–26). London and New York: Routledge.

Bonoli, G., & Taylor-Gooby, P. (2000). *European welfare futures: Towards a theory of retrenchment/Giuliano Bonoli, Vic George and Peter Taylor-Gooby* (190p.). Cambridge: Polity Press.

Clark G. L., & Whiteside N. (2003). *Pension security in the 21st century*. Redrawing the Public-Private Debate. Oxford: Oxford University Press.

Daly, M. (2000). *The gender division of welfare: The impact of the British and German welfare states/Mary Daly* (273p.). Cambridge: Cambridge University Press.

Dyson, K. H. F., & Featherstone, K. (1999). *The road to Maastricht: Negotiating economic and monetary union/Kenneth Dyson and Kevin Featherstone* (859p.). Oxford: Oxford University Press.

Esping-Andersen, G. (1985). *Politics against markets*. Princeton: Princeton University Press.

Esping-Andersen, G. (1990). *The three worlds of welfare capitalism*. Cambridge: Polity Press

Esping-Andersen, G. (1994). Welfare states and the economy. In N. J. Smelser & R. Swedberg (Eds.), *The handbook of economic sociology*. Princeton: Princeton University Press, pp. 712–732

Esping-Andersen, G. (Ed.). (1996). *Welfare states in transition*. London: Sage;

Esping-Andersen, G. (1999). *Social foundations of post-industrial economies*. Oxford: Oxford University Press

Esping-Andersen, G. (2005). *Putting the horse in front of the cart: Towards a social model for mid-century Europe*. Gøsta Esping-Andersen, Universitat Pompeu Fabra

Esping-Andersen, G., & Sarasa, S. (2002). The generational conflict reconsidered, *Journal of European Social Policy*, *12*(1), 5–21.

Esping-Andersen, G., Gallie D., Hemerijck, A., & Myles, J. (2002), *Why we need a new welfare state*. Oxford: Oxford University Press.

Fajertag G., & Pochet, P. (2000). *Social pacts in Europe/edited by Giuseppe Fajertag and Philippe Pochet – Brussels: European Trade Union Institute* (ETUI) (195p.). Brussels: Observatoire Social Européen (OSE), 1997.

Ferrera, M. (2005). *The boundaries of welfare: European integration and the new spatial politics of solidarity.* Oxford: Oxford University Press (forthcoming).

Ferrera, M., & Gualmini, E. (2000). Italy: Rescue from without? In F. W. Scharpf & V. A. Schmidt (Eds.), *Welfare and work in the open economy, Volume II. Diverse responses to common challenges.* Oxford: Oxford University Press.

Ferrera, M., Hemerijck, A., & Rhodes, M. (2000). *The future of social Europe: Recasting work and welfare in the new economy.* Oeiras: Celta Editora.

Ferrera, M., & Hemerijck, A. (2003). Recalibrating Europe's welfare regimes. In J. Zeitlin & D. M. Trubek (Eds.), *Governing work and welfare in the new economy: European and American experiments.* Oxford: Oxford University Press.

Flora, P. (1986). *Growth to limits: The western European welfare states since world war II.* (Vols. 1–4). Berlin and New York: De Gruyter.

Fox, L., & Palmer, E. (1999). *New approaches to multi-pillar pension systems: What in the world is going on?* World Bank.

Hemerijck, A., & Schludi, M. (2000). Sequences of policy failures and effective policy responses, in F. W. Scharpf & V. Schmidt (Eds.), *Welfare and work in the open economy – from vulnerability to competitiveness.* Oxford: Oxford University Press.

Huber, E., & Stephens, J. D. (2001). *Development and crisis of the welfare state.* Chicago: University of Chicago Press.

Immergut, E. M., Anderson, K. M., & Schulze, I. (2007). *The handbook of pension politics in western Europe.* Oxford: Oxford University Press.

Jenson, J., & Saint-Martin, D. (2003). New routes to social cohesion? Citizenship and the social investment state. *The Canadian Journal of Sociology, 28,* 77–100.

Korthouwer, G. (forthcoming). *Party politics as We knew it? Electoral failure, intraparty dynamics and welfare reforms in continental Europe.* Dissertation. Amsterdam: University of Amsterdam.

Klammer, U. (2007). SOZIALES – INTERNATIONALES – Europäische Sozialstaaatlichkeit – Entwicklung, Koordination und Gestaltung von Sozialsystemen in der Europäischen Union. *Soziale Sicherheit: Zeitschrift für Sozialpolitik: die sozialpolitische Monatschrift der Gewerkschaften, 56,* 285–289.

Korpi, W. (1983). *The democratic class struggle.* London: Routledge & Kegan Paul.

Levy, J. (1999). Vice into virtue? Progressive politics and welfare reform in continental Europe. *Politics and Society, 27*(2), 239–273.

Leibfried, S., & pierson, P. (2000). Social policy. In H. Wallace & W. Wallace (Eds.), *Policy making in the European union,* (4th edn., pp. 267–291) Oxford: Oxford University Press.

Lynch, J. (2005*Age in the welfare state: The origins of social spending on pensioners, workers, and children.* Cambridge: Cambridge University Press.

Marshall, T. H. (1950). *Citizenship and social class and other essays.* Cambridge: Cambridge University Press.

Martin, A., & Ross, G. (2004). *Euros and Europeans: Monetary integration and the European model of society.* Cambridge: Cambridge University Press.

Organization for Economic Co-operation and Development. (1981). The welfare state in crisis: an account of the Conference on Social Policies in the 1980s, OECD, Paris, 20–23 October 1981.

Organisation for Economic Co-operation and Development. (1994). The OECD jobs study: evidence and explanations/Organisation for Economic Co-operation and Development, OECD, Paris.

Organisation for Economic Co-operation and Development. (2008). Growing unequal?: income distribution and poverty in OECD countries/Organisation for Economic Co-operation and Development, OECD, Paris.

Palme, J. (2005). Features of the Swedish pension reform. *The Japanese Journal of Social Security Policy*, 4(1), 42–53.

Pierson, P. (1998), Irristesistible forces, immovable objects: Post-industrial welfare states confront permanent austerity. *Journal of European Public Policy*, 5(4), 539–560

Pierson, P. (Ed.). (2001). *The new politics of the welfare state*. Oxford: Oxford University Press.

Ruggie, J. (1982). International regimes, transactions, and change: Embedded liberalism in the postwar economic order. *International Organization, 36*, 379–415.

Scharpf, F. W. (2003). WRR lecture De vitaliteit van de nationale staat in het Europa van de 21e eeuw/lectures uitgesproken door: F. W. Scharpf, H. A. F. M. O. van Mierlo. – Den Haag: Wetenschappelijke Raad voor het Regeringsbeleid, 52p.

Scharpf, F. W., & Schmidt, V. A. (Eds.) (2000). *Welfare and work in the open economy* (2 Volumes). Oxford: Oxford University Press.

Schmid, G. (2008). *Full employment in Europe: Managing labour market transitions and risks.* Glos: Edward Elgar Publishing.

Schmidt, V. A. (2000). Values and discourse in the politics of welfare state adjustment. In Fritz W. Scharpf & Vivien A. Schmidt (Eds.), *Welfare and work in the open economy. Vol. 1: From vulnerability to competitiveness.* Oxford: Osford University Press.

Stiller, S. (2007). *Innovative agents versus immovable objects: The role of ideational leadership in german welfare state reforms.* Dissertation. Nijmegen: University of Nijmegen.

Taylor-Gooby, P. (Ed.). (2004). *New risks, new welfare. The transformation of the European welfare state.* Oxford: Oxford university Press.

Van Gerven, M. (2008). *Reforming social security rights in Europe; A study of path-dependent but not predetermined change.* Helsinki: Social Insurance Institution Finland.

Van Kersbergen, K. (1995). *Social capitalism: A study of christian democracy and the welfare state.* London: Routledge.

Weishaupt, J. T. (2008). *The emergence of a new labor market paradigm? Analyzing continuity and change in an integrating Europe.* Dissertation. Madison: University of Wisconsin-Madison.

Zeitlin, J., Pochet, P., & Magnusson, L. (2005). The *open method of co-ordination in action. The European employment and social inclusion strategies.* P.I.E.-Peter Lang.

Chapter 6
Gender, Marriage, and Family in Post-industrial Society: An International Perspective

Ryan Sheppard

Introduction

The family retains a central position across societies, despite massive changes wrought largely by globalization and other macrosocial forces. As a basic social unit and institution, the family performs many functions for both its members and the larger society, including reproduction, socialization of children, economic support, and care for the young, the ill, and the aged. The family's relative ability or inability to perform these functions well can ease or exacerbate a host of social problems.

In recent decades around the world, families have been shaped and buffeted by macrosocial forces, including the expanding global economy, the global diffusion of post-modern ideologies such as individualism, and social movements promoting greater educational and economic opportunities for women. Far from being insulated from these forces, families experience new opportunities, for example, for greater income from remittances sent by parents working overseas, and new and increasing vulnerabilities such as the postdivorce feminization of poverty and an increasing dependency ratio that jeopardizes the well-being of the growing elderly population.

Yet, families are far from passive recipients of macrosocial forces. While family trends such as increased cohabitation, divorce, and nonfamily child care are often met with mixed reactions, it is important to recognize that these and other family shifts often stem from the efforts of families and their members to cope with large social changes – to adapt and survive, to maintain themselves, to pursue upward mobility, and to press for changes in social structures and public policies. Families have responded to industrialization, for example, by reducing family size and delaying childbearing, and they have dealt with economic uncertainty and downturns, partly by constructing dual-earner arrangements that often necessitate nonfamily child care. The responses of various family members, of course, are not necessarily in concert, for example, as young adults

R. Sheppard (✉)
Department of Sociology and Anthropology, St. Olaf College, NorthField, MN, USA
e-mail: sheppard@stolaf.edu

J. Powell, J. Hendricks, *The Welfare State in Post-Industrial Society*,
DOI 10.1007/978-1-4419-0066-1_6, © Springer Science+Business Media, LLC 2009

relocate in pursuit of higher education and a career foothold and thus distance themselves from their families and the intergenerational ties that could, in the long run, help sustain their elderly relatives. Families also shape large social trends and policies as they press for support in such areas as parental leave and child care.

If our goal is to formulate social policies that help rather than hinder families, that reduce rather than reinforce social inequalities, and that ease rather than exacerbate social problems, it is crucial that we assess the impact of postmodern conditions and virtually all social and economic policies on families, and reconsider public priorities.

This chapter focuses on several major post-1950s areas of change in families around the world, including shifts in family/household composition, marriages and cohabitating unions, fertility and family size, and child care. It describes a range of trends and issues, and it highlights ways in which these areas are interrelated with gender and shaped by globalization, post-industrialism, changes in the welfare state, and new solidarities.

Changing Household Composition and Family Structure: An Overview

Family structure and household composition have changed dramatically in recent decades in post-industrial societies and around the world. Major trends include decline in married couple and nuclear family households (married heterosexual couples and their dependent children) and increase in households of single adults, lone parents and their children, cohabiting heterosexual couples, and gay/lesbian couples and families. Collectively, these trends present a massive diversification of family forms. Considered from a global perspective, they also point to a range of new vulnerabilities and to changes in the nature of identity politics as new family patterns take root.

The decrease in nuclear family households is especially striking in the more developed countries. A study of the United States, Canada, Japan, Denmark, France, Germany, Ireland, Netherlands, Sweden, and the United Kingdom, comparing the early 1980s with the early 2000s, found that all 10 countries experienced a decline in married couple households (with children and overall) from an average of 61.5 percent of all households to 55.3 percent, an increase in single-parent households, primarily female-headed, from an average of 5.4 percent of all households to 6.5 percent, and an increase in one-person households from an average of 27 percent to 32.5 percent. As a percentage of all households with children, single-parent households in six of these countries (United States, Canada, Japan, Denmark, Ireland, and the United Kingdom) increased from an average of 11.9 percent in the early 1980s to 18.3 percent by the early 2000s. Average household size decreased in the EU nations (EU15) from 2.8 in the early 1980s to 2.4 by the early 2000s (Martin and Kats 2003).

Similar trends have appeared across world regions. Research published by the United Nations Programme on the Family indicates that decrease in marriage and increase in one-parent families, especially female-headed, and one-person households have occurred around the globe, although regions and countries vary greatly in the extent of change. In Bulgaria, for example, one-person households increased from 16.9 percent of all households in 1965 to 22.4 percent by 2001, 63 percent of them female and 80 percent of those over 50 years of age (Philipov 2003). These trends suggest that more than mere demographic transitions are at play and that how we conceptualize and provide for the family may be in for significant reformulation. The shifts in family types evident in Japan, the United States, and Bulgaria are not isolated from patterns elsewhere in the world, and as these governments and others plan investments in social welfare, they would do well to consider the patterns and trajectories of family changes. We can expect emerging needs to tax public priorities and, in seeking support, to compete with already-established needs.

A host of interrelated factors, including forces of postmodernization, have been driving these changes in household composition and family forms. Across world regions, more young adults are postponing marriage and childbearing, choosing instead to concentrate on work-related priorities. In Japan, for example, median age at first marriage for women increased from 25 years in 1975 to 27 in 2000 (Kashiwase 2002). In Egypt, the percentage of women aged 15–19, who are married, fell from 22 percent in 1976 to 10 percent in 2003 (Rashad et al. 2005). The average age of women at first childbirth increased across many industrialized countries, including all EU members, between 1980 and 2000, although it decreased slightly in the United States from 25.7 years in 1980 to 24.8 years in 2000 (Clearinghouse staff 2003a). Such shifts in marriage, work, and childbearing are not isolated from other aspects of adulthood and aging and must be considered as new policies and social welfare programs are implemented.

In Europe and the United States, the increase in one-person households reflects age-related factors. While one-person households among the elderly result mainly from death and widowhood, reflecting population aging, and those among the middle-aged reflect increase in separation and divorce, choice plays a large role among younger adults. Young adults increasingly leave home to live alone before cohabiting or marrying, partly due to urbanization, increase in education and employment opportunities, especially for women, and an increase in living-together-apart (LAT) relationships (Cliquet 2003). These trends may significantly alter the nature of intergenerational linkages in the decades ahead.

Cohabitation has also contributed to the delay and decline in marriage. In the United States, for example, the number of cohabiting couples nearly tripled between 1977 and 1994 (Batalova and Cohen 2002). It appears that increase in cohabitation and single parenthood, along with the ideological shifts these changes imply, will impact relationships and support in later life.

The larger proportion of single-parent households reflects an increase in births to nonmarried women, as well as divorce, dissolution of cohabiting unions, spouse migration, and death. A study of 11 industrialized countries (nine European countries, the United States, and Japan) found that births to unmarried women as a percentage of all live births increased dramatically in all 11 countries between 1980 and 2000, from a 34 percent increase in Denmark to a 625 percent increase in Ireland. By 2000, the 11 countries averaged almost 30 percent of births to unmarried women, although many were to cohabiting couples (Martin and Kats 2003). In Western Europe and the United States, nonmarital childbirths partly result from accidental pregnancies but increasingly are due to deliberate choice, especially among women who are better educated, employed, and older (Cliquet 2003).

Rates of divorce climbed in many countries in the latter decades of the 1900s. Measured in terms of the number of divorces per 100,000 persons per year, the divorce rate between 1960 and 1998–2000 almost tripled in Japan and France and almost doubled in the United States (United Nations Statistics Division 1968, 1976, and 2000). Regardless of possible subsequent remarriages, the vulnerabilities produced by divorce, especially for women, will tend to affect the experiences of well-being and old age.

While one-parent households in Western Europe and the United States are now produced less by widowhood and more by divorce and unplanned pregnancy, one-parent households in other world regions are often caused by migration and widowhood, due to the displacement and death that accompany war and civil unrest (De Silva 2003) and the poverty and desire for a higher living standard, which may prompt one parent to seek employment in a distant location (Varia 2007). The migration of a marital partner or parent, of course, alters the meaning of marital and family units.

Changing Unions: Marriage, Cohabitation, and Divorce

Massive changes in marriage and its surrounding trends have led to what Cherlin (2004) labels the "deinstitutionalization" of marriage, a state in which decisions about marriage are guided less by social norms than by personal fulfillment and individual choice. Globalization has fostered the proliferation of individualism, a cultural factor implicated in the delays and decreases in marriage and the increase in singlehood, cohabitation, nonmarital childbearing, and divorce. Social movement organizations at national and international levels have advocated for women's equality in the paid labor force and thus their increased independence from marriage and a male breadwinner and for gay/lesbian rights to legally recognized marriage and domestic partnerships.

Marriage is no longer universally viewed as essential to the transition to adulthood. In the United States, for example, young adults of the early twentieth century tended to leave home, enter the labor force, get married, and start having children by their early twenties, but today's young adults face an environment in which extended education is more valuable, jobs and economic conditions are less certain, entry into adulthood is more ambiguous, and the old social timetables no longer apply (Furstenberg et al. 2005). Although marriage remains one central marker of adulthood, young Americans now define adulthood by such elements as establishing an independent household, gaining employment, attaining financial independence, cohabiting, and beginning parenthood (Shanahan et al. 2005).

In some areas of the world, however, early marriage remains significant despite its decline and is usually accompanied by early childbearing, high fertility, and substantial disadvantages for women. In Benin, Colombia, India, and Turkey, for example, early female marriage is associated with early childbirth, marriage to much older men, and lower educational attainment (Jensen and Thornton 2003). As women move through life and approach old age, these inequalities may be compounded and lead to even greater disadvantages.

Cohabitation has increased in many countries, including nearly all Western countries. In North America and across Europe, more couples now cohabit before marriage and after separation, divorce, and widowhood. In Europe, by 2000, cohabitation rates varied from 30 percent of all couples in Sweden, 24.5 percent in Norway, and 17.5 percent in France (Ambert 2005), with southern European countries having far lower rates (Cliquet 2003). In the United States, about half of all couples now cohabit before marriage (Cherlin 2004). As norms about living together shift to reflect these trends, the realignment will touch many other aspects of life.

Cohabitation less frequently leads to marriage than in past decades, raising the question of whether it is replacing marriage. In the United States, for example, the rate of cohabiting couples marrying within three years of cohabitation dropped from about 60 percent in the 1970s to about 35 percent by the 1990s (Ambert 2005). Sweden combines its high cohabitation rate with one of the lowest marriage rates in the developed world, reflecting a decrease in religious and cultural pressure to marry, widespread feminist concerns over family-based oppression and patriarchy, and the provision of government benefits to individuals regardless of their family and relationship forms (Whitehead and Popenoe 2005).

Benefits of cohabitation include convenience, sexual access, economic advantages, relationship testing, and, in many countries, legal rights that are now similar to those for married couples (Ambert 2005). Cohabitation is expected to continue its rise, reflecting increase in individualism, antimarriage attitude, economic uncertainty, contraception, and women's independence (Batalova and Cohen 2002).

Same-sex couples have increased in social visibility and legitimation in recent decades, due to the efforts of gay liberation social movements of the late 1960s to mid-1970s and ongoing international organizations that advocate for the rights of sexual minorities, including the right to marry, such as the International Gay and Lesbian Human Rights Commission and the International Lesbian and Gay Association. Legal recognition of same-sex relationships began with registered partnerships in Denmark in 1989 and legal marriage in the Netherlands in 2001. By 2006, same-sex couples could legally marry in several countries, including Belgium, Canada, the Netherlands, and Spain, and had legal recognition of relationships in at least 19 countries, including nine EU members (Harding and Peel 2006). However, same-sex marriage remains hotly contested in the United States, where the 1996 Defense of Marriage Act enables states to refuse to recognize same-sex marriages licensed by other states (Cherlin 2004). A survey conducted across 27 countries in six continents indicates that lesbian, gay, and bisexual individuals strongly support equal relationship choices and status, including legal recognition of same-sex relationships, especially marriage (Harding and Peel 2006). Many same-sex couples have children, including 33 percent of women and 22 percent of men in same-sex relationships in the United States, according to the 2000 Census (Cherlin 2004).

Criteria for mate selection have been changing around the globe. As individualism and women's paid labor have increased, people have come to select mates more on the basis of individual choice, romantic love, and partnership and less on the basis of parental choice and gender-role-based criteria. A study of 37 cultures in 33 countries around the world found that mutual attraction and love were among the top three mate selection factors in 34 of the 37 cultures studied (Buss et al. 1990). The increasing individualism that accompanies the spread of post-industrial ideologies challenges long-held traditions and the relevance of custom in the lives of young adults.

Research on mate preferences in the United States, between 1939 and 1996, found that mutual attraction and love became the top preference for men and women by the 1980s and that women and men have converged in the characteristics desired in a mate (Buss et al. 2001). Both sexes increased their mate-selection emphasis on physical appearance, perhaps due to mass media images and the growth of diet, cosmetics, and cosmetic surgery industries. Both sexes also increased their emphasis on good financial prospects, men more so than women, and decreased their emphasis on virginity. Men and women became more similar in their mate-selection emphasis on domestic skills, as men's preference for this decreased, yet the two differed in that men emphasized good looks more than women did and women emphasized good financial prospects more than men did.

The Changing Character of Marriage

Marital spouses now focus more on the emotional character of marriage, placing greater emphasis on communication, partnership, support, and self-fulfillment. In the most developed countries, marriage has shifted from being a covenant based on responsibilities and mutual fulfillment to a private relationship centered on personal satisfaction (Ambert 2005).

Research in the United States has identified a shift toward "individualized" marriage based on self-development and negotiation of marital roles and rules and away from marriage based on social norms and breadwinner/homemaker gender roles (Cherlin 2004). Internationally also, husbands and wives expect more role-sharing between partners (Roopnarine and Gielen 2005). Spouses seek greater intimacy and personal growth through open communication and expression of feelings between partners and evaluate their marriages based more on self-development and expression of feelings than on satisfaction in the roles of husband and wife (Cherlin 2004). The dramatic increase in individualism, self, and individual choice reflects the globalization of culture through mass media and mass consumption, with 'Western' nations dominating the globalized culture (Karraker 2008). As others in this volume note, the flow of global ideologies touches virtually every society regardless of its state of industrialization or postmodernism.

In many areas of the world, distributions of labor and power in marriage have been shifting, with wives earning more income and having more decision-making power and autonomy and husbands doing somewhat more domestic labor and child care than in the past. Globally, the proportion of women working outside the home increased from about one-third in the 1950s to about one-half by the late 1990s. Recent estimates show regional variation from 14 percent in North Africa to 76 percent in East and Central Europe. The rise in women's labor force participation reflects changes in families' needs for women's income and an increased demand for women's labor (UNESCO 2004), particularly in the manufacturing sector in less developed countries and the service sector in more developed countries. As more women move into paid employment, issues of equality will arise, of course, but the point here is that as women increase their employment, families are being reconfigured and redefined.

A study of couple families with at least one child under age six in seven European countries and the United States found that all countries studied showed a decrease in the percentage of male breadwinner couples and an increase in partial dual-earner couples (man working full-time and woman part-time) in the 1980s and 1990s. The most common income-earning arrangement in 1984 was a male breadwinner (man working full-time and woman not employed), but by 1999, dual-earner (both working full-time) was the dominant pattern in the United States (36.5percent), and partial dual-earner was dominant in the Netherlands and the United Kingdom (Martin and Kats 2003). Among all married-couple households in the United States, with and without children, about 56 percent were dual-income families by 2002 (AmeriStat staff 2003a, 2003b).

As women's employment and earnings have grown, an increasing minority of women have come to outearn their husbands. In the United States, for example, the percentage of women in dual-earner marriages earning more than their husbands increased from 22 percent in 1990 to 28 percent by 2002 (AmeriStat 2003), impacting the marital balance of power and decision-making.

Overall, however, women continue to earn less than men. A study of 20 developed countries (16 in Europe, plus Australia, Canada, Israel, and the United States) between 1991 and 2000 found that the average wage of men was about 26 percent higher than that of women with identical education, working hours, marital status, and age. Among the countries studied, wage inequality was highest in the Netherlands (48 percent) and Germany (46 percent), lowest in Hungary (12 percent) and Italy (15 percent), and 33 percent in the United States (Mandel and Seymonov 2005). In 2006, the European Commission responded by adopting a "Road map for Equality between Women and Men," outlining EU priorities for 2006–2010, including achieving gender equality in paid labor and eliminating gender stereotypes in education, employment, and mass media, to be addressed by the EU's Directorate-General for Employment, Social Affairs, and Equal Opportunities (European Commission 2006). Action priorities include, for example, monitoring gender pay gaps, promoting female entrepreneurship, supporting exchanges of good practices in schools' efforts to address gender roles, and promoting "gender mainstreaming" in policy areas, such as pensions and health care (assessing policy implications for women and men to avoid perpetuating gender inequality).

As women's paid labor has increased, attitudes about marriage and gender roles have shifted. By the early 2000s, adults in most areas of the world tended to favor greater egalitarianism in income-earning and domestic labor. In 2002, the Global Attitudes Project asked adults around the world to state the type of marriage that most appealed to them. Majorities in Europe, the Americas, Asia, and Africa stated a preference for both spouses to share income-earning, household labor and child care. In predominantly Muslim countries, such as Egypt and Pakistan, however, a majority favors a gendered breadwinner/homemaker division of labor (Speulda and McIntosh 2004).

Women continue to do the majority of household labor and child care regardless of their income-earning status (Roopnarine and Gielen 2005). Men's participation in domestic labor has increased somewhat, but is still often framed as "helping out around the house" (Adams 2004).

Yet some couples tend to have greater equality in the division of household labor. Younger men are more willing to do household labor than the older ones (Adams 2004), and premarital cohabitors tend to have greater equality, although women still tend to do the majority of domestic labor (Batalova and Cohen 2002). A study of couples in 22 countries found that greater equality in the division of household labor is associated with more education, liberal attitude, younger age, and marriage in which the wife earns more than the husband, the wife works full-time, or the husband does not work full-time (Batalova and Cohen 2002).

Marital power has further shifted as authoritarian values have declined, with parents in developed societies expressing less desire for hierarchical family relationships (Roopnarine and Gielen 2005). By 2003, 83 countries had passed laws establishing equal rights in marriage, although 38 recognized the husband as household head and 57 mandated wives' obedience to husbands (Gautier 2005).

In many less developed countries, discriminatory laws and practices are being contested and changed. As of 2000, Egyptian women can initiate divorce without a husband's consent. Morocco's recent family law, based on new interpretations of Islamic law and passed in 2004, promotes gender equality by increasing women's legal age for marriage to 18, establishing women's self-guardianship rights, and allowing spouses to compose their own marriage contracts (Rashad et al. 2005).

These shifts in the gendered division of marital power are synchronous with international efforts to curb violence against women. The number of countries with specific domestic violence laws grew from 45 in 2003 to 60 by 2006, with an additional 29 addressing domestic violence through other venues, such as family law, and an increasing number of countries establishing national plans to end violence against women (United Nations 2006). Yet rates of domestic violence remain comparatively high in some developing countries. A study of nine developing countries, including Cambodia, Colombia, Egypt, India, and Zambia, found that more than one in six married women reported being physically abused by her husband (Lalasz 2004). Higher risk was associated with having a husband who gets drunk often or displays controlling behavior, having a mother who was abused, and being married young, while lower risk was associated with making decisions jointly with one's husband.

Divorce and Dissolution

Divorce rates increased in most world regions in the later 1900s. Measured by the number of divorces per 100,000 persons per year, from 1960 to 1998–2000, the divorce rate almost tripled in Japan and France, nearly doubled in the United States, where it was already high; increased slightly in Mexico, where it remained relatively low; yet dropped by nearly half in Egypt (Demographic Yearbooks 1968, 1976, and 2000, United Nations Statistics Division). In Western Europe, divorce rates were still increasing in the 1990s, but were stabilizing or decreasing slightly in countries where they were already high, including the United Kingdom, the United States, and northern European countries (Cliquet 2003). In Central and Eastern Europe, divorce rates rose after independence from the Soviet Union, beginning in the late 1980s, but only slightly in many countries (Philipov 2003).

A study of the dissolution of marital and cohabiting unions in 15 European countries and the United States between the late 1980s and late 1990s found that 20 percent to 30 percent of marriages in the European countries and 42 percent of marriages in the United States dissolved within the first 15 years, as did 40 percent of unions overall (married and cohabitation unions) in the European countries and 60 percent in the United States. Among couples with children, both married and cohabiting, dissolution rates were lower but significant. Ten of the European countries studied had dissolution rates of 20 percent or more by 15 years after the time of becoming a parental union; the comparable rate in the United States was 38 percent (Andersson 2002).

Divorce increases the number of one-parent families, most of them female-headed, even though most divorced individuals eventually remarry or cohabit. A comparison of 15 countries, including 11 EU countries plus Israel, Japan, New Zealand, and the United States, found that divorced and separated mothers constituted the largest portion of lone mother families by the late 1990s and early 2000s, except in Italy and Ireland (Clearinghouse staff 2003b). Because many divorced women, including mothers, become sole earners, the consequences of divorce are compounded: mothers often face a lifetime of sole earner and parenting responsibilities, and divorce depresses the socio-economic status of children and thereby their life course trajectories.

While some view rising divorce rates as an alarming marker of the weakening of marriage, divorce rates also reflect a growing freedom to end unsatisfying marriages (Cherlin 2004; Adams 2004). The rising divorce rates indicate that longstanding traditions and norms are being replaced by ideologies and values that reflect other shifts accompanying postmodernization. Researchers would do well to attend to how these emerging trends are likely to play out over the life course and how they might inform public policies.

A range of interrelated factors has shaped divorce trends, many of them linked to globalization. Many developed countries liberalized their divorce laws starting in the1970s (Sorrentino 1990), and by the mid-1980s, nearly all had done so (Martin and Kats 2003). New "no fault" laws have facilitated divorce; they recognize divorce by mutual consent and sometimes by unilateral choice, enable couples to negotiate many of the details of their divorces, and have helped reduce the social stigma of divorce (Cherlin 2004).

Economic factors related to women's paid labor, economic development, and labor migration have also fostered divorce. From Hungary to the United States to China, the increase in women's paid labor and economic independence has enabled women to more easily leave unsatisfying marriages (Adams 2004). In East and Southeast Asia, divorce rates tend to be higher in countries with greater per capita gross domestic product, perhaps due to better-educated populations, greater income-earning options for women, and stronger individual interest in careers and personal development (Quah 2003). In South and Central Asia, when a wife or husband leaves temporarily for income-earning and then returns, problems of reintegration and adjustment to family can increase the risk of divorce, especially in the first year after returning (Quah 2003).

Religion and cohabitation rates are also linked to divorce. A study of 15 European countries and the United States between 1989 and 1997 found that the United States had consistently higher rates of dissolution than the European countries, and several heavily Catholic European countries consistently had the lowest rates (Andersson 2002). In most of the European countries, 20 to 30 percent of all marriages ended within the first 15 years, but the rate was lower in the heavily Catholic countries like Italy, Spain, Slovenia, and Poland, at no more than 10 percent, and considerably higher in the United States, at 42 percent. Unions overall – marriages plus cohabiting unions – showed even higher rates of dissolution. Among the European countries, about 40 percent of unions ended within the first 15 years, with rates lowest in the heavily Catholic countries, whereas the comparable rate in the United States was about 60 percent, with 20 percent of unions ending within the first year. These higher union dissolution rates reflect the much higher dissolution rates of unions begun through cohabitation. In almost all countries studied, unions begun as cohabitation dissolved by the 15-year mark by at least double the rate of those begun as marriages: 45–55 percent in most of the European countries, but again lower in the Catholic countries, and more than 70 percent in the United States. Among couples with children, 10 of the European countries studied had dissolution rates of 20 percent or more by 15 years after the point of becoming a parental union, with an across-countries average of 18.7 percent. Again, the United States' rate was higher at 38 percent.

Not surprisingly, the spread of modern values, including individualism and egalitarianism, also contribute to divorce. Jelin and Diaz-Munoz (2003) discuss these factors in South America, yet their description applies across the range of post-industrial countries:

> The increase in divorce rates and separation should be examined in light of complex socio-cultural processes linked to individuation. The spread of modern values of personal autonomy, free choice of a partner based on romantic love, the growing social expectation of being able to act on one's wishes and feelings – all these have their counterpart in the freedom to sever ties when there is no more love, when the costs of maintaining a conflictual relationship exceed those of ending the conjugal bond . . . (p. 7).

Changing Fertility and Family Size

In the face of economic shifts and the diffusion of industrialization, family size has declined around the world. Europeans now tend to have only one or two children, Asians two or three, and Sub-Saharan Africans five or six (Population Reference Bureau staff 2008). The demographic transition – a long-term reduction in mortality and fertility rates – began earlier and slower in the now post-industrial countries and more recently and rapidly in the developing countries, where average family size is larger but decreasing. Many consider fertility far too high globally and within developing countries, yet fertility decline has been so extensive in some developed countries that many consider it too low. As this section notes, globalization has shaped reduction in fertility partly through mass media; post-industrial influences have shaped fertility, as nongovernmental organizations and supranational organizations, such as the United Nations, have worked to expand family planning programs around the world; and many post-industrial nations with low fertility have developed new social welfare policies designed to elevate fertility.

Demographic data show declines in global, regional, and national fertility, with family size tending to vary with level of economic development. Demographers commonly measure birth rates – a proxy for family size – with "total fertility rate" (TFR), which measures the average number of children women are expected to have over their childbearing years (ages 15–49) if age-specific birth rates remain constant. World TFR decreased from about 5.0 in 1950 to 2.7 by 2007 (Population Reference Bureau staff 2007). In most of the more developed countries of the world, fertility had fallen to 1.6 by 2008 (Population Reference Bureau staff 2008), well below the "replacement level" of 2.1 (Population Reference Bureau 2004). By 2008, the TFR had dropped to 3.2 in developing countries, excluding China, and 4.7 in the least developed countries, rates that are double and triple the TFR of more developed countries (Population Reference Bureau staff 2008), although a few developing countries have TFRs at or below 2.1, including China, Korea, Thailand, and Brazil (Population Reference Bureau staff 2004). Family size and fertility also vary within countries. In the United States, for example, fertility rates of African Americans, Latinos, and recent immigrants are well above the national TFR of about 2.0 (Population Reference Bureau staff 2004).

Like other shifts, the decline in family size has multiple causes, most importantly decrease in the number of children desired and increase in contraceptive access and use (Population Reference Bureau staff 2004). Various demographic, economic, and social factors have prompted women and couples to desire fewer children. As the nature of production shifts from primarily agricultural to predominantly industrial and manufacturing, parents' need for children's agricultural labor decreases. Fertility declines have typically been preceded by mortality declines, especially in infant mortality, so that more children survive and more women achieve their desired family size by age 30 (Quah 2003). Modernization, urbanization, mass media, and increase in women's education have helped spur the desire for fewer children. They help explain fertility changes in Kenya, for example, where women surveyed in the 1970s wanted an average of seven or more children, but those surveyed in the 1990s wanted less than four, and in Senegal and Cote d'Ivoire, where research suggests that exposure to television and films helped promote beliefs that women can control their childbearing and that having fewer children may be beneficial (Population Reference Bureau staff 2004).

Access to family planning and contraception has increased around the world. Globally, the percentage of married women of childbearing age using contraception rose from less than 10 percent in the 1960s to more than 60 percent by 2007, but regional variation is extensive, with contraceptive use in 2007 at 73 percent in North America, 67 percent in Europe, 66 percent in Asia, and 28 percent in Africa (Population Reference Bureau staff 2007). In Europe, contraceptive use soared with the "contraceptive revolution," as use at first intercourse increased from one-third of women born in the 1940s and 1950s to over two-thirds of women born in the 1970s (Ulrich 2001).

Demographers find that contraceptive use is the largest factor shaping fertility rates and that the variation in use is largely due to differences in income, education, gender roles, and government policies (Population Reference Bureau staff 2004). Denmark and the Netherlands provide easy access to contraception through mandatory sex education since the 1970s, family planning services that work with schools, and adequate government funding. In the United Kingdom, however, funding for family planning services has been inadequate and services are less accessible to teenagers (Amu and Appiah 2006).

Legal access to the "abortion pill" – RU 486 or Mifegyne – began in Europe in the 1990s and in the United States in 2000 respectively, although practical access varies by government funding, clinic, and women's social class. In most European countries where Mifegyne is legal, the already low abortion rates have declined or remained stable. Abortion remains a hot issue in Germany, the United States, and France, where opposition is rooted in ethical and religious beliefs (Crighton and Ebert 2002).

By 2008, the most developed nations had an average contraception use rate (by married women aged 15–49) of 69 percent, with a TFR of 2.6, for example, in France, 79 percent and 2.0; in the United States 73 percent and 2.1; and Spain at 72 percent and 1.4, but the rate in the least developed nations was 27 percent, with a TFR of 4.7 (Population Reference Bureau staff 2008). In Mali, for example, less than 9 percent of women were using contraception in 2008 and the TFR was 6.8 (Population Reference Bureau staff 2004).

In recent decades, organized family planning programs (FPPs) have targeted "unmet need" for contraception in less developed countries, providing access to contraception and helping reduce fertility and family size. The increase in FPPs around the world partly reflects the increasing role of supranational organizations and NGOs in shaping national policies and programs. When concerns grew in the mid-1900s that rapid population growth in developing countries might intensify poverty and slow economic development, various organizations moved to shape the population policy and help fund family planning services. The United Nations held meetings on global population in 1954 and 1965; the International Planned Parenthood Federation formed in 1952; international programs to support national family planning programs in developing countries began in the 1960s;, and the United Nations Fund for Population Activities (now the UN Population Fund) was founded in 1969. At the 1984 World Population Conference, nearly all governments agreed that family planning services should be available to all, and by the early 1990s, most developing countries had developed national population policies. Women's groups became involved and asserted that government programs often neglected women's reproductive rights and overall health, used coercive tactics sometimes, and should instead offer comprehensive reproductive health programs designed to promote women's power over sexuality and childbearing, thus enabling women to have the number of children they desire. The 1994 International Conference on Population and Development in Cairo created a 20-year Programme of Action to promote comprehensive reproductive health care that places women's needs for more control over sexuality and reproduction at the center, includes services related to family planning (including abortion where legal), pregnancy, and sexually transmitted infections, and works to eliminate practices harmful to women, such as forced marriage and genital cutting. At UN-organized meetings in 2004, participants assessed progress, shared strategies, and noted that developing countries lacked sufficient resources and many of the more developed countries had failed to meet their pledges for assistance (Population Reference Bureau staff 2004).

The Cairo conference has had far-reaching impacts. International concerns over human rights and comprehensive reproductive health services prompted China to modify its approach to its "one-child" policy in 1995 by offering counseling, choices in contraceptive methods, and reproductive health care in FPPs in at least some counties and by criminalizing coercive enforcement of the one-child policy in 2002. Cairo also prompted India to modify its government-sponsored FPPs. In 1996, India shifted from an emphasis on numerical goals for contraceptive use to a broader reproductive health approach, and in 2000, it began emphasizing on more integrated reproductive services, combined with child health services, all directed at reducing family size from 3.2 to 2.1 by 2010 while addressing women's needs and preserving human rights (Population Reference Bureau staff 2004).

In many of the most developed countries of the world, however, fertility concerns have focused on how to increase low fertility. In the United States and Europe, for example, decline in fertility occurred before WWII, increased afterward, and declined again in the 1980s and 1990s, reaching below-replacement fertility rates by 1999, raising concerns about possible negative consequences and prompting UN meetings on low fertility in 2000. An older age structure can strain social security systems and pension plans, afflict national health budgets, increase the dependency ratio, reduce economic growth, and threaten international economic and political standing. In response, government policies could work to encourage childbearing, increase the number of working-age immigrants, and reduce the effects of aging (for example, by raising the retirement age) (Population Reference Bureau staff 2004). While fertility patterns may at first glance appear far removed from the experience of aging, the two are, in fact, closely related.

Low-fertility countries now employ a range of pronatalist family support policies designed to increase fertility rates or prevent further declines. Family allowance policies help offset the cost of having children, including direct expenses and lost income, and may include cash payments at the birth of a child and monthly payments throughout childrearing years. Flexible work policies help by offering family leave, part-time arrangements, and flexibility in work arrival and departure times, which can enable parents to reduce latch-key time. Additional family-friendly employment policies make it easier to combine paid labor with child rearing and, sometimes, also promote gender equality. They include child care assistance (via government child care programs or tax benefits) and parental and family leave. Parental leave policies, discussed below, vary greatly across countries that use them (Population Reference Bureau staff 2004). Japan's Child Care Support Plan, begun in

2004, seeks to increase fertility by increasing support for child rearing, work/ family reconciliation, and child care (United Nations 2007).

Parental Leave Policies

Maternity, paternity, and parental leave policies provide parents with job-protected time off from paid employment, sometimes with income, at or near the time of childbearing or adoption. Their purposes vary across protecting maternal and child health immediately after childbirth, supporting domestic labor, especially when children are young, reducing work/family tensions, and enabling parents to provide regular care for children at home during early childhood years (Kamerman and Gatenio 2002a).

Parental leave policies have been driven by increase in mothers' labor force participation and concerns over possible negative outcomes for infants and young children placed in day care (Kamerman and Gatenio 2002a). An analysis of six European Union (EU) countries found that women's political pressure, especially through national machineries such as human rights committees, women's bureaus, and Equal Employment Opportunity Commissions is necessary for the introduction or expansion of social-care policies, including parental leave and public child care (Bleijenbergh and Roggeband 2007). Maternal employment policies are also shaped by the percentage of women in parliament (Lambert 2008).

Policies promoting maternity leave have a relatively long history and are now near-universal. Paid maternity leaves began as early as the 1880s when Germany enacted a paid maternity policy. In 1919, the International Labor Organization (ILO) promoted a 12-week paid maternity leave for women working in commerce and industry. The massive movement of women into the paid labor force in the 1960s and 1970s prompted countries in the Organisation for Economic Co-operation and Development (OECD) to enact longer maternity leaves with greater income replacement and to view leaves as an important part of child care and infant care policies. The 1980s and 1990s saw an international trend to establish parental leave as an addition to maternity leave, to expand leave policies, and to use leave policies to promote gender equity. In 1992, the EU mandated a paid 14-week maternity leave, which it expanded to a three-month parental leave in 1998. In 2000, the ILO recommended a 14-week job-protected maternity leave with public-funded income replacement at a reasonable standard of living (Kamerman and Gatenio 2002a).

As of 2004, 128 countries representing every major world region provide childbirth-related leave. Among countries offering maternity leave, the average leave offered is about 16 weeks, and OECD countries offer an average of 18 months total childbirth-related leave, including paid and unpaid maternity leave, paternity leave, and parental leave. Maternity leave is the most common leave, but many countries, especially the more developed countries, are extending leaves to fathers through paternity leaves and gender-neutral parental leaves. Denmark, Italy, Norway, and Sweden urge greater father participation in early child care by mandating that one month of paid parental leave be taken by fathers on a "use it or lose it" basis (Kamerman and Gatenio 2002a).

Benefit levels vary and are usually funded and paid through the same system that pays sick leave benefits. In about half of the leave-providing countries, paid leave replaces 100 percent of lost wages, and some countries provide paid leave plus a one-time-per-child birth allowance. By 2002, 23 of 29 OECD countries provided at least 50 percent income replacement during leave, and 16 of these provided 70–100 percent replacement. Paternity leave benefits are usually 100 percent. If maternity leave is followed by parental leave, the benefit tends to be lower (Kamerman and Gatenio 2002a).

Denmark, for example, offers 18 weeks maternity leave at 90 percent pay, two weeks paternity leave at 100 percent, and 10 weeks parental leave at 60 percent; the United Kingdom offers a minimum of 18 weeks maternity leave with 6 weeks at 90 percent and 12 weeks at a flat rate that varies by employment, plus 13 weeks parental leave up to a child's fifth birthday; Spain offers 16 weeks maternity leave at 100 percent pay with 10 weeks of that transferable to the father (Kamerman and Gatenio 2002a); India and China offer 12 weeks at 100 percent pay; Egypt offers 3 months at 75 percent; and Chad offers 14 weeks at 50 percent (Kamerman 2004). The list of countries providing no leave (and no pay) is populated largely by least developed and Middle East countries, but the United States and Australia are the only developed countries that fail to provide any income during leave (Kamerman 2004).

Reflecting large variability between and within countries, not all parents are eligible and user rates vary. In nearly all OECD countries offering childbirth-related leaves, benefits are only available to women who have some minimum work history and benefit amount may be determined by the duration of work history. Except for the work requirement, however, the leaves tend to be universal and thus available to all families regardless of income. In OECD countries, parental leave "take-up rates" (user rates) tend to be over 90 percent among women, but low among men (Kamerman and Gatenio 2002a). The European Commission's gender- and family-related priorities for 2007 and 2008 include reducing the gender-income gap and improving job security for employees on maternity leave (European Commission's Directorate-General for Employment, Social Affairs, and Equal Opportunities, no date). The United States offers no specific maternity, paternity, or parental leave, but an annual two-week unpaid family leave for childbirth, adoption, care of a sick family member, or personal illness, depending on the length of employment and size of the employer, leaving 45 percent of workers ineligible and many others unable to afford to take the leave to which they are entitled (Kamerman and Gatenio 200a).

Importantly, a wide range of policies can be used to help countries increase low fertility or decrease high fertility, but no single approach will work in all cases. To be effective, fertility policies must respond to preexisting social-institutional frameworks (e.g. typical family organization; state-subsidized child care systems; and women's labor force participation rates), which vary across countries. McDonald recommends that countries seeking to increase fertility base their policies on research and theory regarding the causes of low fertility in their particular country – whether it reflects rational choice, concerns with gender equality, or other factors (McDonald 2002).

Child Care

Families have retained their central functions of providing child care and child socialization, but shifts in patterns of family caregiving have been shaped by modernization, globalization, and post-industrial influences, including the increase in women's labor force participation, organized political pressure from women, and migrant domestic workers. This section focuses on child care centers, domestic migrant workers, child-rearing leaves, and family allowances.

While the proportion of women working outside the home has increased to about one-half globally, paid labor by mothers in many countries has increased even more dramatically. By the early 2000s, employment by mothers with children under three years in the 20 OECD nations averaged 57.5 percent, with a high of 80.1 percent in Austria (Clearinghouse staff 2005b).

Yet the time parents spent on parental primary care (with the child as the main focus of attention) in 2000 was similar to that in 1965. Time diaries indicate that mothercare in the United States decreased between 1965 and 1985 and then increased from 1985 to 2000, and care by married fathers was stable from 1965 to 1985 and then increased. Similar trends occurred in Canada, France, the Netherlands, the United Kingdom, and Australia. In the United States, mothers increased the primary care by cutting back on housekeeping time, free time, and social time; fathers decreased time on personal care; and both increased time multitasking (Cohn 2007).

At the same time, parents have increasingly turned to nonparental child care arrangements. Among children under three years, the percentage in formal child care centers varies, for example, from 64 percent in Denmark, 54 percent in the United States, and 40–50 percent in Sweden, Canada, and Norway, to 13 percent in Japan, and less than 10 percent in the Republic of Korea, Brazil, the Netherlands, and Mongolia. Enrollment in pre-primary education (3–5-year olds) varies widely with France at 100 percent, many developed countries at over 90 percent (including Cuba, the Netherlands, Italy, Spain, Kuwait, New Zealand, Denmark, and Israel), the United States at about 57 percent, and least developed countries clustered at the bottom with less than 5 percent enrollment, for example, in Myanmar and Sierra Leone (Heymann et al. 2004).

'Early childhood education and care' (ECEC) programs for children below compulsory school age provide physical care, education, and socialization and are heavily subsidized by government in most countries (Clearinghouse staff 2005a). ECEC programs began over 100 years ago as private charities, shifted to public entities largely after WWII, and experienced major expansions in the 1970s. Goals include providing early childhood education, boosting child development, easing maternal employment, and providing child protection. National programs vary in their emphasis on education, peer interaction, and the promotion of center-based care versus home-based parental care, as well as their duration (part-day or full-day), national or local authority, eligibility criteria (universal, working parents, poor, or special needs), funding strategies, and caregiver status (parent, professional, paraprofessional) (Clearinghouse staff 2005a). Research indicates that high-quality child care is associated with positive child outcomes (Clawson and Gerstel 2002).

France offers a national, voluntary, government-paid program. 'Crèches' are nursery-like programs for children under age three, staffed by high school graduates. 'Ecoles maternelles,' for children ages three to six, are preschool education programs that focus on early education and have a national curriculum and well-educated, well-paid teachers. Nearly 100 percent of parents enroll their children in ecoles maternelles. Taking a different approach, Denmark offers a nonschool child care system for children, from birth to age six whose parents are employed. The Danish system has a largely unstructured curriculum and college-educated staff, and children mainly spend time playing with their peers. Public funding covers most expenses, leaving parents to pay about one-fifth of actual cost. In Sweden, parental leave is so extensive and highly used that very few children under one year are in public care (Clawson and Gerstel 2002).

In the United States, public-funded programs, such as Head Start, are reserved for low-income families, and subsidies for poorer families are often under-funded and unavailable. Overall costs are similar to those in France but are not public-funded for most. American parents have shown an increased desire for placements in child care centers and preschools, but many struggle to find acceptable and affordable care. Waiting lists are often long, staff pay is low, and turnover is high. Because child care is expensive – full time care often costs more than one year's tuition at a public university – parents sometimes choose lower quality care for its lower cost. Others arrange child care with relatives or work different shifts to care for children themselves, and a relatively few affluent parents hire nannies. In the United States, almost half of the children under one year now spend regular time in nonparental care, and 46 percent of the three-year olds and 64 percent of four-year olds spend significant time in child care centers. Nearly half of the three- to four-year olds with employed mothers are in two or more child care arrangements (Clawson and Gerstel 2002).

Domestic Migrant Workers: Transnational Mothers

Nothing highlights the impact of globalization on family issues more than the fact that an increasing minority of affluent families in post-industrial countries arranges for child care and other household labor by employing immigrant women from poorer countries, such as Mexico and the Philippines, many of whom become primary income providers for the families they leave behind. The transnational families thus created are part of a larger group of families whose members are spread across nation-states, but who maintain a family identity and whose migrant members generally contribute economically to the family (Bryceson and Vuorela 2003). While transnational split-household families are a longstanding phenomenon, the families of migrant domestic workers illustrate a shift from families characterized by absence of fathers to those characterized by absence of mothers (Karraker 2008). The fact that migrant domestic workers find it advantageous, regardless of difficulty, to be away from their families speaks to the privatization of child care and other forms of domestic labor, and the absence of mothers and their employment in distant locales may become a more significant issue in coming decades.

These arrangements form "global care chains" – international flows of labor in which undervalued caregiving jobs are passed from women in First World countries to migrant women from Third World countries who themselves pass caregiving to female relatives or poorer hired domestic workers (Hochschild 2000). Migrant domestic workers are responding to an increasing demand for cheap, flexible care-giving workers in oil-rich nations and more developed countries where women's labor force participation has increased, more married parents have dual-earner households, and many families have achieved suffi-cient affluence to afford private household help (Anderson 2000). These arrangements release affluent women (and men) from traditionally gendered domestic labor, yet reinforce a gender ideology that defines domestic labor as women's work.

Domestic labor has become one of the largest employment areas for female immigrants from Third World countries to more developed countries (Anderson 2000). Women constitute 50–75 percent of the legal migrants leaving the Philippines, Indonesia, and Sri Lanka, many of them seeking domestic labor jobs abroad (Varia 2007). Remittances from Filipino domes-tic workers to the Philippines come from a range of countries. In 2005–2006, the top 10 included the United States, Canada, Italy, the United Kingdom, Japan, Hong Kong, Singapore, and Taiwan, along with Saudi Arabia and the United Arab Emirates (UAE). New hires increased from under 60,000 in 1992 to over 90,000 by 2006 and shifted toward the Middle East, the region of seven of the top 10 countries hiring the largest number of new migrant domestic workers in 2005 (Sana 2007).

Many migrant domestic workers are overworked and underpaid, experience criminal abuses, and face a huge debt burden as the domestic worker recruitment industry shifts more fees to workers (Varia 2007). Labor-sending countries often promote international labor migration to gain income from remittances, and labor-receiving countries often rely on migrant labor while excluding migrant workers from protective labor laws. The potential for exploitation is huge, yet relatively few intergovernmental agencies or NGOs are focusing on the issues.

Those measures that do exist tend to focus on improving conditions for migrant domestic workers, including minimum wage laws, strict regulation of recruitment systems, and increasing worker-protective cooperation between labor-sending and labor-receiving nations (Varia 2007). Hong Kong and South Africa provide model legislation that includes minimum wage, overtime pay, paid leave, and freedom to form trade unions; and migrant domestic workers there have better working conditions, more awareness of their rights, and greater access to legal remedies. Noting the role of globalization, Varia (2007) advocates a human rights approach to migrant domestic workers that establishes international regulations and enforcement mechanisms. Treaties such as the Convention to Protect the Rights of Migrant Workers and Their Families outline an international regulatory framework, but labor-receiving countries have been slow to ratify such agreements and the UN has focused on the contributions workers' remittances make to economic development at the expense of focusing on workers' rights.

Many migrant mothers experience pain over separation, especially as they provide daily care for other parents' children (Parrenas 2002). Children gain economically but face family disruption. At minimum, they experience an altered, mother-absent household structure, and many go to live with female relatives (Dreby 2006; Hongdaneu-Sotelo and Avila 1997). Children miss their absent mother, are sometimes consumed by thoughts of reunification, and may have trouble concentrating in school (Parrenas 2002). Children in mother-away families may suffer more than those in father-away families because of the added task of accepting the altered role of mother as a provider, rather than mother as a caregiver (Parrenas 2005).

Scholars have emphasized the ways in which transnational families demonstrate adaptation and resilience as they work to arrange emotional and financial support and maintain family relationships across nation-states (Bryceson and Vuorela 2003). Children and spouses often maintain contact with the absent parent through letters, phone calls, and e-mail; and children may receive abundant love and support from extended kin networks (Parrenas 2005). Many mother/child relationships are persistently loving, and children may understand and accept the reasons their mothers are away (Parrenas 2002).

Child-Rearing/Family Leave and Family Allowance Policies

In addition to childbirth-related leave policies, many countries, including most OECD countries, also offer extended childrearing leaves. These full-time and part-time leaves enable a parent to stay at home or work part-time with benefits often until the child's third year and sometimes until the eighth year, although the leaves are paid at a lesser benefit, which is sometimes equivalent to the subsidy for ECEC care, and are sometimes termed a "mother's wage" (Kamerman and Gatenio 2002a). Many countries also offer job-protected family leaves to care for ill children and other family members, sometimes with pay (Kamerman and Gatenio 2002a); and some offer paid or unpaid discretionary leaves, which could be used for sick child care or to attend to a child's educational needs (Heymann et al. 2006).

A study of 160 countries found that at least 37 guarantee parents paid leave to attend to child illness. Of 30 countries providing data on the duration of leave, 47 percent guaranteed 11 or more days, 20 percent guaranteed 7–10 days, and 33 percent 1–6 days. Twenty-seven countries guaranteed wage replacement, with 19 offering 80–100 percent of wages and a total of 26 offering at least 50 percent. In addition, Greece and Switzerland guarantee paid leave or work flexibility so that parents can meet their children's teachers; and at least 34 countries offer discretionary leave, which could be used for this purpose, including 17 offering paid leave. The United States offers only 12 weeks per year as unpaid for all leave types, including sick child leave, but not including leave related to child education, and eligibility varies with employment duration and employer size (and applies to only 60 percent of mothers) (Heymann et al. 2006).

A study of five EU countries found that child care and family leave policies were adopted to promote parental care and choice but are also attractive to politically right governments that want to control child care spending, appeal to parents facing work/family tensions, and reduce unemployment. The low benefits accompanying these leaves tend to reinforce caregiving by mothers at home, with women paying economic penalties (Morgan and Zippel 2003).

Many countries also offer child and family allowances – monthly cash payments to parents based on the number of children at home, usually paid through general revenue, but sometimes with employer contributions. The purposes vary from redistributing income (to reduce family's economic burden of childrearing or to reduce poverty) to strengthening labor force attachment (by linking benefits to employment) and increasing social cohesion. Benefit levels are generally modest at less than 10 percent of earnings, may decrease with higher income, and vary from a standard rate per child to more for the first child or for later children, to higher when children are younger or older. Eligibility is usually universal, but may be employment-dependent, residency-dependent, or income-related. Allowances are provided from birth to the age of adulthood or completion of formal education (Kamerman and Gatenio 2002b).

Eighty-eight countries offer child/family allowances. The United Kingdom, for example, provides benefits that are larger for the first child, provided to residents only, and last to ages 16–19. France's benefits begin only with second child, are for residents only, vary by child age, and last to age 20. Norway and Finland offer parents the alternative of subsidized child care placement in a child's early years. At least 13 countries offer benefits lasting until age 18 or older, including Australia, Belgium, Canada, Denmark, France, Germany, Italy, Norway, and Spain. The United States offers tax-related programs, but not direct child/family allowance (Kamerman and Gatenio 2002b).

Conclusion

Families, marriage patterns, and gender issues are not insulated from ongoing economic and social changes, many of them wrought by globalization. As this chapter noted, families are affected by macroeconomic shifts from agriculture to manufacturing and service economies, and by the increasingly global flow of labor, the global diffusion of post-industrial ideologies including individualism, the spread of norms that foster an increasingly wide array of family forms, and social movements forged by and for women and sexual-orientation minorities.

Industrialization and other macroeconomic shifts have prompted a decrease in family size and a rising dependency ratio. Increased employer demands and decreased job security have prompted many young adults to move away from family, as they prioritize education and early career phases, thereby contributing to long-term vulnerabilities for the elderly. Global stratification and global labor flows have produced split families, as migrant domestic workers from poorer countries provide care labor for affluent families in wealthier countries, creating disruption and hardships for the children and spouses left behind. The global spread of individualism and the shifting social norms have stimulated an increase in divorce that renders women more susceptible to poverty and often leaves children without the support of a second parent. Social movements and employer demands have led to a massive rise in women's labor force participation that has prompted increasing demands for family benefits, such as parental leave and child allowances, and has shifted the balance of marital power and provided economic resources that facilitate divorce, while the persistent gender pay gap leaves women and their children economically vulnerable.

The economic and social changes described in this chapter present families with a host of new and growing vulnerabilities that call for new and shifting policies and social welfare programs. This is especially true for women, whose increased labor force participation is combined with lower pay, disproportionate responsibility for child care and domestic labor, and increasing divorce rates, as well as for children facing poverty and insufficient child care and for elderly people facing poverty, economic insecurity, and social isolation, as the dependency rate increases and young adults prioritize education and career.

Adequately responsive public policies cannot be formulated in isolation from emerging family patterns and the recognition of their interrelationships with economic and social changes. To be sure, many public policies have shifted to address the changes described above, as exemplified by the EU's provision of parental and family leaves, state-sponsored child care and early child education, and child allowances. Yet, adequate social welfare policies are often lacking, and current policies sometimes reinforce the already-existing inequalities. As we have seen, some intergovernmental agencies and NGOs work to reduce the exploitation of migrant domestic workers serving in global care chains, but policies fail to enhance parents' ability to earn sufficient income without splitting their families, to say nothing of reducing global inequality, thus failing to meet the problem of split-household families at its root. Although child care and family leave policies in EU countries appeal to parents facing work/family tensions, the low benefits that accompany these leaves tend to reinforce caregiving by mothers at home, thus increasing women's economic vulnerability.

As we look to the future, questions remain about the extent and manner in which new policies will address family, marriage, and gender issues: How will new priorities fare in the face of competition from the already-established social needs? To what extent will new family-related policies reflect the interrelationship between family/gender issues and ongoing economic and social changes under conditions of increasing globalization? To what extent will new policies that target ongoing economic and social changes adequately address the impacts of such policies on marriage, family, and gender? As policymakers consider their options, they would do well to reflect on the European Commission's "gender mainstreaming" model and consider mainstreaming issues of family, marriage, and gender by continually assessing the implications that *all* social and economic policies have for family, marriage, and gender issues. In doing so, policymakers may foster ways in which families can better assure the well-being of their members and simultaneously ease a host of social problems.

References

Adams, B. N. (2004). Families and family study in international perspective. *Journal of Marriage and Family, 66*(5), 1076–1088.

Ambert, A. (2005). *Divorce: Facts, causes, and consequences*. Ottawa, Ontario, Canada: The Vanier Institute of the Family. http://www.vifamily.ca/library/cft/divorce_05.html

AmeriStat staff. (2003a). *More U.S. women outearning their husbands*. Washington, D.C.: The Population Reference Bureau.

AmeriStat staff. (2003b). *Traditional families account for only 7% of U.S. households*. Washington, D.C.: The Population Reference Bureau. http://www.prb.org/Articles/2003/TraditionalFamiliesAccountforOnly7PercentofUSHouseholds.aspx

Amu, O., & Appiah, K. (2006). Teenage pregnancy in the United Kingdom: Are we doing enough? *The European Journal of Contraception & Reproductive Health Care, 11*(4), 314–318.

Anderson, B. J. (2000). *Doing the dirty work?: The global politics of domestic labour*. London: Zed.

Andersson, G. (2002). Dissolution of unions in Europe: A comparative overview. Paper presented at the conference on *Divorce in a Cross-National Perspective: A European Network* in Florence, Italy, November 14–15, 2002. http://www.demogr.mpg.de/papers/working/ wp-2003-004.pdf

Batalova, J. A., & Cohen, P. N. (2002). Premarital cohabitation and housework: Couples in cross-national perspective. *Journal of Marriage and the Family, 64*(3), 743–755.

Bleijenbergh, I., & Roggeband, C. (2007). Equality machineries matter: The impact of women's political pressure on European social-care policies. *Social Politics: International Studies in Gender, State & Society*, doi:10.1093/sp/jxm018.

Bryceson, D. F., & Vuorela, U. (2003). Transnational families in the twenty-first century. In D. F. Bryceson & U. Vuorela (Eds.), *The transnational family: New frontiers and global networks* (pp. 3–30). Oxford, UK: Berg.

Buss, D. M., Angleitner, A., Asherian, A., Biaggio, A., Blanco-Villasenor, A., Bruchon-Schwreitzer, M., et al. [54 co-authors] (1990). International preferences in selecting mates: A study of 37 cultures. *Journal of Cross-Cultural Psychology.* Doi: 10.1177/0022022190211001.

Buss, D. M., Shackelford, T. K., Kirkpatrick, L. A., & Larsen, R. J. (2001). A half century of mate preferences: The cultural evolution of values. *Journal of Marriage and Family, 63*(2), 491–503.

Cherlin, A. J. (2004). The deinstitutionalization of marriage. *Journal of Marriage and the Family, 66*(4), 848–861.

Clawson, D., & Gerstel, N. (2002). Caring for our young: Child care in Europe and the United States. *Contexts, 1*(4), 28–35.

Clearinghouse staff. (2005a). Early childhood education and care. *Clearinghouse on international developments in child, youth and family policies.* New York, NY: Columbia University School of Social Work. http://www.childpolicyintl.org/

Clearinghouse staff. (2005b). Table 2.31b: Mother's employment rates by age of youngest child, in 2002, percentage. *Clearinghouse on international developments in child, youth and family policies.* New York, NY: Columbia University School of Social Work. http://www.childpolicyintl.org/

Clearinghouse staff. (2003a). Table 2.12 Mean age of women at first childbirth. *Clearinghouse on international developments in child, youth and family policies.* New York, NY: Columbia University School of Social Work. http://www.childpolicyintl.org/

Clearinghouse staff. (2003b). Table 2.18 Percentage of different types of lone mother families: most recent data. *Clearinghouse on international developments in child, youth and family policies.* New York, NY: Columbia University School of Social Work. http://www.childpolicyintl.org/

Cliquet, R. (2003). Major trends affecting families in the new millennium: Western Europe and North America, in *Major trends affecting families: A background document.* New York, NY: UN Programme on the Family. http://www.un.org/esa/socdev/family/Publications/ mtcliquet.pdf

Cohn, D. (2007). *Do parents spend enough time with their children?* Population Reference Bureau. Washington, D.C.: Population Reference Bureau. http://www.prb.org/Articles/2007/DoParentsSpendEnoughTimeWithTheirChildren.aspx

Crighton, E., & Ebert, M. (2002). RU 486 and abortion practices in Europe: From legalization to access. *Women & Politics, 24*(3). http://eucenter.scrippscollege.edu/pdfs/Crighton-Ebert.pdf

De Silva, I. (2003). Demographic and social trends affecting families in the south and central Asian region. *Major trends affecting families: A background document.* 2003. New York, NY: United Nations Programme on the Family. http://www.un.org/esa/socdev/family/Publications/mtdesilva.pdf

Dreby, J. (2006). Honor and virtue: Mexican parenting in the transnational context. *Gender & Society, 20*(1), 32–59.

European Commission's Directorate-General for Employment, Social Affairs, and Equal Opportunities. (n.d.). *Gender equality.* Brussels, Belgium: European Commission. http://ec.europa.eu/social/main.jsp?atId = 418&langId = en

European Commission. (2006). *A Roadmap for equality between women and men: 2006–2010.* Luxemburg: Office for Official Publications of the European Communities. http://ec.europa.eu/employment_social/emplweb/gender_equality/publications_en.cfm

Furstenberg, F. F., Jr., Rumbaut, R. G., & Settersten, R. A., Jr., (2005). On the frontier of adulthood: Emerging themes and new directions. In R. A. Setterten Jr., Frank F. Furstenberg Jr., & Ruben G. Rumbaut (Eds.), *On the frontier of adulthood: Theory, research, and public policy.* Chicago, IL: The University of Chicago Press.

Gautier, A. (2005). Legal regulation of martial relations: An historical and comparative approach. *International Journal of Law, Policy, and the Family, 19*(1), 47–72.

Harding, R., & Peel, E. (2006). 'We do'? International perspectives on equality, legality, and same-sex relationships. *Lesbian & Gay Psychology Review, 7*(2), 123–140.

Heymann, J., Earle, A., Simmons, S., Breslow, S., & Kuehnoff, A. (2004). *The work, family, and equity index: Where does the United States stand globally?* Boston, MA: Harvard School of Public Health, The Project for Working Families. http://www.hsph.harvard.edu/ globalworkingfamilies/images/report.pdf

Heymann, S. J., Penrose, K., & Earle, A. (2006). Meeting children's needs: How does the United States measure up? *Merrill-Palmer Quarterly, 52*(2),189–215. http://muse.jhu.edu/journals/merrill-palmer_quarterly/v052/52.2heymann.pdf

Hochschild, A. R. (2000). Global care chains and emotional surplus value. In W. Hutton, & A. Giddens, (Eds.), *On the edge: Living with global capitalism.* London: Jonathan Cape.

Hongdaneu-Sotelo, P., & Avila, E. (1997). "I'm here, but I'm there": The meanings of Latina transnational motherhood. *Gender & Society, 11*(5), 548–571.

Jelin, E., & Diaz-Munoz, A. R. (2003). Major trends affecting families: South America in perspective. *Major trends affecting families: A background document.* New York, NY: UN Programme on the Family. http://www.un.org/esa/socdev/family/Publications/mtjelin.pdf

Jensen, R., & Thornton, R. (2003). Early marriage in the developing world. *Gender and Development, 11*(2), 9–19.

Kamerman, S. (2004). Maternity and parental leaves, 1999–2002 (Table 1.11). *Comparative child, youth and family policies and programs: Benefits and services.* New York, NY: Clearinghouse on International Developments in Child, Youth and Family Policies, Columbia University School of Social Work http://www.childpolicyintl.org/

Kamerman, S., & Gatenio, S. (2002a). Mother's day: More than candy and flowers, working parents need paid time-off. *Issue brief,* Spring 2002, Clearinghouse on International Developments in Child, Youth and Family Policies, Columbia University School of Social Work, New York, NY: Clearinghouse http://www.childpolicyintl.org/

Kamerman, S., & Gatenio, S. (2002b). Tax day: How do America's child benefits compare? *Issue brief,* Spring 2002, Clearinghouse on International Developments in Child, Youth and Family Policies, Columbia University School of Social Work, New York, NY: Clearinghouse http://www.childpolicyintl.org/

Karraker, M. W. (2008). *Global families.* Boston, MA: Pearson.

Kashiwase, H. (2002). Shotgun weddings a sign of the times in Japan. *Population Today.* (July 2002) http://www.prb.org/Articles/2002/ShotgunWeddingsaSignoftheTimesinJapan.aspx

Lalasz, R. (2004). *Domestic violence in developing countries: An intergenerational crisis.* Washington, D.C.: Population Reference Bureau. http://www.prb.org/Articles/2004/DomesticViolenceinDevelopingCountriesAnIntergenerationalCrisis.aspx

Lambert, P. A. (2008). The comparative political economy of parental leave and child care: Evidence from twenty OECD countries. *Social Politics: International Studies in Gender, State & Society, 15*(3), 315–344.

Mandel, H., & Seymonov, M. (2005). Family policies, wage structure, and fender gaps: Sources of earnings inequality in 20 countries. *American Sociological Review, 70*(6), 949–967.

Martin, G., & Kats, V. (2003). Families and work in transition in 12 countries, 1980–2001. *Monthly Labor Review, 126*(9), 3–31. http://www.bls.gov/opub/mlr/2003/09/art1full.pdf

McDonald, P. (2002). Sustaining fertility through public policy: The range of options. *Population* 57, 416–446. http://www.cairn.info/article.php?ID_REVUE=POPE&ID_NUMPUBLIE=POPE_203&ID_ARTICLE=POPE_203_0417

Morgan, K. J., & Zippel, K. (2003). Paid to care: The origins and effects of care leave policies in Western Europe. *Social Politics: International Studies in Gender, State & Society, 10*:49–85.

Parrenas, R. S. (2005). *Children of global migration: Transnational families and gendered woes.* Palo Alto, CA: Stanford University Press.

Parrenas, R. S. (2002). The care crisis in the Philippines: Children and transnational families in the new global economy. In B. Ehrenreich & A. R. Hochschild (Eds.), *Global women: Nannies, maids, and sex workers in the new economy* (pp. 39–54). New York: Metropolitan.

Philipov, D. (2003). Major trends affecting families in Central and Eastern Europe. *Major trends affecting families: A background document.* New York, NY: United Nations Programme on the Family. http://www.un.org/esa/socdev/family/Publications/mtphilipov.pdf

Population Reference Bureau staff. (2008). *World population data sheet, 2008.* Washington, D.C.: Population Reference Bureau.

Population Reference Bureau staff. (2007). World population highlights. *Population Bulletin, 62*(3). Washington, D.C.: Population Reference Bureau.

Population Reference Bureau staff. (2004). Transitions in World Population. *Population Bulletin, 59*(1). Washington, D.C.: Population Reference Bureau. http://www.prb.org/Source/ACFFF4.pdf

Quah, S. R. (2003). Major trends affecting families in East and Southeast Asia. *Major Trends Affecting Families: A Background Document.* New York, NY: United Nations Programme on the Family. http://www.un.org/esa/socdev/family/Publications/mtrendsbg.htm

Rashad, H., Osman, M., & Roudi-Fahimi, F. (2005). *Marriage in the Arab world.* Washington, D.C.: Population Reference Bureau. http://www.prb.org/Publications/PolicyBriefs/MarriageintheArabWorld.aspx

Roopnarine, J. L., & Gielen, U. P. (2005). Families in global perspective: An introduction. In J. L. Roopnarine & U. P. Gielen (Eds.), *Families in global perspective* (pp. 3–13). Boston, MA: Allyn & Bacon.

Sana, E. A. (2007). *Filipino migrant domestic workers: An overview.* Presentation to the Asian Domestic Workers Assembly, June 16–17, 2007, Astoria Plaza, Pasig City. http://www.mfasia.org/mfaResources/ACGFMD-Filipino%20Migrant%20Domestic%20Workers.pdf

Shanahan, M. J., Porfeli, E. J., Mortimer, J. T., & Erickson, L. D. (2005). Subjective age identity and the transition to adulthood: When do adolescents become adults? In R. A. Setterten Jr., F. F. Furstenberg Jr., R. G. Rumbaut (Eds.), *On the frontier of adulthood: Theory, research, and public policy.* Chicago, IL: The University of Chicago Press.

Sorrentino, C. (1990). The changing family in international perspective. *Monthly Labor Review 113*(3), 41–58

Speulda, N., & McIntosh, M. (2004). *Global gender gaps.* Washington, D.C.: Pew Research Center. http://pewglobal.org/commentary/display.php?AnalysisID=90

Ulrich, R. E. (2001). *Most European women use contraceptives, yet some still have surprise pregnancies.* New York, NY: Population Reference Bureau. http://www.prb.org/Articles/2001/MostEuropeanWomenUseContraceptives.aspx

UNESCO. (2004). *Global monitoring report 2003/4: Lessons from good practice.* New York, NY: UNESCO. http://portal.unesco.org/education/en/ev.phpURL_ID=24165&URL_DO=DO_TOPIC&URL_SECTION=201.html

United Nations. (2006). *In-depth study on all forms of violence aginst women: Report of the Secretary-General,* New York, NY: United Nations http://daccessdds.un.org/doc/UNDOC/GEN/N06/419/74/PDF/N0641974.pdf?OpenElement

United Nations. (2007). *Follow-up to the tenth anniversary of the international year of the family and beyond.* New York, NY: United Nations. http://daccessdds.un.org/doc/UNDOC/GEN/N07/434/53/PDF/N0743453.pdf?OpenElement

United Nations Statistics Division. (1968, 1976, 2000). *Demographic Yearbooks.* New York, NY: United Nations. http://unstats.un.org/unsd/demographic/sconcerns/mar/marDYB.htm

Varia, N. (2007). Globalization Comes Home: Protecting Migrant Domestic Workers' Rights. *Human Rights Watch world report 2007.* http://www.hrw.org/wr2k7/essays/globalization/globalizationcomeshome.pdf

Whitehead, B. D., & Popenoe, D. (2005). Marriage and family: What does the Scandinavian experience tell us? *The state of our unions: The social health of marriage in America.* Piscataway, NJ: The National Marriage Project at Rutgers, The State University of New Jersey. http://marriage.rutgers.edu/Publications/SOOU/TEXTSOOU2005.htm

Chapter 7
Health and Health Care in Post-industrial Society

Robin Gauld

Introduction

The post-industrial era has seen extraordinary changes across a spectrum of issues that revolve around health and health care. These include the challenges that confront the health of the developed world population, the philosophies underpinning health policy, the issues deemed to be central to health policy, and the structures for health care delivery.

This chapter overviews these changes. Its scope is global, as the issues under discussion are germane to most developed world societies. In this sense, the processes of globalization have ensured that differing countries have pursued broadly similar health policy agendas. Ideologically, their views about policy and service delivery structures have also coincided. The chapter draws upon the example of New Zealand to provide an illustration for how the issues have impacted on a national health system and to describe the types of policies that have been implemented. Where relevant, other country experiences are also discussed. The chapter focuses on the developed world, although some of the issues are also relevant to developing countries. For instance, international institutions, such as the World Bank and International Monetary Fund, routinely required neoliberal policy solutions to be implemented in the health systems of developing countries (Callahan & Wasunna 2006: Chapter 4; Walt & Buse 2006).

The chapter begins with an overview of neoliberalism and social democracy, which have been the two ideological influences on health policy and systems since the 1980s. It then discusses the issues central to contemporary health care and a mixed social democratic neoliberal agenda. Finally, for illustration, the case of New Zealand is discussed.

R. Gauld (✉)
Department of Preventive and Social Medicine, University of Otago, Dunedin,
New Zealand
e-mail: robin.gauld@otago.ac.nz

J. Powell, J. Hendricks, *The Welfare State in Post-Industrial Society*,
DOI 10.1007/978-1-4419-0066-1_7, © Springer Science+Business Media, LLC 2009

Changing Philosophies Behind Health Policy

Neoliberalism

Through the 1980s and into the 1990s, many of the developed world's health systems endured reforms inspired by a wave of neoliberalism that intoxicated policymakers and their advisors. This 'health reform' era saw health systems subject to radical changes. The preceding postwar era was marked by policies intended to build civil society and expand service coverage, for example, by building hospitals and creating government infrastructure to administer public health care funding and service delivery. Such arrangements tended to include central planning and administration of health systems and leadership at the service delivery level by medical and other health professionals. In contrast, neoliberal theory encapsulated a series of ideas which, combined, amounted to an attack on the existing government and public services and on health professions.

As Ham notes, there were essentially three components of neoliberal approach when applied to health (Ham 1997: 8–9). First, health systems required the private market forces to improve their efficiency and increase the range of available services. Driving this was a belief that central planners were incapable of producing ideas for the health system improvement. But, also, several countries in the mid-1980s saw the election of right-wing governments with a preference for markets, public sector downsizing, and privatization. The preference for markets saw the creation of a split between health care purchasers and providers and the introduction of contracting between these two parties, within previously integrated hierarchical health systems. Of course, in tandem with the purchaser-provider split, many countries reformed the organization of health care delivery. This included creating new corporate structures to manage hospitals and requirements that publicly owned and/or -funded agencies compete with one another.

Second, and in keeping with 'managerialism,' was a desire to implement robust health services management systems. This was propelled by perceptions that health professionals lacked appropriate expertise in management, such as experience in running private business, and were incapable of making objective managerial decisions due to their allegiance with professional colleagues. Improved management also required an orientation toward 'customers,' dedication to improved service performance through developing workforce objectives and incentives and devolving responsibility for these to appropriate units, and a focus on contracting out of services to induce competition and reduce costs. Very importantly, it required a concerted effort to improve performance in areas such as hospital average length of stay, waiting times for elective treatments, and health outcomes. To empower and provide incentives for improved hospital and other local service management, such responsibilities were decentralized. This meant that budgetary, human resource, and service organization decisions were a managerial responsibility and largely separate from the central government intervention.

Third, was the reform of budgetary systems and the creation of financial incentives to improve performance. A core idea, applied across government systems, was that funding ought to be oriented toward 'outputs and outcomes' instead of being simply based on prior expenditure and utilization patterns. Thus, policymakers required that providers develop information systems as well as methods for micromanagement of workforce activities. This was so that funders (or purchasers) would be able to see exactly what they were paying for. They would also be able to see how these activities were contributing to the desired policy outcomes (long-term health policy objectives).

The neoliberal period saw the development of various other budgeting and funding initiatives. These included prospective global budgets, an annual sum of money paid over to a provider who would then carry the responsibility for cost overruns. Global budgets were also applied to purchasing (commissioning) agencies. These proved effective in areas such as drug buying. New Zealand's Pharmaceutical Management Agency, formed in the early-1990s, used its purchasing power to drive down prices of publicly purchased prescription drugs. This, combined with other strategies, allowed it to keep within its budget. To provide incentives to improve service efficiency and quality, diagnosis-related group methods emerged. These pay a fixed sum for predetermined procedures (for example, birth by caesarian section), as opposed to paying for each individual provider and process involved, and can feature incentives for performance improvement. Finally, patient charges for public health care services were introduced as a revenue generator and to stem service demand.

Social Democracy

Toward the end of the 1990s, changing political leadership and recognition of a general failure of neoliberalism as a policy theory saw many countries implementing health system changes based on social democratic ideals. However, while following new goals, governments have often retained and continued to pursue ideas and structures developed in the neoliberal era. Thus, in many developed countries, health policies embody a genuine concern for social democratic goals, such as expanding services, for proactive involvement in improving people's lives, for democratizing planning and governance processes, and also for strong accountability and the continued use of market mechanisms to improve performance. Yet, the rise of social democracy has provided a fertile ground for responding to a range of emerging issues seen to be crucial to health system and population health improvement.

First, is the notion that health systems and services should be coordinated or integrated. This is partly a response to the fact that neoliberal arrangements, particularly managerialism, decentralization, and contracting, perpetuated gaps between service providers that are typical of health care delivery systems. In other words, they did little to ensure that services such as primary and secondary care or public and private providers were linked. Where competition resulted in a failure to promote sharing of information across systems, this has led to a duplication of services, such as laboratory tests and collection of basic patient information. Despite the rhetoric of being customer focused, neoliberal era arrangements also failed to be patient-centered. They were overly oriented toward improving management systems and accountability, with little regard for the patient experience.

In response, it is strongly argued today – from organizations, such as the OECD, to national policymakers – that health systems ought to be patient-centered (Hofmarcher, Oxley & Rusticelli 2007). Funding and organizational models should be aimed at fusing links between or 'integrating' the various service providers. In contrast with the 'hands-off' approach of neoliberalism, integration naturally requires proactive involvement of management and service providers in building coordinated care systems. Integrated care programs are often developed around specific services, such as care for the elderly or treatment of diabetes. They may involve all providers that come in contact with patients from primary care providers to hospital specialists. Key aims include ensuring that services are carefully coordinated, that the patient's experience is 'seamless,' and that services are delivered by an appropriate provider. For example, primary medical care is provided by a community-based practitioner, not a hospital specialist. There is considerable anticipation that health information technology will facilitate service integration. Britain's Health Action Zones are also an example of integrated service delivery, with a range of different providers working together to improve health outcomes among deprived populations (Bauld & Judge 2002).

Second, is a concern with the quality of health care. Quality is a wide-ranging concept and extends to whether patients are screened for possible disease or have access to required care. Several studies published through the 1990s demonstrated that medical error is commonplace and often results in disability and death (for example, Brennan et al. 1991). The sources of error are often simple, such as incorrectly prescribed medicines or surgical mistakes. However, studies of errors and various government reports have highlighted that mistakes frequently occur as a result of failures within the systems that health professionals work. Again, this has highlighted a need for proactive and hands-on involvement of management, professionals, and patients in the crafting of quality improvement programs.

The drive for quality improvement has led to calls for a range of initiatives. These include health system redesign, with close attention to organizational structures that provide support for high quality clinical practice and delivery of appropriate care (Institute of Medicine 2001). This, of course, has created an environment in which health professionals have again become crucial to development, in collaboration with management, of robust patient care systems. It has also created a demand for patient involvement in care planning, for service expansion, and for more health spending. The development of systems to monitor quality and provide transparency has also received attention, with elements of managerialism seen in accountability structures and a quest for data on service standards and quality variations. The application of information technology, complete with coordinated system standards and architecture, has again been viewed as an important tool for quality improvement (Chaudry et al. 2006).

Very important has been the effort to implement funding models that provide incentives for improved performances. Central to this have been pay for performance and for results schemes which reward organizations and health professionals for components of health care delivery. Such schemes can include payments for the percentage of patients screened or vaccinated, who receive appropriate care and are satisfied, the rate of error and hospital readmission, and for the use of information technology in clinical practice (Heath et al. 2007; Rosenthal, M. et al. 2004; Rosenthal, M.B. et al. 2006). While they can produce positive improvements, as with any system of performance indicators and incentives, performance payments carry the risk of failing to deliver improvements in areas not subject to measurement (Bevan & Hood 2006).

Third has been a concern with health inequalities, again prompted by data and by changing political views about the right to equal treatment and outcomes. Services have been found to be failing some groups of patients, particularly ethnic minorities. Data also show that some groups live much longer and healthier than others (Wilkinson 2005). In response, policymakers have made reducing inequalities a key goal for their health systems. This is partly a quality issue of ensuring that every patient receives the same level of care, regardless of who they are. It is also an issue of ensuring access to services by reducing barriers and reaching out to underserved communities and changing people's behavior. This often involves health services working closely with other service sectors, such as local government, education, welfare, and housing (Asthana & Halliday 2006).

Fourth, the growing burden of noncommunicable and chronic diseases, such as heart disease, cancer, and diabetes, has prompted a view among policymakers and researchers that health systems require reorientation. The world is experiencing an increasing incidence of noncommunicable diseases, including heart and respiratory diseases, cancer, and diabetes. Heart disease, the biggest single killer, is now responsible for some 30 percent of global deaths (World Health Organization 2007). Noncommunicable diseases are the key cause of death across the developed world. In addition, the prevalence of conditions such as obesity has grown at an alarming rate, virtually doubling in many countries since the 1980s. In 2005, across the OECD countries, some 14.6 percent of the people were obese. However, prevalence differs starkly among countries. In the United States and Mexico, over 30 percent were obese. The United Kingdom, Greece, Australia, and New Zealand were all over 20 percent. Countries with less than 10 percent incidence of obesity included France, Norway, and Switzerland, with Japan and South Korea around 3 percent (OECD 2007a). A concern is that type-2 diabetes, a contributor to which is thought to be obesity, is also on the rise. Diabetes is expensive to treat and associated with other costly health conditions (World Health Organization 2005).

Instead of being focused on the treatment of illness and leaving individuals to take responsibility for their health and personal behavior, services and planning need to be aimed at identifying and managing those at risk of chronic diseases. This has meant a focus on population-based strategic planning and service delivery and community-based programs. Health promotion and the role of public health practitioners has been particularly important, especially given the need to arrest the growth of obesity and counter behavior that contribute to heart diseases and other chronic illnesses. Again, the chronic disease focus has required new ways of funding and organizing services to ensure that patients at risk are identified and receive appropriate intervention. It has also required that health professionals and agencies adopt a public health focus concerned with broader determinants of health.

Fifth, international agencies such as the WHO, along with national governments, have renewed calls for emphasizing primary care within health systems. Research shows that primary care does play an important role (Starfield et al. 2005) and several countries have implemented primary care reforms (Saltman et al. 2006). Underpinning these has been the idea that strong primary and family care should provide the 'gateway' to the health system. Such services should be community-based, with patient involvement in planning and governance; should feature a range of providers, including general practitioners (family physicians); and should closely manage health of their patients.

Some countries have pursued arrangements in which primary care services carry the budget for secondary hospital care and other services. In this way, budgetary responsibility is decentralized, and patients will also have a 'medical home' from which their care is coordinated. There will also be an incentive for primary care providers to proactively manage patient health to reduce the likelihood of costly hospitalization. Clinical governance, which has seen a revitalization of the role of health professionals (as opposed to generic managers of the neoliberal era) in the governing of provider organizations, has also been increasingly common (Malcolm & Mays 1999; Shaw et al. 2007).

Sixth, health care costs across the developed world have continued to spiral. Data shows that, without exception, health care demand and expenditure in OECD member countries are increasing. The 4 percent OECD average increase in health expenditure shown in Table 7.1 is well above the 2.5 percent average growth of OECD economies. In practice, this means that an increasing proportion of the economy, and in turn of the government budget, is being consumed by health care (OECD 2007a). This trend is of concern to all affected countries, and a common theme in reports by governments and international organizations who routinely assert that the rate of increase is 'unsustainable.'

Table 7.1   Annual average growth rate in real health expenditure per capita, 1995–2005

Country	Annual average growth (%)
Luxembourg*[1]	7.6
Korea	7.6
Ireland	7.2
Turkey[3]	6.3
Poland*	5.2
Iceland	5.0
Hungary*[1]	4.9
Australia*[1]	4.7
Greece*	4.7
New Zealand	4.3
United Kingdom	4.2
OECD	4.0
Sweden	3.8
Portugal*	3.8
Slovak Republic*[2]	3.7
United States	3.6
Mexico*	3.6
Finland	3.5
Norway*	3.4
Belgium*	3.2
Canada	3.2
Italy	3.2
Spain*	3.0
Netherlands*[1]	3.0
Denmark*	2.8
Switzerland	2.8
Japan[1]	2.6
Czech Republic*	2.5
Austria	2.4
France*	2.3
Germany	1.8

Annual average growth (%)

Source: OECD (2007a).

The general consensus on dealing with this situation is that the options are to increase taxes and service funding, boost private funding of health services (insurance and point of service payments), improve efficiency of health services and systems, or explicitly ration service access. Indeed, from around the early-1990s, 'rationing' and 'prioritization' have risen to the top of many government health policy agendas. Improving service efficiency has also been central to the rhetoric and actions of policymakers and managers. Yet, reducing expenditure growth and service access are far from straightforward exercises which tend to be resisted by both the public and health professionals. In democratic societies, rationing and expenditure decisions can also be highly political (Ham & Robert 2003).

Equally perplexing is determining what it is that is driving the growth. Partly, it is the increasing scope of health systems and services as governments pursue new policies and health objectives. Expansion is also driven by technological advancements: the capacity to treat the previously untreatable and the emergence of new drugs and therapies. Another driver is the expanding range of interventions available to patients seeking to enhance lifestyle, physical performance and appearance. As noted above, population aging is a further contributor to expenditure growth. The health workforce cannot be overlooked and, with an international shortage of doctors, nurses, and other professionals, governments face constant pressure to raise remuneration levels and improve working environments.

Despite the increased expenditure, there is evidence in some countries, particularly the United States, that system performance remains questionable and may even be declining (Commonwealth Fund Commission on a High Performance Health System 2008). In response, various alternatives have been suggested. There have been endeavors in the United States, mostly outside of the government, to produce plans for a 'high performing health system' that provides universal coverage, equitable access, is affordable (bearing in mind that private insurance is the backbone of the US funding), efficient, and protects people from the financial costs of catastrophic illness (for example, Committee for Economic Development 2007; Commonwealth Fund 2006).

Beyond the United States, performance improvement includes attempts to increase private sector involvement in public services delivery, offering patients 'choice' and innate incentives for providers to reduce costs, and improve efficiency. Efforts also involve setting health system goals and targets and increased application of methods that restrict access to services and new technologies, drugs, and therapies. Decentralization of global budgets and planning responsibilities to local agencies has also featured. Countries with social insurance have continually sought ways to increase contributions, reduce coverage, increase efficiency, and boost competition (Gauld et al. 2006; Hassenteufel & Palier 2007).

In short, the social democratic period has seen the emergence of a complex health policy agenda in which governments are taking a proactive approach to the issues outlined above. The period is notable for a series of underlying assumptions:

- that policymakers and planners assume a hands-on approach in developing programs designed to better coordinate services, improve quality and efficiency, and change people's behavior to improve their health;
- that health professionals will be central to service governance and decision-making;
- that services will be democratized, with the public being encouraged to contribute to decision-making; and
- that various neoliberal constructs, such as contractual arrangements and performance incentives, continue to be central to service funding and organization.

The Example of New Zealand

New Zealand is an electoral democracy, so political parties and politicians are deeply involved in shaping public policy that accords with their political ideologies. It has a unicameral parliamentary system, meaning that once a government has the support of enough members of the house, it can simply drive through change with few barriers. Prior to the introduction of a proportional representation voting system in 1996, which has since delivered coalition governments, New Zealand was referred to as an 'elective dictatorship,' known for producing hastily implemented and sweeping policy changes.

New Zealand has a 'national' health system that is largely tax-funded and administered by government agencies and public entities. It also has a recent history of successive ideologically driven reforms to its health system funding and organizational arrangements.

New Zealand created the world's first national health system in 1938. That said, the country has frequently looked abroad, especially to the United Kingdom, for policy lessons. The creation of the national health system in 1938 required bargaining with the medical professionals, who were predominantly in private practice. The resulting institutional arrangements remain in place today. These are of general practice (family medicine), being largely provided by private practitioners, albeit with considerable government subsidies to keep patient charges down, while the public sector dominates hospital services. In an anomalous situation, there have always been charges on primary care medicine for patients, while all public hospital services – for both inpatients and outpatients – have been free. New Zealand's health system has a tradition of being centrally administered by a government agency, and of health professionals serving in key decision-making posts at regional planning and hospital levels. In 2005, at 9 percent of the GDP, New Zealand sat on the OECD average for health expenditure. Public funding accounted for just under 80 percent of the total (OECD 2007b).

New Zealand public policy was heavily influenced by neoliberal ideas from around 1984 to 1999. Initially, this was under a traditionally left-leaning Labour government (1984–1990), then a conservative National government (1990–1999). State trading functions were corporatized, then privatized, and the state sector was deregulated with all civil service jobs openly contestable. New departmental chief executives, on terminal performance contracts with government ministers, were required to deliver specific 'outputs.' In the broader labor market, trade unions were outlawed, as was collective bargaining, and replaced by individual employment contracts. The Reserve Bank was granted independence from the government and was required to focus solely on maintaining a stable inflation rate (Boston et al. 1996).

Concerned about the health system performance, especially hospital administration and efficiency, the 1984–1990 Labour government commissioned a series of health system reviews. One of these, chaired by a pro-market businessman with no prior experience in health care, suggested market-oriented structures along the lines of internal market reforms being implemented in the Britain by the Thatcher government (Gibbs et al. 1988). It was not until 1991, however, under the National government, that these ideas were put into practice. The health system was then radically reformed with purchasing and providing split. Four new Regional Health Authorities were created to undertake purchasing and to contract any provider – public or private – for the delivery of publicly funded services. A Public Health Commission was created to purchase public health services (Bandaranayake 1994). Public hospitals were restructured into Crown Health Enterprises, governed by executive boards and managed by generic managers largely recruited from the private sector. These hospitals were expected to return a dividend to the government on funds received from purchasers. With competitive contracting for funding, costs were intended to be cut and efficiency improved.

In one of the earlier manifestations of explicit rationing aimed to limit state responsibility for increasing health care costs, there was also an attempt to define a basket of 'core services' – either a specific list of government-funded services, or definition of people (e.g. lower socioeconomic groups; those with high health care needs) eligible for public service provision. This was so that both the government and the new purchasers would know exactly what services they were responsible for buying. The public, for their part, would have clear guidelines for which services they could expect to have publicly funded. In primary care, general practitioners, who were previously mostly sole operators, grouped into new networks of Independent Practitioner Associations – with broad similarities to Britain's GP fund-holding groups – to improve their bargaining power with the purchasers.

The reforms were short-lived, with multiple problems. The attempt to define core services failed, so there were no clear limitations on what was to be purchased or which services were to be the private responsibility of individuals to pay for. The Crown Health Enterprises (hospitals) were unable to cut costs or close 'unviable' services and, for the most part, required additional government funding to develop their 'businesses.' Morale among health professionals suffered, and there were few private competitors for hospital and other service contracts (New Zealand is, after all, a country of only four million people spread across a wide geographic area). This meant Regional Health Authorities (the purchasers) simply contracted with existing public hospitals and service providers. A brief attempt at public hospital part-charges proved costly to administer and was deeply unpopular, producing considerable political discomfort (Gauld 2001).

On the upside, there were some efficiency gains, information was improved, and the Independent Practitioner Associations revitalized general practice. There were experiments with primary care fund-holding (or budget holding), with savings able to be reinvested in additional patient services. Contracting was particularly beneficial to indigenous Maori who were able to establish a wide range of independent 'by Maori, for Maori' services (Barrett 1997). The debate on core services evolved into one around elective services and, in the mid-1990s, New Zealand was among the first to introduce a clinical scoring system for assessment of patients referred for nonurgent surgical and other services (e.g. hip and knee joint replacements, cataract surgery). This system, where patients would receive a score across a range of clinical criteria, was designed to bring confidence in patients, transparency in the clinical assessment process, and prioritize patients for treatment based on their relative scores.

Patients scoring over a certain point threshold would be booked for surgery; those under would be referred back to primary care (Gauld & Derrett 2000; Hadorn & Holmes 1997).

Following the 1996 election, the health system was re-reformed. The four purchasers were combined into a single national purchaser. Hospitals were no longer required to return a profit. Instead, they were to focus on 'public service,' but were also to be 'business-like.' In line with international trends and discussions in the preceding section, there was a shift in emphasis toward reducing inequalities, developing national service standards to reduce variations in waiting times and service delivery capacity, and toward service integration. A number of integration projects, for example, were commissioned by purchasers, with varied performance (Russell et al. 2003). Yet the purchaser-provider split remained at the heart of the system and hospital governance was largely by appointees with backgrounds in management and business directed to run hospitals in a 'business-like' manner (Gauld 2001).

Following the 1999 election, a re-elected Labour government, which had distanced itself from its romance with neoliberalism in the 1980s, brought further health system reforms (Devlin et al. 2001). The reforms, implemented from 2001, were in keeping with the new government's social democratic orientation, and goals of democratizing and decentralizing health care decision-making, reducing inequalities, improving service access, particularly for disadvantaged groups, and reorienting the health system toward collaboration and public health improvement. Getting the reforms in place was, like any reform process, exhaustive for the health sector (Gauld 2003b, 2003a). The government has since taken a 'steady as we go' approach of allowing the sector to bed down.

New structures included 21 region-based District Health Boards (DHBs). Each is funded on the characteristics of the population it serves and was built around the existing hospital groups. Each has the responsibility for planning and funding services from primary care to hospital care for its district's population. The government's preference is for funding public services. Thus, the use of the private sector for publicly funded elective surgery is restricted. That said, DHBs occasionally purchase private services when they are unable to meet demand and New Zealand's Accident Compensation Corporation (a quasi-social insurance agency that funds victims of accidental injury) routinely buys the services of both public and private providers. This scenario differs from some European countries that have reintroduced competition within their health systems. For example, in the United Kingdom, since 2004, government policy has been to fund private 'independent sector treatment centers' to create provider competition and give patients 'choice' among service providers (Pollock & Godden 2008). In Denmark, similar policies allow government-funded patients to choose between public or private service providers (Strandberg-Larsen et al. 2007). Other countries pursuing competition include Germany and the Netherlands (Enthoven & van de Ven 2007; Lisac 2006).

Contracting continues to be central to the New Zealand DHB funding process, but there is limited explicit competition. Instead, the government has chosen to build capacity within the public sector and drive performance with a series of national goals and targets laid out in the New Zealand Health Strategy (this document provides a focus for all health policy and service development) and other documents (King 2000; Minister of Health 2007). These social democratic goals (see box) have been offset by the application of neoliberal performance management tools. DHB performance expectations and service goals are contained in annual contracts and plans and are regularly reviewed by the government which keeps a very tight reign on DHBs. There are a range of financial and other sanctions on DHB management for poor performance. For example, DHBs that fail to manage within budget will be subject to reduced autonomy and increased central government control. Those failing to deliver elective surgery on target face financial penalties. As such, some DHBs purchase elective services from private providers. Others resort to restricting the number of patients allowed to be placed on waiting lists, while 'dumping' those unable to be treated within the government's targeted time frame of six months. Affected patients have the option of paying privately for treatment or attempting to re-enter the public system.

New Zealand Health Strategy
- Good health and well-being for all
- Focus on disadvantaged populations
- Collaborative approaches to service development and delivery
- Equitable access to services, regardless of ability to pay
- Quality health care
- Consumer and community participation

The 21 DHBs each feature a mix of elected and appointed members. They are required to consult the community in their planning and need assessment and to coordinate services. Despite the rhetoric and new democratic structures, the DHBs remain under firm central government control and must adhere to a range of national policies as set out in their annual contracts. Staff employed by the DHBs, including chief executives, are similarly motivated by contractual obligations. Despite substantial funding increases since 1999 (averaging 7–8 percent per annum), service demand continues to increase and funding remains tight. As such, DHBs are perpetually looking to reduce costs and streamline services, leading to charges among health professionals that this is the primary focus of 'management.' Despite all this, DHBs are expected to collaborate with one another and to link with other sectors with the potential to improve health, including local government, housing, and education. To date, and due to funding constraints and a predominant focus on maintaining hospital services, there has been limited cross-sectoral activity. There have long been suggestions that 21 DHBs are too many, especially given the requirements for collaboration and the substantial transaction costs associated with 21 separate funding and planning bodies (Gauld 2005).

Since 2003, embracing the notion discussed above of strengthening primary care, the government has promoted the formation of new Primary Health Organizations (PHOs). These capitalize on the organizational efforts of GPs through the 1990s, but require a broader professional base and community orientation. There are presently around 80 PHOs covering 97 percent of the population. The Ministry of Health initially drove the PHO formation but subsequently handed over the responsibility to District Health Boards, which provide the PHO funding. Each PHO must have a list of formally enrolled patients on which capitation funding is calculated (previously GPs simply maintained a patient register and were paid a fee for service). They must also show evidence of a range of primary care provider members, not just GPs, and a nonprofit governance structure that includes community representatives. Considerable new funding was made available for PHO formation (an additional 6–7 percent of the government's health budget), providing incentives for this, and also to reduce patient part-charges. This said, charges remain high at around NZ$30 per consultation for those on higher income and NZ$10–20 for those on lower income. Charges serve as a considerable barrier, especially for people from lower socioeconomic groups, and vary widely among individual medical practitioners, PHOs, and regions. Extra funding is also available for 'care plus' initiatives designed for people with chronic diseases, for 'services to improve access,' and for health promotion (Gauld & Mays 2006). To this end, individual PHOs have developed a wide range of initiatives targeted at the most at-risk and hard-to-reach people, who have a high incidence of costly hospital admissions for conditions amenable to primary care intervention (Ministry of Health 2005). The government has continued to drive PHO performance with a controversial pay for performance scheme, with payments for the achievement of various public health and financial objectives (District Health Boards New Zealand 2005).

Through the swing first toward and then away from neoliberalism, the quality of care has failed to make its way up in New Zealand's health policy agenda. This may be due to the focus since the late-1980s on health system restructuring. While political leaders talk of the importance of quality, patient-centered care, and quality is one of the goals of the New Zealand Health Strategy (see box), there remains no national policy for quality improvement. Similarly, there is no body or organization that performs an oversight or quality advocacy function. As such, the entire health system, from DHBs to hospitals and primary care, has failed to embrace a quality culture. Clinical service quality is, therefore, highly variable, with consequences for patient care and outcomes. New Zealand's situation differs markedly from that of other countries. The United Kingdom, for instance, has taken a concerted approach to quality improvement, creating a series of national agencies designed to promote improved standards of clinical service delivery (Klein 2007; Salter 2007; Williams & Osborn 2006). Even the United States, where health services are characterized by competition and fragmentation among providers, has a national effort to collect standardized quality data in an effort to reduce clinical performance variations and drive quality improvement (Kelley et al. 2006).

Conclusion

This chapter overviewed key changes in health and health care in the post-industrial society. It used the example of New Zealand to show how a global policy agenda has been responded to by the national government. The chapter discussed the theoretical evolution from neoliberalism to the present emphasis on social democracy, albeit with the continued influence of neoliberal constructs. The New Zealand case demonstrated how the intersection of these two theories has played out in practical policy. The country pursued issues of inequality and service access and also applied targets and performance management through its policies. Of course, as the chapter discussed, in the social democratic period, other countries have more firmly applied neoliberal ideals to the pursuit of social democratic outcomes. Britain and Denmark are both using competition in the belief that this will increase service access and patient-centeredness. In this sense, there has been a renewed endeavor to 'marketize' the health care component of the welfare state while creating new opportunities for-profit service providers.

The changes discussed in this chapter also illustrate how changing ideologies impact on health policy and service delivery structures. While the influence of neoliberalism remains in the global and national health policy agenda (even in New Zealand, where the government has a strong center-left philosophy), there can be seen the emergence of a new policy constituency. This is evident in the inevitable requirement for policymakers to be involved in issues such as service coordination and quality improvement, in the democratization of governance and planning, and in the aim to improve overall population health.

References

Asthana, S., & Halliday, J. 2006, *What works in tackling health inequalities? Pathways, policies and practice through the lifecourse.* Bristol. The Policy Press.
Bandaranayake, D. (1994). Public health and the reforms: The New Zealand experience. *Health Policy, 29,* (1–2), 127–141.
Barrett, M. (1997). Maori health purchasing: Some current issues. *Social Policy Journal of New Zealand, 9,* 124–130.
Bauld, L., & Judge, K. (Eds.). (2002). *Learning from health action zones.* Chichester: Aeneas Press.
Bevan, G., & Hood, C. (2006). Have targets improved performance in the English NHS? *British Medical Journal, 332,* 419–422.
Boston, J., Martin, J., Pallot, J., & Walsh, P. (1996). *Public management: The New Zealand Model.* Auckland: Oxford University Press.

Brennan, T. A., Leape, L., Laird, N. M., Hebert, L., Localio, A. R., Lawthers, A. G., Newhouse, J. P., Weiler, P. C., & Hiatt, H. H. (1991). Incidence of adverse events and negligence in hospitalized patients: Results of the Harvard Medical Practice Study. *New England Journal of Medicine, 324*, (6), 370–376.

Callahan, D., & Wasunna, A. (2006). *Medicine and the Market: Equity v. choice.* Baltimore: Johns Hopkins University Press.

Chaudry, B., Wang, J., Wu, S., Maglione, M., Mojica, W., Roth, E., Morton, S., & Shekelle, P. (2006). Systematic review: Impact of health information technology on quality, efficiency, and costs of medical care. *Annals of Internal Medicine, 144*, 742–752.

Committee for Economic Development (2007). *Quality, affordable health care for all: Moving beyond the employer-based health-insurance system.* Washington, DC: Author.

Commonwealth Fund. (2006). *Framework for a high performance health system for the United States.* New York: Author.

Commonwealth Fund Commission on a High Performance Health System (2008). *Why not the best? Results from the national scorecard on US health system performance.* New York: Author.

Devlin, N., Maynard, A., & Mays, N. (2001). New Zealand's new health sector reforms: Back to the future? *British Medical Journal, 322*, (7295), 1171–1174.

District Health Boards New Zealand. (2005). *Performance management programme,* District Health Boards New Zealand. Available at: http://www.dhbnz.org.nz/SITE_Default/SIG/SITE_PHO_ PMP/default.asp.

Enthoven, A., & van de Ven, W. (2007). Going Dutch: Managed-competition health insurance in the Netherlands. *New England Journal of Medicine, 357*, (24), 2421–2423.

Gauld, R. (2001). *Revolving doors: New Zealand's health reforms.* Wellington: Institute of Policy Studies and Health Services Research Centre.

Gauld, R. (2003a). The impact on officials of public sector restructuring: The case of the New Zealand health funding authority. *International Journal of Public Sector Management, 16*, (4), 303–319.

Gauld, R. (2005). New Zealand. In R. Gauld (Ed.), *Comparative health policy in the Asia-Pacific,* (pp. 200–224). Maidenhead: Open University Press.

Gauld, R. (Ed.) (2003b). *Continuity amid chaos: Health care management and delivery in New Zealand.* Dunedin: University of Otago Press.

Gauld, R., & Derrett, S. (2000). Solving the surgical waiting list problem? New Zealand's 'Booking System'. *International Journal of Health Planning and Management, 15*, (4), 259–272.

Gauld, R., Ikegami, N., Barr, M. D., Chiang, T.-L., Gould, D., & Kwon, S. (2006). Advanced Asia's health systems in comparison. *Health Policy, 79*, 325–336.

Gauld, R., & Mays, N. (2006). Reforming primary care: Are New Zealand's new primary health organisations fit for purpose? *British Medical Journal, 333*, 1216–1218.

Gibbs, A., Fraser, D., & Scott, J. (1988). *Unshackling the hospitals: Report of the hospital and related services taskforce.* Wellington: Hospital and Related Sercvies Taskforce.

Hadorn, D., & Holmes, A. (1997). The New Zealand priority criteria project. Part 1: Overview. *British Medical Journal, 314*, 131–134.

Ham, C., (Ed.) (1997). *Health care reform: Learning from international experience.* Buckingham: Open University Press.

Ham, C., & Robert, G. (Eds.). (2003). *Reasonable rationing: International experience of priority setting in health care.* Buckingham: Open University Press.

Hassenteufel, P., & Palier, B. (2007). Towards Neo-Bismarckian health care states? Comparing health insurance reforms in bismarckian welfare systems. *Social Policy and Administration, 41*, (6), 574–596.

Heath, I., Hippisley-Cox, J., & Smeeth, L. (2007). Measuring performance and missing the point? *British Medical Journal, 335*, 1075–1076.

Hofmarcher, M. M., Oxley, H., & Rusticelli, E. (2007). *Improved health system performance through better care coordination. OECD Health Working Paper No. 30*. Paris: OECD.

Institute of Medicine. (2001). *Crossing the quality chasm: A new health system for the twenty-first century*. Washington: National Academy Press.

Kelley, E., Arispe, I., & Holmes, J. (2006). Beyond the initial indicators: Lessons from the OECD health care quality indicators project and the US national healthcare quality report. *International journal for quality in health care, 18*, 45–51.

King, A. (2000). *The New Zealand health strategy*. Wellington: Minister of health.

Klein, R. (2007). The new model NHS: Performance, perceptions and expectations. *British Medical Bulletin, 81–82*, (1), 39–50.

Lisac, M. (2006). Health care reform in Germany: Not the big bang. *Health Policy Monitor*. Survey No 8, November.

Malcolm, L., & Mays, N. (1999). New Zealand's independent practitioner associations: A working model of clinical governance in primary care? *British Medical Journal, 319*, 1340–1342.

Minister of Health. (2007). *Health targets: Moving towards healthier futures 2007/08*. Wellington: Author.

Ministry of Health. (2005). *A difference in communities: What's happening in primary health organisations*. Wellington: Author.

OECD. (2007a). *Health at a glance 2007*. Paris: Author.

OECD. (2007b). *OECD health data*. Paris: Author.

Pollock, A. M., & Godden, S. (2008). Independent sector treatment centres: Evidence so far. *British Medical Journal, 336*, 421–424.

Rosenthal, M., Fernandopulle, R., HyunSook, R., & Landon, B. (2004). Paying for quality: Providers' incentives for quality improvement. *Health Affairs, 23*, (2), 127–141.

Rosenthal, M. B., Landon, B., Normand, S. T., Frank, R. G. & Epstein, A. M. (2006). Pay for performance in commercial HMOs. *New England Journal of Medicine, 355*, 1895–1902.

Russell, M., Cumming, J., Slack, A., Peterson, D., & Gilbert, A. (2003). Integrated care: Reflections from research. In R. Gauld (Ed.), *Continuity amid chaos: Health care management and delivery in New Zealand*. Dunedin: University of Otago Press.

Salter, B. (2007). Governing UK medical performance: The struggle for policy dominance. *Health Policy. 82*, 263–275.

Saltman, R. B., Rico, A., & Boerma, W. (Eds.). (2006). *Primary care in the drivers seat? Organizational reform in European primary care*. Maidenhead: Open University Press.

Shaw, K., MacKillop, L., & Armitage, M. (2007). Revalidation, appraisal and clinical governance. *Clinical Governance: An International Journal, 12*, (3), 170–177.

Starfield, B., Shi, L., & Macinko, J. (2005). Contribution of primary care to health systems and health. *The milbank quarterly, 83*, (3), 457–502.

Strandberg-Larsen, M., Neilsen, M. B., Vallgarda, S., Krasnik, A., & Vrangbaek, K. (2007). *Denmark: Health system review*. Copenhagen: Health systems in transition, European Union Observatory on Health Systems and Policies.

Walt, G., & Buse, K. (2006). Global cooperation in international public health. In M. Merson, R. E. Black, & A. Mills (Eds.), *International public health: Diseases, programs, systems, and policies*. Boston: Jones and Bartlett. (pp. 649–680).

Wilkinson, R. (2005). *The impact of inequality: How to make sick societies healthier*. New York: The New Press.

Williams, S. K., & Osborn, S. S. (2006). The development of the national reporting and learning system in England and Wales. 2001–2006. *Medical Journal of Australia, 184*, (10), s65–s68.

World Health Organization. (2005). *Preventing chronic diseases: A vital investment*. Geneva: Author.

World Health Organization. (2007). *World health statistics 2006*. Geneva: Author.

Chapter 8
Post-industrial Society and Aging in a Global World: The Demographic Context of Social Welfare

Jason L. Powell and Cynthia Leedham

Introduction: From Industrialism to Post-industrialism

The challenges posed by welfare in the post-industrial society need to be set within the global context of the demographic changes, the stories by which people live, and the flow of people, technology, money, and ideologies around the world (Appadurai, 1996). Post-industrial societies are characterized by aging of the population, in some cases mitigated by immigration of young, fertile people from less prosperous countries in search of work and economic security. A question only recently receiving attention is whether in the future, young immigrant populations in post-industrial societies will be willing to support an aging population of native residents. The population of Third World countries is aging in a dramatic fashion, albeit from a lower base and, because the overall population of the Third World far exceeds that of post-industrial societies, sheer numbers of older people in Third World countries will in the future far exceed those in post-industrial societies. This trend alone will pose global political challenges as well as challenges for countries faced with a population explosion of elders. In addition to the quandaries of population aging associated with development, some African countries face devastation wrought by AIDS, which depletes the population of those cohorts in mid-life who could otherwise be counted upon to support children and frail elderly.

The very nature of post-industrial societies is dependent on relationships with the Third World. The process of deindustrialization, by which these societies became post-industrial, with their economies focused on the provision of services and information technology, resulted from multinational corporations moving manufacturing from advanced industrial societies to Third World countries, where costs in terms of wages, benefits, and safety precautions are far less than in advanced industrial societies (Bluestone & Harrison, 1982). Workers in Third World countries may be paid as little as dollars a day, below the local living wage, and far below the wages paid to workers in

J.L. Powell (✉)
School of Sociology and Social Policy, University of Liverpool, Liverpool, UK
e-mail: j.l.powell@liv.ac.uk

J. Powell, J. Hendricks, *The Welfare State in Post-Industrial Society*,
DOI 10.1007/978-1-4419-0066-1_8, © Springer Science+Business Media, LLC 2009

advanced industrial societies. The use of child labor is a recurrent problem and one driven by economic considerations. The advent of factories in Third World countries generally provides low wage jobs, but not an adequate living wage, and disrupts local social systems, as workers move to cities where factories are located in search or work. Furthermore, not only do post-industrial societies consume products manufactured in Third World countries, they also lure skilled services workers, such as physicians, to provide medical care. The United States' economy is said to be dependent on low paid, often undocumented low skilled workers in agriculture and other service jobs.

This chapter will discuss the broad dynamics of global aging, outline the basic features of post-industrial societies, and survey global trends in population aging and their consequences. While the case studies in this book focus on post-industrial societies, it is important to understand the global dynamics of aging and so, in this chapter, we look at a broad spectrum of aging, including the demographics of aging in sub-Saharan Africa and Latin America.

New Sites of Vulnerability

The rapid increase in population aging across the globe signals one of the most important demographic changes in human history. In the latter half of the last century, the world's developed nations completed a long process of demographic transition (Phillipson, 1998): a shift from a period of high mortality, short lives, and large families to one with a longer life expectancy leading to an aging population with far fewer children (Powell, 2005). This transformation has taken many years across the globe, but particularly in Europe and North America, as small unit families moved from agrarian modes of production to urban cities; basic public health measures steadily reduced the risk of contagious diseases; and modern medicine has prolonged lives to unprecedented lengths (Giddens, 1993). In developing countries, this demographic transition is well under way, though these countries vary widely at their places along the spectrum. Low birth rates and the resultant population decrease have received considerable media attention, particularly in Europe and parts of eastern Asia (Bengtson & Lowenstein, 2004). In fact, Hendricks and Yoon (2006) go so far as to characterize aging patterns in Asia as a silver tsunami due to the rapidity of the demographic changes. While the proportions of older people in a population are typically highest in more developed countries, the most rapid increase in sheer numbers of elderly are actually occurring in the less developed world (Cook and Powell, 2007). Between 2006 and 2030, the increasing number of older people in less developed countries is projected to escalate by 140 percent as compared to an increase of 51 percent in more developed countries (Krug, 2002).

Demographers have identified three key demographic transitions:

The first demographic transition refers to the process by which a fall in death rate, followed by a fall in birth rate, results in a numerically stable but aging population characterized by low and roughly equivalent birth and death rates. This process started in Western and Northern Europe, with improvements in health and nutrition leading to a population explosion beginning around 1800, followed by an eventual decline in birth rate and gradual population aging extending over the late 19th and the 20th centuries (Cohn, 2007). As implied by the Hendricks and Yoon characterization above, this first demographic transition is occurring in developing countries at a much more rapid (although variable) pace than was the case for Europe and the United States, with resultant policy challenges. Some developing countries, such as those in Latin America, are among the world's fastest aging regions (Kaneda, 2008; United Nations, 2005). The same demographic aging process that unfolded over more than a century in France will occur in two decades in Brazil (OECD, 2007). Sub-Saharan Africa has the slowest rate of population aging and the smallest proportion of elderly, but it is projected to see the absolute size of its older population grow by 2.3 times between 2000 and 2030, even though in 2050, the projected percentage of persons over age 65 is less than 7.49 percent for many sub-Saharan African countries (Kaneda, 2008, United Nations, 2005).

The second demographic transition refers to a further decline in birth rates to below the replacement rate of 2.1 children per woman, which, in combination with gains in life expectancy at older age, is resulting in extreme population aging and, in some countries, population shrinkage. This second demographic transition began in Europe and the United States, four decades ago, due to a combination of factors, including women's increased participation in the workforce and the growing emphasis on self-fulfilment (Cohn, 2007).

A third demographic transition was recently identified as resulting from an interplay of historical factors and flow of people. As life expectancy increases and the post-World War II Baby Boom generation begins its exit from the workforce, they are being succeeded by a smaller generation, which includes a large share of immigrants and their children – who did not always receive a warm welcome in the United States and elsewhere. In the case of the United States, in California, nearly half of the population consists of immigrants or their children. Myers highlights the potential for political conflict this presents and the need for the older white generation, which tends to be more politically active than younger immigrants, to vote not only to preserve social support for the elderly but also to support integration and expanded educational opportunities for immigrants so that they will have the needed skills to replace retirees in the workforce and be able to shoulder the taxes needed to support them (Cohn, 2007; Myers, 2007; cf. Chapa, Hayes-Bautista & Schink, 1988). Mather (2007) refers to this state of affairs as the growing demographic divide between generations, fuelled by immigration and higher fertility rates among immigrants, resulting in a population over 60, with a large majority of non-Hispanic whites and substantial and growing proportion of racial and ethnic minorities in younger generations. While Myers and others are writing about the United States, immigration is also an issue in Europe. For instance, in 2001 in Leicester, England, almost 40 percent of the population was of foreign origin, and the city is well on its way toward becoming the first British city where white Britons are in a minority (Leicester City Council, 2001; Hickley, 2007; Hope, 2007).

The interplay of the factors described above has led to a wider demographic divide between populations which has received increasing attention in recent years (Haub, 2007a; Population Reference Bureau, 2007). At one extreme are the mostly poor countries of sub-Saharan Africa with relatively high birth rates, low life expectancies, and low rates of population aging. At the other extreme are the mostly rich European countries with low birth rates, extreme aging of the population, and impending population loss. In 2007, Germany, for instance, had a total fertility rate (lifetime births per woman) of 1.3, a life expectancy at birth of 79 years, 14 percent of the population below 14 years, and 19 percent of the population aged 65 years and older. The GNI ppp per capita in 2006 US dollars (defined as purchasing power of per capita income equivalent to the amount in 2006 US dollars) was $31,280. On the other hand, in 2007, Zambia had a total fertility rate of 5.5, a life expectancy at birth of 38 years, 46 percent of the population below 15 years, and 2 percent of the population aged 65 and older. The GNI ppp per capita in 2006 US dollars for Uganda in 2007 was $1,000. The population of Germany was estimated at 82.3 million in mid-2007. It was projected to fall to 79.6 million by mid-2025 and 71.4 million by mid-2050. The population of Zambia was estimated at 11.5 million in mid-2007 and was projected to rise to 14.8 million in mid-2025 and 18.4 million in mid-2050. Overall the population of Eastern Africa was projected to rise from 294 million in mid-2007 to 650 million in mid-2050 (Population Reference Bureau, 2007; Haub, 2007b). This pattern of continued dramatic population growth in Third World countries and population shrinkage in Europe, along with the trend of an increasingly aged white population face-to-face with a young predominantly immigrant population in countries like the United States, poses the challenge of ensuring global access to opportunity if there are not be to major conflicts.

The dynamics of global population aging are not, however, as straightforward as the concept of a great demographic divide between populations would make them seem. Largely thanks to immigration, the population of the United States is not aging as rapidly as the populations of other developed countries. In 2007, the total fertility rate in the United States was 2.1, right at the replacement rate, and the total US population is projected to increase from 302.7 million in mid-2007 to 349.4 million in mid-2025 and 419.9 in mid-2050 (Haub, 2007b). There are, however, concerns about population aging in Southeast Asian countries, such as Japan, Korea, and China (Haub, 2007b).

Aging and Post-industrialism

In addition to population aging, the turn of the twenty-first century is characterized by the development of "post-industrial society" (Ritzer, 2007). This book is concerned precisely with the challenges faced by welfare systems in post-industrial societies in the context of globalization and global aging.

A post-industrial society is one in which an economic transition has occurred from a manufacturing-based economy to a service-based economy, also characterized by a diffusion of national and global capital and mass privatization. The prerequisites to this economic shift are the processes of industrialization and liberalization. This economic transition spurs a restructuring in society as a whole.

Within the realm of economic activities, there is a transition from manufacturing of goods to the provision of services. Production of such goods as clothing and steel declines, and services such as selling fast food and offering advice on investments or other non-tangibles increase. Although services predominate in a wide range of sectors, health, education, research, and government services are the most decisive for a post-industrial society. This shift from durable manufacturing to the production of services and information presupposes the transfer of manufacturing operations by multinational corporations to developing countries, where cheap labor is plentiful and safety and environmental regulations are less stringent and less costly than in developed nations. This shift also leads to widening inequalities within the post-industrial society. Semiskilled workers who had been making relatively high wages in manufacturing industries, such as the automobile industry, are forced into low wage, unskilled service jobs lacking adequate benefits, while system analysts, scientists, and other highly educated workers command high wage jobs with good fringe benefits. In the United States, this has led to increasing numbers of people who are medically uninsured, who are not covered by private retirement pension, and whose social security benefits will not be sufficient to meet their needs. As noted above, the importance of blue-collar, manual work (e.g., assembly line workers) declines and professional (doctors and lawyers) and technical work (computer programmers) come to predominate. Of special importance is the rise of scientists (e.g., specialized engineers, such as genetic or electric).

Instead of hands-on know-how, theoretical knowledge is increasingly essential in a post-industrial society. Such knowledge is seen as the basic source of innovation (e.g., knowledge created by those scientists involved in the *Human Genome Project* is leading to new ways of treating many diseases). Advances in knowledge also lead to the need for other innovations, such as ways of dealing with ethical questions raised by advances in cloning technology. All of this involves an emphasis on theoretical, rather than empirical, knowledge and on the codification of knowledge. The exponential growth of theoretical and codified knowledge, in all its varieties, is central to the emergence of the post-industrial society.

In the post-industrial society, there is a focus on assessing impacts of new technologies and, where necessary, exercising control over them. The hope is, for example, to better monitor things like nuclear power plants and to improve them so that accidents like that at Chernobyl can be prevented in the future. The goal is a surer and more secure technological world outside the rigid power containers of the nation-state. To handle such assessment and control, and more generally the sheer complexity of the post-industrial society, new intellectual technologies are developed and implemented. They include, among others, cybernetics, game theory, and information theory.

This is ironic in view of the lack of concern for workers' safety and environment in manufacturing operations moved to developing countries. The explosion at the Union Carbide factory in Bhopal, India, which killed hundreds of people is a blatant example of the consequences of moving risky businesses offshore. As Beck (1992) points out, the lack of concern for the environment may come back to bite those responsible for it. We live in a global risk society where all will suffer from the effects of pollution and global warming. The rise of manufacturing in developing countries is a major contributor to the emission of greenhouse gases, but the governments of developing countries argue that they should not bear the brunt of cutting back on emissions before they have had an opportunity for economic development and that developed countries, like the United States, which are major consumers of world's remaining non-renewable energy resources, should cut back.

A new relationship in the post-industrial society between scientists and the new technologies they create, as well as systematic technological growth, lies at the core of the post-industrial society. This leads to the need for more universities and university-based students. In fact, universities are crucial to the post-industrial society. Universities produce experts who can create, guide, and control new and dramatically changing technologies.

Daniel Bell underscored that changes to the post-industrial society are not merely social structural and economic; but the values and norms within the post-industrial society are altered as well. Rationality and efficiency become the paramount values within the post-industrial society. Eventually, according to Bell, these values cause a disconnection between social structures and culture. Many of today's unique modern problems can be generally attributed to the effects of the post-industrial society. These problems are particularly pronounced where the free market dominates. They can include economic inequality and the outsourcing of domestic jobs with its attendant problems. The economic turmoil that faced the world in mid-2008 is a case in point that resonates around the globe.

The various dimensions of global aging and its impacts, such as demography, socioeconomic issues, health, intergenerational support, activities in later life, social security, dependency rates, and human right issues are intimately related to the advent of the post-industrial age (Phillipson, 1998). In the next section, we will consider the size and growth of the world's older population around the globe, in America, Europe, Asia, and Africa, and conclude by highlighting some of the important social and economic policy challenges which arise from this discussion.

Contested Identity

With the growth in the proportion and numbers of older people around the world, continued increase in life expectancy in most countries, and the population above 85 years old being the fastest growing segment of the population in many developed countries, population aging is changing the face of both global and national societies in a number of ways. The leading causes of death now are those diseases that typically affect older adults. Noncommunicable diseases, such as cancer, cardiovascular diseases, stroke, and other cerebrovascular diseases, are becoming a growing burden, particularly in developed countries. Yet, it should be remembered that low-income countries in Africa and elsewhere still struggle with infectious diseases and one-third of deaths worldwide are due to infectious diseases. HIV/AIDS is among the leading causes of death in developing countries, and malaria causes almost as many deaths in low-income countries as coronary heart disease in high income countries of North America, Europe, and Japan (World Health Organization, 2007; University of California at Santa Cruz, no date.)

Family structures are changing. As people live longer and have fewer children, family structures are transformed, leaving older people with fewer options for care. Family structure and the availability of support for elders are also affected by the migration of young adults in search of work from developing to developed countries and from rural areas to major cities.

At the same time, social insurance systems are evolving. As social insurance expenditures escalate, an increasing number of countries are evaluating the sustainability of their policies supportive of one or another form of social insurance. Meanwhile, developing countries are facing the muddle posed by large numbers of people outside the formal economy who are, therefore, not covered by social security systems and whose traditional family sources of support are eroding. Some less developed nations will be forced to confront issues, such as social support and the allocation of resources across generations, without the accompanying economic growth that characterized the experience of aging societies in the West. In other words, some countries 'may grow old before they grow rich' (Cook & Powell, 2007: 17).

New economic hurdles are also emerging. Population aging will have dramatic effects on social entitlement programs, labor supply, trade, and savings around the globe and may demand new fiscal approaches to accommodate a changing world.

Patterns of work and retirement are shifting. Shrinking ratios of workers to pensioners and people spending a larger portion of their lives in retirement increasingly challenge existing health and pension systems in developed countries (Bengtson & Lowenstein, 2004; Krug, 2002; Estes, 2001).

Aging can no longer just be viewed as a 'national' problem, but one that affects transnational agencies and communities. Local or national interpretations of aging had some meaning in a world where states were in control of their destiny. They also carried force where social policies were being designed with the aim or aspiration of levelling inequalities and where citizenship was still largely a national affair, or where there was some degree of confidence over what constituted 'national borders.' The crisis affecting each of these areas, largely set in motion by different aspects of globalization, is now posing acute challenges for understanding 'global aging' in the 21st century.

The next section looks at four key regions across the globe: (i) aging in America; (ii) aging in Europe; (iii) aging in Asia; and (iv) aging in Africa. We will provide essential facts with regard to the demographics of aging in each region and then briefly explore some of the social implications of aging in the region in global context.

(i) *Aging in the Americas:* Since the turn of the 20th century, the life expectancy of people born in North America (including Mexico) has increased by approximately 25 years and the proportion of persons 65 years or older has increased from 4 percent to over 13 percent (Estes, 2001). By 2030, one in five individuals in the United States is expected to be 65 years or older, while people aged 85 and older make up the fastest growing segment of the population. Because the aging population is not only growing rapidly but also getting older, as evidenced by the average age of the population: "In 1990, fewer than one in ten elderly persons was age 85 or older. By 2045, the oldest old will be one in five. Increasing longevity and the steady movement of baby boomers into the oldest age group will drive this trend" (Longino, 1994: 856).

In 2000, there were 34 million people aged 65 or older in the United States that represented 13 percent of the overall population (Estes, 2001). By 2030, there will be 70 million over 65 in the United States, more than twice their number in 2000. Yet Longino (1994) believes that thanks to better health, changing living arrangements, and improved assistive devices, the future may not be as negative as we think when we consider an aging population (1994).

Furthermore, as noted above, population aging in the United States is not as extreme as in many post-industrial societies, largely because of immigration. In 2007, the index of aging in the United States was only 83.9 as compared to 201 for Japan, and 182.3 for Germany (United Nations, 2007), and the total fertility rate was 2.1 for women in the United States as compared to 1.3 for Japan and Germany (Haub, 2007b). While this situation makes for lower age dependency ratios, it does pose the problem of potential conflict between a younger generation composed in substantial part of immigrants and a largely aging population (Cohn, 2007).

Other important social changes will also accompany population aging in the United States. For example, divorced persons constitute a small proportion of older populations currently, reflecting cohort differences in the likelihood of divorcing. This will soon change in many countries as younger populations with higher rates of divorce and separation enter later life. In the United States, for example, 9 percent of people aged 65 and above are divorced or separated, compared to 17 percent of people aged between 55 and 64 and 18 percent of people aged between 45 and 54 (Manton and Gu, 2001). This trend has gender-specific implications: Nonmarried women are less likely than nonmarried men to have accumulated assets and pension wealth for use in later life, and older men are less likely to form and maintain supportive social networks.

While there are variations between countries, Latin America is among the world's fastest aging regions with the percent of elderly projected to double between 2000 and 2030, as noted above (Kaneda, 2008). By 2050, the population aged 65 and above as a percentage of the working age population aged between 15 and 64 in Latin America will be roughly equivalent to percentages found in developed countries today (Haub, 2007a). By 2002, some countries, including Cuba, Argentina, Chile, and Uruguay, had below average fertility rates, mortality rates, and rates of natural population increase and relatively high life expectancy at birth, in the mid- to late 1970s (Brea, 2003a). In Brazil, Colombia, Costa Rica, Ecuador, Mexico, Panama, Peru, the Dominican Republic, and Venezuela, the population structure was still relatively young in 2002 due to high fertility rates in the past, but there had been a pronounced decrease in fertility since 1965, with average fertility declining from 6.2 children per woman between 1965 and 1970 to 2.8 children per woman in the late 1990s. Although the fertility rate was still higher than mortality, it was trending down resulting in slowing of population growth and increasing aging of the population (Brea, 2003a). In some countries, such as the smaller Central American and Caribbean countries, the process of population aging has been accelerated by younger adults emigrating to the United States in search of work, leaving behind middle-aged and older adults. This process has been aggravated by migration of younger adults from rural to urban areas within the same country, further depleting the financial and social support of older rural residents (Brea, 2003b).

The viability of pension systems in the face of population aging is a major concern in both the United States and Latin America, and there has been a move toward privatization of pensions and defined contribution plans. Recent changes in the pension systems of countries such as Chile, under pressure from international financial institutions, have been a focus of worldwide interest (Huber & Stephens, 2000). Yet, in considering the debates surrounding the privatization of pension programs in Latin America, one needs to bear in mind that, as Sanchez (2008) notes, pensions in Latin America generally cover only those employed in the formal sector, which constitutes less than half of the population. Those who are employed outside the formal system in day labor or subsistence farming are outside the pension system. Sanchez (2008) also notes that, according to a socioeconomic database established by CEDLAS (The Center for the Study of Distribution, Labor, and Social Affairs at the Universidad Nacional de La Plata, Argentina) and the World Bank, in Nicaragua, only 7 percent of the people above 60 have access to health insurance, in El Savador 14 percent, and in Guatemala 21 percent as compared to 96 percent in the United States. (See Rofman & Lucchetti, 2007, and Social Security Administration, 2008 for details of pension coverage in Latin America.)

In developing countries, privately managed savings accounts have been strongly advocated (Estes, 2001). This has paralleled a move from defined benefit pension systems to defined contribution pension systems, which shift risk from employers to employees in the United States. These changes may be seen as part of the shift toward rationality and efficiency (and away from concern with social welfare), which Daniel Bell sees as being associated with the post-industrial society.

Two decades ago, nearly every South American nation had pay-as-you-go (PAYG) systems similar to the Social Security system in the United States. Some countries granted civil servants retiring in their age groups of 50 plus full salaries for life. Widening budget deficits changed that. In 1981, Chile replaced its public system with retirement accounts funded by worker contributions and managed by private firms. The World Bank encouraged 11 other Latin nations to introduce similar features. For example, in Chile, the government addressed its fiscal budget deficit by mobilizing a $49 billion of pension fund assets that make it easier for companies and corporations to fund investments in the local currency with bond offerings, and most workers have some retirement benefits from this (OECD, 2007). At the same time, the downside has been that those people who cannot afford a private pension have been left to a low state pension, which has intensified poverty (Estes, 2001).

For the future, there is no safety guarantee that private pension schemes are protected and pay out for people who invest their savings in such provision. In a deregulated US pension system, the issue of corporate crime has highlighted the continuing problem of private pension provision. In one example, this was seen clearly with the energy corporation of Enron's embezzlement of billions of dollars of employee private pension schemes (Powell, 2005). This debate amounts to a significant global discourse on pension provision and retirement age, but one which has largely excluded perspectives which might suggest an enlarged role for the state and those which might question the stability and cost effectiveness of private schemes. The International Labour Organisation (ILO) concluded that investing in financial markets is an uncertain and volatile business: that under present pension plans, people may save up to 30 percent more than they need, which would reduce their spending during their working life; or they may save 30 percent too little – which would severely cut their spending in retirement (Phillipson, 1998; Estes et al., 2003).

Holtzman (1997), in a discussion of the World Bank's perspective on pension reform, has argued for reducing state PAYG schemes to a minimal role of basic pension provision. This position has influenced both national governments and transnational bodies, such as the ILO, with the latter now conceding to the World Bank's position with their advocacy of a mean-tested first pension, the promotion of an extended role for individualized and capitalized private pensions, and the call for Organisation for Economic Cooperation and Development (OECD) member countries to raise the age of retirement.

There is also the impact of IGOs (Intergovernmental Organizations) on the pension debate in Latin America. The IGO is, by definition, an organization with international membership, scope, or presence to provide pension alternatives to that provided by the individual member states in Latin America. The IGOs have sovereign states as their members. Their scope and aims are most usually in the public interest but may also have been created with a specific purpose. The function of such arguments is to create a sense of inevitability and scientific certainty that public pension provision will fail. In so far as this strategy succeeds, it creates a self-fulfilling prophecy. If people believe the 'experts' who say publicly sponsored PAYG systems cannot be sustained, they are more likely to act in ways that mean they are unsustainable in practice.

Increasingly, the social infrastructure of welfare states is being targeted as a major area of opportunity for global investors. The World Bank has expressed the belief that the public sector is less efficient in managing new infrastructure activities and that the time has come for private actors to provide what were once assumed to be public services. This view has been strongly endorsed by a variety of multinational companies, especially in their work with the World Trade Organisation (WTO). The WTO enforces more than twenty separate international agreements, using international trade tribunals that adjudicate disputes. Such agreements include the General Agreement on Trade in Services (GATS), the first multilateral legally enforceable agreement covering banking, insurance, financial services and related areas (Estes et al., 2003).

(ii) *Aging in Europe*: The population structure of western European countries has changed since the turn of the 20th century. Whereas in 1901, just over 6 percent of the population was at or above 65 years, that figure rose steadily, reaching 18 percent in 2001 (Powell, 2005). At the same time, the population of younger people under 16 years fell from 35 to 20 percent. As European countries reach a relatively high level of population aging, the proportion of workers also tends to decline. European countries, including France, Germany, Greece, Italy, Russia, and Ukraine, have already seen an absolute decline in the size of their workforce. By 2025, the number of people aged between 15 and 64 is projected to dwindle by 10.4 percent in Spain, 10.7 percent in Germany, and 14.8 percent in Italy. In countries where tax increases are needed to pay for transfers to growing older populations, the tax burden may discourage the future workforce participation. The impact on a nation's gross domestic product will depend on increase in labor productivity and state's ability to substitute capital for labor. Less developed countries can shift their economies from labor-intensive to capital-intensive sectors as population aging advances. Options for most European nation-states may be more limited. The 'rolling back' of pensions forced through by neoliberal governments, such as Margaret Thatcher's administration (1979–91) in the United Kingdom, was just one symptom of a shift in European history: the 'graying of the baby boom generation' (Phillipson, 1998). The percentage of 60-year olds and older are growing at 1.9 percent a year in Europe. This is 60 percent faster than the overall global population. In 1950, there were 12 people aged 15–64 to support each one of the retirement age. Currently, the global average is nine. It will be only four-to-one by 2050 in Europe (Powell, 2005). By then, the number of older people will outnumber children for the first time. Some economists fear that this will lead to bankrupt pensions and lower living standards. It is interesting that, in Germany, this fear is becoming a battleground for political electioneering.

For example, Germany has the largest total population in Europe and the third oldest population in the world, which presents both critical questions on public finances to provide pensions and healthcare and an opportunity for innovations in the marketplace. Currently, aging has started to figure prominently in political discussions prior to the 2009 elections, as political parties vie for the elderly votes. The current Merkel administration (2007-) has been criticized for increasing pensions while opponents talk about a "war of generations" requiring young people to pay for taxation for the care of elders.

The population of Britain, like that of other European countries is aging rapidly. In the United Kingdom, the percentage of people of working age, i.e. 16–64, is projected to drop from 64 percent in 1994 to 58 percent in 2031. There are only enough young people to fill one in three of the new and replacement jobs that will need to be taken up over the next decade (Powell, 2005). As the number of workers per pensioner decreases, there will be pressure on pension provision. This is evident now in areas of such as pensions and long-term care and the erosion of State Earnings Related Pay is forcing people to devise their own strategies for economic survival in old age (Phillipson, 1998). In the Britain, as elsewhere, private pensions are slowly being introduced to prevent the 'burden' of an aging population. These are ways in which the state continues to rely on apocalyptic projections, such as 'demographic time bomb,' about aging populations to justify cuts in public expenditure (Powell, 2005). Older people take much of the responsibility for our social and civic life and for the care of children, the sick and the very old in the community. Yet the gap between wealth and poverty, choice and the absence of choice for older people is stark and growing more pronounced (Phillipson, 1998).

(iii) *Aging in Asia*: Just as Asian economies have taken flight, Asia has experienced the greatest demographic changes in the world and the most dramatic growth in the number of older persons. The future challenge of providing for the older adult population is especially urgent in the world's two biggest nations – India and China (Kim & Lee, 2007). By 2030, in China, there will be only two working-age people to support every retiree. Yet only 20 percent of workers have government- or company-funded pensions or medical coverage (Cook & Powell, 2007). China, in particular, has been identified as having four 'unique characteristics' of population aging (Du & Tu, 2000).

1. *Unprecedented speed*: The proportion of population that is older is growing faster than Japan, the country previously recognized as having the fastest rate, and much faster than nations in Western Europe, for example.
2. *Early arrival of an aging population*: Before modernization has fully taken place, with its welfare implications "it is certain that China will face a severely aged population before it has sufficient time and resources to establish an adequate social security and service system for the elderly" (Du & Tu, 2000: 79).

3. *Fluctuations in the total dependency ratio*: The Chinese government estimates are that the country will reach a higher 'dependent burden' earlier in the twenty-first century than was previously forecast.
4. *Strong influence of the government's fertility policy and its implementation on the aging process*: The government policy of one child per family means fewer children being born, but with more elderly people, a conflict arises between the objectives to limit population increase and maintaining a balanced age structure.

The combination of such factors means that the increased aging population is giving rise to serious concerns among Chinese policymakers.

India is slated to have the largest population in the world before 2030, exceeding the population of China, but it has a relatively young population due to continued high fertility rates in some regions. In 2005, about 36 percent of the population was below 15 years, more than half of the population was below 25 years and only 4 percent of the population was 65 or older (Haub & Sharma, 2006). In 2007, the index of aging in India was only 26.1 (United Nations, 2007). India is an extremely complex region, with very diverse ethnic, linguistic, geographic, and demographic features, and it has been described as "a collection of many countries held together by a common destiny and a successful democracy" (Haub & Sharma, 2006: 3). Patterns of aging vary considerably within India, and life expectancy at birth ranges from 57.1 years in Madhya Pradesh to 73.6 years in Kerala. Similarly, while in most states the total fertility rate has declined by just over two children per woman, the total fertility rate in 2003 ranged from a high of 4.4 in Uttar Pradesh to 1.8 (below the replacement rate) in Kerala (Haub & Sharma, 2006). The complexities of the demographics of aging and economic development in the diverse regions of India are beyond the scope of this chapter, but we will note that India faces significant challenges due to the sheer numbers of older people in its population, coupled with high rates of poverty and the fact that only 11 percent of Indians have pensions, and they tend to be civil servants and the affluent. With a young population and relatively big families, many of the older adult population still count on their children for support (Cook & Powell, 2007).

Kim and Lee (2007), among others (**), assert that the growing older adult population is beginning to exert pressure on economies of the east Asian countries. Three decades ago, major industrialized countries had begun to grapple with the similar problem. With increasing reduction in fertility rates, more east Asian economies, such as Japan, Hong Kong, South Korea, Singapore, and Taiwan, are expected to turn into "super-aging societies" by 2025 (Kim & Lee, 2007). However, the magnitude of the future impact depends on the (in)ability of individual economies to resolve the demographic burden through changes, such as increased pension reform, immigration policy, and extension of retirement age. Like Western countries, Asia will ultimately have to tackle issues related to pension reform and the provision of long-term health care services (Cook & Powell, 2007).

Japan, the fastest aging nation in the world, faces an enormous challenge due to the population aging trends. Already, 17 out of every 100 of its people are above 65 years, and this ratio will near 30 in 15 years. From 2005 to 2012, Japan's workforce is projected to shrink by around 1 percent each year – a pace that will accelerate after that. Economists fear that, besides straining Japan's underfunded pension system (Cook & Powell, 2007), the decline of workers and young families will make it harder for Japan to generate new wealth.

(iv) *Aging in Africa*: Economic security, health and disability, and living conditions in later life are policy concerns throughout the world, but the nature of the problem differs considerably from continent to continent and between and within countries – especially within Africa.

In Africa, older people make up a relatively small fraction of the total population, and traditionally, their main source of support has been the household and family, supplemented in many cases by other informal mechanisms, such as kinship networks and mutual aid societies. In 2005, Nigeria ranked among the top 30 countries in the world on the basis of the size of its population aged 60 and above. Nigeria had the largest older population in sub-Saharan Africa, with over 6 million people aged 60 and above; South Africa had just over 3.4 million. Congo and South Africa are projected to have nearly 5 million older people in 2030. Burkina Faso, Cameroon, Cote d'Ivoire, Madagascar, Mozambique, Niger, Senegal, and Uganda are all projected to have their older populations grow to over one million people by 2030 (Building Blocks, 2004). Very little careful empirical research has been undertaken on long-term trends in the welfare of older people, but there are a number of reasons to believe that traditional caring and social support mechanisms in Africa are under increasing strain (OECD, 2007).

African economies, among the poorest in the world, are still heavily dependent on subsistence agriculture, and the average income per capita is now lower than it was at the end of the 1960s. Consequently, the region contains a growing share of the world's poor. In addition, reductions in fertility and child mortality have meant that, despite the huge impact of the HIV/AIDS epidemic across much of the region, both absolute size and proportion of the population aged 60 and above have grown and will continue to grow over the next 30 years (Estes et al., 2003).

In Africa, older people have traditionally been viewed in a positive light as repositories of information and wisdom. While African families are generally still intact, social and economic changes taking place can weaken traditional social values and networks that provide care and support in later life. Africa has long carried a high burden of disease, including malaria and tuberculosis; today, it is home to more than 60 percent of all people living with HIV – some 25.8 million in 2005. The vast majority of those affected are still in their prime wage-earning years, at an age when, normally, they would be expected to be the main wage earners and principal sources of financial and material support for older people and children in their families. Many older people have had to deal with the loss of their own support while absorbing additional responsibilities of caring for their orphaned grandchildren. Increasingly, then, it appears that African societies are being asked to cope with population aging with neither a comprehensive formal social security system nor a well-functioning traditional care system in place (Building Blocks, 2004).

One of the biggest issues in global aging is that a majority of world's population of older people (61 percent, or 355 million) lives in poorer African countries. This proportion will increase to nearly 70 percent by 2025. For many countries, however, population aging has been accompanied by reduction in per capita income and declining living standards. Epstein (2001) noted that between 1950 and the late 1970s, life expectancy increased by at least 10 percent in every developing country in the world, or on average by about 15 years. However, at the beginning of the twenty-first century, life expectancy remains below 50 in more than 10 developing countries and, since 1970, has actually fallen or barely risen in a number of African countries (Phillipson, 1998). The AIDS epidemic is certainly a major factor here, but development loans requiring the privatization of health care have also had an impact. Epstein (2001) reports, for example, that by the mid-1990s, the African continent was transferring four times more in debt repayment than it spent on health or education. More generally, Help Age International (2000: 8) argues:

> Older people's poverty is still not a core concern in the social, economic and ethical debates of our time. Their right to development is routinely denied, with ageing seen as a minority interest or case for special pleading. Poverty and social exclusion remain the main stumbling blocks to the realisation of the human rights of older people worldwide.

Issues of Equality and Global Aging

Although global aging represents a triumph of medical, social, and economic advances, it also presents tremendous challenges for many regions of the world. Population aging strains social insurance and pension systems and challenges existing models of social support traditionally given by family structures (Bengtson & Lowenstein, 2004; Hendricks & Yoon, 2006). The evidence is incontrovertible, global aging will have dramatic effects on local, regional, and global economies. Chris Phillipson (1998) has argued that the rise of globalization exerts unequal and highly stratified effects on the lives of older people in different nation-states (Phillipson, 1998; Estes, 2001).

Post-industrial countries in the developed world face a variety of issues related to extreme aging of their populations.

The magnitude and absolute size of expenditure on programs for older people have made these the first to be targeted with financial cuts, as nation-states with extensive social programs targeted to the older population – principally health and income support programs – find the costs of these programs escalating as the number of eligible recipients grows and the duration of eligibility lengthens due to global pressure (Bengtson & Lowenstein, 2004).

This is related to the fact that few countries have fully funded programs; most countries fund these programs on a PAYG basis or finance them using general revenue streams. Governments may be limited in how much they can reshape social insurance programs by raising the age of eligibility, increasing contribution rates, and reducing benefits. Consequently, shortfalls may need to be financed using general revenue. Projections of government expenditure in the United States and other OECD countries show increase in the share of gross domestic product devoted to social entitlements for older populations. In some cases, this share more than doubles as a result of population aging (OECD, 2007). When individual and family resources, such as public and private pension, financial assets, and property, are included, pensions and eldercare costs will increase from 14 percent of capitalist nations' gross domestic product to 18 percent by 2050 (Walker & Naeghele, 2000).

Population aging will give rise to shortfalls in the labor force, both because of the likelihood that an individual will be in the labor force varies systematically by age (Phillipson, 1998) and because, in the case of Europe, most state-funded pension systems encourage early retirement, with the result that 85.5 percent of adults in France retire from employment by 60 years, and 62 percent of Italian adults retire from employment by 55 years (Estes, 2001). Thus, lower proportion of the population in the labor force in highly industrialized nations threaten both productivity and the ability to support an aging population (Krug, 2002).

Since, according to the life cycle theory of consumption, family households accumulate wealth during their working years to maintain consumption in retirement, there will be a scarcity of capital and high interest rates in nations with high proportions of elders who have left the workforce (Gilleard & Higgs, 2001). In some countries, labor force shortfalls – and the aging of the population – are mitigated by the use of immigrant workers. Currently, 22 percent of physicians and 12 percent of nurses in the United States are foreign born, representing primarily African countries, the Caribbean, and Southeast Asia (OECD, 2007). The United States is also dependent on large numbers of migrant workers, primarily from Mexico, many of whom are undocumented, for agricultural labor. The foreign-born workforce also is growing in most OECD countries, and even in countries like South Korea and Japan, which have strong cultural aversions to immigration, small factories, construction companies, and health clinics are relying more on 'temporary' workers from the Philippines, Bangladesh, and Vietnam (OECD, 2007). This reliance on immigrant labor can, however, be a two-edged sword for aging post-industrial countries. In the United States, there is concern about whether a younger generation with a large share of immigrants will be willing to support a predominantly white aging population. (Cohn, 2007; Myers, 2007; Chapa et al., 1988)

Developing countries, too, face their own hurdles. The increase in sheer numbers of older people in developing countries at a time when global forces are shattering the family support systems before these countries have had a change to build wealth and create institutionalized systems of support for elders poses a major policy challenge. Patterns of population movement and migration sparked by globalization may produce changes that disrupt the lives of older people (Phillipson, 1998). The brain drain of skilled health care workers to the United States has a negative effect on the infrastructure of the country of origin, and the departure of these young people – and migrant workers from Mexico – erodes the family support system of the elders they leave behind. One must not forget either that the elderly comprise up to one-third of refugees in conflict and emergency situations – a figure which was estimated at over 53 million people worldwide in 2000 (Estes, 2001). In less developed countries, older people (especially women) have been among those most affected by the privatization of health care and the burden of debt repayments to the World Bank and the IMF (Estes, 2001).

Population aging is also very much a global affair, which affects and is affected by trends such as global economic downturns as well as patterns of migration and the mutual effect which different regions of the world have on one another. There are an increasing number of international agencies concerned with global aging. The World Bank (1994) foresees growing "threats" to international stability resulting from different demographic-economic regions being pitted against one another (Phillipson, 1998). The United Nations (2002) has also identified urgent policy challenges, including the need to reverse recent trends toward decreasing labor force participation of workers in late middle and old age despite mandatory retirement in certain Western countries, such as the United Kingdom (Powell, 2005).

Globalization has produced a distinctive stage in the social history of population aging, with a growing tension between nation-state-based solutions (and anxieties) about growing old and those formulated by global institutions (Phillipson, 1998). Globalization, defined here as the process whereby nation-states are influenced (and sometimes undermined) by transnational actors (Powell, 2005), has become an influential force in shaping responses to population aging. Growing old has, itself, become relocated within a transnational context, with international organizations (such as the World Bank and the International Monetary Fund) and cross-border migrations, creating new conditions and environments for older people (Phillipson, 1998).

References

Appadurai, A. (1996). *Modernity at large: Cultural dimensions of globalization*. Minneapolis, MN: University of Minnesota Press.

Beck, U. (1992). *Risk society: Towards a new modernity* (M. Ritter, Trans.) Thousand Oaks, CA: Sage.

Bengtson, V. L., & Lowenstein, A. (Eds.) (2004). *Global aging and challenges to families*. New York: De Gruyter.

Building Blocks. (2004). *Africa-wide briefing notes – supporting older carers*. Brighton: HIV AIDS Alliance and HelpAge International.

Bluestone, B., & Harrison, B. (1982). *The deindustrialization of America: Plant closings, community abandonment and the dismantling of basic industry*. New York: Basic Books.

Brea, J. A. (2003a). Population dynamics in Latin America. *Population Bulletin, 58*(1). Washington, DC: Population Reference Bureau.

Brea, J. A. (2003b). *The graying of Latin America*. Washingrton, DC: Population Reference Bureau. Available at: http://www.prb.org/Articles/2003/TheGrahingofLatinAmerica. aspx?p = 1

Chapa, G, Hayes-Bautista, D. E., & Schink, W. O. (1988). *The burden of support: Young Latinos in an aging society*. Stanford, CA: Stanford University Press.

Cohn. D. (2007). *The divergent paths of baby boomers and immigrants*. Washington, DC: Population Reference Bureau. Available at: http://www.prb.org/Articles/2007/Divergent PathsofBabyBoomersandImmigrants.aspx?p = 1

Cook, I. G., & Powell, J. L. (2007). *New perspectives on China and aging*. New York: Nova Science.

Du, P., & Tu, P. (2000). Population ageing and old age security. In X. Peng & Z. Guo (Eds.), *The changing population of China* (pp. 77–90). Oxford: Blackwell.

Epstein, H. (2001). Time of indifference. *New York Review of Books*, April 12, pp. 33–38.

Estes, C. (2001). *Social policy and aging*. Thousand Oaks, CA: Sage.

Estes, C., Biggs, S., & Phillipson, C. (2003). *Social theory, social policy and ageing*. Milton Keynes: Open University Press.

Giddens, A. (1993). *Sociology*. Cambridge: Polity Press.

Gilleard, C., & Higgs, P. (2001). *Cultures of aging*. London: Prentice Hall.

Haub, C. (2007a). *Global aging and the demographic divide*. Washington, DC: Population Reference Bureau. Available at: http://www.prb.org/Articles/2008/globalaging.aspx.

Haub, C. (2007b). *2007 World population data sheet*. Washington, DC: Population Reference Bureau.

Haub, C., & Sharma, O. P. (2006). India's population reality: Reconciling change and tradition. *Population Bulletin, 61*(3). Washington, DC: Population Reference Bureau.

Help Age International. (2000). *The mark of a noble society*. London: HelpAge International.

Hendricks, J., & Yoon, H. (2006). The sweep of Asian aging: Changing mores, changing polilcies. In H. Yoon & J. Hendricks (Eds.), *Handbook of Asian aging* (pp. 1–22). Amityville, NY: Baywood.

Hickley, M. (2007). White Britons will be a minority in a dozen towns within 30 years. *MailOnline*, 24 December 2007. Available at: www/dailmail.co.uk/news/article-504354/ White-Britons-minority-dozen-towns-30-years.html?

Holtzman, R. A. (1997). *A world bank perspective on pension reform*. Paper prepared for the joint ILO-OECD Workshop on the Development and Reform of Pension Schemes, Paris, December.

Hope, C. (2007). U.K. cities to have white minorities 'in 30 years'. Telegraph.co.uk, 17 September 2007. Available at: haatp://www.telegraph.co.uk/news/uknews/1563191/ UK-cities-to-have-white-minorities-'in-30-years'.html

Huber, E., & Stephens, J. D. (2000). The political economy of pension reform: Latin American in comparative perspective. United Nations Research Institute for Social Development. Available at http://www.unrisd.org/80256B3C005BCCF9/(httpPublications)/

International Monetary Fund. (2006). The economics of demographics. *Finance and Development, 43*(3). Available at: http://www.imf.org/external/pubs/ft/fandd/2006/09/

Kaneda, T. (2008). *A critical window for policymaking on population aging in developing countries*. Washington, DC: Population Reference Bureau. Available at: http://www. prb.org/Articles/2006/ACriticalWindowforPolicymakingonPopulationinDeveloping Coun...

Kim, S., & Lee, J-W. (2007). Demographic changes, saving and current account in East Asia. *Asian Economic Papers, 6*(2) p. 55.

Krug, E. G. (2002). *World report on violence and health*. Geneva: World Health Organisation.

Leicester City Council. (2001). *Area profile for the city of Leicester: Demographic and cultural.* Available at: http://www.leicester.gov.uky/index.asp?pgid = 1009

Longino, C. F. (1994). Pressure from our aging population will broaden our understanding of medicine. *Academic Medicine, 72,* 841–847.

Manton K. G., & Gu, X. (2001). Changes in the prevalence of chronic disability in the United States black and nonblack population above age 65 from 1982 to 1999. *Proceedings of the National Academy of Sciences, 98,* 6354–6359.

Mather, M. (2007). *The new generation gap.* Washington, DC: Population Reference Bureau. Available at: http://www.prb.org/Articles/2007/NewGenerationGap.aspx?p = 1

Organisation for Economic Cooperation and Development (OECD) Directorate for Employment, Labour and Social Affairs. (2007). *Disability trends among elderly people: Re-assessing the evidence in 12 OECD countries* (Interim Report). Paris, France: OECD.

Phillipson, C. (1998). *Reconstructing old age.* London: Sage.

Population Reference Bureau. (2007) World Population Highlights. *Population Bulletin, 62,* No. (3).

Powell, J. L. (2005). *Social theory and aging.* Lanham, UK: Rowman and Littlefield.

Ritzer, G.(2007). *The McDonaldization of society* (5th ed.). Stage: New York.

Rofman, R., & Lucchetti, L. (2007). *Pension systems in Latin America: Concepts and measurements of coverage.* World Bank, Social Protection Discussion Paper No. 0616. Washington, DC: World Bank.

Sanchez, M. (2008). With aging comes hardship in Latin America. *Washingtonpost.com,* Friday July 25, 2008.

Social Security Administration. (2008). *Social security programs throughout the world: The Americas, 2007.* SSA Publication No. 13-11804. Washington, DC: Author.

United Nations Department of Economic and Social Affairs Population Division. (2002). *World population ageing 1950–2050.* New York: Author.

United Nations Department of Economic and Social Affairs Population Division. (2007). *World population ageing 2007.* New York: Author.

United Nations Population Division. (2005). *World population prospects: The 2004 revision.* New York: Author.

University of California at Santa Cruz (no date). Cause of Death. *UC Atlas of Global Inequality.* Available at http://ucatlas.ucsc.edu/health/causeprint.html

Walker, A., & Naeghele, G (2000). *The politics of ageing in Europe.* Milton Keynes: Open University Press

World Health Organization. (2007). The top 10 causes of death. *Fact Sheet No. 310* March 2007. Available at: www.who.into/mediacentre/factsheets/fs310/en/print.html

Chapter 9
On the Road to Welfare Markets: Institutional, Organizational, and Cultural Dynamics of a New European Welfare State Settlement

Ingo Bode

Introduction

Accounts of the development of welfare states in what is widely referred to as the post-industrial era often place an emphasis on changes in the needs of the citizenry, in the character of social risks, or in the administrative foundations (e.g., the resourcing) of public welfare provision, with all this laying the ground for, or materializing in, 'new politics' (see Pierson 2001 or Armingeon & Bonoli 2006). Granted, given a shrinking role of 'true' industrial work in advanced Western societies, a marked growth of female employment alongside novel ways of ensuring social reproduction, and, not least, the intensification of information- and science-based economic agency, many typical features of the postwar settlement have disappeared. Yet major classical social divisions persist or even grow; moreover, there is an intriguing resemblance between past patterns of social deprivation and those affecting, inter alia, senior citizens, the working poor, or lone mothers today; and, concerning the political economy of capitalism, different modes of resourcing welfare provision (taxes versus social security contributions) have, after all, exhibited a limited impact on how welfare regimes evolve. Hence the scope of the aforementioned changes appears at times overstated in the analysis of what actually happens to Western welfare states (on this, see Bode 2008a).

By the same token, looking at developments in the post-industrial era, much less attention has been awarded to the far-reaching transformation of the *institutional, organizational, and cultural infrastructure* social welfare provision is based on, including the material consequences of this transformation. In particular, major Western societies have seen, over the last two or three decades, paradigmatic change in how the respective roles of the market and of nonmarket spheres are understood and related to one another. While the market economy appears to conquer ever wider parts of the globe, its social regulation is no longer concentrated on nonmarket forces. Rather, the combination of

I. Bode (✉)
Institute for social policy and the organisation of social services,
Department of Social Work, University of Kassel, Germany
e-mail: ibode@uni-wuppertal.de

J. Powell, J. Hendricks, *The Welfare State in Post-Industrial Society*,
DOI 10.1007/978-1-4419-0066-1_9, © Springer Science+Business Media, LLC 2009

'market means and welfare ends' (Taylor-Gooby et al., 2004) has been discovered as a new approach to the provision of social support and income replacement, with the market agenda also affecting the organizational settlement by which social policies are implemented. Welfare states, then, are ever less welfare *states*. Rather, they create and develop welfare *markets*, that is, social welfare provision operated by market actors.

Concerning Western Europe, scholars rooted in the academic community of social policy analysis have, if sporadically, undertaken a reflection on this phenomenon (Lai 1994, Wistow et al. 1996, Taylor-Gooby 1999, Dean et al. 2000, Hyde & Dixon 2001, Means et al. 2002, Powell 2003, Beresford 2005). While this has brought valuable insights in the properties of welfare markets, the available body of work refers to dispersed fields and themes so that the theory of welfare markets is still in its infancy. Widely glossing over national particularities, this article first provides a brief review of what can be deemed elements of a society-centered middle-range theory of welfare markets. Referring to Western Europe mainly, it discusses institutional varieties of welfare markets and organizational landscapes taking shape with their proliferation; subsequently, some evidence on the impact of welfare markets is sketched. Finally, it presents findings from a comparative assessment of what is coined here the *cultural* embeddedness of welfare markets, critical to the very societal dynamics occurring with the rise of these markets.

Social Welfare Going Market

It is commonsense knowledge that, within the post-industrial (mainstream) economy, market-based forms of social coordination have been soaring worldwide. From the perspective of political sociology, however, it is important to see that, concurrently, the overall *infrastructure* embedding capitalist economies has been subject to marketization as well (see Slater & Tonkiss 2001; Smart 2003; Miller 2005). This affects the very institutional framework in which the market economy itself is embedded. Thus, the market rationale, always endemic to the economic system of Western European nations, has now spilled over to genuinely *nonmarket* spheres, including those regulated by social policies.

Indeed, the postwar settlement exhibited a (far) clear(er) separation between the mainstream economy and social politics. A key objective of the latter was the *control of basic social risks* arising from the market interplay, or from problems of human existence, the market appeared unable to cope with on its own. These risks embraced work incapacity or a sharp drop in personal income. Welfare state institutions were addressing *basic human needs*, which were not, or were insufficiently, satisfied by the mere market mechanism. Decent housing, good health, and basic provision of commodities were meant to be guaranteed by society independently of the capricious dynamics of (labor) markets. Moreover, to an extent depending on the prevailing welfare state regime, the typically uneven outcomes of market interaction were expected to be smoothed out interpersonally through various *mechanisms of social redistribution*, with the (para-)fiscal system being a prime lever.

All this was ensured by *comprehensive implementation machineries* based on law and hierarchical coordination. There was a legal codification of social welfare provision that often, if implicitly and incoherently, drew on the concept of social citizenship (Bode 2008a). Moreover, the various European jurisdictions contained (more or less) clear-cut procedures to *directly implement* public programs. Even in more liberal countries (Slater & Tonkiss 2001: 132–139), a 'welfare consensus' existed, which made the state setting limits to the market to secure the social well-being of the citizens in need.

Nowadays, the infrastructural embeddedness of markets has by itself become subject to marketization, stimulated by the 'idea that regulation, where absolutely unavoidable, should be "market-like"' (Kuttner 1998: 36). While the institutions of the welfare state were for long being viewed as 'the most prominent of those instruments aiming at "embedding" ... the market mechanism' (Leitner & Lessenich 2003, 327–328), this mechanism is now inherent to the embedding infrastructure itself. The overall movement is linked to the reform agenda known under the label of *New Public Management* (Pollitt 2007), which has profoundly affected the implementation machinery of the welfare state. It has promulgated numeric standards of performance and increased competition, with the wider objectives being: improving cost-efficiency, introducing 'customer orientation,' and ensuring higher transparency and accountability. In fields as varied as child care, higher education, or job training, the reform agenda has led to innovations such as purchaser-provider splits, contracting out, interagency rivalry, public-private partnerships, and business reengineering within public or nonprofit agencies (see Bönker & Wollmann 2000; Gilbert 2002; Ascoli and Ranci 2002; Clarke et al. 2007).

However, it would be erroneous to contend that, in the new marketized welfare state, 'everything is for sale' (Kuttner 1998). First of all, it is obvious that contemporary Western societies continue to include 'islands of respite from marketisation' (ibid: 56). Evoking the considerable importance of these islands in the day-to-day life of Western citizens, critics indeed warn against a 'myth of marketisation' (Williams 2004), arguing that nonmonetarized work, informal exchange, and civic action are more than ever cornerstones of public life. Second, the implementation of welfare markets has often shown their inherent limitations. In health care, for instance, it has frequently proved difficult to organize competition among a limited number of providers, to guarantee frictionless service provision through volatile contract policies, or to sidestep well-established suppliers holding valuable expertise and skills (Beil-Hildebrand 2002, Powell & Exworthy 2002, Harrison 2004).

Third, deregulation does not mean nonregulation. In fact, the newly emerging markets often appear as 'distorted, managed, and limited' (Slater & Tonkiss 2001: 140). There are tendencies toward the *deliberate control* of competitive public service provision, manifesting itself in the proliferation of quality inspectorates and watchdog bodies. While the bureaucratic agencies emblematic of the 'golden age' of the welfare state appear to be on the retreat, it is, in many instances, new quangos rather than full-fledged businesses that have taken their place (Talbot 2004). And where private firms have become entrusted with service provision, they often comply with 'quasi-market' regulation imposing binding standards on their organizational practice.

This is why many view quasi-market mechanisms as mere means to improve the efficiency and/or the quality of public service provision without generating effects counteracting the wider objectives of the welfare state as we have known it. Proponents of this governance model argue that welfare markets simply enhance the well-being of citizens through procedural perfection (Le Grand 2007). They are assumed to ensure a better match between the welfare state and major societal transformations and meant 'to transform the spend shift culture of the old-style buro-political regime into a leaner, meaner managerial system' (Jordan 2004: 86). Below some of these promises are reviewed against the available evidence.

However, from a sociological perspective, the chief question is as to whether processes of marketization, as fuzzy and limited they may appear, bring about pathbreaking changes in the way social welfare is conceptualized and organized, including with respect to social citizenship. The remainder of this chapter therefore focuses on the very societal dynamics triggered by the introduction of welfare markets, in particular with respect to the new roles of market actors and those involved in the regulation of social welfare provision.

Institutional Varieties of Welfare Markets

Welfare markets can be conceived as competitive spheres in the delivery of social welfare, embracing the allocation and the management of benefits or services designed to improve a person's social situation. Various patterns of marketization (co)exist in the field of social welfare provision. First of all, marketization occurs where public spending is cut or capped, as welfare recipients subsequently rely to a higher degree on income or services available on the mere (labor) market. This is mostly referred to as privatization although this notion embraces further phenomena (see, e.g., Spulber 1997: 76–93; Walker 2001). However, privatization per se is not amenable to the rise of *welfare* markets since, as such, it may simply stand for a dislocation of the production of personal well-being, that is, a move from the collectivity to the individual. Private (co-)payments in health care, the individual employment of personal assistants (at home), or the purchase of private insurance may indeed take place without any institutional regulation.

A second pattern of marketization is salient where such regulation exists, albeit without any deliberate mechanism to promote the social well-being of particular groups of individuals. This is the case where welfare states, possibly after having provided (more) inclusive social insurance schemes in the past, grant tangible advantages to citizens taking steps to protect themselves against social risks. In many countries, indeed, enormous fiscal subsidies 'underpin private provision ... either through tax incentives or public subsidies' (Walker 2001: 139). Again, this *by itself* does not make deferred income provision or personal service delivery subject to a full-fledged welfare market.

Rather, the realm of welfare markets begins where *some* purposeful social policy objectives are pursued by means of distinctive regulations. Drawing on this definition, one can perceive a third variety of marketization, which goes along the emergence of true welfare markets, namely, the instigation of managed care or quasi-markets for the delivery of social services. This is a field addressed by the bulk of the literature dealing with the marketization of welfare, including under the headline of 'social markets' (Le Grand and Bartlett 1993; Wistow et al. 1996; Taylor-Gooby 1999; Brandsen 2004). Arrangements falling into this category may be labeled *managed welfare markets*.

In these markets, public bodies or quangos operate as key players but devolve the delivery of services upon independent providers, including from the nonprofit sector. They are prompted to operate as (quasi-)businesses seeking good return on investment, not least through tough human resource policies. Managed welfare markets generally dwell on a purchaser-provider split and often imply public tenders. Usually, they operate through fixed-term contracts with selected service suppliers and are based on different modes of payments (per capita reimbursement, capped block grants, performance-related payment). Frequently, managed-care agencies purchase services from different suppliers to safeguard an encompassing and multitiered provision for one (group of) person(s). This model is particularly widespread in health care (Gooijer 2007).

Quasi-markets often go alongside a growing role left to private firms, replacing in-house services of local authorities or nonprofit providers. In former times, the latter had (more or less) largely been involved in input-based partnerships with public authorities (Katz & Sachße 1996), mostly via arm's length funding, rough accountability requirements and retrospective compensation schemes concerning expenses related to unforeseen contingencies. This awarded service providers leeway to orient their practice to self-identified and spontaneous needs or citizen claims. A widely alleged drawback was limited public control of client responsiveness and cost efficiency. Regardless of whether such concerns were justified, the move to welfare markets has profoundly changed the terms under which the nonprofit sector is involved in social welfare provision (Taylor 2002; Chapman et al. 2008; Bode forthcoming).

Importantly, the establishment of welfare markets entail a decentralization of financial responsibility and a new role set for welfare bureaucracies, which become 'by-distance-managers' of service or policy delivery. Agreements between purchasers and providers are frequently 'one-way contracts,' with the latter being told 'what they are expected to provide in performance terms' (Talbot 2004: 14). Providers are urged to follow predetermined input-output ratios and to struggle for efficiency gains to outperform competing suppliers.

They often have to comply with tight performance standards set by agencies that (spot) purchase on behalf of welfare recipients or of a population of clients.

In many places, indeed, strong rivalry among suppliers has surfaced, including between different types of them. Nonprofit agencies, facing commercial firms as (new) competitors, frequently seek to adopt methods from the for-profit sector with the intention to enhance numeric output efficiency, potentially at the expense of wider objectives, such as political advocacy (see Carmel & Harlock 2008); should the market 'award' traditional aims of the nonprofit sector, such as responsiveness to intangible needs, such as human attention (e.g. by faith-based action) practices may be different, however.

As a matter of principle, quasi-markets involve interagency coordination through both 'competition and regulation' (Brandsen 2004: 18). At least when the objective is to ensure frictionless services, quasi-markets need mechanisms that readjust dynamics not foreseen by the contract to avoid disruptions in service delivery. This is why contract failures may become 'the subject of discussion, negotiation and eventual consensus rather than punitive action' (Talbot 2004: 14) and may be conducive to the building of quasi-networks, rather than quasi-markets (Powell & Exworthy 2002). That said, quasi-markets may also involve a systematic neglect of contingency, as well as providers defecting from formal agreements undercover. This, in turn, may trigger political protest and lead regulators or managing bodies to respecify their contract policies. Thus, the practical use of quasi-markets is prone to create 'its own new political and organisational dynamic, producing more diversification ... and [ever] new regulations' (Smith 2002: 95, see also Clarke 2004: 125).

A further variety to be discussed here is *subsidized welfare markets*. This model may be combined with managed welfare or quasi-markets, yet in essence, it stands on its own. While it has a longer tradition in the field of tax-advantaged saving, it has become a key element of the 'enabling state' agenda originating in the Anglo-Saxon world (Gilbert 2002: 32–44). Based on the idea of making welfare recipients self-conscious customers (Mann 2006), the model applies to both deferred income schemes (insurance plans) and social service systems. Thus, welfare states award monetary advantages enticing citizens to purchase products from an open supplier market (consisting of insurance companies, care providers, job trainers, etc.). Pension systems based on tax-exempted saving schemes resort to this mechanism almost by tradition – although, as noted above, they are residualistic arrangements, since they often do not go beyond granting rough economic incentives. The so-called 'Riester pension' scheme in Germany (see Schmähl 2007) is emblematic of a more interventionist approach, as the state not only pays direct subsidies to holders of private saving plans but also heavily regulates the content of these plans. Further varieties of 'adapting private pensions to public purposes' (Whiteside 2006) exist throughout Western Europe. Granted, market mechanisms remain vital here, as the decision on whether and how to ensure protection against social risks is laid in the hands of the individual 'consumer.' As the supply side is highly differentiated and often opaque, these mechanisms are often framed by norms rooted in social policies.

In fields such as social care or training for jobless citizens, (quasi-)statutory subsidies also adopt the form of a voucher handed over to individuals eligible for public support (Lundsgaard 2006; Hipp & Warner 2008). A widespread variety of this is arrangements known under the label of *direct payments* (Leece & Bornat 2006). Originating in claims of the disability movement and, more generally, of academic middle-class citizens interested in having more discretion over the use of public services, the basic idea behind these arrangements is yielding opportunities for 'buying independence' (Glendinning et al. 2000). Welfare recipients and users of public services are meant to be enabled to make informed decisions on how and when social support is to be provided. In as much as case managers are involved in the process of assessing needs, selecting services, or employing a personal assistant, and to the extent that services or assistants are under public quality inspection, direct payment schemes overlap with managed welfare markets. Direct payments also exist in the form of allowances useable for a list of services, the range and character of which is defined by (quasi-)public bodies. This is, for instance, the case for German long-term care insurance and, implicitly, the French 'personal care allowance' (Morel 2007). Here as well, subsidies are granted for paying providers that compete on a market; yet the services supplied are under tight regulation. Conversely, direct payments may imply a tendency toward (more) spot purchase of services and less quality assurance, especially where underfunding and lack of case management are salient. Given the limited take-up rates internationally, direct payments thus far prove 'a component of, rather than a competitor to . . . [publicly managed] social care systems (Lyon 2005: 241). They may, however, exhibit an inbuilt tendency to crowd out the ultimate public responsibility for good quality and broad coverage.

Importantly, scholars investigating movements of marketization have seen traditional (social) policy takers becoming capricious and fuzzy customers of a new welfare industry. Indeed, subsidized welfare markets appear as a trigger of what has been termed welfare consumerism (Powell & Wahidin 2005: 79; Baldock 2003; Newman & Kuhlmann 2007). Welfare consumerism has a wider societal background (see below), but is certainly pushed by charters or programs like the recently introduced 'choose and book' system in the British National Health Service. This example illustrates that it can also pervade managed welfare markets.

The New Organizational Settlement

Welfare delivery, including its marketized forms, take shape *through organizational action*, hence the need to consider the very agencies which make welfare markets work. Different types of organizations have to be distinguished here. To begin with, there are traditional players, such as government authorities managing social services. These are professional bureaucracies (Mintzberg 1983), composed of a large operational core, a small technostructure and a slim strategic apex. Historically, a complex division of labor developed within the public administration of the modern welfare state. In many countries, social welfare provision was incumbent on local authorities, with this tradition bringing a strong divide between local and central governance. Nowadays, the rise of welfare markets often changes central state agencies into 'market managers' and makes local welfare bureaucracies develop new, and often volatile, organizational routines, including business-like budgeting and competitive contracting. This goes alongside the emergence of novel collective actors, such as watchdogs, quality inspection agencies, or pension protection funds. Thereby, the role set in the public sector is profoundly altered, as evident by the extensive (international) debate on 'multi-level governance' (Bache and Flinders 2004) or the 'dispersed state' (Clarke 2004: 116).

That said, the welfare state has never stood on its own feet alone. Throughout the twentieth century, the management and delivery of social welfare and health care provision was often devolved to specialized agencies, which became a cornerstone of what has more recently been referred to as 'welfare mix' and has been understood by some as a distinctive pattern of the post-industrial age (see Graefe 2004). Indeed, many Western countries set up quasi-independent welfare schemes overseen only 'ex post' by the centralized bureaucracy. These schemes were based on a management involving major stakeholders, such as employer associations, trade unions, or medical pressure groups, which all exerted influence on the schemes' agenda, including in liberal welfare states (Birkinshaw et al. 1990, Giaimo 2002). The organizational practice of many of these agencies was largely shaped by associational self-governance (Anheier & DiMaggio 1990).

Some countries completely left the administration of social welfare provision to such groups or networks formed by them, for example, in the case of mainland European social security schemes. This implied a strong 'nexus between industrial relations and social policy' (Crouch 2000: 103), commonly referred to as corporatism. As the scope of social protection ensured by corporatist agencies is decreasing with the rise of welfare markets, this nexus is now prone to become weaker. However, in some respects, it is revived through new functions awarded to social partners, such as the brokering of defined contribution pension schemes, like in Germany or (more timidly) in France. Welfare markets have provided these actors with new intermediary roles, with the result of both a more managerial approach to the governance of the schemes and the maintenance of some associational accountability.

Similar developments affect organizations involved in the provision of social and health care. While, in some countries, statutory bodies crystallized as lead agencies throughout the twentieth century, other care systems were based on institutionalized partnerships between nonprofit organizations and public bodies. Thus, nonprofit organizations were often operating as coopted partners of the (local) welfare state (Katz & Sachße 1996). They remained accountable to a (more or less) democratic constituency while being bound to consensual agreements with strong public actors. The introduction of welfare markets has created a new situation for many of them. On the one hand, they face an intrusion of commercial competitors into their inherited domains. While expectations concerning loyal cooperation in the local arena persist (for example, within publicly promoted care networks), pressure to bid for public tenders and outperform their likes in a managed competition are proliferating (Ascoli & Ranci 2002; Chapman et al. 2008, for the case of England). Many of the affected organizations have reconceptualized themselves as 'social enterprise' busy on markets for human services and keen to develop unique 'selling points' (Kerlin 2006).

In addition, novel actors take the center stage. First of all, alongside public and nonprofit sector delivery, commercial organizations, shaped by private hierarchical governance and often keen to make profits, become major social policy players. Concerning pension regulation, associations of actuaries, insurance companies, and pension funds now widely set the tune. Financial advisers have become viewed as experts in social security, including on questions relating to state-subsidized retirement schemes. Engaging in advertisements for insurance products or personal services, they structure perceptions about self-care, thrift, and wise choice. They also publicly comment on the future of statutory pillars, for example, by portraying them as insufficient or by arguing that additional fiscal subsidies are needed to make potential plan holders solvent. Liberal welfare regimes are familiar with this; however, only with the crowding-out of public pension schemes, these actors have become full-fledged players in the social policy arena there.

Professionals from the growing private care industry are in a similar, though more contested, position as they participate in the debate as to how to ensure service quality and responsiveness to clients on a competitive market. Providers interested in return on investment may develop some role ambiguity here. While making profits is far from being the only, or driving, motive of professionals in a (more) marketized care sector (Matosevic et al. 2007), things may evolve with what is referred to as 'cartelization' of social care provision (Scourfield 2007).

Moreover, as noted above, the instigation, or extension, of the market-based social welfare provision has gone alongside the establishment of new regulating agencies, or the broadening of the remit of the existing ones. Agencies responsible for inspecting the quality of care or the soundness of pension schemes have come to deploy their proper policies. In many cases, such agencies are also entrusted with registering care providers or certifying saving plans. While these organizations are loosely accountable to the government, their legitimacy is mostly taken for granted. Their remit consists of offering 'independence and control while at the same time marrying the public and private sectors' (Flinders 2004: 892). The establishment of welfare markets then goes alongside the creation of a new type of organizations of which the internal governance rationale often appears as muddled (see Talbot 2004).

Also, organizations concerned with user interests tend to adopt a new role. Traditional interest groups (pensioner groups, charities concerned with issues of old age, associations of welfare recipients) are now led to address citizens in their role of consumers, rather than as a mere object of political claims. Consumer issues are also a point of reference for agencies which are providing ratings of providers operating on welfare markets. While this is fairly widespread in the financial services industry, ratings have also begun to play a role for the evaluation of quality in health and social care provision. In some places, quasi-public inspection agencies publish data on quality outcomes (for hospital and residential care).

Finally, think tanks participate in the shaping of welfare markets. Some scholars have seen the overall extension of market principles in old-age provision as being successfully promoted by a number of highly influential 'messaging' organizations (Béland & Wadden 2000). Concomitantly, there are more social policy-oriented think tanks that advocate more or better market regulation. Concerning the United Kingdom, one should mention the Pension Policy Institute, the Institute for Public Policy Research, or Catalyst. In France, the role of providing 'biased' expertise is mostly taken by scientific institutions, even though small industry-sponsored think tanks exist in the pension field. The same holds for Germany where a powerful think tank (the Bertelsmann Foundation), adopting arguments from the financial industry, proved a key player during the introduction of a private pension pillar. Overall, the role of think tanks is assumed to be growing since welfare state administrations and regulators increasingly draw on nongovernmental experts or consultants (James 2004).

The Impact of Welfare Markets

A systematic review of findings on the material impact of welfare markets would require a lengthy investigation on what has happened in several social policy domains over the last 20 years. Such evaluation is not available thus far (Beresford 2005) and cannot be provided here either. In general, *social* outcomes of marketization are tricky to measure, but there are also problems in checking its impact on cost-efficiency given, for instance, the existing cost-shunting mechanisms (Powell & Exworthy 2002). Some basic observations can be made, though.

One major issue referred to by the wider literature is transaction costs related to the governance of welfare markets. These are often viewed as outweighing efficiency gains. Evidence suggests that subsidized welfare markets, unless classical social policy aims are taken from the welfare state's agenda, need recurrent monitoring and regulatory intervention as these markets constantly create incentives to exploit information advantages held by those who control the production process. Health care is a field where such concerns have been discussed most thoroughly (Marini & Street 2007).

Investigating the case of educational services provided to the unemployed, Hipp and Warner (2008) have argued that the creation of voucher systems meant to make jobseekers choose appropriate service providers has entailed

problems in market formation. They and others also point to profound information asymmetries affecting both market inspectors and customers, as quality
monitoring proves tricky in social and health care, for instance. Moreover, price
dumping policies reduce the range of available providers. As to the impact on
the organizations involved in welfare markets, doubts have been raised concerning the willingness and capability of nonprofit agencies to cope with the
new contracting agenda (McLaughlin 2004, Chapman et al. 2008). Thus, welfare markets may be, and often have already been, amenable to the growth of
the commercial sector. In addition, these markets produce both winners and
losers among providers, with the destruction of capital (knowledge, facility
investment, etc.) as an inevitable consequence.

Assessments of the social impact of market-oriented welfare reform suggest
that the recourse to market mechanisms in the incentive system of welfare
providing agencies may disadvantage citizens with limited 'marketability.'
This seems to be the case with publicly subsidized pension plans (Mann 2006,
Schmähl 2007) and also with social support (or activation) provided to marginalized citizens, as delivery under competitive pressure may impede providers
from fostering those most difficult to work with (van Berkel & van der Aa 2005;
Bredgaard & Larsen 2008). A much discussed issue is organizations creaming
off 'easy-to-care' clients; (profit-seeking) suppliers, if paid on a capitation basis,
benefit from providing services to those on which they expect to spend relatively
few resources. True, proponents of quasi-markets have anticipated such tendencies, yet they were quite optimistic as to the efficacy of control mechanisms
through which they can be avoided (Le Grand & Bartlett 1993).

As to the 'consumer agenda' linked to welfare markets, the evidence is
inconsistent. On the one hand, direct payments to the disabled have been
found to improve the well-being of those empowered to purchase services on
a free provider market (Leece & Bornat 2006). On the other hand, the 'choice
agenda' has often not altered the range of options available to mainstream
social and health care users (Perri6 2003; Beresford 2005, Clarke et al. 2007). All
this may explain why Brandsen (2004: 19), summarizing the international
experience with quasi-markets, deplores a 'loss of equity in provision' and an
'increase in social segregation,' that is, developments pertaining to the issue of
social equality.

Culture Matters

If, notwithstanding the drawbacks mapped in the precedent section, welfare
markets have remained unchallenged internationally, this may be due to *cultural
factors*. Leichsenring (2004: 13) has argued that, in the recent past, 'public services
and social services in particular could catch-up in their professional and societal
image only by taking on board the "professional approaches" coming from ...
business-based concepts.' Moreover, it appears that contemporary belief systems

of those in the driving seat of the welfare state as well as of wider sections of the (more individualistic) middle classes accommodate the establishment of welfare markets. These belief systems, however, sit uneasy with the ideological foundations of social modernity, and the question arises as to how far this has an impact on the public sensemaking around welfare markets.

An extensive press review the author of this chapter has conducted on the issue of old age provision in the United Kingdom, France, and Germany (Bode 2008b) sheds light on the ambiguity inherent in the new cultural settlement. The study was based on a collection of articles published by quality newspapers, ranging from 2001 to 2006. Using qualitative content analysis, it focused on utterances from collective stakeholders, such as care and pension industry, trade unions, public interest groups, and journalists (assumed to provide a synthesis of the debate). Basically it brought to the fore that, across European nations, traditional patterns of collective sensemaking coexist nervously with novel, more or less neoliberal, readings.

The novel readings emphasize values such as cleverness, consumer autonomy, individual responsibility, and (cost-) efficiency. However, in the eyes of those defending these ideologies, the performance of the latter is mostly premised on conditions which set limits to the reach of market governance. For instance, both resolute statutory inspection of the activities of independent welfare providers and (publicly organized) financial education are viewed as a 'must' for welfare markets to work properly. In addition, references stemming from the postwar settlement continue to be evoked at many instances and permanently challenge the novel readings even in liberal welfare regimes. Thus, debate about pension and care reforms in Britain has revived sensemaking processes typical of the postwar settlement, with a strong emphasis on values, such as social deservedness and human dignity, deemed to entitle citizens to decent care and income security in later life.

On the whole, the collective sensemaking around welfare markets reflects a fuzzy and uneasy compromise between the new and the traditional (modern) ideologies. Social rights to pension and care provision are still an issue, yet the public pledge for them is becoming less authoritative even as the actual level (or quality) of benefits and services is widely accepted to become *flexible* – that is, less reliable. Moreover, while human dignity is awarded great attention, concerning, for instance, ill-treatment in elderly care, a strong emphasis is now placed on '*consumer dignity*,' that is, rights to equal opportunity and fair information in the face of a competitive supply structure.

Statutory enactment of the social welfare provision is still in demand, yet the role of the state is permanently challenged by pleas for greater individual responsibility. Here, the fuzzy compromise says that public bodies, apart from providing basic provision, should concentrate on *context steering*, rather than direct intervention. Public agency, then, is widely accepted to become less imperative. Finally, there is a new understanding of what is to be seen as sound management of welfare provision. It is now '*best value*' arrangements that are viewed as a satisfying and working approach to the management of welfare provision. They are deemed to ensure measurable outcomes beyond mere (average-) cost-efficiency – for instance, through service frameworks imposed on private providers or through limits set to the tradability of retirement plans in the equity market. However, there is no longer a symbolic priority on *guaranteeing* a given outcome by (re)adjusting budgets or regulations to emerging needs.

Conclusion

Assessing the impact of welfare markets requires the analysis not only of social outcomes, as delicate as this may appear, but also of the very institutional, organizational, and cultural dynamics accompanying their implementation. Only the consideration of both the structural dynamics triggered by choice, competition, and commercial practice and the framing of the 'market play' – through the agency of bureaucracies, civil-society-based initiatives, and commercial actors, on the one hand, and through the cognitive frames proliferating in the public sphere, on the other – will provide us with deeper insights into the distinctive evolutionary forces to which social welfare provision is exposed in the age of marketization.

As things stand now, welfare markets appear as an *uneasy and open configuration*, with high outcome volatility and constant pressure to readjust the 'rules of the game.' Concerning what can be referred to as post-industrial welfare regimes, this has at least three implications: first, while publicly regulated and sophisticated patterns of the social welfare provision do persist in the 'marketized' post-industrial settlement, these patterns conform less systematically to the model which has (as a tendency) informed major social policies throughout the postwar decades. Basic rights to social welfare provision, though still prominent in many policy fields (take the example of child care), become more *implicit* simply because, concerning the realization of these rights, much is now left to the market game. In this sense, we witness a shift in the nature of social citizenship. That said, welfare markets – secondly – do not lend themselves to become a consistent reform model, as they follow disparate orientations and can barely be an end in itself. Rather, they function, and are widely perceived, as a pragmatic policy vehicle travelling on unknown roads, with a route-finder regulators tend to constantly recode; third, since present day cultures of the welfare market(s) are anything but well-entrenched and since these cultures appear to provoke permanent re-regulation, they are prone to changes like chameleons, depending on fads and fashions, on windows of opportunities available to a large (and growing) range of stakeholders, as well as on recurrent pressure from those torn between values such as individual freedom and individual choice, on the one hand, and social security and human dignity, on the other. Western European welfare states thus enter a stage of permanent reconfiguration and conceptual ambiguity. In this precise sense, the 'anything goes' narrative of postmodern accounts of the post-industrial society contains a kernel of truth.

References

Armingeon, K., & Bonoli, G. (Eds.). (2006). *The politics of post-industrial welfare states.* London: Routledge.

Anheier, H. K., & DiMaggio, P. (1990). "A sociological conceptualization of the nonprofit organizations and sectors". *Annual Review of Sociology, 16,* 137–159.

Ascoli, U., & Ranci, C. (Eds.). (2002). Dilemmas of the welfare mix: The new structure of welfare in an Era of privatization. New York: Kluwer Academic / Plenum Publishers.

Bache, I., & Flinders, M. (Eds.). (2004). Multi-level Governance. Oxford: Oxford University Press.

Baldock, J. (2003). "On being a welfare consumer in a consuming society." *Social Policy & Society, 2*(1), 65–71.

Beil-Hildebrand, M. (2002). "Going to market: The german health care reform experience." *Policy, Politics & Nursing Practice, 3*(4), 313–324.

Béland, D., & Waddan, A. (2000). "From Thatcher (and Pinochet) to Clinton? Conservative think tanks, foreign models and US pension reform". *The Political Quarterly, 71*(2), 202–210.

Beresford, P. (2005). "Redistributing profit and loss: The new economics of the market and social welfare." *Critical Social Policy, 25*(4), 464–482.

Birkinshaw, P., Harden, I. et al. (1990). *Government By Moonlight: The hybrid parts of the state.* London: Unwin Hyman.

Bode, I. (2008a). Social citizenship in post-liberal Britain and post-corporatist Germany – curtailed, fragmented, streamlined, but still on the agenda. In: K. Clarke, T. Maltby, & P. Kennett (Eds.), *Social policy review 20.* Bristol: Policy Press.

Bode, I. (2008b). The Culture of welfare markets. The international recasting of pension and care systems. New York/London: Routledge

Bode, I. (forthcoming). Creeping marketization and post-corporatist governance: The transformation of state-nonprofit relations in continental Europe. In: S. Phillips & S. R. Smith (Eds.), *Governance and regulation in the third sector.* London: Routledge

Bönker, F., & Wollmann, H. (2000). The rise and fall of a social service regime: Marketisation of German social services in historical perspective. In: H. Wollmann, and E. Schroeter (Eds.), *Comparing public sector reform in Britain and Germany.* Aldershot: Ashgate.

Brandsen, T. (2004). *Quasi-market governance: An anatomy of innovation.* Utrecht: Lemma Publishers.

Bredgaard, T., & Larsen, F. (2008). "Quasi-markets in employment policy: Do they deliver on promise?" *Social Policy & Society, 7*(3), 341–352.

Carmel, E., & Harlock, J. (2008). "Instituting the 'Third Sector' as a governable terrain: Partnership, procurement and performance in the UK. *Policy & Politics, 36*(2), 155–171.

Chapman, T., Brown, J., & Crow, R. (2008). "Entering a brave new world? An assessment of third sector readiness to tender for the delivery of public services in the United Kingdom." *Policy Studies, 29*(1), 1–17.

Clarke, J. (2004). *Changing welfare, changing states: New directions in social policy.* London: Sage.

Clarke, J., Newman, J., Smith, N., Vidler, E., & Westmarland, L. (2007). *Creating citizen-consumers: changing publics and changing public services.* London: Sage.

Crouch, C. (2000). Employment, industrial relations and social policy. In: N. Manning, & I. Shaw (Eds.). *New risks, new welfare. Signposts for social policy.* Oxford: Blackwell.

Dean, J., Goodlad, R., & Rosengaard, A. (2000). "Citizenship in the new welfare market: The purposes of housing advice services." *Journal of Social Policy, 29*(2), 229–245.

Flinders, M. (2004). "Distributed public governance in Britain." *Public Administration, 82*(4), 883–909.

Giaimo, S. (2002). *Markets and medecine: The politics of health care reform in Britain, Germany and the United States.* Ann Habor: University of Michigan Press.

Gilbert, N. (2002). *Transformation of the welfare state: The silent surrender of public responsibility*. Oxford: Oxford University Press.

Glendinning, C., Halliwell, S. et al. (2000). *Buying independence: Using direct payments to integrate health and social services*. Bristol: Policy Press.

Gooijer, W. de (2007). *Trends in EU health care systems*. Berlin/New York, Springer.

Graefe, P. (2004). "Personal Services in the Post-industrial Economy. Adding Nonprofits to the Welfare Mix." *Social Policy & Administration, 38*(5), 456–469.

Harrison, M. D. (2004). *Implementing change in health systems: Market reforms in health systems in the United Kingdom, Sweden and The Netherlands*. London: Sage.

Hipp, L., & Warner, M. E. (2008). "Market Forces for the Unemployed? Training Vouchers in Germany and in the USA." *Social Policy & Administration, 42*(1), 77–101.

Hyde, M., & Dixon, J. (2001). Welfare ideology, the market and social security: Toward a typology of market-oriented reform. In. id (Ed.), *The marketisation of social security*, Westport (Conn.)/London, Quorum Books.

James, O. (2004). Executive agencies and joined-up government in the UK. In C. Pollitt, & C. Talbot (Eds.), *Unbundled government: A critical analysis of the global trend to agencies, quangos and contractualisation*. London: Routledge.

Jordan, B. (2004). Personal social services. In: N. Ellison, L. Bauld, & M. Powell (Eds.), *Social Policy Review 16*. Bristol, Policy Press.

Katz, M. B., & Sachße, C. (Eds.). (1996). *The mixed economy of social welfare: Public/private relations in England, Germany and the United States*. Baden-Baden: Nomos.

Kerlin, J. A. (2006). "Social enterprise in the United States and Europe: Understanding and learning from the differences." *Voluntas, 17*(3), 247–263.

Kuttner, R. (1998). *Everything for sale: The virtues and the limits of markets*. New York: Alfred A. Knopf.

Lai, O.-K. (1994). "Farewell to welfare statism! more happiness in welfare market? Putting consumption in (Post) modern context." *International Journal of Social Economics, 21*(1), 43–54.

Le Grand, J. (2007). *The other unvisible hand: Delivering public services through choice and competition*. Princeton, Princeton University Press.

Le Grand, J., & Bartlett, W. (1993). The Theory of Quasi-Markets. In: id. (Ed.), *Quasi-Markets and Social Policy*. London: Macmillan.

Leece, J., & Bornat, J. (Eds.). 2006. Developments in direct payments. Bristol: Policy Press.

Leichsenring, K. (2004). Providing integrated health and social care for older persons – A European overview. In: Id (Ed.), *Providing integrated health and social care for older persons. An European overview of issues at Stake*. Aldershot: Ashgate.

Leitner, S., & Lessenich, S. (2003). "Assessing Welfare State Change: The German Social Insurance State between Reciprocity and Solidarity." *Journal of Public Policy, 23*(3), 325–347.

Lundsgaard, J. (2006). "Choice and long-term care in OECD countries: Care outcomes, employment and fiscal sustainability." *European Societies, 8*(3), 361–383.

Lyon, A. (2005). "A systems approach to direct payments: A response to 'Friend or foe? Towards a critical assessment of direct payments." *Critical Social Policy, 25*(2), 240–252.

Mann, K. (2006). "Three steps to heaven? Tensions in the management of welfare: Retirement pensions and active consumers." *Journal of Social Policy, 35*(1), 77–96.

Marini, G., & Street, A. (2007). "A transaction cost analysis of changing contractual relations in the English NHS". *Health Policy, 83*(1), 17–26.

Matosevic, T., M. Knapp, J. Kendall, C. Henderson, & J.-L. Fernandez (2007). "Care-home providers as professionals: Understanding the motivations of care-home providers in England". *Ageing & Society, 27*, 103–126.

McLaughlin, K. (2004). "Towards a 'Modernized' voluntary and community sector?" *Public Management Review, 4*(6), 555–562.

Means, R., R. Smith & H. Morbey (2002). *From community care to market care? The development of welfare services for older people.* Bristol, Policy Press.

Miller, M., (Ed.). (2005). *Worlds of capitalism – Social institutions, governance, and economic change in the Era of Globalization.* London/New York: Routledge.

Mintzberg, H. (1983). *Structures in fives: Designing effective organisations.* Englewood Cliffs, N.J.: Prentcie Hall.

Morel, N. (2007). "From Subsidiartiy to 'Free Choice': Child- and Elder-care policy reforms in France, Belgium, Germany and the Netherlands." *Social Policy & Administration, 41*(6), 618–637.

Newman, J. & Kuhlmann, E. (2007). "Consumers enter the political stage? The modernization of health care in Britain and Germany." *Journal of European Social Policy, 17*(2), 99–111.

Perri6 (2003). "Giving consumer of British Public Services more choice: What can be learned from recent history?" *Journal of Social Policy, 32*(2), 239–270.

Pierson, P. (2001). "Post-industrial pressures on the mature welfare states". In: id (Ed.), *The new politics of the welfare state.* Oxford: Oxford University Press

Pollitt, C. (2007). Convergence or divergence? What has been Happening in Europe? In: id, S. Van Thiel, & V. Homburg (Eds.), *New public management in Europe.* Adaptation and Alternatives, Basingstoke: Palgrave Macmillan.

Powell, J. L., & Wahidin, A. (2005). "Ageing in the 'Risk Society." *International Journal of Sociology and Social Policy, 25*(8), 70–83.

Powell, M. (2003). "Quasi-markets in British health policy: A longue durée perspective." *Journal of Social Policy, 37*(7), 725–741.

Powell, M., & Exworthy, M. (2002). Partnerships, Quasi-networks and Social policy. In: C. Glendinning, P. Martin, & K. Rummery (Eds.), *Partnerships, New Labour and The Governance of Welfare.* Bristol: Polity Press.

Rathgeb Smith, S. (2002). Privatization, devolution, and the welfare state: Rethinking the prevailing wisdom. In B. Rothstein & S. Steinmo (Eds.), *Restructuring the welfare state: political institutions and political change.* New York/Houndmills Basingstoke: Palgrave Macmillan.

Schmähl, W. (2007). "Dismantling an earnings-related social pension scheme: Germany's new pension policies." *Journal of Social Policy, 36*(2), 319–340.

Scourfield, P. (2007). "Are there reasons to be worried about the 'Cartelization' of residential care?" *Critical Social Policy, 27*(2), 155–180.

Slater, D., & Tonkiss, F. (2001). *Market society: Markets and modern social theory.* Cambridge: Polity Press.

Smart, B. (2003). *Economy, culture and society: A sociological critique of Neo-liberalism.* Buckingham: Open University Press.

Spulber, N. (1997). *Redefining the state: Privatisation and welfare reform in industrial and transitional economies.* Cambridge: Cambridge University Press.

Talbot, C. (2004). The Agency Idea. Some times old, sometimes new, sometimes borrowed, sometimes untrue. In C. Pollitt, & C. Talbot (Eds.), *Unbundled Government: A critical analysis of the global trend to agencies, quangos and contractualisation.* London: Routledge.

Taylor, M. (2002). Government, the third sector and the contract culture: UK experience so far. In U. Ascoli, & C. Ranci (Eds.), *Dilemmas of the welfare mix: The new structure of welfare in an era of privatization.* New York etc.: Kluwer / Plenum.

Taylor-Gooby, P. (1999). "Markets and motives: Trust and egoism in welfare markets." *Journal of Social Policy, 28*(1), 97–114.

Taylor-Gooby, P., Larsen, T., & Kananen, J. (2004). "Market means and welfare ends: The UK welfare state experiment." *Journal of Social Policy, 33*(4), 573–592.

van Berkel, R. & van der Aa, P. (2005). "The marketisation of activation services: A modern panacea? Some lessons from the Dutch experience." *Journal of European Social Policy, 15*(4), 329–343.

Walker, C. (2001). The Forms of privatization of social security in Britain. In: J. Dixon, & M. Hyde (Eds.), *The Marketisation of Social Security*. Westport (Conn)./London: Quorum Books.

Whiteside, N. (2006). "Adapting private pensions to public purposes: Historical perspectives on the politics of reform." *Journal of European Social Policy*, *16*(1), 43–54.

Williams, C. C. (2004). "The myth of marketisation: An evaluation of the persistence of non-market activities in advanced economies." *International Sociology*, *19*: 437–449.

Wistow, G., Knapp, M., et al (1996). *Social care markets: Progress and prospects*. Buckingham: Open University Press.

Part II
Social Welfare in Post-industrial Societies: International Comparisons

Chapter 10
A Nordic Welfare State in Post-industrial Society

Jorma Sipilä, Anneli Anttonen, and Teppo Kröger

Introduction

Transition from industrial to post-industrial societies has fundamentally challenged social policy arrangements of Western welfare states. The concept of welfare state offers broader social protection, growing consumption, family wages, strong labor unions, better public services, and a state apparatus that was able to control the national economy. To use the slogan introduced by Berman (1982) a post-industrial society refers to a social landscape where 'all that is solid melts into air.' In particular, the state is no more able (or willing) to protect citizens against new social risks. In this article, our aim is to study the transition to post-industrial societies by paying attention to the globalization of the economy and the aging of the population. Due to deep ongoing social and economic changes, it has become increasingly difficult to maintain a Nordic welfare state model based on the principle of universalism.

The effects of globalization on the development of welfare state are unclear. We do not yet know the specific extent to which globalization will alter socio-political systems and indeed change the course of the entire welfare state models. We might even imagine that globalization could actually unify various welfare models, which would bring them closer together, as opposed to coming between them. It could, however, do exactly the opposite, as globalization could well have significantly different effects in, for example, Europe and Asia. In this article, we examine the relationship between the Nordic welfare state model and some of the changing conditions caused by globalization, focusing specifically on the Finnish perspective. The emphasis of our study is on the provision of social services.

The Nordic welfare state model would never have evolved without a strong state and the trust created by the development of a state democracy. As international market forces were tightening their grip on nation-states and leading them toward what appeared to be permanent financial and economic crises, the

J. Sipilä (✉)
Department of Social Work Research, University of Tampere (until July 31, 2009);
Institute for social research, University of Tampere, Tampere,
Finland (from August 1, 2009)
e-mail: jorma.sipila@uta.fi

J. Powell, J. Hendricks, *The Welfare State in Post-Industrial Society*,
DOI 10.1007/978-1-4419-0066-1_10, © Springer Science+Business Media, LLC 2009

general consensus was that large welfare state models, based on a system of public funding, simply had no future. A number of analyses were carried out in the 1990s in which the Nordic welfare states appeared to be the clearest victims of globalization (see, e.g., Lindbeck 1997).

Today, assessments like these have become outdated. The Nordic countries have thrived in the face of increasing globalization, and the Nordic welfare state model has experienced a revival in international forums and discussions. Finland is somewhat an exception among the Nordic states, and the results of our analysis are not necessarily applicable to our Nordic neighbors. It is, however, precisely because of these differences that an examination of the Finnish case can contribute a significant amount of new information to the theoretical and political discussions surrounding the Nordic welfare model.

Although we will focus mainly on highlighting the differences between the Nordic states and their welfare models, there are also a number of similarities between them. International comparisons (Anttonen et al. 2003; Rostgaard & Fridberg 1998) reveal that the Nordic welfare states have an extremely high level of social service provision compared to most other countries. Accordingly, the Nordic welfare state is not only a 'social insurance state,' but also a 'social service state' or 'caring state' to a great extent (Anttonen 1997).

When describing the Nordic welfare state model, reference is often made to the principle of universalism, which lies behind service provision (Anttonen 2002; Esping-Andersen 1990; Kautto et al. 1999; Kuhnle 2000). Explanations as to why the principle of universalism developed in these countries have focused on social democracy, Protestantism, agrarianism, the strength of women's movements, cultural homogeny, and the generally high level of public support for the state (Anttonen & Sipilä 2000).

Universalism is a multidimensional concept (see, e.g., Sainsbury 1996: 18–19). Its primary reference is to the assurance of the availability of benefits and services to all citizens. Second, it refers to the extension of a virtually uniform set of benefits to citizens all over the country. Third, universalism implies that a majority of citizens actually rely on and use these benefits when in need. Fourth, universalism includes the idea that citizens may have a legal right to benefits. Overall, universalism is difficult to achieve without tax financing.

In the context of the provision of services, universalism refers to both the extension of services to all and the application of universal standards, that is, the assurance that everyone is treated equally and no one receives any kind of special treatment. In this way, universalism refers to both the complete extension of benefits and services (to whom they are extended) and the content of these benefits and services (what is being provided). Universalism is considered strong if everyone is included in the same system and receives the same benefits or services. These benefits are usually determined by social service professionals on the basis of need, i.e. they must establish whether each specific case warrants the extension of the benefit in question. It is also important to remember that in the Nordic countries, the operative responsibility for service provision rests with fairly independent local authorities.

The strongest forms of universalism can be found in school systems, day care systems, and the sphere of the provision of basic social security. In elder care, of all the Nordic countries, only the Danish model can truly be considered universal (Anttonen & Sointu 2006). The Finnish model is an example of weak universalism (Kröger, Anttonen, & Sipilä 2003). As the elderly population is not the most popular target of social investments, the social policies related to the elderly are particularly prone to privatization and informalization. The state has a keen interest in the effective utilization of the financial and human resources of the elderly and those who care for them.

Popular support for universal programs is clearly strong and stable in Nordic societies. Rothstein (2000; see also Kumlin & Rothstein 2003) suggests that this support is based on such values as trust, reciprocity, and solidarity. Universalism as opposed to selectivism in social policy seems to strengthen the sense of trust in a society. However, we can also argue that a general sense of trust is a precondition to the development of universalism in social policy. Thus, universalism and trust are inherently linked.

Over the past two decades or so, many European welfare states have adopted what Pierson (2001) calls the *new politics of the welfare state*. The introduction of new welfare politics has led to retrenchment, rather than the further expansion of social services and benefits (Julkunen 2001). Bonoli et al. (2000) have identified the main reasons for this shift toward retrenchment policies as globalization, the weakening of national (and class) solidarity, and neoliberalism. Some scholars have also highlighted that major reorganization and reorientation has indeed taken place in all Western welfare states (e.g. Goldberg & Rosenthal 2002; Kuhnle 2000).

Eitrheim and Kuhnle (2000: 54) present a thorough evaluation of the changes which have taken place in Nordic social policies over the course of the 1990s. On the one hand, they conclude that the Nordic welfare states are currently less generous than they have been in the past, as various measures have been taken to, among other things, reduce benefit levels, shorten benefit periods, and tighten eligibility rules. On the other hand, they note that universalism is still the leading principle in the Nordic social policy. The following trends can be identified while evaluating the field of the Nordic social service provision: the informalization of care (Rostgaard 2004; Szebehely 2003), the privatization of the management and provision of public care services (Szebehely 2004), and the marketization, companization, and entrepreneurization of service provision (Trydegård 2003). Moreover, the principles of selectivism and means-testing have continued to gain a stronger foothold, particularly in the field of elder care. Conversely, there has been an increase in the universalism of child care services and to some degree services for disabled persons also. Thus, there are clearly a number of trends to be identified.

Impact of Globalization on Welfare Politics

There are many incentives for a state to practice welfare politics. The inherent risks related to wage labor, the efficient use of the labor force, the political struggles facilitated by democracy, and shared cultural values are all constant and ongoing justifications for broad collective activity. During the period of the rise of the nation-state, the main driving force behind these activities slowly began to be the state.

What, then, are the economy-driven European states of today aiming to achieve by practicing welfare politics? The answer to this question can be summarized in the following three themes:

1) The state eases social risks by preventing their occurrence and related socio-economic consequences.
2) The state invests in people (in human and social capital) by supporting and promoting their development and education from birth.
3) The state promotes social unity by preventing marginalization and discrimination.

States use welfare politics as a means of limiting, reforming, investing in and supporting the public, the main aim being the facilitation and maintenance of individuals' ability to be active members of the labor force and productive members of society. The fulfillment of this mandate poses a number of major long-term challenges, which individual actors are not always able or willing to meet. The question now is whether the state is still able to meet them.

Over the past few decades, financial capital and the production of goods have essentially freed up intra- and international constraints. The swift and fluid movement of financial capital tends to avoid countries which impose the heaviest restrictions. Internationally mobile workers are also able to choose both the country and region in which they want to live often wanting to avoid the redistribution of income (see, e.g., Kaufmann 2000). The Nordic countries have recently begun taxing capital income less heavily than earned income in the interest of boosting international capital investments (Ganghof 2005).

Countries which practice welfare politics will also inevitably encounter other problems. Globalization eats away at the very foundation of welfare politics by heightening economic disparity, which thus increases the burden of social equalization, and by decreasing public confidence, which makes finding political solutions increasingly difficult. There are a number of reasons why both citizens' solidarity and their confidence in the state's ability to protect and organize their rights have decreased in recent years. Today, fewer citizens belong to labor organizations or other interest groups which aim at protecting their rights. Today's workers see themselves not only as workers but also as consumers, taxpayers, beneficiaries, and, increasingly often, owners. The income disparity which began to rise sharply in Finland in the 1990s is yet another factor: the rich tend not to rely on the universal benefits provided by the state, seeking security and services elsewhere (Taimio 2007). Immigration also tends to dilute people's confidence in the state as a solidifying and stabilizing force, as many immigrants come from countries in which people feel they can only rely on their families for support.

The main aim of welfare politics is to use political means to intervene in the relationships between citizens and markets. As such, it is clear that the formation of a new kind of relationship between markets and politics has shaken the very foundation of welfare politics. We should not, however, exaggerate the impact or degree of the changes which have taken place thus far. The weakening of the state's hold over the national economy, businesses, and elite members of the labor force has not led to the collapse of welfare politics – nor, for that matter, has the middle-classization of society. Public opinion polls have found that there continues to be an extremely high level of support in the Nordic countries for welfare politics. Democracy is something that tends to be cherished by all, and so far, nothing or no one has managed to challenge the state's role as its producer and protector. There have been no public suggestions as to how order, safety and security, and basic health care could be ensured without the state.

States' social expenditure has remained high, and it is interesting to note that there has not been a decrease in employers' share of financing social expenditure despite significant pressure in this direction.[1] Despite scathing criticism from the economic elite (see, e.g., Mandag Morgen 2007), the Nordic countries with their high tax rates have been extremely successful members of the global competition economy. Scharpf (2000: 405) aptly points out that it is not that states have lost their ability to aim at providing comprehensive welfare, but rather how they go about it must conform to the limitations of international capitalism.

In Front of Globalization: Finland, an Unusual Nordic Welfare State

Researchers tend to view Finland as a Nordic country and a social democratic welfare state. Despite this, the political role of social democracy has not been particularly strong in Finland, with the exception of a short period before WWI (1905–1918). It is to a large extent because of this that Finland's road to becoming a Nordic welfare state has been rocky and the end result has distinguished it from its Nordic neighbors. In this regard, Finland does not at all resemble Sweden, where the effects of social democracy have run much deeper and been much more permanent.

---

[1] Since dropping in the wake of the recession during the 1990s, the state expenditure for the EU25 has remained at 47% of the GDP since 1999. Employer's share of social expenditure in the EU15 is 11% of the GDP, which it also was in 1990 (Eurostat Online310708).

The Finnish Civil War of 1918 stymied both the political influence of the left and the development of social policy until the end of WWII. Even as late as the 1950s, Finland dedicated the least amount of resources to health care and had the highest male mortality rate in Europe. Finland established its national health insurance in 1963, after Burma, Libya, and Nicaragua. It was not until 1970 that Finland finally shed its distinction as the Western country, which dedicated the least amount of financial resources to its social insurance expenditure.

The democratic development which took place in Finland after WWII brought with it the broad popular support for the state that the creation of a welfare state required. The creation of the Finnish welfare state was characterized by the fact that center-left coalition governments were always forced to find compromises that were able to meet the needs of all Finns, whether they were living in a large city or in one of the lower income developing areas, and regardless of whether they worked in agriculture or industry.

An important aspect of Finnish universalism was to meet social policy needs by providing comprehensive benefits to all. To ensure that people were satisfied with the benefits they received, the state often had to create a range of benefits that were tailored to the diverse needs of the population. Centralized public services were not necessarily of much use to a farmer living in the middle of the woods: what he needed was local services and financial support that would allow him to live as an independent farmer. We might say that, influenced by the political center, the Finnish brand of welfare policy has often included an element of pre-industrial self-service. Now, rather surprisingly, the use of these types of independently arranged services seems to be meeting the needs of the post-industrial society in which we live.

The fundamental core of the political point of departure of the Finnish compromise has been the equal and local provision of welfare services. Over 450 municipalities throughout the country have provided Finland's 5 million inhabitants with health care, education, and social services, and the state has given more financial support to the poorest municipalities. The heavy burden of providing comprehensive benefits has been reflected, for example, in the rather low amount of financial assistance available and the often insufficient supply of services (e.g., Kröger & Vuorensyrjä 2008). The most internationally well-known example of the special character of the Finnish brand of universalism is the care policy innovation introduced in the 1980s, according to which parents who do not need or wish to use public day care to look after their young children receive compensation in the form of a home care allowance. As far as income transfer programs are concerned, the Finnish compromise is characterized by the fact that small allowances are also granted to people who were not receiving any income prior to becoming sick or incapacitated.

Because of the inverted nature of the fundamental core of the Finnish model and often slow pace of its political compromises, Finland was not considered a Nordic welfare state until the 1980s. Things continued along this positive trajectory for 10 years until Finland was hit in 1990 by the deepest recession experienced by any Western nation since the end of WWII. The period of economic recovery, which began in 1995, was marked by the attempt to increase international competitiveness. If there are countries in this world that deserve to be referred to as 'competition states' (Cerny 1999), Finland is definitely one of them. Thus, the traditional Nordic welfare state model has not been as strong in Finland as in Denmark, Norway, and Sweden.

As the title of this book makes reference to the 'post-industrial society,' it is important to note that the Finnish society still has an industrial base. The promotion of industry, and in particular the development and strengthening of technical know-how, has played a central role in Finland's rise as one of the world's most competitive nations.

There has been a great deal of discussion about a crisis within the public sector, which is evident when we examine the rate of social expenditure in relation to Finland's GDP, which quickly came down from its all-time high during the recession (34.2 percent of the GDP in 1993) to below the EU average (26.7 percent of the GDP in 2005) (Eurostat, online310708). Despite this, the number of workers in Finland's social service sector has increased (Statistics Finland, online290708).

The Post-industrial Welfare State: Promoting Social Investment

In the post-industrialism era, the most common answer to the question of what wealthy countries must do to protect their welfare state systems against the growing threat posed by international market forces can be found in the concept of the 'social investment state,' which calls for an increase in the employment rate and increased investment in human capital. This strategy can be found both in the work of some influential social theorists (see, e.g., Esping-Andersen 1996; Giddens 1998, 2000, and 2007) and in the policy guidelines provided by the EU and OECD (European Commission 2004; European Parliament 2000; OECD 2001, 2007).

The strength of the Nordic welfare model appears to center on the significant increase in the investment in human capital, which is impossible to achieve without a significant amount of public funding. Kvist (2006), for example, highlights the benefits of this model as the high number of women in the workforce, the relatively high birthrate, the high quality of the education and health care systems, and the high number of highly educated and highly skilled workers. This high level of social investment is politically possible because the recipients are – in the true spirit of universalism – students, women, the sick, and other members of all social classes. In this sense, the Nordic model appears to embody the concept of the social investment state. If we consider state expenditure in education and family policy as examples of social investments, the Nordic countries have the highest level of social investment of all OECD member countries (OECD online120808).

The survival of the Nordic welfare model is also obviously dependent on popular support. Rothstein (2008) has analyzed why the public tends to find it easier to support universal, rather than selective, social policy. The advantage of the universal model is that benefits are aimed at and made available to the entire community, which means that it is not up to officials to make the often difficult distinction between regular citizens and 'others.' The risks of application fraud and/or human error are avoided when the grounds upon which applications are made are not questioned. In addition, the distribution of costs is easier to justify when all those who receive benefits are taxpaying members of society.

Although the benefits of universalism do not diminish with the globalization of the economy, it does make the establishment of its perimeters more difficult. It has become increasingly easy for wealthy people to avoid paying taxes by seeking out tax havens while continuing to take advantage of social benefits paid for by others, particularly education and health care benefits. Many immigrants find it difficult to integrate into the workforce and are constantly accused of abusing Finland's social welfare system. If there is a decrease in the popular support, universalism needs to survive and thrive; it manifests itself in an unwillingness to participate in the funding of the welfare state. And the other side of the same coin is that if we come to a point at which there is an acute lack of funding, the universal benefits to which this country has become accustomed will dwindle down to the point where selectivism is the only possible remaining option.

To some extent, Finland, too, has had to increase the selectivism of its social politics because of the continuous lowering of the minimum social security benefits. This, in turn, has meant that more people have received individual subsistence subsidies than in previous decades. There has been a significant decrease in the state's level of responsibility when it comes to providing public social security, and in keeping with Titmuss' (1968)[2] famous phrase, the quality and legitimization of the social service system has suffered immensely.

There is a clear correlation between the current and ongoing process of globalization and the individualization of values. Those who have benefited most from this process have openly questioned the importance of solidarity and also of public services in general. Social politics has to have the ability to offer more individualized benefits, which is why monetary benefits are becoming increasingly popular. A prime example of this is that when given the choice, many people would choose monetary compensation over services.[3]

The allocation of resources for social investments and the promotion of universal benefits are good ways of alleviating the pressures caused by globalization, but it is likely that they alone will not be enough to meet the growing need to increase investment in social services as the population ages.

---

[2] 'Separate discriminatory services for the *poor* have always tended to be *poor* quality services.' Titmuss (1968, 134)

[3] In addition to Finland's home care allowance (Sipilä 1995) Germany's Pflegegeld and The Netherlands' personal budget systems are prime examples of this.

Andersen (2008) has noted that the increased need for services poses a particularly significant problem. The cost of care provision puts an increasingly significant strain on the national economy, as there is no correlated increase in productivity. At the same time, the middle class' standards are getting higher and higher, which means that improvements must be made in the quality of public services so that they continue to enjoy the political support of the middle class. According to Andersen, the only way to ensure this happens is by limiting the number of state-financed services.

Obviously, the decrease in the state's responsibility is not well-suited to an increase in social investment. The maintenance of a broad and comprehensive education system and support of young families cannot be the responsibility of individual households. It is hard to secure private funding to fight against discrimination. It is difficult to come to any other conclusion than that state resources must be targeted at essential services and supplementary funding must come from other sources.

It is easy to understand why the state is quite eager to outsource nonessential services to companies and other service providers when we consider the increasing needs of the aging population and the decreasing means of collecting state revenue. As long as it has the support of voters, the state, including both political and administrative elite, is willing to privatize and informalize social politics. Doing so, however, will mean that citizens will have to foot the bill. The procurement of additional funding from employers is not an easy feat in the current global market.

Privatization increases not only the pressure on the state but also the pull of the private sector. On the one hand, private capital investors are interested in expanding into insurance and service markets. On the other hand, an increasing number of people are using private services and buying private insurance. Informalization, for its own part, wants to see the responsibility for the provision of care shifted back to the family.

Changes to the Finnish Welfare State: The Privatization of Care

The road map to privatization has been drawn and redrawn: the role of social security has to be reduced and subsistence security must rely more heavily on private solutions in the future. The efficiency of the production and provision of social and health care services must be improved by purchasing more services from private companies, and there has to be more competition for contracts by ending the subsidization of those voluntary organizations which act as public service providers. The breakthrough of the purchaser-producer model in Denmark is a prime example of the new model, in which all service providers operate in relation to the local monopolized purchaser. The voucher model, on the other hand, in which individuals compare and choose their own service producers, has not received much support in the Nordic countries (Szebehely 2006: 119).

Certain features of this model can, however, be found in the provision of home care services and subsidies to family caregivers.[4]

The complete privatization of the provision of care would require that the individual citizens responsible for funding it have high incomes. They would be forced to purchase home care, support, and housing services from private companies and would have to purchase additional insurance to supplement their retirement plans. Generally, there is fairly little demand for market-priced services and insurance, as most people are only able to purchase a limited amount of services and save a small amount of money to supplement their retirement plans. Privatization does not facilitate the kind of comprehensive coverage and security originally intended by the development of public services and the social security system.

Privatization can, of course, also follow another course. The public sector can make its own purchasing agreements, in some cases covering all of the costs itself. This operational model does not, however, save the state as much money as the privatization of funding, that is, transferring the entire financial burden to households.

In the Nordic countries, the private sector has begun to provide both subsistence security (Mandag Morgen 2007: 22–23) and welfare services (Szebehely 2006: 118–119), and there is more to come. Privatization might well further improve the financial position of people with higher incomes, but in so doing, it would also bypass the fundamental principles of social politics. The more privatized retirement plans are, the more difficult it becomes to implement transfer payments and prevent discrimination. At the same time, it creates problems and increased risks for people who are not used to having to make rational investment decisions. The tightly controlled state social insurance system, on the other hand, allows income distribution policy to be influenced by democracy and increases the security of retirement investments.

The welfare state primarily produces goods and services that the free market is unable to produce. The lack of public resources does not really pose much of a threat to the ability to provide insurance compensation, because most risks can be covered, at least in principle, by purchasing policies from private insurance companies. Insufficient investment in people, however, does pose a major problem. The comprehensive provision of day care, education, and national health services is only possible because of public funding. Somewhat paradoxically, only society itself can create the kind of social trust and stability it needs to survive and thrive.

Privatization does also have its financial limits. Although retirement benefits have improved and more and more elderly people have fairly large income-based pensions, the state's responsibility for caring for the growing elderly

---

[4] Himmelweit (2005: 173) notes that the emphasis in the UK as regards the provision of childcare has shifted from the provision of parental support to the provision of services purchased by municipalities. The trend in elderly care, on the other hand, has taken a rather paradoxical turn toward the payments to individuals for providing care.

population cannot be met with pensions alone. According to our calculations, European public expenditure on old age per elderly has not improved in relation to the GDPs of European countries (Sipilä & Anttonen 2008). As the disparity in the distribution of income increases and there is no correlative decrease in the cost of care services, there will also be no increase in the number of people who are financially able to purchase the care and services they need.

Companies do tend to be effective and efficient in the production of services which are easily productized. If, on the other hand, clients are not able to define the nature of their needs or the quality of the care they receive, or if their needs change quickly, there becomes a need for a broader organization whose sphere of responsibility is not limited to the production of one specific service. Services provided must be flexible enough to meet the needs of its clients, and employees must have the freedom to take a more individualized and human approach when dealing with clients. According to Szebehely (2006: 119–120), the pre-requisites for the provision of quality care include the ability for caregivers and clients to have an ongoing relationship in which there is a sufficient amount of time for interaction and in which the caregiver has the professional autonomy to meet his or her clients' individual needs, particularly the diverse needs of the aging population. Is this possible if the service organization in question does not operate under the watchful eyes of the public?

Changes to the Finnish Welfare State: The Informalization of Care

The care provided in the informal sector is extremely important in terms of the production of welfare. The public actively participates in all aspects of the production of welfare. They care for sick and elderly relatives, they share money, and they raise their children to become active and responsible members of society and try to ensure that they do not end up having social problems.

Over the course of history, the increase, particularly in the number of women in the workforce, has led to the socialization of caring for young children and the elderly, which has been reflected in the increase in the production of public services, particularly social services. The responsibility for carrying out services which were once the responsibility of the government is now being shifted back by the government to families and local communities. The process of informa-lization is not, however, concerned as much with the return of responsibility to families and local communities as with the minimization of the costs associated with the ever-increasing burden of care.

Sipilä and Anttonen (2008) have shown that the governments of European countries are not investing in public care policies to the extent one might expect in light of the massive aging population. Governments promote deinstitutiona-lization as a means of relieving the pressure of increased public expenditure, which results in the provision of less expensive forms of care (OECD 2005). Governments have begun making an increasingly conscious effort to cooperate with private service providers and have introduced benefits that support the provision of informal care and new types of combinations of formal and informal care.

The combination of formal and informal care tends to be favored in social care policy at least partly because households are able to create their own care resources. Families are the government's most important allies, as most of the care is carried out informally and without pay by relatives and members of local communities. For these and other reasons, support for informal care became one of the focal points of social policy innovation in the late 20th century.

The other side of the coin is that there are fewer people available to provide informal care. Himmelweit (2005) highlights two trends which accentuate the importance of supporting informal care. First, wages are generally going to increase, which means that people who do not participate in the labor market will lose more compared to those who do wage work. Second, the division of labor will continue to the extent that people will be less able to efficiently multitask at home.

This will be experienced in the form of the rising opportunity cost of staying at home to care for family members. People who provide care at home feel increasingly as though they cannot afford not to work (Himmelweit 2005). These trends emphasize the need for financial compensation to encourage informal caregiving. It is no longer a question whether governments should support informal care, but how such support should be arranged.

Social research also identifies a slew of other risks linked to supporting the informal care of the aging population. The role of the provision of care still tends to be ignored in the context of economic policy; in which the relationship between formal and informal care and paid and unpaid work is hardly ever discussed. A typical example of the often limited nature of the discussion surrounding welfare politics is the European Employment Strategy's discussion of its objectives regarding the employment of women and the aging population. While it does focus on the topic of parental leave, part-time work, and child care, it has little to say about caring for the elderly (Himmelweit 2005: 169). There should also be discussion, for example, about the potential to combine paid work and informal care by increasing the flexibility of working life.

When discussing social investments, it is also important to note that the objective of increasing paid work naturally leads to a decrease in the amount and availability of unpaid care and volunteer work (Himmelweit 2007: 4). Conversely, the process of informalization decreases the number of women in the labor market, including highly educated women. There has been a lot of discussion regarding the extent to which the support for informal caregiving acts as a trap for women (see, e.g., Sipilä 1995; Kröger et al. 2003).

Swedish studies on the processes of privatization and informalization have found that there is a great deal of disparity in the compensation of diminished public services. Elderly people with little education tend to rely more on their family members for care, while those with a higher level of education tend to compensate for the lack of provision of public care by purchasing private services (Szebehely 2003). In Portugal, however, studies have shown that the provision of care by family members does not compensate for lack of money, as there is more informal aid available to those with a higher social position (Wall et al. 2001).

There is something inherently contradictory about the simultaneous promotion of a high level of employment and elderly people's right to live at home for as long as possible and be cared for by their relatives. Informalization is not conducive to the expectation that people should work longer hours and later into life, nor is it conducive to the fact that a growing percentage of the population lives in single-person households. Almost one million Finns live alone (Tilastokeskus, online310708). Cohabitation significantly increases the availability of informal care (Pickard et al. 2000), while the constant dissolution of unions and marriages weakens the familial safety net and decreases the amount of available care.

The promotion of the provision of care by family members is clearly problematic. On the one hand, governments are obliged to financially support the provision of care by family members, while on the other hand, this support sometimes has undesired effects on the labor market, the careers of caregivers, and sometimes even on those being cared for. To whom and in what forms should resources and support to informal care be allocated? The following is based on Anttonen and Sointu's (2006) identification of the existing forms of support for the provision of care by family members.

In Finland, small subsidies are paid to people caring for family members. These subsidies are particularly important in cases in which the caregiver is highly motivated and has another source of income. A large proportion of people who are caring for a loved one are retired people caring for their husband or wife. They want recognition for their work (Sointu & Anttonen 2008), and the provision of a subsidy is a good way of giving them the recognition they want and deserve. These subsidies have been found to be relatively unimportant for people who are members of the paid workforce.

As the burden on the working people caring for family members increases, their earned income decreases. To be able to continue caring, caregivers have to be able to take care leave and must receive either subsistence security or a salary for its duration. There are two different principles when it comes to the organization of subsistence security: poverty prevention or the replacement of lost wages. The use of minimum subsistence subsidies as a means of covering one's basic living expenses and avoiding poverty generally attracts women with weak positions in the workforce. There is good reason to be critical of this system here in Finland, where international comparisons have shown that there is a significant gap between the income levels of men and women. Earnings-related career benefits would be better equipped to treat working caregivers more fairly and equally, although such a system does not exist here in Finland.

In Norway, Sweden, and Denmark, the responsibility of municipalities has been emphasized and there has been a great deal of criticism of the support given to family caregivers. In keeping with this, people providing care for family members have been given employment contracts, although the number of contracts has decreased significantly in Sweden and Norway since the early 1970s. The main problem in all Nordic countries regarding the support of those providing care would appear to be its unsystematic nature and inability to react quickly to changing situations (Sand 2005, 222–227).

From the perspective of caregivers, there are a number of advantages to actually being employed to care, particularly when the caregiver does not plan to return to his or her previous place of employment after taking care leave. The provision of earnings-related benefits is better suited to shorter periods of care leave. Although it is not the most inexpensive possible option, the total cost is almost always lower than that of home help. All in all, the support of informal care is still quite a new strategy in the field of social politics. It appears that this is the direction in which social politics in general must move, which is why it is so crucial that we compare and consider all available and potential options.

A New Form of Universalism Suited for the Post-industrial Society?

The main idea of welfare politics has been to transfer the responsibility for taking risks to the public at large. The trends of the post-industrial society toward formalization and privatization, on the other hand, are doing exactly the opposite, as they rely on individual citizen's own resources. When we view the universal model as emphasizing the state's responsibility for ensuring the well-being of all citizens and providing basic services, the inherent contradictions between it, on the one hand, and informalization and privatization, on the other hand, become obvious.

Most Finns would never expect that the same level of universalism be applied to social services as health care services. It seems natural to expect and demand that all sick patients be treated equally, whether they are rich or poor, young or old. All patients deserve to be treated equally. In the case of home help and institutional nursing home care, however, the need for such services is always compared to the availability of informal care. People who live alone and have no family members to care for them are given priority when it comes to the provision of home care, and nursing homes do their best to get families to care for their own elderly relatives at home. If the elderly relative is being cared for at a nursing home, relatives are often asked to come to help feed and care for their relatives (Kröger 2005). People who are more well-off tend to be encouraged to use private services, so as not to use public services 'needed' by those with less money. This is a far cry from universalism.

The support of caring for family members is a goal-oriented form of informalization. The provision of subsidies is an invaluable tool, as the Ministry of Social Affairs and Health has its sight set on cutting the number of available places in Finnish nursing homes (STM 2008). But as the forms of support available to family caregivers increase, so do the risks associated with the provision of informal care. The governmental support for the provision of care by family members should also include the responsibility for ensuring the quality and stability of the care relationship in question. Public actors should not support tired caregivers, the unfair distribution of labor, problematic relationships, or the lack of skills. Kröger (2005, 250–252) notes that the success of informal care relies heavily on the ability to ensure that formal and informal care work parallel to one another.

This could well allow for the application of the principle of universalism. The application of universalism in the provision of care by family members could mean that a caregiver would be eligible to receive a public subsidy in an amount to be determined according to the scope or size of the service to be provided, but that in addition to money, it would also include services and follow-up evaluations. Thus, in the spirit of the Danish model, public services, and informal care would complement as opposed to replacing one another (Szebehely 2006, 117–118).

It is difficult to apply the concept of private funding to the principle of universalism, if universalism is understood as dealing with the same societal needs in the same way. On the other hand, the provision of universal services should not take the form of a total institution, which would not allow for the provision of informal care and would restrict the use of personal funds to purchase services. There are examples of universal services successfully applied in ways in which they complement privately funded services. For example, someone living in a city-run nursing home can use his or her money to purchase a pedicure from a private vendor. In cases like this, the purchase of private services takes place in a way that does not weaken the position of other residents.

Isn't it about time we broadened our understanding of universalism? Could the basis of this new understanding be that universal services can always be topped up with private and informal services? Why should clients be prohibited from purchasing additional services from the same public service provider? Why should the local government demand that he or she purchase all additional services or even all services from private service providers? Could a country that is becoming more culturally, linguistically, and religiously diverse and whose citizens often have very different expectations see the replacement of the strict division between public and private services with one that would allow some individual variation in both services and payments?

It is possible to envision a universalism that would provide basic services funded by the government which clients could supplement by purchasing additional services privately. This would allow us to meet the ever-changing needs of a quickly diversifying society without having to dismantle the existing service system and without forcing people with special needs to purchase the services they need from private service providers. Surely giving those receiving home care the possibility to purchase additional care from public service providers would not cause universalism to come crashing down. All in all, the provision of this type of service would be advantageous to all involved.

The key question (à la Rawls) is: would this type of system actually increase the availability and quality of the kind of services low-income clients need? If universalism was incorporated into the social security system to support women and the poor (Edebalk 1995) and into the practice of provision of services to support women (Sipilä 1997), what kind of effect has the weakening of the principle of universalism as a result of informalization and privatization? Certainly it increases both gender inequality and the risk of the manifestation of the differences in income distribution in the service system. From the client perspective, however, linking private and informal resources to the public service sector would provide a means of solving at least some of the problems associated with the lack of resources in the public sector, which would likely lead to improved service provision for all.

Perhaps this type of combined system offering extra services would be a less problematic model than the complete segregation of services for the rich and the poor. The biggest threat to universalism is that the public service system will be weakened by a lack of resources to the extent that the majority of the population no longer wants to use it. If this happens, we can say good-bye to the Nordic public service model.

Conclusion

There is a great deal of tension in the balance between global economy and political democracy, with the latter coming under increased pressure due to the increased strain on public resources as the population ages. But the political realities created by globalization will not necessarily look the same tomorrow as they do today. There are no stabilizing scenarios on the horizon.

Even if international corporations continue to get a free ride as taxpayers, they have a keen interest in the provision of highly skilled and educated workers and in the preservation of politico-administrative stability and a strong workforce. States produce both. Most small-and medium-sized businesses operate on a national level and thus understand the importance of future-oriented investments. International corporations, for their own part, often get a free ride as taxpayers and employers, but anyway, they pay wages which are then taxed by the government.

On the other hand, it is also possible that the current dominance of international businesses is just a passing phase in history. Throughout history, local regulatory systems have tended to become inherently ineffective until workers and the public in general have taken their integration to a higher level. The progression of political integration and increase in international risks will create the possibility for new international regulations.

In conclusion, let us reiterate Scharpf's (2000) view that it is not that states have lost their ability to aim at welfare, rather that how they go about it must conform to the limitations of international capitalism. None of us can be sure how permanent these limitations are. It is, however, likely that Finnish universalism has not yet reached the end of its line.

References

Andersen, T. (2008). Pohjoismainen malli – tulevaisuuden näkymät ja haasteet. *Yhteiskuntapolitiikka, 73*(4), 402–410.

Anttonen, A. (1997). The welfare state and social citizenship. In K. Kauppinen & T. Gordon (Eds.), *Unresolved dilemmas: women, work and the family in the United States, Europe and the former Soviet Union* (pp. 9–32). Aldershot: Ashgate.

Anttonen, A. (2002). Universalism and social policy: a Nordic-feminist revaluation. *Nora, 10*(2), 71–80.

Anttonen, A., & Sipilä, J. (2000). *Suomalaista sosiaalipolitiikkaa.* Tampere: Vastapaino.

Anttonen, A., Baldock, J., & Sipilä, J. (Eds.). (2003). *The young, the old, and the state: social care systems in five industrial nations.* Cheltenham: Edward Elgar.

Anttonen, A., & Sointu, L. (2006). *Hoivapolitiikka muutoksessa. Julkinen vastuu pienten lasten ja ikääntyneiden hoivasta 12:ssa Euroopan maassa.* Helsinki: Stakes.

Berman, M. (1982). *All that is solid melts into air: the experience of modernity.* New York: Simon & Schuster.

Bonoli, G., George, V., & Taylor-Gooby, P. (2000). *European welfare futures: towards a theory of retrenchement.* Cambridge: Polity Press.

Cerny, P. G. (1999). Globalization and the erosion of democracy. *European Journal of Political Research, 36*(1), 1–26.

Edebalk, P. G. (1995). *Välfärdsstaten träder fram. Svensk socialförsäkring 1884–1955.* Lund: Arkiv.

Esping-Andersen, G. (1990). *The three worlds of welfare capitalism.* Cambridge: Polity Press.

Esping-Andersen, G. (1996). After the golden age? Welfare state dilemmas in a global economy. In G. Esping-Andersen (Ed.), *Welfare states in transition. National adaptations in global economies* (pp. 1–31). London: UNRISD.

European Commission (2004). *Report of the High Level Group on the future of social policy in an enlarged European Union, Report of the High Level Group.* Directorate-General for Employment and Social Affairs, Brussels: EC.

European Parliament (2000). *Presidency Conclusions.* Lisbon European Council 23 AND 24 March 2000.

Ganghof, S. (2005). Globalization, tax reform ideals and social policy financing. *Global Social Policy, 5*(1), 77–95.

Giddens, A. (1998). *The third way: the renewal of social democracy.* Cambridge: Polity Press.

Giddens, A. (2000). *The third way and its critics.* Cambridge: Polity Press.

Giddens, A. (2007). *Europe in the global age.* Cambridge: Polity Press.

Goldberg, G., & Rosenthal, M. (Eds.). (2002). *Diminishing welfare: a cross-national study of social provision.* London: Auburn House.

Himmelweit, S. (2007). Feminism and economics. *ukwatch.net.* March 4th, 2007. http://www.ukwatch.net/article/feminism_and_economics.

Himmelweit, S. (2005). Caring: the need for an economic strategy. *Public policy research, 12*(3), 168–173.

Julkunen, R. (2001). *Suunnanmuutos. 1990-luvun sosiaalipoliittinen reformi Suomessa.* Tampere: Vastapaino.

Kaufmann, F.-X. (2000). Towards a theory of welfare state. *European Review, 8*(3), 291–312.

Kautto, M. et al. (1999). *Nordic social policy: changing welfare states.* London: Routledge.

Kröger, T. (2005). Interplay between formal and informal care for older people: the state of the Nordic Research. In M. Szebehely (Ed.), *Äldreomsorgsforskning i Norden. En kunskapsöversikt* (pp. 243–280). Köpenhamn: Nordiska ministerrådet.

Kröger, T., Anttonen, A., & Sipilä, J. (2003). Social care in Finland: stronger and weaker forms of universalism. In: A. Anttonen, J. Baldock, & J. Sipilä (Eds.), *The young, the old and the state: social care systems in five industrial nations* (pp. 25–54). Cheltenham: Edward Elgar.

Kröger, T., & Vuorensyrjä, M. (2008). Suomalainen vanhustyö pohjoismaisessa vertailussa. Vanhuspalvelujen koti- ja laitoshoitotyön piirteitä ja ongelmia. *Yhteiskuntapolitiikka, 73*(3), 250–266.

Kuhnle, S. (Ed.). (2000). *Survival of the European welfare state.* London: Routledge.

Kumlin, S., & Rothstein, B. (2003). Staten och det sociala kapitalet. In J. Pierre, & B. Rothstein (Eds.), *Välfärdstat i otakt. Om politikens oväntade, oavsiktliga och oönskade effekter* (pp. 146–168). Lund: Liber.

Kvist, J. (2006). Europæiske perspektiver på den nordiske velfærdsstat. In *Nordisk Ministerråds Velferdsforskningsprogram. Programkomitéens sluttrapport* (pp. 128–139). Köpenhamn: Nordiska ministerrådet.

Lindbeck, A. (1997). The Swedish experiment. *Journal of Economic Literature, 35*(3), 1273–1319

Mandag, M. (2007). *What lies ahead for the Nordic model?* Copenhagen: Nordic Council of Ministers.

OECD (2001). Balancing work and family life. Helping parents into paid employment. In *Employment Outlook.* Paris: OECD.

OECD (2005) *Long-term care for older people.* Paris: OECD.

OECD (2007). Finnish policy on reconciling work and family life should strengthen: a country note. In *Babies and bosses: reconciling work and family life – a synthesis of findings for OECD countries.* Paris: OECD.

Pickard, L., Witternberg, R., Comas-Herrera, A., Davies, B., & Darton, R. (2000). Relying on informal care in the new century? Informal care for elderly people in England to 2031. *Ageing and Society, 20*(6), 745–772.

Pierson, P. (2001). Introduction: investigating the welfare state at century's end. In P. Pierson (Ed.), *The new politics of the welfare state* (pp. 1–14). Oxford: Oxford University Press.

Rostgaard, T. (2004). *With due care: social care for young and the old across Europe.* Social Forsknings Instituttet. Copenhagen: The Danish National Institute of Social Research.

Rostgaard, T., & Fridberg, T. (1998). *Caring for children and older people: a comparison of European policies and practices.* Copenhagen: The Danish National Institute of Social Research.

Rothstein, B. (2000). The future of the universal welfare state: an institutional approach. In S. Kuhnle (Ed.), *Survival of the European welfare state* (pp. 217–233). London: Routledge.

Rothstein, B. (2008). Pohjoismainen hyvinvointivaltio ja keskiluokka. *Yhteiskuntapolitiikka, 73*(4), 368–375.

Sainsbury, D. (1996). *Gender, equality, and welfare states.* Cambridge: Cambridge University Press.

Sand, A.-B. (2005). Informell äldreomsorg samt stöd till informella vårdare – en nordisk forskningsöversikt. In M. Szebehely (Ed.), *Äldreomsorgsforskning i Norden. En kunskapsöversikt* (pp. 197–241). Köpenhamn: Nordiska ministerrådet.

Scharpf, F. (2000). The viability of advanced welfare states in the international economy: vulnerabilities and options. *European Review, 8*(3), 399–425.

Sipilä, J. (1995). The right to choose: day care for children or money for parents? *Social Policy Review, 7,* 151–169.

Sipilä, J. (Ed.). (1997). *Social care services: the key to the Scandinavian welfare model.* Avebury: Aldershot.

Sipilä, J., & Anttonen, A. (2008). Mobilising formal and informal resources in meeting old age–related needs – a European comparison. In C. Leggewie, & C. Sachsse (Eds.), *Ermunterungen. Soziale Demokratie, Zivilgesellschaft und Bürgertugenden. Adalbert Everts zum 60. Geburtstag* (pp. 169–201). Frankfurt am Main: Campus.

Sointu, L., & Anttonen, A. (2008) Omaistaan hoivaavan arki: rakastamista, sitoutumista ja jaksamista. In P. Lipponen (Ed.), *Rakas velvollisuus. Omaishoitajan arjen haasteet* (pp. 21–62). Helsinki: Kirjapaja.

STM (2008). *Ikäihmisten palvelujen laatusuositus. Sosiaali- ja terveysministeriö, julkaisuja 2008: 3*. Helsinki: Sosiaali- ja terveysministeriö & Suomen Kuntaliitto.

Szebehely, M. (2003). Den nordiska hemtjänsten – bakgrund och omfattning. In M. Szebehely (Ed.), *Hemhjälp i Norden – illustrationer och reflexioner* (pp. 23–61). Lund: Studentlitteratur.

Szebehely, M. (2004). Nya trender, gamla traditioner. Svensk äldreomsorg i europeiskt perspektiv. In C. Florin, & C. Bergqvist (Eds.), *Framtiden i samtiden. Könsrelationer i förändring i Sverige och omvärlden* (pp. 172–202). Stockholm: Institutet för framtidstudier.

Szebehely, M. (2006). Hälsa och välfärd – kunskapsöversikt över nordisk – välfärdsforskning inom äldreomsorgsområdet. In *Nordisk Ministerråds Velferdsforskningsprogram. Program-komitéens sluttrapport* (pp. 115–122). København: Nordisk ministerråd.

Taimio, H. (Ed.). (2007). *Talouskasvun hedelmät – kuka sai ja kuka jäi ilman?* Helsinki: Työväen Sivistysliitto.

Titmuss, R. M. (1968). *Commitment to welfare*. London: George Allen & Unwin.

Trydegård, G.-B. (2003). Swedish care reforms in the 1990s: a first evaluation of their consequences for the elderly people. In L'État providence nordique. Ajustements, trans-formations au cours des années quatre-vingt-dix. *Revue française de Affaires sociales* 57(4, numero spècial), 443–460.

Wall, K., Aboim, S., Cunha, V., & Vasconcelos, P. (2001). Families and informal support networks in Portugal: the reproduction of inequality. *Journal of European Social Policy*, *11*(3), 213–233.

Chapter 11
Citizenship and Education in Post-industrial Societies

Antonin Wagner

Introduction

As societies around the world grow ever more diverse with respect to ethnic, cultural, and religious backgrounds of their members, a common civic identity becomes the tie that holds them together in democratic polities. Civic identity is not to be confounded with national citizenship, which is based on the place of a person's birth (*jus soli*) or derived from the citizenship of one's parents (*jus sanguinis*), respectively acquired by people without a birthright to national citizenship through naturalization. By contrast to such a legal construct of citizenship, civic identity emanates from the commitment that members of society make to commonly accepted values and virtues. From a legal stand-point, one can distinguish between the status of citizens and other residents, mostly with respect to the right to vote and to be elected to certain offices. Civic identity, however, has to be acquired by both categories of residents in a dynamic process of personal development if it should become the glue that holds political communities together.

In this respect, one has to differentiate between formal citizenship, understood as a legal status, and realized citizenship as full participation in a democratic polity (Wagner, 2008a). It is through education—both formal and informal—that people living together in a society learn to effectively identify with their role as members of a polity and to access the resources necessary to realize their citizenship. As a lever for social inclusion, realized citizenship requires active participation in society, rather than merely passive membership. Hence, all residents of a country should become involved in an arduous learning process, through which they acquire the knowledge, attitudes, and skills necessary to become effective and active citizens in the family, at school, on the job, and through leisure and cultural activities.

Over the last couple of years, the idea that citizenship and education are intertwined concepts has got increasing recognition, not only from national governments but also in the arena of international institutions. The Council of

A. Wagner (✉)
The New School for Management and Urban Policy, New York, USA
e-mail: wagnera@newschool.edu

J. Powell, J. Hendricks, *The Welfare State in Post-Industrial Society*,
DOI 10.1007/978-1-4419-0066-1_11, © Springer Science+Business Media, LLC 2009

Europe has taken the lead in promoting the idea that democracy should be learned and lived on an everyday basis. It declared 2005 as the *European Year of Citizenship* and launched a campaign to put into practice a program of Education for Democratic Citizenship and Human Rights (Council of Europe, 1999). In the United States, where cultural heterogeneity of residents has traditionally been addressed by local governments, states and municipalities have launched similar initiatives. A good example is the New York City Commission on Human Rights (www.nyc.gov/cchr), which helps cultivate mutual respect among New York City's many diverse communities.

Both in Europe and the United States, such public projects lead to the establishment of research institutions dedicated to exploring the connections between citizenship and education. In the United Kingdom, the National Foundation of Educational Research (www.nfer.ac.uk) has recognized citizenship and human rights education as one of its main areas of research. Likewise, in the United States, Tufts University's Jonathan M. Tisch College of Citizenship and Public Service has become known for its commitment to promoting research and scholarship on education for active citizenship (www.activecitizen.tufts.edu). Research institutions of this kind provide a productive environment for publications addressing the relationship between education and citizenship, either from a scholarly/theoretical or a more practical/programmatic perspective. Beyond dealing with issues related to civic engagement in general (Ostrander and Portney, 2007; Ravitch and Viteritti, 2001), theoretical studies often analyze the role of educational policy in fostering citizenship. In research that dates back to the early 1990s, Mosher et al. (1994) have demonstrated how democratically structured school systems help students, faculty, administrators, and staff to become responsible citizens in their respective school community. More recently, the contributors to *Educating Citizens* (Wolf and Macedo, 2004) analyzed the impact of publicly funded school choice on civic cohesion, in countries as diverse as the Netherlands, the United Kingdom, Belgium, Canada, Germany, France, Italy, and the United States. Furthermore, a growing number of reports address a variety of curricular issues relating to education for citizenship and add an important programmatic perspective to the academic scholarship on this topic. An interesting example is provided by the Spanish CIVES Foundation, which was involved in crafting a new mandatory class 'education for citizenship,' aiming to replace more traditional religious instruction and teach civic values consistent with a diverse democracy (Burnett, 2007).

Most of the literature quoted here has a pedagogical focus and puts the emphasis on the idea of education *for* citizenship. By contrast to this trend, the present contribution takes a different approach, not one that emphasizes the programmatic aspects of education, but puts citizenship in the foreground of the analysis: not education *for* citizenship, but citizenship *through* education. On the following pages, citizenship will be framed in the context of political theory and conceptualized as a dynamic institution—rather than a static framework of rights and obligations—resulting from a learning process undergone by the members of democratic societies. The aim is to understand how in a culturally diverse environment individuals come to accept the normative foundations of a just society. Citizens cannot reach consensus by deriving the foundations for their polity from comprehensive—but contradictory—religious, philosophical, and ethical doctrines (Rawls, 1993; Rawls, 1999). Rather, they have to rely on a commitment to what is 'politically reasonable,' not what is 'true.' Through education and by undergoing a learning process, members of society will recognize that values, such as liberty, equality, and democracy, are powerful in their own right 'and over time will come to enjoy historical legitimacy within a political community that endorses and upholds them' (March, 2007: 235). In this way, citizens will gradually create a political culture and recognize that they are better off living together under a democratic regime, than if they were to pursue their own aims and impose their own comprehensive doctrine on others.

To understand how people with diverse cultural identities can be prepared for living together in democratic societies, the following argument traces the concept of citizenship through education back to its roots in Enlightenment philosophy, in particular to the writings of Jean-Jacques Rousseau. 'Citizenship, Education and Social Contract Theory' develops the political and pedagogical framework for the argument. The section will recast Rousseau's theory of the social contract, emphasizing that political communities derive their legitimacy not from divine right or dynastic succession, but from the will of their members. It is through education that these members learn to effectively identify with their role and to acquire the knowledge, attitudes, and skills to become effective citizens. 'Post-industrialism and the Welfare State' applies the concept of citizenship through education to the national welfare state of the twentieth century and the idea of social citizenship associated with it. Now, those (mostly national) inhabitants of a territory are considered citizens who pay (direct and indirect) taxes on their income and contribute to financing the public infrastructure of their economy/society. In this context, income taxation came to function as an important instrument of education, transforming the relationship between citizens and their state. However, as more plural forms of life emerged during the last couple of decades, the notion of national citizenship as a state-centered mechanism of societal integration has increasingly come under assault. 'Citizenship and Local Civil Society' dwells, therefore, on residential or interest-based forms of societal integration. In particular, organizations of local civil society have the potential to enhance civic identity of those members of society who diverge from the majority way of life and advocate the need to complement the nation-state as the dominant integrative device with a wide range of private collective action.

The argument developed here—that citizenship is coupled with education—puts the emphasis on how secular institutions of government and civil society function as mechanisms of societal integration. In the future, however, more and more citizens will—under the influence of immigration from foreign cultures—derive some of their deepest commitments to society from religious comprehensive doctrines they hold in private. In its 'Concluding Remarks,' the contribution will, therefore, assess the role faith-based groups and their doctrines play in the societal learning process of citizens, either as a factor of divisiveness or of support in fostering civic identity in multicultural societies.

Citizenship, Education, and Social Contract Theory

The role of education in forming citizenship has first been emphasized in the eighteenth century by Enlightenment philosophers, such as David Hume, Immanuel Kant, and, more particularly, Jean-Jacques Rousseau. The terms and assumptions of his writings still shape the political practices of today's societies and provide the tools to frame social issues of modernity. In *The Social Contract* (1947), Rousseau lays the foundations of the social contract theory. He describes the transition from the state of nature to the civil state, which 'produces a most remarkable change in man by substituting justice for instinct in his conduct, and endowing his action with the morality they previously lacked' (Rousseau, 1947: 16). This transition is conceived as an act of association through which 'each of us places in common his person and all his power under the supreme direction of the general will' (Rousseau, 1947: 15). It follows from this quote that Rousseau conceives citizenship not as a privilege bestowed by an authority on certain members of society but as a communal arrangement through which people living together in a political community convey to each other rights and obligations.

But where do the rights and obligations of citizenship come from: can they be derived from religious doctrines, do they emanate from the immutable nature of men or are they a mere creation of the human mind itself? Modern positivists hold that all rights derive from human-made law itself, that is, they are found by logical deduction and imposed by government authority or implemented based on some majority rule of democratic decision-making. However, if rights came from the law alone, there would be no basis on which to judge in a noncircular way a given legal system. By contrast to legal positivism, the following argument develops the view that the source of rights must lie outside the law itself. Pre-Enlightenment religious doctrines postulated God as the external source of all laws that apply to human beings. Rejecting the idea of such a supranatural origin of human rights, Rousseau saw human nature as the source from which the rights of citizenship can be derived.

Does this mean that human rights are 'out there,' inscribed in immutable human nature, only waiting to be discovered by men? According to a recent interpretation (Neiman, 2002: 44) of Rousseau's writings, rather the opposite seems to be true. Unlike the classical Greek thought that viewed the natural order as immutable in space and time and the role of human beings within it as eternally fixed, Rousseau stated in several of his writings that human nature is subject to change. Human beings, both as species and as individuals, evolve in the course of time. Human nature has a history, and people's choices have an impact on its course.

In his *Discours sur l'origine et les fondements de l'inégalité parmi les homes* (1964), Rousseau describes human history as a descent from natural innocence to civilized misery, as a long development during which human beings alienated themselves from their own true nature. In the course of time, men passed from self-sufficient decency in the state of nature to the web of dependence and betrayal that makes up the social world in the state of civilization. The noble savages that men once were—though free of evil and suffering in the state of nature—came to spawn the wretched creatures that pass for civilized humanity (Neiman, 2002: 45). According to the *Discours sur l'inégalité*, all vices that currently plague societies can be explained by particular events that occurred in the course of the development of human species, such as the discovery of iron and the cultivation of wheat (Rousseau, 1964: 171), the division of labor, and the private ownership of land (Rousseau, 1964: 173), or simply by human inclinations. A little vanity, and the alienation from our own nature that accompanies it, can take us all the way to the system of injustice now organizing the world (Neiman, 2002: 45).

This narrative seems to contradicts the almost romantically sounding account in *The Social Contract*, where Rousseau describes how the transition from the state of nature to the civil state 'produces a most remarkable change in man by substituting justice for instinct in his conduct, and endowing his action with the morality they previously lacked' (Rousseau, 1947: 16). Yes, if we conceptualize the transition from one state to the other as a pseudochronology (Bertram, 2004: 36), i.e., a sequence in time in which one phase follows the other. No, if we understand—as Rousseau seems to have done in *Discours sur l'inégalité*—the history of human development as dialectical and contingent, and not as deterministic. Despite the tendencies to weakness within human nature, the course humankind takes is not inevitable. There is, however, no denying that defective political institutions corrupt the healthy natural impulses of the otherwise noble savages. Human beings must nevertheless live in society, and there is no resolving the problem of corruption by returning to a fictitious state of nature.

In this situation, a second chance is given to the civilized human beings. In the famous opening sentence of *Émile ou l'Éducation* (1969), Rousseau states that at its core the world is good, awaiting only human action to make it better. *Émile ou l'Éducation*—incidentally published the same year as *Du Contrat social*—is as much a novel as it is a manual of instruction (Neiman, 2002: 52). In it, Rousseau develops his understanding of education as a process meant to undo the descent into misery he described in the *Discours sur l'inégalité*. Through pedagogical intervention, children such as Émile could be protected from the evils of civilization and play a role in shaping a more civilized order. The goal of education is, therefore, not to return to the state of nature (in the sense of the often misunderstood *Retour à la nature*), but to produce something better, something that is equivalent to a synthesis of the state of nature and the state of civilization (Wagner, 2004).

Given the dialectical nature of human development, the problem of citizenship is how to restore through education to civilized men the kind of liberty, independence, and equality equivalent to the happiness they enjoyed in the state of nature. In this respect, citizenship is not only an institutional and political category but in the fullest meaning of the term also a pedagogical one. The purpose of citizenship through education is to form human beings far more noble than anything possible in the state of nature, by properly managing societal institutions and developing the natural human capacities of freedom, reason, and sexuality (Neiman, 2002: 50).

Citizenship through education requires that citizens learn from their own experiences in society, instead of being reminded of their duties by political authorities. In this respect, citizens' rights and obligations are not inscribed in nature, nor are they imposed from above. They rather emerge from below; they are the result of societal learning and come from a collective human experience with injustice. Rights come from wrongs! Based on Rousseau's philosophy, one could define citizens' rights as those societal preferences that experience and history have taught are so fundamental that they are permanently entrenched in society, instead of making them subject to easy changes by shifting majorities.

Education for citizenship is a difficult task to achieve and requires—according to Rousseau's *Émile*—the presence of a perfect tutor who steps in not with words, but with action (Rousseau, 1969, Livre II: 299–425). The tutor's role is not to create the desire in the child to meet the teacher's expectations or to impose his own values on those who are supposed to be educated. The perfect tutor is rather somebody capable of instigating learning processes and producing the kind of self-knowledge that reflects the true needs children gradually develop in life.

Post-Industrialism and the Welfare State

Unlike in Rousseau's *Émile*, in our times the tutor who triggers the collective learning experience and instills a community culture is often not an individual, but a group or a collective. Rousseau knew this and in his writings supported the view that only the community can prescribe socially binding obligations (Wagner, 2004: 279). Citizens' rights, in general, and social rights, in particular, will only continue to shape human destiny if members of society constantly defend their convictions in a dialog with each other. According to Rousseau, the ideal outlet for this communal interaction was to be found in a city state, such as Geneva, where *The Social Contract* was originally published. In this respect, the roots of citizenship lie in the idea of the Greek *polis*, but the full emergence of the institution paralleled the rise of sovereign nations in eighteenth and nineteenth centuries and their progressive mutation to welfare states after World War II. During this period, citizenship has become an increasingly state-centered institution, shaped by the principle of nationality as the rule of territorial organization of political communities (Wagner, 2004).

The emergence of the welfare state in the course of the twentieth century had a profound impact on the social contract under which members of a society lived together. Citizenship through education—that is, the idea that citizenship needs to be realized through a learning process—depends on the particular give-and-take relationship that in a welfare state exists between the government and its citizens. By guaranteeing social rights and providing public services to all residents, the government creates the necessary conditions for able-bodied adults to compete in the labor market and to participate in the economic well-being. Social citizenship is being extended to all inhabitants of a territory as long as they pay taxes and contribute to financing the public infrastructure essential for a functioning labor market. Social rights, therefore, expand the prerogatives of citizenship from those who own property to those who pay taxes on the earnings that result from their contribution to the economy. Citizenship has become an economic good, and taxes are the price that citizens pay for it.

The taxes citizens pay in return for getting access to the services provided by the state are typically based on their income as the most adequate indicator of the ability to contribute to the community. Most welfare states levy, therefore, a direct and progressive income tax on the income earned, instead of an indirect tax on the income spent. Direct taxes require the taxpayers' collaboration in establishing the tax burden and determining the individual price for citizenship. In this respect, direct and progressive taxation is instrumental in realizing citizenship in that it plays an important role as a means of education for democratic participation. Most progressive tax systems suffer, however, from a vicious circle that makes them more and more complicated. The tax breaks, deductions, allowances, and concessions that under progressive taxation are accorded to taxpayers force governments to gather revenue from an ever narrower base of taxpayers and at correspondingly higher and more distorting tax rates. In that respect, tax systems are a good example of what Rousseau would have called deficient institutions that cater to special interests and lead to corruption of the citizenry.

Simplification is the main reason that, since the mid-1990s, many of the newly emerging democracies in Eastern Europe have replaced progressive taxes by proportional taxes. This so-called flat-tax revolution is associated with a proposal originally advanced by Hall and Rabushka (1995), suggesting that income be taxed at a single uniform rate. Tax codes based on a flat tax are easier for the government to administer and easier for citizens to comply with. Simplicity is the best way to fight tax avoidance and flat tax systems seem to be the ideal method for citizens to pay the price for their citizenship. But if flat taxes are simple, are they also fair? As long as a flat tax combines a threshold or a tax-exempt amount of income with a single rate on all income above it, progressivity is achieved indirectly: although income is taxed at the same uniform rate, the rich pay a bigger share of their income in taxes than the poor (Table 11.1).

Table 11.1 Flat-tax revolution in Europe

Country	Introduction of flat-tax	Income tax rate (%) before introduction	Flat-tax rate (%)
Estonia	1994	16–33	22
Latvia	1994	18–33	27
Lithuania	1995	25–10	25
Russia	2001	12–30	13
Serbia	2003	10–20	14
Ukraine	2004	10–40	15
Slovakia	2004	10–38	19
Georgia	2005	12–20	12
Romania	2005	18–40	16
Macedonia	2007	15–24	12
Montenegro	2007	16–24	15
Albania	2007	5–30	10

Source: *Neue Zürcher Zeitung*, October 8, 2007, no. 233, p. 13.

Progressivity under a flat tax can also be assured by offsetting every tax-payer's fiscal burden by a fixed tax rebate (Greene, 1997). For the lowest income bracket, the rebate wipes out the entire tax obligation, for the middle class it still provides a significant reduction in the effective tax rate, while it reduces the amount due by the wealthiest group of people only insignificantly. From a pedagogical standpoint, a tax rebate—either combined with a flat or with a progressive tax—is, however, not an adequate means to advance social citizenship, at least not for the poor. Because people living in poverty earn less than the poverty threshold, they usually don't pay taxes and can consequently not take advantage of a tax rebate. Modern welfare states deal with such households in the framework of an income support scheme that is administered outside the tax code. In this way, the government creates two types of citizens: those who pay taxes and those who get income support and are, therefore, often not considered true citizens, but merely welfare recipients.

More than 60 years ago, Lady Juliet Rhys Williams, a British social reformer, suggested therefore in *Something to look forward to* (1943) that the income support system be integrated into the tax code. The best way to achieve this goal is to tax the first monetary unit that citizens earn, but to offset the tax burden by a rebate or so-called social dividend paid out to each citizen, even those who do not owe taxes at all or whose tax due is smaller than the dividend. In this way, every citizen is a part of the give-and-take relationship between citizens and the government that is at the core of modern societies. From the perspective of citizenship through education, a social dividend, also known as a negative income tax, would be the most appropriate form to tax citizens (Atkinson, 1983).

Changes to the Welfare State

The state's role as an important provider of welfare services and its unique position as a guarantor of social rights led to an enormous growth in public expenditures and a corresponding increase of the tax burden imposed on a country's residents. However, the rapid growth of public expenditures made the welfare state vulnerable to many criticisms. With growing citizen expectations, on the one hand, and the rising costs of welfare associated with technical advance and public demand, on the other, the idea that the state could guarantee universal social rights was increasingly exposed as a fiscal illusion. Furthermore, the large bureaucracies created over the postwar period had failed to deliver services in the quantity and quality that citizens wished to receive. The welfare state was seen as mainly catering to the middle classes and insensitive to the diversity of citizens' preferences, especially the needs of the poor.

As a consequence, the welfare state was forced to reshape the social contract that binds the members of a society together. Thus, new paradigms of citizenship emerged, each envisaging a different social contract between the state and its citizens. The most far-reaching attempt to reorganize the public sector is the privatization paradigm. The main purpose of privatization is to restore citizenship to its original status defined by civil liberties, such as the right to own property and to make free choices. In the framework of this paradigm, citizens are conceived first and foremost as private individuals and consumers, whose freedom of choice has to be protected against government interference. Furthermore, private businesses and nonprofit organizations are seen as attractive means of outsourcing human services that were previously provided in their entirety by the government.

Few modern democracies followed the privatization agenda of completely dismantling the welfare state and replacing it with a market model of welfare. Instead, they took a less radical approach, changing the mechanism through which government distributed welfare to its citizens and consolidating the institution of social citizenship. One can distinguish three such paradigms, each representing a special way in which the social contract with citizens is being reinterpreted and the delivery of social services is rearranged: decentralization, new public management, and private–public partnership (Wagner, 2004: 282) (Table 11.2).

Table 11.2 Consolidating social citizenship

Paradigm	Consolidation of social citizenship
Decentralization	The division of labor between the two tiers of the government is one of complementarity: Income transfers affecting collective social security remain with the national government, whereas services targeting individuals are being provided by local governments in collaboration with private associations.
New public management	Service provision is contracted out to private entities functioning as 'third-party governments.' Contracts are subject to the introduction of efficiency enhancing techniques and performance management. The state remains, however, firmly in control of welfare and retains ultimate responsibility for the delivery of services.
Private–public partnership	This paradigm stresses the critical importance of partnership between public authorities, private enterprises, and the voluntary sector in providing welfare services to local communities. Partnership governance helps to develop vital human resources and to mobilize the energies of disenfranchised citizens.

Although each of these paradigms represents a distinctive proposal for reforming the welfare state, they overlap in that they put the emphasis on local civil society. Instead of simply reducing the role of the state, these reform proposals promote an institutional blend of municipalities, local nonprofit organizations, and community-based trade unions to complement the government in its formerly dominant role. The next section will address the role of these organizations as a mechanism of societal integration in post-industrial societies.

Citizenship and Local Civil Society

The consolidation of the welfare state that took place during the last two decades of the twentieth century has undeniably strengthened the functional and moral ties between the state and its citizens, at least at the national level. However, as more plural forms of society began to emerge during the last couple of decades, with differentiated lifestyles and deeper structures of disadvantage by class, race, and gender, social citizenship at the national level has come increasingly under assault from within and from without the welfare state. In complex and dynamic societies, multiple forms of integration, and thus alternative kinds of citizenship, are necessary to maintain cohesion and stability of society. While some observers put the emphasis on territorial or place-based mechanisms of integration, others attribute the leading role to voluntary associations, affinity groups, and communities of interest.

Initially, citizenship was confined to the social space that corresponded to the territory of a nation. Citizenship was, therefore, defined as national citizenship. As the dominant elites of Western democracies began to restrict the delivery of social services and as the gap was widening between the formal status of national citizenship and the substantive benefits linked to it, more and more people were forced to find their own ways of organizing their daily existence and of practicing their societal commitment. In this context, urban centers emerged as new social spaces in many countries around the world. As territorial entities, they are closer than central government to the issues that people face in their daily lives. They attract residents in need of social services, trying to evade surveillance and control by public authorities and, at the same time, willing to engage with each other. Cities constitute an outlet for civic interaction and an ideal environment to develop a new form of citizenship: residential citizenship (Wagner, 2008a).

The emergence of residential citizenship is tied to the physical spaces of urban centers where social life takes place. In these spaces, people gather to interact, to debate shared concerns, and to resolve their differences. Beauregard and Bounds (2000: 248) suggest that the public realm of the city comprises two types of spaces: public and parochial. Public spaces (such as parks and plazas) provide opportunities for people unknown to each other to come together.

People who congregate as part of the same social network meet in parochial spaces, such as neighborhood playgrounds and church basements. Here, city dwellers initiate social learning processes and craft their interests and identities (Beauregard and Bounds, 2000: 248); in public spaces, they make them known to a citywide or even national audience.

It is this interaction of engaged local residents and their collective action that constitutes the essence of residential citizenship. Rights and responsibilities of local residents are shaped by the social relationships through which citizens acknowledge each other. Their behavior and attitudes are governed from bottom up, rather than from top down, by private initiatives and not so much by the intervention of local authorities (Beauregard and Bounds, 2000: 252). To paraphrase Rousseau, residential citizens place in common their person by interacting with each other, rather than by placing themselves under the direction of the local authority. Their relationship with the local government is, therefore, a mediated one, an indirect, rather than a direct, relationship.

Although not a constituent element of residential citizenship, the local government, nevertheless, plays an important role as a supportive institution. It guarantees the rights and responsibilities that form the substantive core of residential citizenship and raises the revenue necessary to finance the social infrastructure of urban life. Ideally, this requires a flexible source of revenue in form of a local income tax. In the absence of such a tax, jurisdiction over taxation has to be centralized, and adequate instrument of fiscal equalization among the different levels of the government have to be put in place (Wagner, 2004).

Parallel to residential citizenship, some authors (Hirst, 1994; Cohen and Rogers, 1992) advocate associational democracy as a form of identity-based citizenship at the subnational level. The argument they advance is twofold. Since the 1970s, voluntary associations have assumed an increased role in providing social services due to the decline of state activity in the welfare and health sectors. In this area, voluntary associations have a comparative advantage vis-à-vis the state, because they are more sensitive to local needs and capable of providing services to marginalized social groups (Turner, 2001: 203). More importantly, voluntary associations can provide opportunities for democratic involvement, and thus for active citizenship (Turner, 2001: 200). In this respect, they are important vehicles for building communities and enhancing participation of those members of society who are socially, politically, and economically most often excluded. Therefore, associational democracy constitutes an interesting outlet for learning processes leading to active citizenship.

The idea of a citizenry in which people relate to each other (and not only to government bureaucracies) played an especially important role in the history of the United States. Here, citizenship was understood in the context of the so-called associational revolution that in the course of eighteenth and nineteenth centuries spread throughout Europe and the United States. Whereas, in Europe, freedom of association soon clashed with the sovereignty of the state and the spirit of the French Revolution; the right of citizens to associate freely became one of the basic organizing principles of the United States. In the opinion of A. de Tocqueville, 'the most democratic country on the face of the earth is that in which men have, in our time, carried to the highest perfection the art of pursuing in common the object of their common desires and have applied this new science to the greatest number of purposes' (quoted from Zunz and Kahan, 2002: 181).

It is therefore tempting to consider associational democracy as a typical 'American' paradigm, based on Tocqueville's idea of participation and contrasting with a more 'European' framework of a deliberative democracy, influenced by Rousseau's social contract. One should, however, refrain from using such geographic labels to distinguish the two types of society. For one, it has to be taken into account that Tocqueville was of European descent. More importantly, however, his view—so cherished in the United States—that associations play an important role as vehicles of integration in democratic societies has not gone unchallenged, not even in American history. In *The Federalist* (Paper No. 10), James Madison (Hamilton et al., 2006) argued that factions 'are the mortal disease under which popular governments have every where perished' (2006: 52). The proliferation of factions, he goes on, demonstrates and actuates Americans' 'zeal for different opinions concerning religion, concerning government, and many other points. [Factions] have, in turn, divided mankind into parties, inflamed them with mutual animosity, and rendered them much more disposed to vex and oppress each other, than to cooperate for their common good' (2006: 53). Madison's concern about factions echoes Rousseau's, who argues in *The social contract* that special interest groups or 'partial associations' can have a negative impact on societal integration. 'When there are partial associations—Rousseau argues (1947: 27) —it is politic to multiply their number, that they may be all kept on an equality'.

Concerns about the political role of associational life—such as those voiced by Madison and Rousseau—continue to resonate in modern times. Rawls argued in *Political liberalism* (1993: 40) that the concept of a deliberative democracy emphasizes discourse and the use of public reason in the negotiation of the social contract. In that respect, it differs from the idea of associational democracy, with its emphasis on participation in local communities and special interest organizations. In an associational democracy, membership in society is mediated through membership in particular groups, which are often governed by their own comprehensive doctrine. Under such a regime, members of society 'are viewed in public life as members of different groups and each group is represented in the legal system' (Rawls, 1999: 64). Therefore, associational democracies are structured in a hierarchical way, offering their members terms of participation depending on the worth of their potential contribution to associational life and not linked to the equal status of citizenship, as it would be the case in a deliberative democracy (Wagner, 2008b).

Conclusion: New Forms of Solidarity

The purpose of this chapter is to better understand the meaning of citizenship and the often contested role it played at the national and local levels in Western welfare states. Rather than comprehending citizenship within a static framework of rights and obligations bestowed upon a fortunate few, it was conceptualized as a dynamic institution resulting from a lifelong learning process undergone by the members of society. The processes through which people learn to become citizens are embedded in particular institutional environments. In a welfare state setting, the learning process through which people become citizens is based on a give-and-take relationship between the government and the members of society. Citizens pay taxes to their government and in return are provided public goods. As in the course of the twentieth century, public authority was successively devolved to lower level governments and private organizations, third-party governments ended up delivering the services originally provided by the government. As a result, the link between the taxes citizens pay and the services they receive was more and more attenuated. The welfare state ceased to function as the exclusive—or at least the major—vehicle for addressing public problems, while local authorities, voluntary associations, and civil society became major nonpublic sites of education for citizenship.

Despite this important role of local civil society, one should, however, refrain from uncritically celebrating membership in voluntary organizations as an effective mediating institution between individuals and their polity (Wagner, 2008). In multiethnic and culturally diverse societies, more and more citizens will derive some of their deepest commitments to society from comprehensive, but irreconcilable religious/ethical doctrines they hold in private. In conclusion, this essay has, therefore, to assess the role that faith-based groups (and their doctrines) play in the societal learning process leading to citizenship, as a factor either of divisiveness or of support for civic identity among members of society. Particularly, in what way will religious/ethical doctrines affect democratic principles of citizenship: will they facilitate social cooperation—on their own terms and for their own reasons—or will they contribute to tearing society apart?

Islam is such a religious/ethical doctrine par excellence (March, 2007). It is worth special consideration, because particularly in Europe—with a population of at least 13 million Muslims, according to recent estimates—Muslims are citizens of liberal societies in large numbers (Wagner, 2008b). Islamic legal, political, and ethical doctrines have traditionally held that submission to non-Muslim political authority and bonds of loyalty with non-Muslim societies are to be avoided. Therefore, the idea of Muslim citizenship in non-Muslim states is deeply problematic. But in his pathbreaking research on this question, March (2007) presents Islamic sources which could serve to ground a stable social contract among Muslims and non-Muslims in liberal democracies of the West. This author found that classical and modern discourses affirm a certain set of values and principles which prescribe vigorous ethical standards for dealing with non-Muslims, within both Muslim and non-Muslim polities (March, 2007: 236). In particular, there are elements of Islamic jurisprudence insisting on the inviolability of contracts and affirming political obligations and loyalty of Muslims toward non-Muslim states.

In more general terms, March's findings support the insight that citizens of different creeds (and more importantly secular and nonsecular citizens as well) can reach an overlapping consensus supporting a society's public conception of justice, as long as they refrain from truth claims derived from comprehensive doctrines to which they adhere. This position emphasizes Rawls's (1999: 132) principle of reasonable pluralism. In pluralistic societies, citizens act reasonably when they offer one another fair terms of cooperation and recognize that their political ideas may be revised through public deliberation. Against the backdrop of the growing Muslim immigration to Europe, Tibi (1998) coined the term *Leitkultur* (leading or guiding culture) for such an overlapping consensus between citizens holding conflicting comprehensive doctrines. His concept was quickly misunderstood as an attempt by an Arab scholar—turned European— to force a majority culture on Muslim immigrants and other foreign residents. But what Tibi wanted to advocate was merely the need for a European civic identity, the idea of a democratic community whose members are bound together by a social contract.

Rawls's vision for the need of an overlapping consensus and Tibi's concept of *Leitkultur* bring us full swing back to the social contract theory and the institution of citizenship. At a time when processes of political exclusion affect the ethnic and cultural texture of Europe, the formula 'citizenship through education' points to an innovative path of societal integration in culturally diverse democracies of the West. Thus, the social contract theory leads us back to the roots of the modern welfare state and through Enlightenment philosophy also back to its future.

References

Atkinson, A. B. (1983). *The economics of inequality*. Oxford: Clarendon Press.

Bertram, C. (2004). *Rousseau and the social contract*. London and New York: Routledge.

Beauregard, R. A., & Bounds, A. (2000). Urban citizenship. In E. Isin, (Ed.), *Democracy, citizenship and the global city*, (pp. 243–256). London and New York: Routledge.

Burnett, V. (2007, August 8). New secular civics class riling Catholic Church. *International Herald Tribune*, p. 2. http://www.highbeam.com/doc/1P1-142405448.html

Cohen, J. R., & Rogers, J. (1992). Secondary associations and democratic governance. *Politics and Society, 20*(4), 393–472.

Council of Europe (1999). *Declaration and programme on education for democratic citizenship*, adopted by the Committee of Ministers at its 104th Session on 7 May 1999.

Greene, L. (1997). *The national tax rebate: A new America with less government*. Washington, DC: Regnery Publishing.

Hall, R. E., & Rabushka, A. (1995). *The flat tax*. Stanford: Hoover Institution Press.

Hamilton, A., Madison, J., & Jay, J. (Eds.) (2006[1788]). *The Federalist*. New York: Barnes & Noble Classics Series.

Hirst, P. (1994). *Associative democracy: New forms of economic and social governance*. London: Polity Press.

March, A. F. (2007). Islamic foundations for a social contract in non-Muslim liberal democracies. *American Political Science Review, 101*(2), 235–252.

Mosher, R., Kenny, R. A. Jr., & Garrod, A. (Eds.). (1994). *Preparing for citizenship: Teaching youth to live democratically*. Westport, CT: Praeger.

Neiman, S. (2002). *Evil in modern thought. An alternative history of philosophy*. Princeton and Oxford: Princeton University Press.

Ostrander, S. A., & Portney, K. E. (Eds.). (2007). *Acting civically*. Medford, MA: Tufts University Press.

Ravitch, D., & Viteritti, J. P. (Eds.). (2001). *Making good citizens: Education and civil society*. New Haven and London: Yale University Press.

Rawls, J. (1993). *Political liberalism*. New York: Columbia University Press.

Rawls, J. (1999). *The law of peoples*. Cambridge, MA: Harvard University Press.

Rhys-Williams, J. (1943). *Something to look forward to: A suggestion for a new social contract*. London: MacDonald.

Rousseau, J.-J. (1947 [1762]). *The social contract*. New York: Hafner Press.

Rousseau, J.-J. (1964). Discours sur l'origine et les fondements de l'inégalité parmi les homes. In B. Gagnebin & M. Raymond, (Eds.), *Jean-Jacques Rousseau, Oeuvres Complètes* (vol. III, pp. 131–223). Paris: Gallimard.

Rousseau, J.-J. (1969). Émile ou de l'éducation. In B. Gagnebin & M. Raymond (Eds.), *Jean-Jacques Rousseau, Oeuvres Complètes*, (vol. IV, pp. 239–868). Paris: Gallimard.

Tibi, B. (1998). *Europa ohne Identitä?. Die Krise der multikulturellen Gesellschaft*. München: Bertelsmann.

Turner, B. S. (2001). The erosion of citizenship. *British Journal of Sociology, 52*(2), 189–209.

Wagner. A. (2004). Redefining citizenship for the 21st century: From the national welfare state to the UN Global Compact. *International Journal of Social Welfare, 13*, 278–286.

Wagner, A. (2008a). Citizenship through education. A comment on *Social exclusion in Europe: Some conceptual issues*. *International Journal of Social Welfare, 17*, 93–97.

Wagner, A. (2008b). Religion and civil society: A critical reappraisal of America's civic engagement debate. *Voluntary and Nonprofit Sector Quarterly, 37*, 626–645.

Wolf, P. J., & Macedo, S. (Eds.). (2004). *Educating citizens: International perspectives on civic values and school choice*. Washington, DC: Brookings Institution Press.

Zunz, O., & Kahan A. S. (2002). *The Tocqueville reader. A life in letters and politics*, Oxford: Blackwell Publishing.

Chapter 12
England and Wales: The Criminal Justice System in 'Post-industrial Society'

Tim Owen

For David Ridley

Introduction

This chapter examines the current 'state of play' and recent trends in the criminal justice system of England and Wales in the context of developments associated with the so-called 'post-industrial society' (Bell, 1973) and the impact of the processes which have come to be referred to as 'globalization' in terms of crime, citizenship, the welfare state, and challenges to the nation-state. It is the contention here that whilst there is little doubt that the criminal justice system of England and Wales, and for that matter the individual nation-state of the United Kingdom, is being challenged by global and technological processes in the so-called 'post-industrial society,' we should strive to avoid reductionist and essentialist theoretical accounts relying on unitary explanations for complex social phenomena which serve to exaggerate the scale and/or the intensity of 'globalization,' and which underplay the uneven impact of 'globalizing' tendencies. It is the view here that the social world is contingent and *not* determined by macrostructural motor forces. Drawing upon the *anti-reductionist* theories of Sibeon (1996, 2004) and Owen (2006, 2007a, 2007b, 2008, forthcoming), it is suggested here that it is highly doubtful that reliance on unitary explanations of the sort associated with 'crude' globalization and post-industrialism theses will ever be capable of providing an adequate account of policy reproductive processes, trends, and developments in the criminal justice system of England and Wales. The thesis of *post-industrialism* may indeed refer to some important

T. Owen (✉)
Centre for Criminology and Criminal Justice, University of Central Lancashire, Preston, UK
e-mail: towen1@uclan.ac.uk

J. Powell, J. Hendricks, *The Welfare State in Post-Industrial Society*,
DOI 10.1007/978-1-4419-0066-1_12, © Springer Science+Business Media, LLC 2009

contemporary economic trends, some of which have undoubtedly impacted upon the criminal justice system, but it is the contention here that the thesis exaggerates the nature and scale of change.

Arguably, more fruitful analyses lie in the direction of a *post-postmodern*, ontologically flexible approach, which emphasizes *agency-structure, micro-macro*, and *time space*, multi-factorial explanations and methodological generalizations as opposed to substantive generalizations (Sibeon, ibid; Owen, ibid); in the direction of Sibeon's (ibid) *postnational* perspective and methodology which focuses on the subnational, national, and transnational levels of governance, rather than giving causal primacy to any one of these levels on a priori grounds; or in the direction of Cavadino and Dignan's (2006) important, groundbreaking work, which, building on Esping-Anderson's (1990) research, analyses systematic differences in penal systems in the context of 'globalization.' For example, Cavadino and Dignan (ibid) are arguably correct to emphasize that whilst some international trends and pressures may be identified, together with an increase in American cultural domination, this does *not* equate with global homogeneity and uniformity.

Here, the focus is on the agencies and aspects of the criminal justice system of England and Wales that have been affected by the frenetic pace of reform since the election of the New Labour government in 1997. Concerns about change and uncertainty were apparent in the debates about the 'causes' of crime and the role of the criminal justice system at the dawn of Bell's (1973) so-called 'post-industrial society.' Arguably, such concerns also characterize current debates some 35 years on. It appears to be the case that the criminal justice system of England and Wales faces considerable changes and dilemmas, some of which are outlined in what follows. Membership of the European Union has arguably changed the nature of sovereignty, the role of the nation-state, and the nature of citizenship, but that is *not* to say that nation-states and variations between them are unimportant. Trends and developments in the uncertain, 'post-industrial' landscape of the criminal justice system of England and Wales are identified here, and it is contended that an increasing emphasis on cost-effectiveness may possibly conflict with other influences in penal policy. The New Labour government of Gordon Brown arguably faces a dilemma in the pursuit of crime strategies which emphasize politically desirable 'tough on crime' approaches, whilst at the same time taking account of economic issues (Davies et al., 2005). As is hopefully made clear here, the increasingly tougher and more punitive polices which characterize the criminal justice system of England and Wales may lead to higher prosecution costs and the increasing use of imprisonment as punishment.

Davies et al. (2005) describes how there are three distinctive criminal justice systems with separate procedures and agencies in the United Kingdom: England and Wales, Scotland, and Northern Ireland. In this chapter, as has hopefully been made clear, the focus is on England and Wales. As the authors suggest, the organization and jurisdictional limits of criminal justice in England and Wales are determined by 'constitutional distinctions within the United Kingdom and increasingly by the need to respond to issues of crime in the outside world,' especially in the aftermath of the acts of terrorism in New York and Washington DC on 11 September 2001 (Davies et al., ibid: 3). Britain's membership of the European Union also means that, with regard to crime, constitutional, and everyday regulations, 'we are no longer an isolated island in the sea of criminal justice' (ibid). Agencies of criminal justice in the United Kingdom as a whole have inevitably had to comply with aspects of harmonization, integration, and greater cooperation with European partners (member countries).

At this point, it might be useful to define criminal justice. Hudson (2007: 93–94) defines criminal justice as, 'the process through which the state responds to behaviour that it deems unacceptable.' Criminal justice is thus delivered through a series of various stages or processes; prosecution; trial; sentence; appeal; punishment. As Hudson shows, theoretical analysis of criminal justice has focused on, 'the tension between the objective of crime control, and the values of due process' (ibid: 94). Crime control and due process were developed as theoretical models by Herbert Packer to 'illuminate what he saw as the two conflicting value systems that competed for priority in the operation of the criminal justice process' (Sanders and Young, 2007: 19). As Hudson suggests, if crime control is the dominant consideration, 'severe penalties may be imposed: penalties designed to ensure protection of the public through removal or incapacitation of the offender, so that there is no chance of a further offence' (ibid). In contrast, 'due process values emphasize fairness and equality in criminal justice, and respect the rights of offenders, so that there should be proper safeguards through representation, rules of evidence, and the prosecution having to establish guilt according to rigorous standards of proof' (ibid). As Hudson makes clear, the 1980s are generally viewed as being characterised by a dominance of the values of the due process model, while 'there has been a marked swing towards crime control in the 1990s.'

In England and Wales, criminal justice agencies, such as the police, prisons, and probation, depend mainly on central government funding. Policy is established partly by civil servants and by legislation enacted by Parliament. As Davies et al. (ibid: 4) show, there are seven main agencies: police, prosecution, the Criminal Defence Service, courts, probation, prisons, youth justice, and the Serious Organised Crime Agency (SOCA). Regarding the police, there are currently 43 regional police forces, each of which is under the direction of an individual chief constable and local police authorities, with the exception of the Metropolitan Police and the City of London police. Police forces in England and Wales vary in terms of size, with the largest being the Metropolitan Police with 26,800 uniformed officers, and the smallest with just over 1,000 police officers. In England and Wales, in 2004, there were 138,000 police supplemented by 16,000 Specials, 4,000 Police Community Support Officers, and 53,000 civilian employees.

The Crown Prosecution Service (CPS), established in 1985, is divided into 42 areas with the attorney general being answerable in Parliament for the CPS. The CPS in turn is headed by the Director of Public Prosecutions (a senior lawyer). The Crown Prosecution Service is estimated to complete approximately 1.4 million cases a year in the magistrates' courts and around 125,000 in the Crown Court. The Criminal Defence Service is responsible for overseeing the system of legal support of those accused of crimes in terms of advice, assistance, and representation in court by 'full-time public defenders' and contracted private sector lawyers (Davies et al., ibid). In terms of courts, most criminal cases go to the magistrates' courts, while it is the Crown Court which deals with the more serious cases. Officials in the courts include judges, recorders, magistrates, magistrates' clerks, and ushers. Criminal courts come under the Department for Constitutional Affairs' authority, which in turn is responsible for the appointment of judges.

The Probation Service bears the responsibility for preparing presentence reports for courts, supervising community orders, and 'helping prisoners adapt to community life following release' (Davies et al., ibid). The National Probation Service was established by legislation in 2000. Regarding prisons, the Prison Service is an 'executive agency' and is directed in terms of policy by the Home Office. It is organized into 15 regional areas, with a responsibility for 138 prisons. Together with the Probation Service, it constitutes the National Offender Management Service (NOMS) with a responsibility for the management of offenders from the point of sentence to the point of 'resettlement' in the wider community.

The Youth Justice Board is the central board monitoring the work of the youth justice system and that of the Youth Offending Teams (YOTs). The Youth Offending Teams were established across England and Wales by 2000 and are local authority, multiagency teams, which coordinate the work of agencies and volunteers working with young offenders.

The year 2006 saw the establishment of SOCA, the Serious and Organised Crime Agency, which is a national policing agency with considerable powers to combat urgent threats from terrorism and global organized crime. SOCA has around 5,000 agents drawn from the merger of the National Crime Squad, National Criminal Intelligence Service, Special Branch, Serious Fraud Office, and, to a lesser extent, Customs and Immigration Services. SOCA's focus is on drug and human trafficking, which, in theory, provide an 'integrated approach to deal with the threat of cross-jurisdictional crime and international crime organisation' (Davies et al., ibid: 5). There are also a number of smaller criminal justice agencies in England and Wales, which include Coroners, the Criminal Injuries Compensation Authority, the Forensic Science Service, HM Inspectorates, the Parole Board, and the Victim Support. In what follows, we examine the criminal justice system in the context of 'post-industrialism' and 'globalization.'

'Post-industrial Society'

As Sibeon (1996: 82) suggests, in the decade of the 1960s, a number of sociologists and social theorists, such as Daniel Bell, Raymond Aron, Ralf Dahrendorf, and others, 'reacted against' 'structural-functionalists' and Marxists' alleged failure to adequately grasp the significance of social, economic, and political changes associated with movement toward a post-industrial society (Bell, 1973; Touraine, 1974). The argument was along the lines that industrial capitalism, the manufacturing of material goods, and social class interests/ class conflict were the key features of the industrial society. In contrast, post-industrial society (there are parallels here with 'the information society' of Webster (1995) and the 'postmodern society' of Kumar (1995) is conceptualized as being characterized by a centrality of information and knowledge and also by a decline in the importance of manufacturing. Additionally, in such a post-industrial society, there is a 'relative decrease in the numbers employed in manufacturing industry and an expansion of service occupations; the clerical and professional sectors have increased in size' (Sibeon, ibid). Bell (1973) refers to 'codified knowledge' (the idea that bodies of knowledge have been systematized), which becomes a crucial societal resource. Emerging from this are a new 'knowledge class': those involved in the creation and dissemination of information, such as academics, scientists, professionals, and technical experts. This new 'knowledge class' become powerful groupings superseding industrialists and entrepreneurs formerly associated with older, 'industrial' forms of society. In the 'new' post-industrial landscape, policy making is said to be increasingly based on expert knowledge and scientific rationality, rather than on intuitions and 'judgements' (Sibeon, ibid).

Authors like Kasarda (1989) and Judd and Parkinson (1990) have suggested that while consumerism may be a key characteristic of post-industrial society, the ability to 'consume' is not equally open to all citizens. Such writers have drawn attention to post-industrial trends, which include a movement toward highly automated (robotic) production methods associated with deindustrialization, rising levels of unemployment, poverty, urban decline, and a disadvantaged 'underclass.' Scholars like Standing (1986) have made the point that there has been a movement toward the flexibilization of labor leading to increased levels of job insecurity and low wage levels for unskilled and part-time workers. As Sibeon (ibid: 83) reflects, change in labor-market conditions 'coincided with government initiatives in the United Kingdom in the 1980s to de-regulate working conditions and reduce trade union power.' Perhaps, as the latter author suggests, such 'negative' features of post-industrialism are sometimes overlooked in more 'upbeat' descriptions of a 'new' social order based on ideas of a post-industrial society and closely associated notions of an 'information society.'

The thesis of post-industrialism may indeed refer to important contemporary socioeconomic trends, but it is a thesis that has attracted criticisms from those such as Kumar (1978) and Williams (1985). Sibeon (ibid) makes the point that 'theories of postindustrialism, post-Fordism etc., quite often accurately identify certain patterns of change, but they tend to exaggerate the nature and scale of change.' There has been, for example, an overemphasis in the work of some post-industrial/information society theorists on the handling of the kind of complex information which is seen to characterize the post-industrial/

information society. A great number of service sector jobs have become mechanized in the sense of being computerized and routine in nature. Another relevant factor is that 'quite a number of computer experts and "service" professionals are in fact employed in manufacturing industries' (ibid). Additionally, as Lyon (1987) suggests, the notion of 'information' and 'codified knowledge' as organizing principles of society is less than clear. Arguably, the notion of an 'information society' or a 'post-industrial' society is a highly contestable, rather than self-evident, concept. Sibeon (ibid) is quite possibly correct in suggesting that it is difficult to accept the post-industrial thesis because of its tendency toward reductionism and oversimplification. Waters (1995: 18), too, appears to express doubts about the post-industrial thesis (specifically that of Bell (1973)), observing: 'In Bell the emerging society is governed by a single axial principle (the use of theoretical knowledge to produce services) and it is specified as the only possible principle of future social organisation ... all the societies on the planet march resolutely forward to a singular post-industrial future.'

As Sibeon (ibid) observes, many theorists of the post-industrial society appear to 'propound a singular and general substantive theory of social change.' Such general theories of societal change are, however, arguably highly problematic. Giddens (1984: 227–228) has suggested that a little too much is laid at the door of 'post-industrialism' and that in explaining social change, 'no single and sovereign mechanism can be specified; there are no keys that will unlock the mysteries of human social development, reducing them to a unitary formula.' In theories of post-industrialism, social change in general is largely attributed to economic change, and there is 'more than a touch of economic determinism (and therefore reductionism) in the approach' (Sibeon, ibid: 83). Bell (1973) appears to assume that there is a near-inevitability, a 'logic of postindustrialism' (Sibeon, ibid: 84) about the changes he predicted in the 1970s. Arguably, Sibeon (ibid) is correct in arguing that a 'more adequate conception of social change' would recognize that the 'impact of macro-social processes' pertaining to deindustrialization, technological change, the growth of service occupations and professions, the growth of information technology, etc., 'are likely to be variable and differentially shaped by a variety of cultural, economic, and political factors at the subnational, national, and transnational levels of social process.' The role played by *agency* (the ability of an actor to formulate and act on decisions), too, should be considered here. Patterns of social life and their reproduction or change 'are in various ways influenced by the activities of *actors* whose forms of thought and formulations of interests and purposes are not structurally predetermined nor guided inexorably in a single direction by something called 'post-industrialism'' (Sibeon, ibid). It may be the case that actors involved in politics and public policy, the criminal justice system of England and Wales, etc., are affected by some macro processes described by theorists of post-industrialism, such as Bell (1973), but events are not universally or singularly determined by 'post-industrialism' or for that matter by any other macrosocial phenomena (Sibeon, 1996, 2004; Marsh and

Rhodes, 1992a, 1992b; Wilsford, 1994; Dunn and Perl, 1994: 312). It is, therefore, highly unlikely that reductionist metanarratives, such as 'post-industrialism,' which rely on unitary explanations for complex social phenomena, will ever be capable of providing an adequate explanatory account of policy reproductive processes in the criminal justice system of England and Wales. Drawing upon the *antireductionist* theories of Sibeon (ibid) and Owen (2008, forthcoming, 2007a, 2007b, 2006), it is contended here that the social world is contingent and not determined by macrostructural motor forces such as 'post-industrialism.'

Globalization

Recently, Muncie (2007: 186–187) has defined globalization as 'a widely, but often loosely, used term which usually implies an increasing homogeneity of national economies, politics and culture.' He then goes on to observe that such convergence is driven mainly by, 'international flows of de-regulated capital, information and people and dominated by multi-national, neo-liberal economies and technologies' (ibid: 187). Muncie makes the point that global multinational corporations and financial markets 'now seem to provide the economic, political and cultural parameters in which we live' (ibid). For Muncie, 'the sovereignty of individual nation-states and the authority of traditional social institutions seem to be increasingly redundant in the face of these powerful forces' (ibid). Nelken (1997) has made similar observations. However, as Muncie goes on to suggest, despite a widespread acceptance of these notions, the meaning and implications of globalization are the subject of great debate. The concept is sometimes used 'interchangeably with other competing macroconcepts,' such as *transnationalization* (the dissolving of national boundaries); *supranationalization* (transcending national limits); *internationalization* (exchanges of capital and labor); *universalization* (the spread of information and cultural phenomena worldwide); *neoliberalization* (the removal of regulatory barriers to international exchange/transfer); *westernization* (standardization driven by advanced industrial economies); *Anglo-Americanization* (homogenization driven by the United States/United Kingdom alliance); or indeed *modernization* (the diffusion of managerial economies).

As Muncie (ibid) appears to suggest, dispute emerges over the question of whether globalization is 'anything new at all, or rather simply a modern version of *colonization*.' Yeates (2001) has observed that the concept is flawed because it encourages reductionist and economistic readings of societal change. Is the concept able to aid an understanding of contemporary transformations in crime and crime control within the criminal justice system of England and Wales? Arguably, as Muncie (ibid) suggests, there is an 'emergent and growing fear' that global flows of capital, information, and human beings are providing the ideal conditions and opportunities for organised crime to flourish. Criminal 'enterprises,' for example, the Chinese triads, the Russian mafia, and Jamaican

Yardies, and others are often assumed to have made widespread profits in the trafficking of drugs, arms, human beings, in international pornography, prostitution, and international fraud, etc. This 'vision of criminality out of control' (Muncie, ibid) has arguably dramatically increased since the terrorist attacks of 11 September 2001, together with the widespread fear that crime now lacks boundaries. However, with regard to 'serious organised crime,' it is important to appreciate the 'subtlety, complexity and depth of field of the organization of crimes' (Levi, 2007: 799). In doing so, we should arguably keep firmly in mind that 'many different forms of organization can coexist in parallel, and that to be an "organized criminal" does not mean that one has to be a member of an "organized crime syndicate" '(ibid). As Levi (ibid) observes, 'There is no Blofeld figure or SMERSH collective organizing "crime" or "terrorism" worldwide: rather there are layers of different forms of enterprise criminal, some undertaking wholly illegal activities and others mixing the legal and illegal depending on contacts, trust, and assessment of risks from enforcement in particular national markets.'

For Muncie (ibid), globalization carries with it the transformations which are of particular relevance to the study of criminal justice systems. First, according to the author, there is global convergence in terms of criminal justice politics (especially with regard to the 'Anglophone' north), with governments increasingly adopting similar economic, social, and criminal justice policies, as they endeavor to attract international capital and combat crime on an international scale. Second, much 'homogenization' appears to be 'underpinned by a fundamental shift in state/market relations whereby neo-liberal conceptions of the "free market" driven by multi-national corporations encourage the formulation of policies based upon deregulation, privatization, authoritarianism and social inequality than upon social inclusion and welfare protection' (ibid). The author cites the US-led 'war on drugs and terror' as a typical example of such global developments.

O'Malley (2002) has made the point that neoliberalism manifests itself in conservative and social democratic *rationalities*, in authoritarian, retributive human rights and in responsible/restorative *technologies*. Arguably, the effects of globalization are not uniform, and we need to keep in mind the 'diversity of criminal justice reform' (Muncie, ibid: 188). As Nelken (1997) has suggested 'global' is only realized in specific localities, through which it may be challenged, contested, and reworked. For the latter author, the central issue is actually not how globalization produces homogeneity and uniformity, but how it is producing and activating diversity.

In a recent study of the criminal justice system of England and Wales, Davies et al. (2005: 97) draw attention, in the course of a discussion about the cross-jurisdictional and international responses to crime, to the possibility that the free movement of people in the enlarged European Union means that 'criminals have a wide market to deal in and more places to hide both themselves and their assets.' A number of regional and world developments have emerged, together with a greater insight into 'both the nature of crime and other criminal justice systems' as law enforcement agencies increasingly endeavor to share information and attempt to harmonize with and accommodate each others' systems/procedures (ibid: 97–98). In the United Kingdom, the Anti-Terrorism, Crime and Security Act 2001 established new powers to: cut off terrorist funding; allow government departments/agencies to collect and share the information necessary to counter terrorist threats; streamline immigration procedures; protect the security of the nuclear and aviation industries; improve the security of dangerous substances that could be targeted by terrorists; and enhance powers when detainees in custody refuse to cooperate with the police (ibid: 98).

Other forms of international cooperation include bilateral agreements between two countries to fight crime, indicating, as Davies et al. (ibid) suggest, 'the greater cross-jurisdictional awareness among governments of the need to cooperate to deal with a problem that is not restricted within national boundaries.' The UK/USA Drugs Agreement of 1988 provides for cooperation in terms of the investigation of drug-trafficking offences, the freezing and confiscation of the proceeds of drug-related crimes, and allows for the transfer of prisoners with their consent to give evidence and carry out requests to search and seize property. The United Kingdom and Poland signed a mutual cooperation agreement on 27 February 1997 to work together to deal with 'the illegal distribution of weapons, drugs, and organised crime' (ibid: 99). The agreement allows for speedier extradition orders, intelligence gathering on illegal arms and drug sales, etc., and contains powers to confiscate the 'proceeds' of crime that have been made between jurisdictions. Davies et al. (ibid) point how, with regard to the criminal justice system of England and Wales, international cooperation has involved the Forensic Science Service (FSS) conducting DNA tests in 1992, 'in response to the Russian Governments' approach to check the remains of a group of people, thought to be those of the Romanov family, the Russian royal family that disappeared, presumed murdered on the night of 16 July 1918, or soon after' (ibid). Using bone materials, the FSS then concluded that the DNA test did indeed support the theory that the remains found in the mass grave were that of the Romanovs.

In the aftermath of 9/11, international cooperation is also increasing between the 176 member countries of Interpol. In England and Wales, within the National Criminal Intelligence Service (NCIS), Customs and Excise manage a network of Drugs Liaison Offices (DLOs), which cooperate with their counterparts in Europe and the wider world. Arguably, the 'success' of the policing of the Euro 96 football tournament, when an estimated number of between one-quarter and half a million foreign football supporters came to England, was partly due to the role played by the NCIS, which helped to plan the policy of the event, 'by putting together a team of experts on football hooliganism from different forces across the country and liaison officers from each of the competing countries,' as well as relying on the information provided by Interpol (ibid). The NCIS is also involved in efforts to combat international crime gangs. Their involvement was set out in the white paper, *One Step Ahead: A 21st Century Strategy to Defeat Organised Criminals* (2004). As Davies et al. (ibid) show, the paper contains details about the Serious Organised Crime Agency (SOCA), announced by the home secretary in February 2004. SOCA has hi-tech and financial specialists, new powers to combat criminal activity, and there is discussion of ways to make more effective use of the existing legislation such as tax, immigration, and planning laws.

Recently, Cavadino and Dignan (2006) have analyzed systematic differences in penal systems in the context of globalization. They observed that American models, such as 'zero tolerance,' have rapidly spread throughout the discourse and policies of practitioners and governments on a global scale. This has led to a common perception of 'penal convergence' (Reiner, 2007). Whilst some international trends and pressures may be identified, together with an increase in American cultural domination, this does not equate with homogeneity and uniformity. Cavadino and Dignan (ibid) develop further the analysis of Esping-Anderson (1990), which sought to characterize 'varieties' of capitalism. First, they identify *neoliberalism*, which entails a minimal welfare state, extreme differences in wealth and income, formal status egalitarianism, individualism with limited social rights, increasing social exclusion, and the dominance of right-wing politics. Second, they identify *conservative corporatism*, which entails a status-related welfare state and pronounced but not extreme income differentials, and moderately hierarchical status rankings with moderate social rights and some social exclusion. Centrist politics dominates in this model. Third, Cavadino and Dignan identify *social democratic corporatism*, which entails a generous, universalistic welfare state, limited income differentials, an egalitarian status system, together with limited social exclusion, and relatively unconditional and generous social rights. The left-wing political dominance is the case in this model. Fourth, the authors identify *oriental corporatism*, which entails private sector-based, paternalistic welfare, limited income differentials, traditional status hierarchy, quasi-feudal corporatist duties, low levels of social exclusion with some alienation of 'outsiders' present. The center-right political dominance is the case here.

As Reiner (2007: 364) observes, 'the nub of Cavadino and Dignan's analysis is the demonstration that this typology of political economies corresponds to clear differences in the punitiveness of both penal policy and culture.' Arguably, Cavadino and Dignan's important work suggests that the four types of political economy seem to differ in qualitative terms in relation to practice and culture, though not in any linear, evolutionary fashion. Regarding the punitiveness of policy (measured by data on official imprisonment rates), it is possible to discern four essentially different groups. *Neoliberal* countries appear to be the most punitive, with rates ranging from 701 per 100,000 population in the United States to 115 in Australia. *Conservative corporatist* countries are next, with imprisonment rates varying from 93 to 100 per 100,000 people. *Social democracies* are less punitive, with rates from 70 to 73 per 100,000 people. *Oriental corporatist* countries, such as Japan, have the lowest imprisonment rates of 53 (Cavadino & Dignan, ibid: 29–32). Japan appears to be, in terms of the punitiveness of popular attitudes, more punitive than other social democracies or conservative countries and even some neoliberal countries. There appear to be overlaps between groups, but it is interesting to note that England and Wales (along with South Africa and the United States, the majority of the neoliberal group) score the highest. Cavadino and Dignan (ibid: 15) associate neoliberalism with a dominant politics of 'law and order,' whilst conservative corporatism tends to emphasize rehabilitation and social democracies emphasize a rights-based approach.

There is little doubt that individual nation-states are being challenged by global processes in the so-called 'post-industrial society,' but an analysis at merely nation-state level may possibly be limited and limiting as regional governments, federation states, international cities, and multiple forms of community governance 'suggest alternative visions of statehood and citizenship and offer alternative routes of access to decision-making on social and economic issues' (Muncie, ibid). Perhaps, as Muncie (ibid), Robertson (1995), and Bauman (1998) appear to suggest, global neoliberal pressures are subject to mediation and can only ever be 'one amongst many influences on policy and then its influence may pull and push in diverse ways *at the same time*' (Muncie, ibid). Thus, the 'global,' the 'national,' and the 'local' are not exclusive, discrete entities, and 'the key issue is how they interact and are experienced differently in different spaces and at different times' (ibid). Loader and Sparks (2007: 91), too, appear to acknowledge that globalization 'is not merely an "out there" phenomenon, a process impacting only on distant occurrences and relations between states.' Its effects, which Giddens (1991), too, has observed, are also 'experienced *by* and felt *within* localities that can no longer insulate themselves from events and processes happening elsewhere' (Loader and Sparks, ibid).

Although it is essential to acknowledge the challenges to the nation-state posed by global processes, it is contended here that we should avoid falling into the trap of underestimating the significance of the nation-state in any analysis of the criminal justice system of England and Wales. Without denying that senses of nationhood or of 'global order' are socially constructed, 'we should not entertain exaggerated claims that the nation-state is no longer a significant entity' (Sibeon, 1996: 149). There is some support for this view from Anderson (1991: 3), who has also observed that 'nation-ness remains the most universally legitimate value in the political life of our time.' Arguably, we should strive to avoid tendencies to exaggerate the scale and/or the intensity of globalization, attempts to underplay the 'highly uneven impact of globalising tendencies,' and accounts which imply that 'objective and irreversible globalizing forces are at work' (Sibeon, ibid: 153). In the latter author's view, this orientation leads toward an unfortunate reductionism and essentialism, 'insofar as it erroneously assumes the existence of a social process (globalization) that is relatively unified' (ibid). Bretherton (1996: 12) has made similar observations, suggesting that 'Globalization is . . . a set of overlapping processes that are neither inexorable nor irreversible, the impact of which varies in intensity and is highly differentiated in effect. Simply put- globalization is an uncertain process that affects some people more than others.' Not all regions of the world are involved to the same extent in global production, and some such as Sub-Saharan Africa are barely involved at all (Bretherton, ibid: 7). In an attempt to avoid the 'crude and exaggerated globalization approach,' Sibeon (ibid: 158) recommends a 'post-national' perspective and methodology which focuses on the subnational, national, and transnational levels of governance, rather than 'giving causal primacy to any one of these levels on a priori grounds.' Questions like which of these levels is the most important and whether and in what form there are linkages between them 'are empirical questions to be determined in each instance, not matters for theoretical predetermination in advance of empirical enquiry' (ibid).

Crime, Citizenship, and the Welfare State

Walklate (2007: 107) supports the notion that in the United Kingdom, a certain way of 'thinking about the relationship between the citizen and the state' lasted until the 1970s. This was a view in which 'the citizen had social rights and the state had obligations to fulfil those rights provided that the contract between the citizen and the state had been fulfilled' (ibid). Here we can identify the key principle of the welfare state in terms of contractual obligations between citizens and state and notions of less eligibility. Arguably, even within the Beveridge ideal, there were exceptions as to who was included as a full social citizen, with the 'undeserving' excluded from full social citizenship. As Cook (2006: 33) suggests, from the 'dangerous classes' of Victorian Britain to the 'underclass' of the late twentieth century/early twenty-first century, 'the poor have been portrayed as in essence crimogenic,' posing distinct threats to law and order.

At the dawn of Bell's (1973) so-called *post-industrial* age, the Labour government of the United Kingdom in the 1970s 'presided over high rates of inflation that set the economic framework in which changes in public policy were likely to take place' (Walklate, ibid: 108). By the time of the international recession of the mid-1970s, time was arguably ripe for changes in the political climate, in terms of social policy, and in terms of what was regarded as the 'appropriate' relationship between citizen and state. As Walklate (ibid) shows, public expenditure was viewed as being at the center of the economic difficulties being experienced and the plan for reducing the inflation rate by restoring incentives included 'removing what Margaret Thatcher referred to as the "nanny state." ' Arguably, Thatcher's (1977: 97) belief in self-reliance, property ownership, 'paying one's way,' and 'playing a role within the family' as being 'all part of the spiritual ballast which maintains responsible citizenship' is the embryo of the political ideas that changed the direction of the relationship between the citizen and the state in the United Kingdom throughout the 1980s and 1990s (Walklate, ibid). The civil disturbances of 1981 and the concerns they generated (repeated and reiterated in the early 1990s) 'marks that continuing preoccupation with the undeserving; those dangerous classes who live in dangerous places' (ibid). The riots and 'disturbances,' varied in their 'causes,' arguably marked the beginning of a decade in which the criminal justice system of England and Wales was severely tested. In simple terms, changes in direction in the relationship between the citizen and the state were 'primarily about reducing the obligations of the state to provide and increasing the obligations (as opposed to the rights) of the citizen to contribute to society and provide for themselves' (Walklate, ibid: 109). This view appears to be situated within a wider belief in the free reign of market forces and their ability to increase competition, expand consumer choice, and provide a route out of economic problems. As Walklate suggests, in the UK context, for the individual, such expectations were 'encapsulated by "active citizenship." ' Put simply, individual citizens 'no longer fulfilled their obligations to the state through the payment of their taxes or national insurance contributions' (ibid). In these particular economic circumstances, it is 'the welfare of the state, as opposed to the welfare of the individual' which demanded more of them (ibid).

This view of citizenship appears to have taken strong roots in the contemporary political landscape of the United Kingdom, is enshrined in a range of policy initiatives, and is 'clearly present within the world of the criminal justice system' of England and Wales (Walklate, ibid). For example, there has been a rapid growth of Neighbourhood Watch schemes in which active 'good citizens' become the 'eyes' and 'ears' of the police; in Victim Support as a voluntary organization and 'the increasing importance of the symbolism of the victim politically'; and in the generation of 'consumer charters and concerns with consumer satisfaction within policing' (ibid). Arguably, a feature of all of these recent developments is the likelihood that the poor or 'socially excluded' are most likely to be the *objects* of this 'active citizenship,' rather than its *subjects* because they do not possess the power to pay or make claims count. As Walklate (ibid) observes, 'some would describe this as a re-articulation of the principle of less eligibility. Others would say that principle never disappeared.'

Hutton (1995) has made the observation that there has been a dramatic, overwhelming increase in the gap between the rich and the poor since 1979, leading him to talk of the '30-30-40 society,' which emphasizes not only the gap between the 'well-off' and secure and those who are not, but also the increasing numbers who are economically vulnerable. The impact of this growing economic vulnerability for an increasing number of people has been felt 'nowhere less than in the criminal justice system' (Walklate, ibid: 111). This view is also supported by Carlen (1988). Put simply, there appears to be a relationship between an increase in the numbers of those deemed 'the dangerous classes' and the levels of work faced by criminal justice agencies in England and Wales. As Walklate (ibid: 112) observes, 'While the nature of this relationship has been strongly contested (and denied) politically, it nevertheless points up the interconnection between the distribution of social justice and the likelihood of being subjected to the criminal justice system.' For example, as the prison population grows, so does the preoccupation with security. The relationship, as

Walklate (ibid) observes, also points to another problem; if the people who come before the criminal justice system are increasingly likely to be from the 'dangerous classes' – the poor, the unemployed, the unemployable, the homeless, the physically ill, and the mentally disturbed – 'then how might such people be treated justly by it?' The author goes on to pose a further poignant question: 'What does a socially just punishment for a mentally disturbed offender look like who becomes homeless following the implementation of policies designed to provide care in the community and what resources do they have as individuals to manage how they are being dealt with?' (ibid).

Developments and Trends in the 'Post-industrial' Landscape: Clues to the Future?

In the so-called 'post-industrial' age, it appears to be the case that no agency or aspect of the criminal justice system of England and Wales has been left untouched by the 'frenetic pace of reform' (Davies et al., 2005) in the United Kingdom since 1997. In England and Wales, crime policy has become part of the political debates, 'partly in response to rising crime and partly as a result of the reform era of the 1960s and 1970s' (ibid: 416). Rapid social change in this period has shifted the sociocultural roots and arrangements of the population in terms of everyday home-based activities, community, and the workplace. As Davies et al. (ibid) have observed, 'change and consequent uncertainty' was very apparent in the debates about the 'causes' of crime and the role of criminal justice agencies in the 1970s (the dawning of Bell's (1973) *post-industrial society*). In the 1990s, data protection legislation and human rights reforms caused greater levels of uncertainty, 'with tragic consequences in the case of the latter when the Humberside police did not keep effective records about allegations of sexual offences by Ian Huntley' (ibid), the murderer of Holly Wells and Jessica Chapman in Soham in 2003. As the authors observe, very few of the traditional institutions and agencies of criminal justice in England and Wales have remained untouched, as new laws provided new rights and 'intervened into spheres previously regarded as private, such as the home' (ibid). There was also some polarization in terms of the pre-1950s consensus on crime, as reforms imposed changes that are arguably unpopular with the majority of the population, the abolition of the death penalty for murder being one example.

The so-called 'post-industrial society' is arguably one in which uncertainty appears to be rife in many aspects of life, and this includes crime policy. Under the New Labour administration, there has been an increasing emphasis on cost-effectiveness, which may possibly conflict with other influences in penal policy. Governments 'face a dilemma' in the pursuit of crime strategies which emphasize the politically desirable 'tough on crime' approach, whilst at the same time taking account of economic issues (ibid: 417). In the 'post-industrial' landscape, the increasingly tougher and more punitive policies which characterize the criminal justice system of England and Wales may lead to higher prosecution costs and the increasing use of imprisonment as punishment. This appears to have led to a 'tendency towards bifurcation,' whereby the harsher penalties are reserved for the most serious offences/offenders, while 'others are diverted from the system at various stages' (ibid). Increasingly, the use of caution and victim-offender mediation schemes and community sentences play a part here. As Davies et al. (ibid) observe, this can conflict quite obviously with notions of 'just deserts and denunciation' and with the interests of victims who may see their offenders escaping punishment.

Many of the strategies employed by the New Labour in the 'post-industrial' age to ensure that the criminal justice system of England and Wales runs more effectively involve 'new technologies' for both the management of systems and the control of offenders. In theory, offenders can be kept out of the penal system if they are subject to monitoring by electronic tagging, with many town and city centers subject to increasing levels of CCTV surveillance. Additionally, there has been an expansion of 'private policing.' Increasingly, local authorities in England and Wales employ security companies and sometimes have their own municipal version, which they extend to housing estates, council property, and public spaces (i.e., parks). A desire to 'include the community' in both policy and crime prevention is also apparent, and there has been a growth in both auxiliary police and community wardens (ibid).

As Davies et al. (ibid) suggest, diversionary strategies, such as the ones referred to above, can 'increase efficiency in the court process but can lead to public disquiet' on the grounds that offenders may be seen as being 'let off too lightly,' and denunciationists might argue for public trials. Additionally, the diversionary policies of the New Labour raise important issues of due process and justice, in that decisions concerning such offenders are made in private and are thus 'less accountable' (ibid). Such divergence may also possibly disadvantage those who decide to contest their guilt and are viewed as taking up officials' time unnecessarily and who may possibly receive a harsher sentence as a result. Arguably, the diversionary policies also raise the question of the degree to which some minor offences 'may in effect be decriminalised,' for example, the downgrading of cannabis from a Class B to a Class C drug, 'thus carrying lower penalties and symbolically allowing the police to treat possession of the drug more lightly' (ibid).

In the so-called 'post-industrial' age, the 'what works' debate has dominated the agenda about prisons in England and Wales (ibid: 418). What Davies et al. refer to as 'prison reductionist' arguments concerning the high costs of prisons and doubts about the rehabilitation potential of prisons raise questions for the prison system of England and Wales, pertaining to whether the steady increase in the prison population should be accepted or whether there should be moves to reduce the number of offenders in prison. If prisons are to be utilized for the more serious offenders in terms of incapacitation, 'how should regimes be organised and what should they aim for?' (ibid).

Since the election of the New Labour in 1997, legislative reforms have proceeded rapidly with the most all-encompassing being the Criminal Justice Act of 2003. The Act builds on the Auld and Halliday reports and is arguably 'one of the most far-reaching pieces of criminal justice legislation in modern times' (ibid). The great impact of the Act relates to bail, police conduct, the composition of juries, conduct in criminal trials, rules of evidence, sentences, appeals, prison, and probation. Such rapid, sweeping reforms alongside the many 'initiatives' launched by the New Labour since 1997 indicate an all-encompassing approach toward 'modernization' and change. Thirty-five years on, from the publication of Bell's (1973) *post-industrial* thesis, it appears to be the case that the criminal justice system of England and Wales faces considerable change and continuing dilemmas. As Davies et al. (ibid) have observed, it is increasingly clear that criminal justice policy and agencies must be seen 'in a wider, social, cultural, economic, national and international context.' Membership of the European Union has arguably changed the nature of sovereignty and the role of the nation-state, though it is contended here that this is *not* to say that nation-states and variations between them are unimportant (Sibeon, 1996). New rules, regulations, and institutions are forthcoming, and 'new' crimes have to be defined in Brussels and Strasbourg, with new cross-European arrangements introduced. If the United Kingdom remains within the European Union, this will arguably provide 'the major source of change to the criminal justice system in the foreseeable future' (Davies et al., ibid: 415).

Concluding Observations

Notions of the 'post-industrial society' and 'globalization' may possibly refer to some important economic trends over the past 35 years, but they are limited analytical tools with which to analyze the criminal justice system of England and Wales. To conceptualize the complex social processes which have impacted and continue to impact upon the agencies of the criminal justice system, it is necessary to reject 'crude,' reductionist, essentialist, unitary explanations, such as those offered by Bell (1973), which effectively reduce the great complexity of social life to a *single* substantive explanatory principle, such as the 'post-industrial society.' It may well be the case that globalization carries with it transformations which are relevant to the study of the criminal justice system (Muncie, 2007), in terms of a degree of convergence in terms of criminal justice policies, but as Cavadino and Dignan (2006) have recently suggested, the adoption of similar economic, social, and criminal justice policies by governments does not necessarily mean uniformity and homogeneity. There may be evidence to suggest that there is a greater cross-jurisdictional awareness among governments of the need to cooperate to deal with crime 'problems' that are not restricted within national boundaries, for example, the UK/USA Drugs Agreement of 1988. In the aftermath of 9/11, it may well be the case that international cooperation is increasing between the member countries of Interpol. It may also be the case that there have been shifts in the nature of citizenship and that views on 'active citizenship' (Walklate, 2007) have taken strong roots in the contemporary political landscape of the United Kingdom and are enshrined in the criminal justice system. However, the determinist grand narratives of 'the logic of post-industrialism' and 'globalization' are highly contestable. A more adequate and sensible model of social change would arguably recognize that the impact of macrosocial processes pertaining to 'post-industrialism,' 'globalization,' etc., are most likely to be highly variable and differentially shaped by 'a variety of cultural, economic, and political factors at the subnational, national, and transnational levels of social process' (Sibeon, 1996: 84). In any analysis of the criminal justice system of England and Wales, we should avoid accounts which make exaggerated claims that the nation-state is no longer a significant entity (Sibeon, 1996). As Anderson (1991) has put it, 'nation-ness' remains a universally legitimate value in contemporary political life. Any adequate analysis of the current 'state of play' in the criminal justice system in the so-called 'post-industrial' age must surely also recognize the role played by *agency*: patterns of social life and the reproduction of social change are in varied ways influenced by human social *actors* whose ways of thinking and formulations of interests/purposes are *not* structurally predetermined nor guided by inexorable 'post-industrial' motor forces of change.

References

Anderson, B. (1991). *Imagined communities: Reflections on the origins and spread of nationalism*. London: Verso.

Bauman, Z. (1998). *Globalization: The human consequences*. Cambridge: Polity.

Bell, D. (1973). *The coming of post-industrial society*. London: Heinemann.

Bretherton, C. (1996). Introduction: Global politics in the 1990s. In C. Bretherton & G. Ponton (Eds.), *Global politics: An introduction*. Oxford: Blackwell.

Cavadino, M., & Dignan, J. (2006). *Penal systems: A comparative approach*. London: Sage.

Carlen, P. (1988). *Women, crime and poverty*. Milton Keynes: Open University Press.

Cook, D. (2006). *Criminal and social justice*. London: Sage.

Davies, M. et al. (2005). *Criminal justice: An introduction to the criminal justice system in England and Wales*. London: Pearson Longman.

Dunn, J. A., & Perl, A. (1994). Policy networks and industrial revitalization: High speed rail initiatives in France and Germany. *Journal of Public Policy, 14*(3), 311–343.

Esping-Anderson, C. (1990). *The three worlds of welfare capitalism*. Cambridge: Polity.

Giddens, A. (1984). *The constitution of society*. Cambridge: Polity.

Giddens, A. (1991). *Modernity and self-identity: Self and society in the late modern age*. Cambridge: Polity.

Hudson, B. (2007). Criminal justice. In E. McLaughlin & J. Muncie (Eds.), *The sage dictionary of criminology*. London: Sage.

Hutton, W. (1995). *The state we're in*. London: Random House.

Judd, D., & Parkinson, M. (Eds.). (1990). *Leadership and urban regeneration*. London: Sage.

Kasarda, J. (1989). Urban industrial transition and the underclass. *The Annals of the American Academy of Political and Social Science, 501*, 26–47.

Kumar, K. (1978). *Prophecy and progress: The sociology of industrial and post-industrial society*. London: Penguin.

Kumar, K. (1995). *From post-industrial to post-modern society: New theories of the contemporary world*. Oxford: Blackwell.

Levi, M. (2007). Organized crime and terrorism. In M. Maguire et al. (Eds.), *The Oxford handbook of criminology*. Oxford: Oxford University Press.

Loader, I., & Sparks, R. (2007). Contemporary landscapes of crime, order and control: governance, risk, and globalization. In M. Maguire et al. (Eds.), *The Oxford handbook of criminology*. Oxford: Oxford University Press.

Lyon, D. (1987). *The information society: Issues and illusions*. Cambridge: Polity.

Marsh, D., & Rhodes, R. A. W. (Eds.). (1992a). *Policy networks in British government*. Oxford: Oxford University Press.

Marsh, D., & Rhodes, R. A. W. (1992b). Policy communities and issue networks: beyond typology. In D. Marsh and R. A. W. Rhodes (Eds.), *Policy networks in British government*. Oxford: Oxford University Press.

Muncie, J. (2007). 'Globalization', in McLaughlin, E. & Muncie, J. (Eds.), *The sage dictionary of criminology*. London: Sage.

Nelken, D. (1997). The globalization of crime and criminal justice. *Current Legal Problems, 50*, 251–277.

O'Malley, P. (2002). Globalising risk? Distinguishing styles of neo-liberal criminal justice in Australia and the USA. *Criminal Justice, 2*(2), 205–222.

Owen, T. (2008, forthcoming). *Social theory and human biotechnology*. New York: Nova Science Publishers.

Owen, T. (2007a). Culture of crime control: through a post-Foucauldian len, *The Internet Journal of Criminology*. internetjournalofcriminology.com.

Owen, T. (2007b). After postmodernism: Towards an evolutionary sociology. In J. L. Powell and T. Owen (Eds.), *Reconstructing postmodernism: Critical debates*. New York: Nova Science Publishers.

Owen, T. (2006). Genetic-social science and the study of human biotechnology, *Current Sociology, 54*(6), 897–917.

Reiner, R. (2007). Political economy, crime, and criminal justice. In M. Maguire et al. (Eds.), *The Oxford handbook of criminology*. Oxford: Oxford University Press.

Robertson, R. (1995). Glocalisation: Time-space and homogeneity-heterogeneity. In M. Featherstone et al. (Eds.), *Global modernities*. London: Sage.

Sanders, A., & Young, R. (2007). *Criminal justice*. Oxford: Oxford University Press.

Sibeon, R. (1996). *Contemporary sociology and policy analysis: The new sociology of public policy*. London: Kogan Page and Tudor.

Sibeon, R. (2004). *Rethinking social theory*. London: Sage.

Standing, G. (1986). *Unemployment and labour market flexibility: The UK*. Geneva: International Labour Office.

Thatcher, M. (1977). *Let our children grow tall*. London: Centre for Policy Studies.

Touraine, A. (1974). *The post-industrial society*. London: Wildwood.

Walklate, S. (2007). *Understanding criminology: Current theoretical debates*. London: McGraw Hill.

Waters, M. (1995). *Globalization*. London: Sage.

Webster, F. (1995). *Theories of the Information Society*. London: Routledge.

Williams, R. (1985). *Towards 2000*. Harmondsworth: Penguin.

Wilsford, D. (1994). Path dependency, or why history makes it difficult but not impossible to reform health care systems in a big way, *Journal of Public Policy, 14*(3), 251–283.

Yeates, N. (2001). *Globalization and social policy*. London: Sage.

Chapter 13
Canada: New Ideology and Social Assistance in Post-industrial Society

Patricia M. Daenzer

Introduction

Contemporary analyses of the Canadian post-industrial welfare state frequently focus on globalization, the creeping market demon sniffing out social programs, as the cause of current welfare state regressions (Mishra, 1999; Fligstein, 1998; Barlow, 1996). Critiques infer that social programs are no longer structured to adequately assist workers made jobless by the global market machinery. State aid now has to be earned following great suffering and loss of dignity (National Council of Welfare, 1997). Social programs put in place between the 1940s and the 1960s, such as employment insurance, retraining assistance, and social assistance, which fall short of adequate, are now seen as too generous (Tzembelicos, 1996). The neoliberal culture of individual responsibility and competitive market accumulation is now in tension with the more old-fashioned values of the just society. In this free and competitive market climate, generous social programs became the antithesis to the labor exploitation so essential for maximum accumulation at the lowest possible cost (Gindin, 2004).

The global exploitation of labor benefits from unregulated workforces and weakening labor movements. The absence of strong labor organizations leads to the unchallenged flight of capital across borders seeking the lowest labor cost generated by unprotected workers. This market vision to move in and out of global labor sites to exploit and dispose (Bales, 1999) of vulnerable workers depends on support from less protective nation-states and weakened labor (Godard, 2003). The evidence in Canada is that the number of unionized workers across sectors markedly decreased between 1981 and 2004 (Statistics Canada, 2005; Mullaly, 2002: 106). This gutting of organized labor has been the surest sign of a weakened Canadian political commitment to the 'just society' (Goldfield & Palmer, 2007; Barlow & Campbell, 1995). Exposing workers to the inevitabilities of free market competition has created social crises, which remain unsolved. And, yes, of course, there is resistance to market liberalization.

P.M. Daenzer (✉)
Department of Social Work, McMaster University, Hamilton, ON, Canada
e-mail: daenzer@mcmaster.ca, pdaenzer@sympatico.ca

J. Powell, J. Hendricks, *The Welfare State in Post-Industrial Society*,
DOI 10.1007/978-1-4419-0066-1_13, © Springer Science+Business Media, LLC 2009

Burgmann (2002) suggests that there are signs of remobilization and reunification of the working class alongside other resisters in opposition to globalization. Lightman (2003) concurs and sees this challenge as 'unanticipated by the proponents of globalization' (258–259). But, in Canada, alongside this resistance, there is concurrently capitulation to these new market arrangements. State concessions made to accommodate market liberalization are driving Canadians to rely on diminished forms of protective social arrangements. So, once again, charities have increased visibility and significance to stave off the worst fallout from neoliberal ascendancy.

Social assistance programs which were once adequate for protecting displaced labor force members are no longer vital segments of Canadian social programs. In fact, social assistance reforms, to be discussed below, in all Canadian provinces have given Canadians a neoliberal system within a framework which punishes more than enables.

This chapter examines changes over time to this welfare program of last resort: social assistance. I suggest that the context for social program regressions, which impact those made most vulnerable by loss of work, rests in Canada's wavering and situational welfare ideology. I argue that even though globalization has challenged welfare in Canada through increasing labor vulnerabilities, this is not the sole impetus for recent social program retrenchments. I focus on female sole parents, new immigrants, and First Nations peoples, as I discuss how new forms of solidarity emerging from voluntary efforts are growing out of what are considered to be mean-spirited welfare times. This solidarity, however modest at the moment, exists as a threat to the total liberalization of market arrangements in Canada.

Canadian Welfare: Post-industrialism and the Nation-State

A modern cabinet ... must balance particular pressures from interest groups and other sources with its concept of the public interest, and in this difficult balancing act its judgment and convictions are inevitably, and usefully, tempered by necessity ... (C.E.S. Franks. *The Parliament of Canada*, 1987: 11)

The Canadian welfare state is weakened but not dismantled; in fact, Canada's system of social programs is concurrently envied and vilified by our American neighbors. It is envied because it provides what the more collectivist-minded democrats envision for America, and vilified because republican free-market proponents see shades of socialism embodied in social programs, such as our publicly administered universal health care. Socialism, real or imagined, on the borders of America has never been welcomed and would be especially so in Canada. And the American supporters of free market care about events unfolding in our Canadian economy; Canada is their closest playground for market exploits and also their significant trading partner.

Notwithstanding competing American analyses, the Canadian welfare state has been 'in crisis' since the early 1980s (Mishra, 1999, 1990) and is currently balancing tentatively under the strain of self-imposed neoliberalism. In the 1980s, when latent Canadian neoliberalism was most sharply resurgent, globalization should not have been the dominant analysis (Rice & Prince, 2000a: 135–156; Barlow, 1996; Wolfe and Mendhelsohn, 2005). But globalization seemed an expedient new direction which urged Canadian welfare opponents to hatch timely critiques of the 'unaffordable caring state.'

In that convenient analysis, welfare opponents were eager to dispense with the complexities which plagued the Canadian welfare history from its inception and shift the discussion to a far-right direction. Leonard (1997), for example, explores this 'discursive shift' and shows that heightened awareness of the globalization phenomenon altered the welfare discourse by repositioning recipients as burdens (113–115). So, then citizens with social entitlements (Hibbert, 2008) became the problem and impediments to the bright economic promises of globalization. People without jobs, needing state assistance, were seen as a detriment to the work ethic: 'work ethic' became the synonym for market progress.

Globalization was not our most serious problem, but our faltering welfare ideology was. Canada's welfare woes are historical and more complicated than the convenient analysis which is now common. These views mourn the loss of the Canadian postwar 'consensus' on social welfare (Mishra, 1999) and de-emphasize the historical disagreements over, and resistance to, collectivism. In fact, Canada's potential to move toward full development of the Fabian Canadian state was always compromised. It is, then, an optimistic overstatement to suggest that welfare consensus ever triumphed over welfare ambivalence in Canada. Most notable in the Canadian welfare history are the disagreements and uncertainties about how much to redistribute, who deserves redistributed goods, under what conditions should the need be recognized, and who should control the social program resources (Brock, 2008; Leo, 2006; Tzembelicos, 1996).

The most enduring of these disagreements was over jurisdictional control for social programs (see, e.g., Vayda & Deber, 1995: 313–323; Struthers, 1983: 175–207; Smiley, 1987: 20–22). The postwar welfare state was designed to complement a three-tiered structure of federalism. Political power was layered between the federal government (security and law) provinces and territories (education, law, and program delivery) and with municipalities (infrastructure, taxes, and local governance). The system which exists in 2008 is not as straightforward and reflects changes negotiated during the last half-century and the resultant accommodations which appeased some of these jurisdictional disputes.

What is notable in the Canadian welfare history is that provinces wanted the autonomy to shape and administer social programs based on their regional and transient ideology. But the federal government, recognizing that to be the end of Canada's identity as a welfare state, fought, sometimes, through manipulations to hold on to primary jurisdiction for social programs (Banting, 1995, Brock, 2008; Smiley, 1987: 19–22). In fact, Brock (2008) argues that the federal government struggled to hold on to, or reclaim control of, social programs as a way of legitimating itself.

Central control of social programs, it was thought, would entrench rights for Canadians. These rights are articulated as principles which shape the character of the Canadian welfare state. They include 'comprehensiveness, universality, portability, publicly administered programs and accessibility.' Portability and comprehensiveness best materialized if control of programs was held by the federal government.

What this means for the 31.6 million Canadians spread over ten provinces and three territories on a landmass equal to that of the United States was that we could move freely among provinces and territories without constraints of lost social protection due to domiciliary changes. A citizen could expect to walk into a hospital in the far west of Canada and receive health care equivalent to that provided in their eastern home province. Workers who lost jobs in one part of the country could move to another province and expect entitlements to federally controlled jobless benefits. But despite agreements on these valued principles, which framed social programs, provinces would continue to bicker over entitlements to, and adequacy of, transfers from the federal government.

These disagreements about control and adequacy of social programs were not vacuous, egotistical quarrels. Disagreements between federal and provincial governments were political misalignments. A conservative (right of center) government in one province negotiating with a liberal (left of center) government in our national capital sometimes made unfriendly negotiating partners. This is not to suggest, however, that rigid ideological boundaries contoured our democratic political system. In Canada, conservatives can be centrists, and liberals, too, can be centrists. At times, liberals can be right of center and be just as eager to limit welfare expansions. More constant and predictable were the regional demands which differed based on economic conditions and affinity for, or likeability of, the federal government.

That situation unfolding in 13 regional locations in the context of location-specific demands, based on differing needs and social conditions, made deliberations unsteady. Decisions were not always 'tempered by necessity' (Franks, 1987), and outcomes were not always acceptable. The Canadian welfare history, thus, resembles a fraying patchwork quilt displaying uneven political relations between provinces, territories, and the national government.

Between 1966 and 2004, the control, responsibility, and funding of social programs would be renegotiated several times with five outcomes: See Fig. 13.1

Figure 13.1 shows that the foundation policy of Canadian welfare, the CAP, was changed to become the Canada Health and Social Transfer. In 2004, further changes were made to separate health transfer from social transfer. Most recently, in 2004, provinces won the right to control many social programs without unilateral federal interference. These changes permitted provinces to influence social programs with divergent ideologies. Social programs could then more closely reflect the politics of the provincial region or of special interests in the province, instead of reflecting national agreed-upon principles.

1966	Canada Assistance Plan (CAP)	The federal government reimbursed 50 percent of the expenditure for social assistance and social services for provinces and territories. Standards set and enforced by the federal government. Eligibility for programs based on need. Rich provinces can get more because they can spend more.
1977	Established Programs Financing	Federal transfer to provinces and territories to pay for health care and post secondary education. Federal transfer condition is that money must be spent on target programs only.
1996	Canada Health & Social Transfer	The federal government transfers to provinces and territories for health and social programs, but, 25 percent less than under. Standards established under the CAP eliminated, and provinces and territories assume control of not just standards by how money should be spent. People in need receive less and program controls become punitive. Need, then, becomes a bureaucratic discretion.
1999	Social Union Framework Agreement	Agreement reached between nine provinces and three territories to re-entrench rights of Canadians for one quality of social programs across the country. The federal government potentially regains authority to establish and fund social programs only if it receives the OK from at least six provincial governments
2004	Canada Health Transfer	Row 3 above (1996) is split into package health and social programs separately. Health transfers must respect the Canada Health Act (1984). There is a presumption that untangling funding for the two programs will enhance accountability and transparency.
2004	Canada Social Transfer	Row 3 above to untangle social from health transfer monies. These are block transfers from the federal government to provinces and territories targeted at postsecondary education, social assistance, social services, early childhood learning, and development. The federal government conditions don't apply; provinces and territories have discretion, and all provinces receive vertical transfer top ups (equalization payments from rich to poor provinces) to compensate for regional economic variances.

Fig. 1 Changes to funding and control of Canadian social programs, 1966–2004
Sources: Laugesen and Susan (2000), Department of Finance Canada (2003, 2006), Richer (2007: 160), Seguin (2008), Canada Health Act (1985)

The Canadian welfare family of provinces and territories matured in its own troublesome dynamics, and by the time global markets developed more focused interests in Canada, we were well on our way to seriously distorting the foundation of the postwar welfare design. But that postwar welfare program-design, with shared provincial/federal/territorial control and administration, was an uneasy compromise, which inherited prewar troubled relations.

Historians have captured these political rumblings in discipline-specific detail (Struthers, 1983; Owram, 1986; Palmer, 1992). Our challenging geography-driven regional economics and our vastness with varying regional lifestyles added to complexities.

Understanding then that citizens' social needs derive from lifestyles formed around primary occupations, local development stage, and industries, some of these tensions were linked to legitimate regional differences. Provinces in the west of Canada tended to be more agrarian; farming and oil drilling were developed and social needs arose from these significant regional occupations and pace of urban growth. The Maritimes, however, those provinces buttressing the Atlantic Ocean, were heavily into marine occupations, which tended to be seasonal. Maritime workers who were involuntarily displaced from work during off-season periods would, therefore, have different social program needs than those of the more urban industrial regions. Rural life in the inland of British Columbia, for example, when juxtaposed with marine-driven social uncertainties of the Maritimes, demanded federal intervention to even out access to social development opportunities. This came in the form of federal equalization transfer payments to economically disadvantaged provinces and territories for structural-dysfunction episodes during seasonal changes. Provinces and territories exercised full discretion in spending equalization funds.

Intraprovincial differences also created welfare redistribution tensions. In larger provinces such as Ontario, citizens in northern regions have social challenges unfamiliar to those who live in the wealthier and more urban south. These differences are mostly related to local economy, climate, regional occupations, and urban/rural developmental differences in service availability. Prior to the preoccupation with the external enemy of globalization, these contested inter/intraprovincial relations were played out by regional activists and local politicians.

Since postwar welfare gains were won through troubling acrimony and uneasy compromises (Finkel 1995: 221–243), our welfare and protection were always tenuous. This is because Canada's welfare structure was never driven by strong, widely shared national ideology in the way the Nordic regimes are (Olsson, 1993: 74–89). Going forward, our situational ambivalence toward comprehensive and far-reaching welfare commitment (Lightman, 2003: 255–259) provides little assurance that welfare protection will be championed over market interests during any global economic invasion. However, major restructuring of the Canadian welfare state (elimination of programs) would be severely challenged, since the most recent restructuring of social assistance has created great numbers of vulnerable people and increased insecurity.

Impact of Globalization: New Priorities for State Investment

Globalization includes economic, social, demographic, cultural, and political dimensions (Midgley, 2000:14). In its fullest impact, globalization pursues, among other privileges, free trade and the privatization of publicly owned enterprises (Elwood, 2001: 19; Leonard, 1997: 115–119). Canadian critics of globalization are apprehensive about this potential for external market players privatizing publicly operated Canadian institutions. This would strike at the heart of Canadian welfare, a rather sacred element of the Canadian culture.

Most welfare critiques focus on the economic dominance aspect, portraying globalization as an economic giant, which emerged out of the suddenly cleared fog, with a foreign agenda. The surprise is misplaced; the implied nullification of Canadian sovereignty is an overreach (Jiwani, 2000; Barlow, 1996; Rice & Prince, 2000a: 137–143). Canada has been a player on the global scene for some time and the Canadian labor force has been historically dependent on imported global talents to fill the gaps in its labor pool. Canada also exports as much talent as it imports by providing economic and social development services to other countries and economic aid to developing nations and by participating in student exchanges. Canadian philanthropy is articulated both at home and abroad (Mamuji, 2007), and Canada has served six terms on the Security Council of the United Nations.

Some of the globalization critiques are, however, valid, and these logically followed the recent Canadian concern with deficit financing. Social distraction created by the state's concerns over deficit reduction obscured the signals of Canadian fiscal housecleaning in readiness for the newest wave of global economic competition (Jiwani, ibid: 9). Deficit reduction, then, functioned as the precursor to social spending cutbacks. Social welfare funding reductions have led to diminished output capacity of social programs. So globalization itself is not the problem; sacrifices made to domestic affairs are the issue for some critics.

What Canadian opponents of globalization fear most is that, in addition to continued social program reductions, foreign enterprises will make incursions into our publicly administered social programs. The privatization of social programs in Canada will take the nation in a very different direction. But while external reach into Canadian social programs is only possible through Canadian invitation, this fear is supported by the recent events. There is eager-ness by American-owned enterprises to establish a private tier of health care in Canada. While some infringements were already made in some provinces, these were curtailed by the federal government. Universal health care remains the social program of choice in Canada, but its financing and operation are con-tentious. The Province of Alberta has repeatedly attempted to introduce for-profit health care by private companies and continues to feign provincial autonomy in the area of health care delivery. Market culture is also evident in other program areas.

Publicly administered Canadian social programs were never intended as profit-making enterprises. However, changes reflected in social policy language and operations are clearly market-driven. There is now explicit emphasis on work ethics, as though this is a 'new value' for Canadians. The program reminders that work is the expectation and that welfare dependence is immoral nullify the labor invested by citizens in building and maintaining Canada as the proud nation it now is. The invocation of work ethics and personal responsibility as new national requirements is also the management of the expectation process induced by the market. The moralistic intent is to lessen expectations of the state and increase individual guilt. Work for welfare, which is grounded in market ethos, is the boldest articulation of this expectation. While the market ethos induces guilt in workers, there is none evident from capital for the increased loss of primary sector jobs and the attack on citizenship through minimal social protection.

Loss of income in the heightened profit-making market climate represents the most destabilizing aspect for individual citizenship in today's society. Previous aims of the Canadian welfare state thought to be the synchronization between labor supply and demand, enhanced individual capacity for market interaction (cash intake and cash expenditure), and contribution to the national income were loosely linked to citizenship articulation. According to Lister (1997:41), we articulate citizenship when we act to attain our life's goals. What joblessness incurs is the inability to trade individual capacity for rewards, which are enjoyable and status enhancing. While paid work remains central to our post-globalization culture, joblessness and low paid work have become realities for many.

The social programs designed to address loss of income and income deficiencies are provincially administered Social Assistance. Reforms of Social Assistance swept the nation (National Council of Welfare, 1997; Prince, 1998: 2-3) following the period of deficit reductions, which paved the way for less state and more free market in the mid-1990s. Each Canadian province now structures its own program and these retain common features. Social Assistance is a last resort and not a convenient substitute for paid work. The 'assistance' package includes, in principle, directions in locating another job, re-education or retraining to realign skills with market demands, and counseling which reorients the dislocated person with changing labor market demands. Social Assistance has become the most contentious social program during this period of market expansion in Canadian culture.

Changes to the Welfare State

The Canadian post-industrial welfare state represents collaboration between state, market, and nongovernmental organizations (NGOs). The framework for this collaboration rests in political, civil, and cultural rights to the exclusion of social and economic rights. While basic subsistence is guaranteed by social tradition, an individual Canadian has questionable legal basis upon which to compel the state to provide economic subsistence through social programs.

The state uses its redistributive obligation to enable individual progress toward self-fulfillment with a hoped-for outcome of relative social harmony.

State-funded NGOs[1] assist in dispensing services and creating programs which stabilize communities and appease extreme needs. NGOs have received as much as 60 percent of their funding from the state prior to recent cutbacks (Jiwani, ibid, 7). The market benefits from social productivity and social harmony and rewards individual progress.

NGOs operate at the community level and have over the years developed the capacity to mobilize communities to respond to social issues and needs. Shelters for victims of violence, boys and girls clubs, research and development, homes for developmentally challenged persons, new immigrant-orientation centers, after school drop-in centers, and in-home care for the elderly are some of the NGO community services which use state and private funds to assist, care, and advocate for community members. Collectively, Canadian NGOs are indispensable to the Canadian Welfare State, since they dispense thousands of caring and service hours each day. They have, though, become the newest casualties of funding cutbacks, so more recently, much of this work has been volunteer or nonpaid hours (Scott, 2003).

Years of state-NGO collaboration successfully taught provincial and federal governments that the focus had to be on more than individuals and that it made more social sense to mobilize communities[2] to aid in mediating social distress. But this new emphasis on community capacity building has not displaced the ideology of individualism tempered by moderate collective action. The articulated priority of the welfare state remains individual rights with freedom to associate with communities of choice.

Rights articulated in social programs give Canadians programs and services which focus on preventing extreme want and thus curbing social restlessness. State assistance targets one person at a time and also one community at a time. Lessons from the depression and wars taught us that deprivation leads to desperation and then to social unrest. Both state and market, then, had vested interests for involvement in this appeasement enterprise.

Boundaries are very important in the state/market/community collaboration, which keeps citizens appeased and relatively satisfied with their social statuses as worker-citizens with rights. The market boundary is drawn at relatively unchallenged labor commitment and the state sets limits to discourage dependence on social programs so that the commitment to market is ensured. The community functions with expectations of citizen participation and no profits from derived services (market aim). Following recent funding cutbacks, it was not difficult to shift to the current trend of relying on free labor from community members (Curtis (Downloaded 2008)).

---

[1] NGOs have received as much as 60% of their funding from the State and between 1969 and 1996 they multiplied greatly and tripled in number (see Jiwani: 6).

[2] Communities here mean geographic (North End residents) or demographic groups (14–17 boys drop in center) or (seniors social group). It also means cultural groups affiliated by certain statuses (immigrants). These examples are not exhaustive.

The commitment to market by workers is known as the work ethic. However, worker citizens also required assurances. These included income replacement when work displacement occurred, insurances against labor-site accidents, and plans for contingencies when the unexpected disrupted the productive life. More ambitious expectations included retraining during technological labor displacement, re-education to stay abreast of advances in workforce expectations and protection from labor exploitation through unionization. The welfare pact, then, included citizen workers, their community collectives, the state and the market.

This pact which was more 'reluctant' than 'institutionally proactive' (George & Wilding, 1985) is currently altered and workers have had reassurances stripped from their lives without consultation. There is currently angst regarding the preeminence of the collaboration between market and state over a proactive state-worker agenda. Why is this so?

Character changes have altered the welfare pact; the global market is now a relatively faceless entity, with controls operating both within and outside Canadian borders. The Canadian state has not relinquished its sovereignty nor sold out its control over fiscal matters, but in the opinion of the most disadvantaged, its loyalty to protecting Canadian workers is wavering. It is probably fairly accurate to suggest that the state now splits its obligations unevenly between this faceless market force and worker citizens, with the latter incurring more loss. Workers have also lost confidence in their capacity and rights to protect themselves through unionization. This loss of confidence coincides with less state protection and increased uncertainty regarding the intentions or directions of the global market.

Changing Ideologies

Since Social Assistance is the welfare program of last resort, there has always been some measure of stigma associated with having to take money from the state during episodic job displacements. That stigma endured by those who become market casualties, the structure of the reformed Social Assistance programs, and the political expectations which inspired current program reforms all have traces of ideological shifts, which are important to understand the Canadian society.

The post-1990s welfare reforms in Canada reflect ideology leaning further toward liberalism but still left in place a reluctant but pragmatic welfare commitment (National Council of Welfare, 1997). A mix of universal programs with some selective intervention and protective programs now balance commitment between workers and market investors. The influence of labor has been curtailed, universal health care continues to present access hurdles and is under challenge from the private sector, postsecondary education subsidies are less, care and support for children continues to be politically contentious but retains some state commitment. Support for the poorest Canadians is the focus in the following budget excerpt (Canada, 2007, 2006).

> This proposal reflects recognition that the federal government is better placed to provide income support to families with children and that provinces and territories are better placed to tailor child care services and support to the wide variety of needs among Canadian families. The Government's child care proposal builds on the improved support to families with children that resulted from clarification of federal and provincial-territorial responsibilities as part of the 1998 National Child Benefit (NCB) (described below) (Government of Canada Budget, 2006; Chapter 6).

Citizen variations in education, labor location (secondary or primary), gender, cultural affiliation related to immigrant status and ability complicate the competition for state welfare resources. This competition unfolds in numerous ways and is associated with the life scripts of individuals who are themselves competing for rights and protection in the Canadian workforce. Provincial social assistance requirements are structured to address homogeneity and do not respond adequately to the diversity of needs reflected among the poorest populations.

Women have emerged as a particularly vulnerable group in the postwar welfare arrangements. Their social assistance needs are related to tensions derived from their dual parenting and out-of-home working roles. Social Assistance, the social program which traditionally transitioned women from preschool parenting to paid work, was subject to policy reforms in the mid-1990s and women's status as citizen workers altered along with these policy changes.

Under postwar Social Assistance programs, sole female parents with preschool children could receive support under Family Benefits Programs, which took the necessary work of raising children and the need for one parent to be carer as the starting point (Freiler et al., 2001). Family Benefits Programs were a substitute for the state's inability or unwillingness to provide universal child care. Under pre-1990s reforms, there was implicit permissiveness for sole support mothers to work at home as child minders and for the state to support this work in part through provincial and territorial income maintenance programs. Market considerations were not the immediate driving force then as is the case with current social assistance programs.

Under post-1990s reforms, this implicit obligation by the state for sharing responsibility for raising children has been streamlined and made more accountable to the market. Social Assistance is now structured to obligate sole support mothers, who are carers, to own and act on the first responsibility of positioning themselves in the paid workforce outside of their own homes. The post-1990s policy reforms then have clarified the ambiguity in the responsibilities for sole support women carers. In the Province of Ontario, for example, a legislation tabled in the 1960s was repealed and replaced[3] with more punitive legislation

---

[3] The General Welfare Act 1967 and the Family Benefits Act 1967 were repealed and replaced by the Ontario Social Assistance Reform Act 1997.

(Mosher & Hermer, 2005: 7–23). A new legislation tabled in 1997 shifted the primary onus for family survival from the state to parents, with the state only coming to aid during desperate circumstances. In recognition of this shared responsibility and in respect of the market, the Government of Canada recently introduced modest transfer payments for child care going directly to families (Canada, 2007). These transfers are intended to obviate the need for universal child care. Instead of providing child care centers run and operated by the state, cash transfers give parents options to spend in the public market place. Sole support female parents have, on the one hand, inadequate cash transfers to pay for child care and, on the other hand, stringent expectations to position themselves in paid work. Social assistance regulations, the Social Assistance Reform Act 1997, suggest the following in 1(a) and 1(b).

Purpose of Act

1. The purpose of this Act is to establish a program that,

    (a) recognizes individual responsibility and promotes self reliance through employment;
    (b) provides temporary financial assistance to those most in need while they satisfy obligations to become and stay employed;
    (c) effectively serves people needing assistance; and
    (d) is accountable to the taxpayers of Ontario. 1997, c. 25, Sched. A, s. 1. (Statutes of Ontario, 1998)

Parents, in general, however, exist with their own levels of challenges and with varying obstacles. The constant and substantial inflow of newcomer populations from across the international community into the Canadian labor pool means that social programs should reflect Canada's external labor dependence. Social programs appropriate for newcomer populations also serve to legitimate Canada's commitment to linking economic stability to social growth. The newcomers who join the Canadian labor market and society as immigrants and refugees are in principle eligible to receive state aid on the same basis as long-term residents. However, family class immigrants, those sponsored into Canada by relatives who are Canadian residents, are limited in the state aid they may receive. State-sponsored refugees[4] arrive in Canada with commitment from the government of Canada for short-term aid. Family class immigrants are compelled to enter paid work immediately following state programs which orient them to the Canadian labor market. Language, job search assistance, and health care are included in the newcomers' social

---

[4] Refugees are not the subject of discussion here. State sponsored refugees who ultimately gain citizenship in Canada are subject to the challenges experienced by minorities in the Canadian labor force.

package. Yet, current social programs fall quite short of removing obstacles from labor integration for newcomer populations.

In the streamlining of social programs, following the 1990s reforms, the emphasis shifted to short-term assistance for those who lose jobs. Newcomer populations are not challenged by job loss; they are generally locked into secondary labor market jobs without benefits, mobility, or labor protection for long durations. Their needs are largely different from long-term residents. Newcomers' most urgent needs are protection of rights and antiracism protocols. Provincial/territorial and federal governments initiate and fund these programs, but these are postcrisis redress processes consistent with liberal values.

Other historical troubles make achieving the just society through welfare development difficult in Canada. The long-standing unsettled relations with Canada's Aboriginal peoples have detracted from any possibility of the profile of a just and caring nation. The welfare analysis tends to focus more on the state's ability to redistribute wealth through social programs and not enough on Canadian unwillingness to insure basic human rights for Aboriginal peoples. Social welfare has historical association with material needs; but rights to a just and safe existence are social goods, which must be competed for in the open market.[5]

At its very core, though, social programs, however uneven in impact, managed to create some measure of social solidarity in Canada and confidence in our nation's capacity to redistribute the means to minimal protections. That was until our homegrown problems collided with global market issues and internal bickering was subordinated to more external and complex market threats. That solidarity has come in large measure from the mobilization which followed cutbacks to funding for social programs.

New Forms of Solidarity

The uncertainty, the economic threats, and the fear of widespread instability, which gave way to riots during the depression years, have surfaced again in Canada. However, in 2008, these uncertainties are grounded in the knowledge that citizens are protected by basic minimums. Today's cries are for greater protection. Poverty groups have mobilized with other civil society agents and the outcry against neoliberalism ebbs and flows (MacKay, 2002).

Because globalization has become a universally unpopular concept with protest groups, it features as the focus in most mobilized group protests. More importantly, the dissatisfaction which began with the perception that

---

[5] Rights protection can be guaranteed if individuals can afford lawyers who can champion these. Poor people who lack access to financial resources must depend on conditional state aid to seek redress for rights infringement. So, welfare in this case is an out-of-reach privilege.

the state values its market more than citizens has flourished, as labor, NGOs, poverty activists, and academics combine to make statements which can and must be heard. This new show of civil society with an aim is not ignored by the state.

Not only have activists converged with this common aim of protecting entitlements and questioning the social commitment of politicians but their activism has served as an educational tool for those less inclined to heed conflict politics (Torczner, 2000). Advantages abound; easy access to the media through the Internet, the younger media-savvy generation, and the insecurity which causes the otherwise uninterested persons to pay attention have strengthened activism and put our state on guard. We now have increased attentiveness to social demands, but not always necessarily with congruent action. But the impact is discernible: the language of the government in power has recently lost its arrogant tone, there is better transparency, and appeasement is noticeable in policy language.

Because the United States, our closest neighbor, is synonymous with global expansion, cross-border ties on welfare issues are not appropriate. However, anti-globalization has a global movement only because globalization has this demonic characterization. As Canadians, we thrive to keep what we have and to regain what we have lost in the market fray. That battle we confront as Canadians with vested interests and allies from outside our borders are excluded. The struggle for our welfare state is private and symbolically sacred. We Canadians have ideological demons in our closet, which preceded globalization.

In spite of the modest merits of the Canadian welfare state, we have not always depended on redistribution from the state to meet welfare needs. Liberalism was the ideology of the nineteenth century, and the earliest settlers in Canada developed other means of mutual survival alongside their expectation of individualism. Charities continue to exist alongside state welfare programs; these are constant reminders of our ideological heritage. The state grew naturally into individualism, and when concessions were finally made to structure the welfare state, it was imprinted with 'reluctance.' This reluctant welfare model is kept in place by citizens who challenge and by alliances which threaten the tenure of politicians.

Conclusion

The postwar changes which gave Canada its contemporary welfare state were not forged out of consensus. The interventionist state was an uneasy truce between federal, provincial, and territorial governments sharing responsibility for welfare redistribution. But special interest groups also have considerable say in public policies, especially programs which protect market interests from organized labor and labor from market exploitations. Our welfare state inherited both liberal (right of center) and social democratic (left of center) strains, and at times, these collide as competing forces. At other times, we have managed to govern through a combination of both locations.

In 2008 we are seeking new analysis through lenses, which have global reach, and ideological direction, which is strained. Having never sorted out what the ideological starting point for our welfare commitment should be, it will be more difficult now to decide whether global markets are enticing ideology not friendly to the welfare ideal. But welfare has allies, and they are mobilizing.

The left has had a historical role in advancing Canadian social programs (McKay, 2005: 83–91), even though their positive influence on the Canadian welfare state is unacknowledged. Threats of welfare interference from global investors will not go unchallenged. Community mobilization is increasing as social hardships signal to citizens that something is amiss and things should be made right again. The next three to five years will be instructive years.

References

Bales, K. (1999). *Disposable people: New slavery in the global economy.* Berkeley: University of California Press.

Banting, K. G. Parts 1–5. (1995). *Queens forum on social policy.* Video. Canadian Broadcasting Corporation Production, Ottawa, CBC International Sales.

Barlow, M. (1996). *Globalization and the dismantling of Canadian democracy, values and society.* PCDForum Article #17 Release Date March 10, 1996. http://www.pcdf.org/1996/17barlow.htm

Barlow, M., & Bruce C. (1995). *How the liberals abandoned the just society.* Toronto: Harper Collins.

Brock, K. L. (2008). The Politics of asymmetrical federalism: Reconsidering the role and responsibilities of Ottawa. *Canadian Public Policy, 34*(2), 143–161. Toronto: University of Toronto Press.

Burgmann, V. (2002). Labour/LeTravail and Canadian working class history: A view from Afar. *Labour/LeTravail No. 50.* Fall 2002. http://www.historycooperative.org/journals/llt/50/burgmann.html

Canada, Department of Finance: Minister of Finance. (2007). *The budget plan 2007.* Department of Finance, Ottawa, Canada.

Canada, Department of Finance: Minister of Finance. (2006). *The budget plan 2006.* Department of Finance, Ottawa, Canada.

Canada, Department of Justice. (1985). *Canada Health Act (R.S.,1985,c,C-6).*

Curtis, K. A. (Downloaded 2008). The impact of welfare restructuring on the nonprofit and voluntary sector in Canada and the US. http://www.aspect.bc.ca/pdf/curtisCanadian.pdf

Elwood, W. (2001). *The no-nonsense guide to globalization.* London: Verso.

Finkel, A. (1995). Origins of the welfare state in Canada. In R. B. Blake & Jeff Keshen (eds.) *Social welfare policy in Canada. Historical readings* (pp. 221–243). Toronto: Copp Clark.

Fligstein, N. (1998). *Is globalization the cause of the crises of welfare states?* Paper Prepared for the Annual Meetings of the American Sociological Association held in Toronto, Canada, August 1997.

Franks, C. E. S. (1987). *The Parliament of Canada.* Toronto: University of Toronto Press.

Freiler, C. C. F., Felicite S., Brigitte K., & Judy C. (2001). *Mothers as earners: Mothers as carers. Responsibility for Children. Social Policy and the tax system.* Research Report prepared for the Status of Women Canada, Ottawa.

George, V., & Paul W., (1985). *Ideology and social welfare,* 2nd. ed. Routledge & Kegan Paul: London.

Gindin, S. (2004). *Globalization and labour: Defining the problem. Work in a Global Society.* Working Paper Series. 2004-1. Labour Studies Programme, McMaster University, Hamilton.

Godard, J. (2003). Labour unions, workplace rights and Canadian public policy. *Canadian Public Policy, 29*(4), 449–467.

Goldfield, M., & Bryan D. P. (2007). Canada's worker's movement: Uneven developments. *Labour/LeTravail No. 59,* Spring 2007

Hibbert, N. (2008). Citizenship and the welfare state: A critique of David Miller's Theory of Nationality Citizenship and the Welfare State. *Canadian Journal of Political Science/Revue canadienne de science politique, 41*(1), 169–186. New York: Cambridge University Press.

Jiwani, I. (2000). *Globalization at the Level of the nation-state: The Case of Canada's Third Sector.* http://www.ucalgary.ca/~innovative/issues/Inv2000-4.pdf

Laugesen, M., & Susan A. B. (2000). *Support for Healthcare in the Western Welfare State: Australia, Canada, Britain, New Zealand and the United States.* Paper prepared for the Western Political Science Association Annual Meeting, March 25–27. San Jose, California.

Leo, C. (2006). Deep federalism: Respecting community: Difference in national policy. *Canadian Journal of Political Science, 39*(3), 481–506.

Leonard, P. (1997). *Postmodern welfare: Reconstructing an emancipatory project.* London: Sage Publications.

Lightman, E. (2003). *Social policy in Canada.* Toronto: Oxford University Press.

Lister, R. (1997). *Citizenship: Feminist perspectives.* London: MacMillan.

MacKay, K. (2002, Full). Solidarity and symbolic protest: Lessons for labour from the Québec City Summit of the Americas. *Labour/Le Travail #50.*

Mamuji, A. (2007, September). *Canada's official development assistance: Policy shortfalls and possible improvements.* Major Graduate Research paper for Globalization and the Human Condition, McMaster University, Hamilton, Ontario, Canada.

McKay, I. (2005). *Rebels, reds, radicals: Rethinking Canada's left history.* Toronto: Between the Lines.

Midgley, J. (2000, July). Globalization, capitalism and social welfare. *Social Work and Globalization, Special Issue,* 13–28.

Mishra, R. (1999). *Globalization and the welfare state.* Cheltenham: Edward Elgar.

Mishra, R. (1990). The welfare state in capitalist society: Policies of Retrenchment and Maintenance in Europe, North America, and Australia. Toronto: University of Toronto Press.

Mosher, J., & Joe H. (2005). *Welfare Fraud: The constitution of social assistance as crime.* Paper prepared for the Law Commission of Canada. See at: http://osgode.yorku.ca/osgmedia.nsf/O/27IAE

Mullaly, B. (2002). *Challenging oppression: A critical social work approach.* Oxford: Oxford University Press.

National Council of Welfare. (1997). *Another look at welfare reform.* Report #99. http://www.ncwcnbes.ne.net/document/researchpublications/Otherpublications/1997Report-AnotherLook AtWelfareReform/Reports

Olsson, S. E. (1993). *Social policy and welfare state in Sweden.* Lund: Arkiv.

Owram, D. (1986). *The government generation: Canadian intellectuals and the state 1900–1945.* Toronto: University of Toronto Press.

Palmer, B. (1992). *Working class experience: Rethinking the history of Canadian labour 1800–1991. Toronto:* McClelland & Stewart Inc.

Prince, M. J. (1998). Holes in the safety net, leaks in the roof: Changes in Canadian welfare policy and their implications for social housing programs. *Housing Policy Debate, 9*(4).

Rice, J., & Michael P. (2000a). A double movement: Implications of globalization and Pluralization for the Canadian welfare state. S. McBride & J. Wisemen (Eds.), In *Globalization and its Discontents*. Basingstoke, England: Macmillan.

Rice, J. R., & Michael J. (2000b). *Changing politics of Canadian social policy*. Toronto: University of Toronto Press.

Richer, K. (2007). The federal spending power. (PRB 07 36E) Library of Parliament. Parliamentary information and research Service. Law and Government Division. http://www.parl.gc.ca/information/library/PRBpubs/prb0736-e.html

Scott, K. (2003). *Funding matters: The impact of Canada's new funding regime on nonprofit and voluntary organizations*. Report prepared for the Canadian Council on Social Development. Ottawa.

Seguin, G. (2008). *Canada assistance plan: Canadian Health and Social Transfer; Canada Health Transfer, Canada Social Transfer*. Canadian Social Research Links. http://www.canadiansocialresearch.net/cap.html

Smiley, D. V. (1987). *The federal condition in Canada*. Toronto: McGraw-Hill Ryerson.

Statistics Canada. (2005). Diverging trends in unionization. *Perspectives, 6*(4). http://www.statcan.ca/english/freepub/75-001.XIE/1040575-001-XIE.pdf

Struthers, J. (1983). *No fault of their own: Unemployment and the Canadian welfare state 1914–1941*. Toronto: University of Toronto Press.

Torczner, J. (2000, July). Globalization, inequality and peace building: What social work can do. *Social Work and Globalization. Special Issue,* 123–146.

Tzembelicos, A. C. (1996). *Canada: State of the Federation. The Series*. Social Programs. Chronology of Events July 1995–June 1996. Queens University, School of Policy Studies, Institute of Intergovernmental Relations. http://www.queensu.ca/iigr/pub/SOTF.html Downloaded August 17th, 2008.

Vayda, E., & Raisa B. D. (1995). The Canadian health care system: A developmental Overview. In R. Blake & J. Keshen (Eds.), *Social welfare policy in Canada* (pp. 313–325). Mississauga: Copp Clark.

Wolfe, R., & Mendhelsohn, M. (2005). Values and interests in attitudes toward trade and globalization: The continuing compromise of embedded liberalism. *Canadian Journal of Political Science, 38*(1), 1–24.

Chapter 14
United States: Social Welfare Policy and Privatization in Post-industrial Society

Michael Reisch

Introduction: Globalization and Social Welfare Policy in the United States

It is widely acknowledged that the US welfare state evolved differently from those of other industrialized nations (Karger & Stoesz, 2002; Chatterjee, 1996). Pragmatic, rather than ideological, in origin, it relied less on the national government and more on the private sector than its European counterparts (Midgley, 1997). In comparison to the welfare states of Western Europe, the US version had more limited goals and never developed a national network of services or a fully integrated income maintenance system. Other unique features of the US welfare system include decentralized government intervention and a critical role for the nonprofit sector, as both funder and provider of services (Young, 1999). The US social welfare system has also frequently been used to maintain prevailing racial, gender, and class inequalities (Reisch, 2005; Schram et al., 2003; Schram et al., 2007).

Until the late 1970s, proponents of the US welfare state assumed that limited government intervention could ameliorate the socioeconomic problems produced by capitalism without fundamentally altering the structure or values of the nation's political-economic system (Axinn & Stern, 2008). Over the past three decades, however, an alternative view of the welfare state emerged, which regards such intervention as antifreedom and antithetical to the market's self-correcting mechanisms (Hayek, 1949; Friedman, 1962). According to this perspective, welfare state policies discourage entrepreneurial activities, innovation, and risk; reduce the role of the voluntary sector and diminish civil society; increase the dependency of benefit recipients; and expand state power to the point where it creates a potential threat to liberty (Popper, 1997). This view of the welfare state sees it as socially disruptive, wasteful, inefficient, and destructive of individual freedom. Although it is based on several untested ideological assumptions – that political and social democracy cannot coexist; that freedom

M. Reisch (✉)
School of Social Work, University of Maryland, Baltimare, MD, USA
e-mail: mreisch@ssw.umaryland.edu

J. Powell, J. Hendricks, *The Welfare State in Post-Industrial Society*, DOI 10.1007/978-1-4419-0066-1_14, © Springer Science+Business Media, LLC 2009

and equality are conflicting social goals; that inequality is neither economically nor socially harmful; that markets can solve the problems of stigma and discrimination and enhance free choice; that social welfare policies only benefit the poor; and that health care and social services "commodities" are identical in character to traditional industrial goods – this perspective provides much of the ideological rationalization for economic globalization and its consequences today (Greve, 2006).

At the heart of this rationale is the assumption that twentieth century levels of social welfare provision threaten the efficacy of the twenty-first century market system (Beck, 2000). All corrective measures to reduce the social costs of private enterprises, therefore, run counter to the short-term logic of the market system (Sodersten, 2004). Since the late 1970s, the United States has been a global leader in this regard – reducing the overall social spending, initiating efforts to shred existing safety nets, and transferring social costs from the public to the private and nonprofit sectors with deleterious social effects (Zunz et al., 2002).

In combination with market developments, this approach to social welfare produced four major consequences. First and foremost, it contributed substantially to a marked increase in socioeconomic inequality. The United States is now the most unequal of all industrialized nations, more unequal than at any time since data were first collected (Smeeding, 2008; Bernstein, 2007). Increase in socioeconomic inequality is also reflected in growing racial and class disparities in health and mental health, education, housing, and the justice system (Navarro, 2007).

Second, employment has become more precarious and less remunerative for millions of Americans due to a sharp drop in average wages and benefits and a marked growth in unemployment, part-time employment, and underemployment (U.S. Bureau of the Census, 2008a). Third, there has been a parallel decline in the social character of work. This has contributed to the growing alienation of large segments of population and increased incidence of drug and alcohol abuse, domestic violence, and mental illness (Macarov, 2003). These developments have exacerbated the growing isolation of American social life, reduced daily interracial and interclass contact, and heightened intergroup suspicion and hostility. They have also created additional barriers to the formation of alliances across racial and class lines around issues of mutual concern.

At the same time, as the response to the recent global financial crisis demonstrates, the government is less able to influence the consequences of emerging forms of economic organization, production, and distribution (Walzer, 2003). This last point is particularly important in understanding the relationship of globalization to issues like welfare state transformation. In effect, globalization has revealed the anachronistic structure of political institutions and traditional social welfare organizations and the declining significance of political boundaries and allegiances, particularly in regard to their span of control and speed in responding to economic, political, and social problems. Ironically, this has occurred in an era in which the increased mobility of capital and information has affected the rapidity with which problems emerge. Thus, the role of the welfare state has become more significant, even as state-sponsored policies undermine its foundation (Greve, 2006).

The economic roots of this transformation date back to the early 1970s. After 25 years of modest downward income redistribution, the United States experienced over two decades during which both wages and welfare benefits stagnated. Concurrently, the nation's tax system became increasingly regressive and the value of income transfers to the most vulnerable segments of the population sharply declined (Danziger & Gottschalk, 2004). Closely related to an increase in economic inequality was the growth of chronic and "severe poverty," particularly among African Americans and Latinos (U.S. Bureau of the Census, 2008b). Explanations for these complementary phenomena include the impact of deindustrialization, outsourcing of production, technological innovations, class and racially based gaps in education, foreign competition and trade imbalances, and the decline of unions (Reisch & Gorin, 2000).

Another important development was the reorganization and transformation of employment, which some observers have referred to as the "end of work" (Rifkin, 1995). This has been accompanied by what Head (1996) termed "lean production" aimed at expanding productivity and reducing labor costs. This type of corporate reengineering in manufacturing industries quickly spread to the service sector, resulting in the displacement of many lower-level workers and middle-level managers. The introduction of managed care produced similar effects in hospitals, mental health centers, and child welfare agencies. Thus, globalization transformed the very nature of service provision in the post-industrial United States.

Post-industrialism and the Nation State: Work and Welfare, Identity and Citizenship

Major policy shifts like the Personal Responsibility and Work Opportunity Act of 1996 (PRWORA), also known as welfare reform, served several interrelated purposes in shaping the context of the post-industrial welfare state. First, they helped drive down the wage scale and reduce the cost of production, with the ostensible goal of making US firms more competitive in the world market. Second, they strengthened the drive for greater workforce discipline and compliance, as more workers seek fewer jobs, particularly in the low-wage service sector of the economy. Third, they promoted a general reduction in the role of the government, which has significant implications not only for the totality of social policy but also for government policies in the areas of trade, banking, and environmental regulation, with disastrous consequences as the recent economic crisis demonstrates. Finally, by questioning the legitimacy of the social welfare system itself and government's effectiveness in administering social programs, they created an opportunity for the private sector to acquire new and vast resources of capital: the Social Security Trust Funds (Piven, 2005).

Cities and Citizenship in the Post-industrial United States

Modern social policies in the United States emerged as a response to two conflicting developments: the belief of the elite that the control of urban problems and population and the consequences of industrialization was a prerequisite for stable, long-term economic growth and the desire of organized workers, reformers, intellectuals, and professionals, to use cities as laboratories of social reform or as vehicles through which to initiate structural changes in the economy and society. For the elite class, these policies became effective instruments of social control. They helped maintain the wage scale at below subsistence levels and reinforced the values of the dominant culture. For the working class and low income persons, however, particularly women and persons of color, welfare programs became an integral part of the ongoing survival strategies (Allen & Kirby, 2000). These contradictions forged the US social welfare system into a unique synthesis of moral stigma and economic safety net (Axinn & Stern, 2008).

As long as the well-being of cities and their population was regarded as critical to the nation's prosperity and as long as the organized advocates for social welfare identified with urban problems and the need for their resolution, US social policies slowly expanded to address what were perceived as predominantly urban problems. During the past three decades, however, the critical role that central cities play in the US economy has declined, while, as a result of dramatic demographic shifts, the urban population are comprised increasingly of immigrants, migrants, and people of color (U.S. Bureau of the Census, 2008b). In the calculus of the global marketplace and domestic politics, such populations are frequently regarded as expendable.

In some cases, as in the original provisions of PRWORA, their social rights were denied because of their immigration status. More recently, conservative politicians in the 2008 election contrasted these urban populations with "real Americans." These developments reflect a well-orchestrated assault on the structural components of the US welfare state accompanied by the expectation that recipients of services rely on the uncertainties of the marketplace, rather than legal entitlements, to satisfy their basic human needs (Prigoff, 2001).

Race and Welfare Reform

For many years, race has played a significant role in the development of US welfare policies (Schram et al., 2003; Lieberman, 1998). Even during periods of reform, such as the 1930s and 1960s, persons of color faced discrimination in the application of eligibility standards and the distribution of social benefits; they also suffered the effects of white backlash against the modest gains they received (Brown, 1999). Over the past 40 years, significant changes in welfare policies – including the introduction of work requirements in the late 1960s and early 1970s and the contraction or elimination of a broad range of supportive services – have had dramatic consequences for persons of color (Schiele, 1998; Bobo & Smith, 1998). The perpetuation of racial stereotypes in the mass media and the use of racial codes for partisan political purposes have reduced public support for welfare programs as a whole (DeParle, 2004; Clawson & Trice, 2000). In the decade before the passage of PRWORA, racial stereotyping played a major role in shaping public opinion about the goals and assessment of welfare reform (Schram et al., 2003; Reisch, 2003).

Political Realignment

Attacks on the urban poor, immigrants, and racial minorities coincided with a major shift in the locus of US economic and political power to the so-called "sun belt" – a shift that initially went unnoticed. This power shift was driven by the same logic as the process of globalization and was abetted by political changes of considerable magnitude. The power of states in which the old "New Deal coalition" of organized labor, white ethnics, African Americans, and intellectuals did not exist increased. The policy devolution that ensued exacerbated income disparities among and within regions produced by government cutbacks (Piketty & Saez, 2003).

Perhaps the most significant policy development of the past generation, however, has been the unstinting attack on the government as a potential problem solver. Myths about the causes of poverty and the so-called "underclass" were repeated with such frequency that many Americans now view social policies as their source, rather than their solution. This attack on social welfare served four essential purposes.

First, it transferred the social costs of economic transformation to the least vulnerable and most stigmatized segments of the population. Second, it compelled communities to rely increasingly, if not exclusively, on marketplace solutions for complex economic and social problems. Third, it drove a political wedge, based on race, between the various (potentially unified) elements of the working and middle classes. Finally, it diverted the focus of political debate away from the structural causes of inequality in the United States toward a discussion of individual or cultural deficiencies (Macarov, 2003; Piven 2005).

This political onslaught was accompanied by significant changes in the social and cultural landscape of the nation that diluted any latent sympathies for the low-income people. There was a dramatic decline in daily interactions between the poor and the non-poor, white and non-white segments of the population, as a result of suburban growth, urban gentrification, and the changing character of poverty accompanied by the growing privatization of social life and loss of public space (Fisher & Karger, 1997). Overt, politically coded attacks further isolated urban populations from the US mainstream. These attacks fueled criticism of the social welfare system and rationalized the dismantling of the US welfare state (Katz, 2001).

Changes to the Welfare State: Ideology, Multiculturalism, Marketization, Privatization

For most of nineteenth and twentieth centuries, social policy making in the United States rested on several assumptions about the relationship between the state and social welfare. One assumption was that industrialization and its consequences would lead to a gradual expansion of government's role in addressing what Titmuss (1969) called the "diswelfares" produced by industrialization. A second assumption was that publicly funded social welfare systems would ameliorate these negative effects by collectivizing what Kapp (1971) referred to as the "social costs of private enterprise." Third, that the expansion of state-sponsored welfare policies would sustain the legitimacy of government at all levels and expand the rights of citizenship. Fourth, that the evolution of the welfare state would enhance the role of professionals within it and, ideally, improve the relationship of these professionals with their clients. Finally, and perhaps of greatest significance today, that both the problems social welfare systems addressed and the policy solutions they proposed would be shaped by finite political and economic borders (Axinn & Stern, 2008; Jansson, 2005; Patterson, 2001).

Developments during the past 30 years, however, have produced new political-economic realities and challenged many of these prevailing assumptions. The pressures of economic globalization within a world system in which market values are ascendant have transformed the underlying values, goals, and consequences of welfare provision. This is best illustrated by the impact of the 1996 Personal Responsibility and Work Opportunity Reconciliation Act and the growing movement to privatize social welfare in the United States.

The Privatization of US Social Welfare

For the past three decades, critics of the US welfare state have suggested that the privatization of social and health care services would increase both their effectiveness and efficiency. Although the preference for market-oriented solutions among the proponents of privatization is clear, its meaning remains ambiguous. In general, it refers to a transfer to nongovernmental responsibility of some or all of the roles in creating or distributing a good or service formerly produced or distributed by the government (Hacker, 2002). There have been two broad categories of privatization: the government "load shedding" or "cost shifting" in which both responsibility for service delivery and financing are transferred from public to private auspices and policies which "empower" the so-called "mediating institutions" through government grants and contracts (Macarov, 2003).

This ambiguity gives rise to several important, as yet unsolved questions: (1) Does privatization refer to a shift to nonprofit, nongovernmental organizations (NGOs) or for-profit organizations or both? (2) What will be the impact of applying private sector models of organization and service delivery to social goods which were formerly the responsibility of the government? (3) Which forms of government support for private sector activities – taxes, subsidies, capital development, or training – are most effective? (4) Finally, what are the ultimate purposes of privatization?

Advocates of privatization base their arguments on several questionable premises. First, that privatization is a novel concept or, alternatively, that where it has been tried, it has worked. Actually, there is a long history of privatization of welfare in the United States dating back to colonial times. The expansion of public sector involvement in social welfare was, in part, a response to the abuses of the private sector (Patterson, 2001; Katz, 2001).

A second assumption is that the commodities produced by social welfare systems are equivalent in the marketplace to other economic goods; that is, the demand for such goods equals the supply and that the market can adequately match human needs and financial resources. There is a complementary assumption that the consumers of social services have free choice and unimpeded access to such goods and that the providers of social services compete freely in the marketplace. None of these assumptions has been validated by either historical or contemporary events (Macarov, 2003).

Third, the private sector is more efficient and effective in the implementation of social welfare services than the government. This assumption ignores the myriad ways in which the government has borne the social costs of private enterprises (e.g., unemployment insurance), the efficiency of government bureaucracy, like the Social Security Administration, and the historic role which the government has played in supporting the efficiency (i.e., profitability) of the for-profit sector through capital formation, grants, and contracts for research; the expansion and protection of markets; and the construction of the nation's physical and social infrastructure. It also ignores the reality that the goods produced by government services have qualitative characteristics that are not easily subjected to standard cost-benefit analysis. Finally, it overlooks the fact that most of the efficiencies achieved by privatization have occurred by lowering workers' wages and benefits, reducing services, diminishing the quality of staff development and training programs, imposing fees on clients, and focusing service provision on new, less difficult, and more affluent service consumers (Twombly, 2001).

A fourth assumption is that the marketplace is a more democratic and pluralistic mechanism for the distribution of social goods than the government and that the privatization of services can occur without affecting the nature, quantity, and quality of services and their overall pattern of distribution (i.e., their distributional equity). Privatization threatens to reproduce marketplace inequalities in the service sector and undermine the basic mission of the non-profit sector itself (Alexander et al., 1999). A recent component of the movement toward privatization – the promotion of faith-based social services – also threatens to undermine some of the civil rights gains of the past several decades.

Religious Provision of Social Welfare in Post-industrial Society

Through the Civil War, religious ideas were the most important influence on the development of the US social welfare (Leiby, 1978). During the Progressive Era, they contributed significantly to the development of major social welfare institutions, such as the Charities Organization Societies, and settlement houses. They helped to fill gaps in social service provision to low income families, racial minorities, and other socially disadvantaged groups which had been created by government inaction and the neglect of secular nongovernmental agencies. In addition, they provided new services and expanded access to services that were denied to their congregants by mainstream churches or their secular counterparts. Today, faith-based organizations continue to deliver services to hard-to-reach populations, such as ex-offenders, drug and alcohol abusers, and perpetrators of domestic violence (Cnaan et al., 1999). Over 90 percent of religious congregations provide at least one social service (Chaves, 2004), and the established sectarian agencies receive significant amounts of government funding.

Most contemporary religious social service programs, however, are small, short-term, and staffed by clergy or lay volunteers, absorbing only a tiny fraction of church budgets (Ammerman, 2005). Although the passage of "Charitable Choice" legislation expanded the role of faith-based services, serious questions remain about their efficacy, accountability, and discriminatory potential. There is little reliable research which demonstrates their effectiveness and scant evidence, indicating which types of programs produce the best results or how they compare to their secular counterparts (Chaves, 2004). In addition, because religious organizations are exempt from states' education, training, and licensing requirements, there is a danger of creating a two-tiered system of service provisions. The most controversial aspect of faith-based service provision, however, is the exemption religious organizations receive from Title VII of the 1964 Civil Rights Act. This allows them to receive public funds even if they discriminate in hiring, client screening, and program content (Kaminer, 2002).

In sum, the drive to privatize the US social welfare has served three major purposes. It explicitly discredits the underlying principles of the welfare state that individuals have certain rights (entitlements) to the basic goods required to address their "common human needs" (Towle, 1952). It allows policymakers to avoid tough fiscal decisions that serious responses to contemporary social problems require. Finally, it facilitates the transfer of vast amounts of public dollars into private hands, which amounts to a public subsidy of private profit. Privatization, in short, underscores and complicates those features of the US welfare system which have often been characterized as "American exceptionalism."

American Exceptionalism

US social welfare policies have focused primarily on problems of poverty, rather than inequality. Even after the modest reforms of the New Deal and the War on

Poverty, the United States lagged considerably behind other Western nations in its degree of social provision. This "American exceptionalism" has been explained in several ways: ideologically, as a consequence of the nation's Calvinist roots and emphasis on individualism; politically, as a result of the absence of working class, left-wing political parties to advocate for social democratic or socialist alternatives; demographically, as a means of stigmatizing certain populations, particularly people of color and, thereby, rationalizing institutional racism and sexism and their effects; and, culturally, as a way to reinforce hegemonic values and prevailing hierarchies (Rank, 2004; Abramovitz, 1998; Lieberman, 1998).

Since low-income groups lack power in the US society, they have always borne the brunt of the social costs of growth and change. Yet, the normative structure of the US welfare state has exacerbated the problems these groups experience through its emphasis on work over income maintenance, its preference for marketplace solutions, and its distrust of an activist state. Rationales for these approaches have appeared in both moral and pseudo-scientific forms since the eighteenth century (Jansson, 2005).

During the past three decades, several macro-level developments reinforced and intensified these tendencies. These included a marked increase in income and asset inequality; the strengthening of capital's power over labor; the growing insecurity of employment among all classes; the declining social character of work; the destabilization of communities; and the decline in the public faith in government's ability to address these issues (Reisch, 2005). The contraction of social welfare benefits and the spread of regressive modes of taxation have further undermined public confidence in the state's potential to develop and implement ameliorative policy solutions. They have been abetted by an increasingly antiwelfare ideology.

Antiwelfare Ideology

For decades, opponents of the welfare state sought to redefine the nation's social contract. They exaggerated the costs of welfare programs and focused public attention on a minority of recipients – African American adolescent mothers – to promote the myth of welfare failure (Schiele, 1998; Quadagno, 1996). In creating a wedge issue based on symbolic appeals to racial and gender biases, antiwelfare propagandists deliberately undermined the foundations of the US welfare system itself. Many of the myths disseminated as analysis at the height of the welfare reform debate of the late 1980s and early 1990s not only distorted data on welfare participation and benefit levels but also deliberately mislead the public about the nature of dependency in modern industrial society (Patterson, 2001). From an ideological standpoint, therefore, welfare reform can best be understood as the spearhead of a broader campaign to reduce government's role in addressing the problems generated or overlooked by economic globalization (Deacon, 1999; Prigoff, 2001).

The Impact of Welfare Reform

Most research on the impact of PRWORA has focused on the extent to which recipients of Temporary Assistance to Needy Families (TANF) have made a successful transition from welfare to work (DeParle, 2004). Measured solely in these terms, welfare reform has been a considerable success. In the first seven years after its implementation, the nation's welfare caseload dropped over 50 percent and, in some states caseloads decreased nearly 70 percent (US Department of Human Services, 2004). Yet, these indicators of success mask two other consequences of PRWORA: the increasing concentration of TANF recipients in urban areas and the conversion of long-standing racial stereotypes about welfare recipients into statistical reality.

In addition, amid the proclamations about the success of welfare reform, relatively little attention has been paid to its impact on the living standards of low-income households, the quality of life in low-income neighborhoods, or the availability of support services to these communities (Rank, 2004; Chow et al., 2005; Danziger et al., 2008). Yet, there is ample evidence that welfare reform has intensified the economic and social problems confronting low-income neighborhoods, with particularly deleterious effects on populations who are most dependent on the services small nonprofit community-based organizations provide (Bischoff & Reisch, 2000; Reisch & Bischoff, 2001; Abramovitz, 2005). The reduction in caseloads appears to represent, therefore, a shift in emphasis and responsibility for needed social support from the public to the nonprofit, private, and for-profit sectors. Recent studies have also found that the dramatic decline in welfare caseloads does not provide an adequate measure of the consequences of welfare reform, particularly when they are placed in the context of the overall effect of the legislation on the availability of essential services and the capacity of community-based organizations to deliver them (Reisch & Sommerfeld, 2003; Abramovitz, 2005). What welfare reform has done, in effect, is to create a neoliberal US workfare regime.

The US Workfare Regime

Political-economic theorists like Jessop (2002) have described the emergence of a Post-Fordist neoliberal workfare regime as the successor to the Keynesian-style welfare state that first appeared in the 1930s. They focus their analyses on the role played by welfare provision in balancing patterns of production and social demand (Esping-Andersen, 2002). They posit that, in a globalizing world economy, the classic pattern of accumulation and growth in industrial societies is created by *both* social and economic regulation. It produces significant alterations in the institutional fabric of welfare states to prepare recipients for "the pursuit of a competitive edge in a global economy" (Jessop, 1999: 353). Once conceived as a component of citizenship, welfare benefits have been transformed into a means to enhance corporate, rather than individual, well-being (McDonald et al., 2003).

Through this lens, PRWORA had a significant impact on the structure and substance of the US welfare state. It completed a generation-long process of devolving responsibility for public assistance to the states, eliminated the half-century-old concept of entitlement for low-income children and families, and brought to fruition the long-standing preference of US policymakers for work as the primary means of income support for the poor. By expanding, even mandating the role of the private sector and, most notably, religious organizations in policy implementation and service provision, it made their role critical to the legislation's definition of success. Researchers in numerous US cities have determined, however, that the underlying assumptions of PRWORA have not been validated by events since its passage. Although welfare reform – combined with a period of relative economic prosperity in the late 1990s – dramatically reduced caseloads (the official benchmark of success), it also produced substantial changes in the client populations served by community-based organizations and the character and mission of the agencies on which the low-income people were increasingly dependent (Abramovitz, 2005; Reisch & Bischoff, 2001; Fink & Widom, 2001).

Another consequence since the 1990s is that the relationship between the government and the nonprofit sector in the US welfare state most closely conforms to what Young (1999) termed the "supplementary perspective" – that is, private organizations have become the "support of last resort," providing goods and services that the state has eliminated or significantly reduced. This development raises two critical questions for policymakers, service providers, and scholars: To what extent can the private sector, particularly small community-based nonprofit organizations, replace the state in terms of financing or service provision, and what are the consequences of this shift in the locus of social welfare responsibility for low-income families, those who assist them, and the private sector as a whole (Reisch & Sommerfeld, 2003)?

To date, researchers have answered these questions largely in pessimistic terms. Welfare reform has encouraged the spread of market mechanisms in the nonprofit sector with deleterious effects on agencies' mission, culture, values, and norms of employment. The combination of privatization and devolution has forced these agencies to take on responsibilities that they lack the resources and, in many cases, the capacity to bear. The transformation of the US welfare state has also heightened intra- and interorganizational conflicts and produced recurring ethical dilemmas around such issues as confidentiality, informed consent, client self-determination, and divided professional loyalties (Alexander, 1999; Abramovitz, 2005; Reisch, 2003).

These changes and their future implications represent a significant and complex challenge to the limited US social safety net, one which jeopardizes the historically delicate framework of relationships between the public and nonprofit sectors (Young, 1999). Particularly since the 1960s, this relationship has shaped the size and direction of government funding, the distribution of societal responsibilities, and the balance of power around social welfare issues. Over the past decade, the dismantling of welfare state provision has produced both undesirable and potentially harmful consequences in this arena (Twombly, 2001; Reisch & Sommerfeld, 2003; Abramovitz, 2005; DeParle, 2004).

Welfare State Transformation and Social Work

The forces transforming the US welfare state have also influenced the nature of the professions within it, particularly the character and purpose of social work. In the United States, social workers in both public and nonprofit organizations have wrestled with the contradictions between their ethical imperative to work for social justice and their need for elite support. To some extent, US social workers are reaping the consequences of a problem they helped create. Many of their long-standing criticisms of the nation's welfare system were appropriated by conservatives to justify welfare reform. During the past decade, the failure of the organized social work profession to proffer a viable alternative to PRWORA or its antecedents put many social workers in the ironic position of defending the policies and programs they had fiercely criticized for nearly half a century. This contributed substantially to the marginalization of social workers from the major policy debates of the 1990s, a condition that persists today (McDonald & Reisch, 2008).

For example, the ideological basis of PRWORA created a peculiar contradiction between its emphasis on individualism and self-sufficiency and the chronic dependency of TANF recipients and those who purport to assist them on external political factors largely beyond their control. Ironically, in the new regime, independence is defined as acquiescence to the values and goals of neoliberal institutional forces, whose center of power has shifted from the state to the corporate sector. One consequence is the increasing depersonalization of relationship between individuals and institutions. This reflects both the growing power imbalance in all sectors of the US society and the increasing privatization of social life. Another consequence appears in the changing functions of social work interventions: from personal maintenance to behavior modification; from long-term stability to short-term outcomes; and from voluntary to compulsory participation in the welfare system's rules.

Several factors contribute to the powerlessness of clients and workers in the transformed welfare state. First, critical resources are increasingly controlled by forces outside the reach of their organizations. These forces, which possess a monopoly of strategic resources, are guided by fundamentally different premises about the purpose and nature of welfare systems. Second, the principal actors within the welfare system, including many policymakers, have scant influence over decisions regarding environmental uncertainties. Finally, these actors often cannot even anticipate what these decisions will be. This produces an interesting paradox in which change can only occur through structural challenges to the hegemonic regime, yet those who promote change must operate from a situation of resource, power, and information deficiency. The resolution of this paradox will have profound implications for our entire society, not merely for those who rely for their survival on its begrudging compassion (McDonald & Reisch, 2008).

New Forms of Solidarity: Intergenerational and Cross-National Linkages

There is an increasingly fractious debate among advocates, activists, and policy-makers as to how best to respond to the consequences of economic globalization and the welfare state transformation (Piven, 2005). Some activists even reject the idea of using globalization as the basis for analysis and strategic development. Others propose new approaches that emphasize the resurgence of communities of identity or the creation of alternative economic and political institutions at the local level, such as cooperatives and ecovillages, through which communities can become self-sufficient centers of alternative, life-sustaining culture (Delgado, 2000; Jacobson, 2001). Whether such approaches can produce sustainable progressive change in the current political-economic context is unclear.

Despite these differences, there is widespread acknowledgement that previous strategies, which viewed communities and even nations in isolation from the international environment, are no longer adequate. Yet, the persistence of views often based on identity politics within contemporary movements and movement-based organizations hinders their ability to develop coherent strategies or broad, effective coalitions (Fisher & Karger, 1997). In addition, "no mechanisms currently exist than can aggregate neighborhood mobilization of needs into a viable public discourse..." (Gottdiener, 1987: 285, quoted in Fisher & Kling, 1993: xiii). Thus, the formation of a viable response to globalization is hampered both by the existence of seemingly intractable social divisions and the absence of organizational structures that provide a basis for unity. The challenge for the future is how to combine long-standing identity-based conceptual frameworks into effective policies and political strategies (Afshar & Barrientos, 1999; Naples, 1998).

Sometimes, this struggle is reflected in the agendas of activist groups that seek inclusion at the expense of clarity and fail to link proposed solutions to the problem – globalization – that sparked their initial mobilization (Manski, 4 April 2000, e-mail communication). At other times, it is reflected in the persistent tension between advocates of universal human rights (Broadbent, 1998) and those who view such concepts as "self-interested attempts to protect the social welfare securities of the people in developed countries from being undercut by competition from the developing world" (Deacon, 1999, p. 24) and "instruments [that] only work to the advantage of the powerful and the dominant, and make the world more oppressive" (Third World Network, 1996). These views are particularly prominent outside the West (Korean Academy of Social Welfare, 2007).

Some international organizations have attempted to overcome such divisions and organize a consensus around a strategy of sustainable human development, which would include the following elements:

- satisfaction of basic human needs for food, shelter, health care, education, and natural resources, such as clean water;
- expansion of economic opportunities for all people in long-term environmentally and socially viable ways;
- protection of the environment through future-oriented management of resources;
- promotion of democratic participation, especially by marginalized populations, in the fundamental economic and political decisions that affect their lives; and
- encouragement of adherence to internationally recognized human rights standards (Bread for the World, 1995).

Some organizations, including the International Forum on Globalization, have attempted to forge coalitions of community leaders, scholars, and service professionals into a "Community of Communities." The development and sustenance of such coalitions will require cooperation among groups that have a long history of antagonistic relations or that are largely ignorant of each other's existence. These include international trade unions, environmental groups, civil and women's rights organizations, transnational NGOs, academic researchers, and even some liberal economists. In some nations, such as Canada, efforts to create such coalitions are much further along than in the United States. (Deacon, 1998).

Conclusion

There are several reasons why economic globalization will have a lasting impact on social welfare in the United States in the foreseeable post-industrial future. First, the welfare state – particularly in the United States – emerged in response to the social consequences of industrialization. Its ideological roots, strategies, and organizational forms are closely linked, therefore, to its relationship to the overall political-economy (Patterson, 2001). Although the theories, policies, and programs of the US welfare state have not yet adapted to recent structural and cultural changes, the creation of effective responses to globalization will become even more important if the current worldwide economic crisis worsens as expected.

Second, a persistent focus of welfare state policies has been the collectivization of the social costs of private enterprise through the expansion of government responsibility for social and economic provision. US social welfare policies have achieved the greatest success when they have integrated issues of employment/unemployment, income distribution, equitable fiscal policies, occupational safety and health, and workers' political rights (Rose, 1997). In the twenty-first century, policymakers will have to create new approaches to respond effectively to the new global economy and the growing gaps in employment, income, and wealth it has created (Reich, 2001). Among liberal economists, there is widespread acceptance of the premise "that socially regulated capitalism rather than unfettered capitalism and state socialism does better at meeting human needs" (Deacon, 1998: 16). This will require "a focus on broadly formulated issues and programs, articulated through multicultural coalitions and alliances, as central instruments for the achievement of policy goals, and the engagement of the state as an arena for struggle and change" (Fisher & Kling, 1993: 319).

At its best, the US welfare state recognized the connections between private troubles and public issues (Reisch & Andrews, 2001). The welfare state of the future will have to incorporate principles of social justice, self-determination, empowerment, and democratic participation both in the design of its policies and in their processes of implementation and evaluation (George & Wilding, 2002; Greve, 2006). Otherwise, economic globalization "is likely to marginalize and exclude a majority of the world's population from participation in productive economic activity and from its rewards" (Prigoff, 2001: 2). It would be a cruel irony if the welfare state, an institution created to democratize industrial society, had the opposite effect in its post-industrial successor.

References

Abramovitz, M. (1998). *Regulating the lives of women: Social welfare policy from colonial times to the present*, 2nd ed. Boston, MA: South End Press.

Abramovitz, M. (2005). The largely untold story of welfare reform and the human services, *Social Work, 50*(2), 175–186.

Afshar, H., & Barrientos, S. (Eds.) (1999). *Women, globalization, and fragmentation in the developing world*, New York: St. Martin's Press.

Alexander, J. (1999). The impact of devolution on nonprofits: A multiphase study of social service organizations, *Nonprofit Management and Leadership, 10*(1), 57–70.

Alexander, J., Nank, R. & Stivers, C. (1999). Implications of welfare reform: Do nonprofit survival strategies threaten civil society? *Nonprofit and Voluntary Sector Quarterly, 26*(4), 452–475.

Allen, K., & Kirby, M. (2000). *Unfinished business: Why cities matter to welfare reform.* Washington, DC: Brookings Institute.

Ammerman, N. T. (2005). *Pillars of faith: American congregations and their partners,* Berkeley. CA: University of California Press.

Axinn, J. & Stern, M. (2008). *Social welfare: A history of the American response to need,* 7th ed. , Boston: Allyn and Bacon.

Beck, U. (2000). *What is Globalisation?* Cambridge, Polity Press.

Bernstein, J. (2007, December 13). *Updated CBO data reveal unprecedented increase in inequality,* Economic Policy Institute, http://www.epi.org.

Bischoff, U. M. & Reisch, M. (2000). The impact of welfare reform on community-based non-profit organizations: Implications for policy, practice, and education, *Journal of Community Practice, 8*(4), 69–91.

Bobo, L. & Smith, R. (1998). From Jim Crow racism to laissez-faire racism: An essay on the transformation of racial attitudes in America. In W. Katkin, N. Landsman, & A. Tyree, eds.,

Beyond pluralism: The conception of groups and group identities in America, Urbana, IL: University of Illinois Press.

Bread for the World. (1995). *Hunger 1995: The causes of hunger*. Washington, DC: Author.

Broadbent, E. (1998). The challenge to economic and social rights: Thoughts on citizenship in the welfare state in the North Atlantic world, *Global Society, 12*(1), 15–29.

Brown, M. (1999). *Race, money, and the American welfare state*, Ithaca, NY: Cornell University Press.

Chatterjee, P. K. (1996). *Approaches to the welfare state*. Washington, DC: NASW Press.

Chaves, M. (2004). *Congregations in America*. Cambridge, MA: Harvard University Press.

Chow, J. C., Johnson, M. A., & Austin, M. J. (2005). The status of low-income neighborhoods in the post-welfare environment: Mapping the relationship between poverty and place. *Journal of Health and Social Policy, 21*(1), 1–32.

Clawson, R., & Trice, R. (2000). Poverty as we know it: Media portrayals of the poor. *Public Opinion Quarterly, 64*(4), 53–64.

Cnaan, R., Wineburg, R., & Boddie, S. (1999). *The newer deal*. New York: Columbia University Press.

Danziger, S., & Gottschalk, P. (2004). *Diverging fortunes: Trends in poverty and inequality*. New York: Russell Sage Foundation.

Danziger, S., Marsh, S., & Klum, K. (2008). Community services after welfare reform: Changing needs, shrinking resources, report prepared for the Charles Stewart Mott Foundation. Ann Arbor, MF: University of Michigan Program on Poverty and Social Welfare Policy.

Deacon, B. (1999, January). *Towards a socially responsible globalization: International actors and discourses*. GASPP Occasional Papers, Helsinki, Finland.

Delgado, M. (2000). *Community social work practice in an urban context: The potential of a capacity-enhancement perspective*. New York: Oxford University Press.

DeParle, J. (2004). *American dream: Three women, ten kids, and a nation's drive to end welfare*. New York: Viking Press.

Esping-Andersen, G., Gallie, D., Hemerijck, A., & Myles, J. (2002). *Why we need a new welfare state*. New York: Oxford University Press.

Fink. B., & Widom, R. (2001). *Social service organizations and welfare reform*. New York: Manpower Demonstration Research Organization.

Fisher, R., & Karger, H. J. (1997). *Social work and community in a private world: Getting out in public*. New York: Longman

Fisher, R., & Kling, J., (Eds.) (1993). *Mobilizing the community: Local politics in the era of the global city*. Newbury Park, CA: Sage Publications.

Friedman, M. (1962). *Capitalism and freedom*. Chicago, IL: University of Chicago Press.

George, V., & Wilding, P. (2002). *Globalization and human welfare*. New York: Palgrave.

Greve, B. (2006). *The future of the welfare state: European and global perspectives*. Burlington, VT: Ashgate.

Hacker, J. S. (2002). *The divided welfare state: The battle over public and private social benefits in the U.S*. New York: Cambridge University Press.

Hayek, F. J. (1949)., *Individualism and economic order*. Cambridge UK: Routledge & Kegan Paul.

Head, S. (1996, February 29). *The new ruthless economy, The New York review of books, 43*, 47–52.

Jacobson, D. (2001). *Doing justice: Congregations and community organization*. US: Fortress Press.

Jansson, B. (2005). *The reluctant welfare state*, 5th ed. Pacific Grove, CA: Brooks/Cole.

Jessop, B. (1999). The changing governance of welfare: Recent trends in its primary functions, scale, and modes of coordination. *Social Policy & Administration, 33*, 348–359.

Jessop, B. (2002). *The future of the capitalist state*. Cambridge, UK: Polity Press.

Kaminer, W. (2002). *Free for all: Defending liberty in America today*. Boston, MA: Beacon Press.

Kapp, J. W. (1971). *The social costs of private enterprise.* New York: Schocken.

Karger, H. J., & Stoesz, D. (2006). *American social policy: A pluralist approach,* 5th ed. Boston, MA: Allyn and Bacon.

Katz, M. B. (2001). *The price of citizenship: Redefining the American welfare state.* New York: Henry Holt.

Korean Academy of Social Welfare, ed. (2007). *Human rights and social justice: Rethinking Social Welfare's Mission.* Seoul, Korba: Author.

Leiby, J. (1978). *A history of social welfare and social work in the United States.* New York: Columbia University Press.

Lieberman, R. (1998). *Shifting the color line: Race and the American welfare state.* Cambridge, MA: Harvard University Press.

Macarov, D. (2003). *What the market does to people: Privatization, globalization and poverty.* London: Zed Books.

Manski, B. (2000, April 16). *To our friends and allies in progressive campus organizations.* e-mail communication.

McDonald, C., Harris, J., & Winterstein, R. (2003). Contingent on context? Social work in Australia, Britain, and the USA. *British Journal of Social Work, 33*(2), 191–208.

McDonald, C., & Reisch, M. (2008). Social work in the workfare regime: A comparison of the U.S. and Australia. *Journal of Sociology and Social Welfare, 35*(1), 43–74.

Midgley, J. (1997). *Social welfare in global context.* Thousand Oaks, CA: Sage Publications.

Naples, N. A., (Ed.) (1998). *Community activism and feminist politics: Organizing across race, class, and gender.* New York: Routledge.

Navarro, V. (2007). *Neoliberalism, globalization and inequalities: Consequences for health and quality of life.* Amityville, NY: Baywood Publications.

Patterson, J. (2001). *America's struggle against poverty in the 20th century.* Cambridge, MA: Harvard University Press.

Piketty, T., & Saez, E. (2003). Income inequality in the United States, 1913–1998, *Quarterly Journal of Economics, 118* (updated through 2005 at http://emlab.berkeley.edu/users/saez

Piven, F. F. (2005). *Institutions and agents in the politics of welfare cutbacks,* paper prepared for the Conference on Making the Politics of Poverty and Inequality: How Public Policies are Reshaping American Democracy, Madison, WI: Institute for Research on Poverty.

Popper, K. (1997). *The lesson of this century.* London, UK: Routledge.

Prigoff, A. (2001). *Economics for social workers: Social Outcomes of economic globalization with strategies for community action,* Belmont, CA: Brooks/Cole.

Quadagno, J. (1996). Race and American social policy. *National Forum, 76*(3), 35–59.

Rank, M. R. (2004). *One nation underprivileged: Why American poverty affects us all,* New York: Oxford University Press.

Reich, R. (2001). *The future of success.* New York: Alfred A. Knopf.

Reisch, M. (2005). American exceptionalism and critical social work: A retrospective and prospective analysis. In I. Ferguson, M. Lavalette, & E. Whitmore (Eds.), *Globalisation, global justice and social work,* (pp. 157–172). London, UK: Routledge.

Reisch, M. (2003). Welfare reform, globalization, and the transformation of the welfare state. In M. R. Gonzalez, (ed.), *Community organization and social policy: A compendium,* 2nd ed. San Juan, PR: Editorial Edil.

Reisch, M., & Andrews, J. (2001). *The road not taken: A history of radical social work in the United States,* Philadelphia: Brunner-Routledge.

Reisch, M., & Bischoff, U. (2001). Welfare reform strategies and community-based organizations: The impact on family well-being in an urban neighborhood, in F.F. Piven, J. Acker, M. Hallock, S. Morgen, (eds.), *Welfare, work, and politics,* (pp. 333–346). Eugene, OR: University of Oregon Press.

Reisch, M., & Gorin, S. (2000). The nature of work and the future of the social work profession. *Social Work, 46*(1), 9–19.

Reisch, M., & Sommerfeld, D. (2003). Welfare reform and the future of nonprofit organizations. *Nonprofit Management and Leadership, 14*(1), 19–46.

Rifkin, J. (1995). *The end of work*. New York: Tarcher/Putnam.

Rose, N. (1997). The future economic landscape. In M. Reisch & E. Gambrill, (Eds.), *Social Work in the 21st Century* (pp. 28–38). Thousand Oaks, CA: Pine Forge Press.

Schiele, J. (1998). The personal responsibility act of 1996: The bitter and the sweet for African American families. *Families in Society, 79*(4), 424–432.

Schram, S. F., Soss, J., & Fording, R. C. (Eds.) (2003). *Race and the politics of welfare reform*. Ann Arbor, MI: University of Michigan Press.

Schram, S. F., Soss, J., Fording, R.C., & Houser, L. (2007). *Deciding to discipline: A multimethod study of race, choice, and punishment at the frontlines of welfare reform*. Paper presented at the annual meeting of the American Political Science Association, Chicago, IL.

Smeeding, T. (2008, February). Poorer by comparison. *Pathways*, 3–5.

Sodersten, B. (Ed.) (2004). *Globalization and the welfare state*. New York: Palgrave MacMillan.

Third World Network. (Ed.). (1996). *Barking up the wrong tree: Trade and social clause links*, http://www.twnside.org/sg/south/twn/title/tree-ch.htm.

Titmuss, R. (Ed.). (1969). *Essays on the welfare state*. Boston: Beacon Press.

Towle, C. (1952). *Common human needs*. New York: American Association of Social Workers.

Twombly, E. D. (2001). Welfare reform's impact on the failure rate of nonprofit human service providers, *Charting Civil Society*, no. 9, Washington, DC: Urban Institute, Center on Nonprofits and Philanthropy.

U.S. Bureau of the Census. (2008a). *Poverty in the U.S.*, Washington, DC: U.S. Government Printing Office.

United States Bureau of the Census. (2008b). *Statistical abstract of the United States, 2008*. Washington, DC: U.S. Government Printing Office.

U.S. Department of Health and Human Services. (2004). *Change in TANF caseloads*. Washington, DC: Administration for Children and Families.

Walzer, M., (Ed.) (2003). *Toward a global civil society*. New York: Berghahn Books.

Young, D. (1999). Complementary, supplementary, or adversarial? A theoretical and historical examination of nonprofit-government relations in the United States. In E. Boris and E. Steuerle, (Eds.), *Nonprofits and government: Collaboration and conflict*. Washington, DC: Urban Institute Press.

Zunz, O., Schoppa, L., & Hiwatari, N. (2002). *Social contracts under stress: The middle classes of America, Europe, and Japan at the turn of the century*. New York: Russell Sage.

Chapter 15
Australia: Contemporary Issues and Debates on the Social Welfare System

Mel Gray and Kylie Agllias

Introduction

The single most important event that has molded changes to welfare policy across the developed Western world in the so-called post-industrial nation state is the advent of computer technology and the World Wide Web in what has been dubbed the information age or knowledge-based society. This technology enables policy researchers to search the Internet for clues as to what is being done elsewhere and morph together policies with bits from everywhere as they see fit. Australia is no exception, and while historically it evolved a unique welfare system, in contemporary times, it increasingly bears the hallmarks of policy development in the United States and the United Kingdom, with whom it most identifies. For the most part, however, even in the face of economic globalization, welfare policy remains the province of nation-states, albeit influenced by international conventions and human rights charters. We believe that claims that globalized capitalism has reduced the nation-state's control of its territorial boundaries are overzealous. We agree with Hardy (2007) that global capitalism 'has not necessitated the downfall of the nation-state for the reason that global culture fails to adequately center the ethnonationalist identity that citizens of a nation-state feel within their local community.' Instead, the nation-state has become more open to multilateral transactions and accustomed to engaging with other nations and cultures. Consequently:

> The nation-state is still required to provide a locus of stability in ethnic identity and an umbrella of protection from the rest of the world. The notion that globalising capitalism will erode the affinity that individuals hold with their nation and replace it with supranational blocs neglects that civilisational and cultural divergence are as politically and socially inflammatory as always. Weakened and transformed it may be, but the nation-state is here to stay for the immediate future (Hardy, 2007).

Australia is a land of immigrants and a multicultural society with a strong sense of social justice. The notion of 'fair go' for all is deeply imbedded in the

M. Gray (✉)
Institute of Social Wellbeing, University of Newcastle, New South Wales, Australia
e-mail: mel.gray@new castle.edu.au

J. Powell, J. Hendricks, *The Welfare State in Post-Industrial Society*,
DOI 10.1007/978-1-4419-0066-1_15, © Springer Science+Business Media, LLC 2009

Australian culture and has always been part of its national identity. Against this backdrop, in most parts of the developed Western world, contemporary welfare policy has arisen because of a perception that past welfare-state systems have failed to deal effectively with the problem of the poor. The dominant idea is that welfare treats the symptoms rather than the causes of poverty. So in post-welfare states, rather than a 'requiem for welfare' (Brodkin, 2003), what we are witnessing is an attempt to address the problem of poverty by relating it to joblessness. However, those who work in the welfare sector know that poverty is not related solely to a lack of money – or jobs – and that there are myriad factors that color the lives of those who need help and care. We recognize that poverty is not related solely to unemployment, but what we aim to do in this chapter is to show that there has always been a strong relationship between work and welfare in Australia. This has been coupled with an expectation of self-reliance on the part of those able to work and compassion for those unable to do so. The pivotal issues and critiques in contemporary debates on welfare in Australia revolve around this relationship between work and welfare. To demonstrate this relationship, we begin with a brief overview of the period of colonial settlement, continuing with the erection of the wage-earner's welfare state before examining the neoliberal welfare reform era of the present times. In so doing, we show that, while social spending on welfare has increased in dollar terms, this does not mean that values are comparable across time mainly because of more recent improvements in data collection and reporting enabled by developments in computer technology (Whiteford, 2006). As we shall see, unemployment benefits, which became the pivotal target of welfare reform, were never a part of welfare in the wage-earner's welfare state. In this respect, Australia has always differed from other OECD countries, in that income support for the working sick is provided through industrial awards that fall outside of public spending. In many other countries, these are provided through the social security system (Whiteford, 2006). From 1990 onwards, the OECD data for Australia included state and territory workers' compensation and from 1995 public service pensions, which amounted to an estimated $6 billion and $9.3 billion in 2001, respectively (Whiteford, 2006). Welfare payments have always been 'residual,' noncontributory, flat-rate entitlements financed from government revenue and applied only to those who were unable to work. Most importantly, as we shall see from our historical analysis, the patterns of Australia's welfare system were set soon after federation, when the first welfare payments were introduced. They included the Commonwealth Age Pension introduced in 1909, Invalid Pension in 1910, and one-off Maternity Allowance in 1912. According to Schut, Vrooman, and de Beer (2001), Australia is a textbook example of a liberal or residual system. But in truth, over the years, the government has assumed greater control of the welfare system, erecting a huge and costly welfare bureaucracy, which absorbs increased welfare expenditure that includes administration overheads as well as direct benefits to recipients. In the strictest sense, it is the latter which is the province of 'residual' welfare, that is, mechanisms put in place for the social protection of citizens in times of need.

The Colonial Settlement Period

There seems to be some agreement that the development of the Australian society was motivated in the settler years by the desire to devise a social system wherein everyone would be able to earn a decent living wage regardless of their social station. This was especially motivated by a desire not to emulate the English welfare system based on the Poor Laws and workhouses. The shortage of skilled labor in Australia at the time meant that not only could high wages (compared with similarly placed workers in England) be commanded but also a strong labor movement was able to emerge which helped reinforce the payment of a level of wages that would enable a worker to survive occasional bouts of unemployment and sickness. Thus Australia's welfare system 'bears the hallmark of settler societies with strong labour movements' (Murphy, 2006, p. 44.03). This had direct consequences on the evolving role of colonial governments and private associations in assisting those in need. Both showed a preference for a labor-related system, wherein wage arbitration and the delivery of high wage outcomes were the *principle means* of social protection, which has been described by Castles (1985) as 'Australian exceptionalism' or the 'wage-earner's welfare state' (102). This form of welfare state is characterized by a strong relationship between industrial relations and social welfare policy (Ramia & Wailes, 2006) and a comparatively autonomous, highly fragmented nongovernment sector. The separation of the deserving and nondeserving rested on the logic that those who were fit and able to work did not need benefits, or if there were likely to be a gap between jobs, then a fit and able person deserved some sort of social protection. As a result, a culture of charity and mutual aid remained underdeveloped in Australia, with some exceptions, especially Victoria (see Murphy, 2006).

Federation and Beyond: 1901–1980s

The colonial settlement period ended with federation in 1901 at which time, the Australian Constitution, approved by the House of Commons, established the political structure, that is, a federal system of government in which the legislature or parliament makes the law and the executive or government, including ministers and the public service, administers the law. Independent of government is the High Court, which deals with matters relating to the constitution and the judiciary or courts that interpret and apply the law.

Federalism shares the political responsibility of governing between federal and state parliaments. Policy is administered through three tiers of government, with different levels of responsibility: the national, federal, or Commonwealth level of government, state and territory government, and municipal or local government. Each tier of government has particular responsibilities, which are sometimes shared as follows:

The federal government undertakes responsibility for immigration, social security, communication, foreign affairs, trade, and control of income tax, and sets the broad economic policy parameters within which all tiers of government have to operate. It addresses broadscale policy issues and provides funds through untied grants to the states which administer the various social programs according to a range of Commonwealth and State and Territory Agreements. For example, the federal government sets the overarching policy arrangements for housing, education, disability, health, and welfare and then hands over the funds and responsibility to the states and territories to administer public housing, schools, hospitals, and disability, aged care, health and community services (see Table 15.1). In the event that there is an inconsistency or conflict between federal and state laws, the federal law always prevails. The head of the federal government is the prime minister.

Table 15.1 Levels of government and responsibility for social welfare provision

Federal welfare provision	State welfare provision (e.g., NSW)	Local welfare provision
Department of Education, Employment and Workplace Relations	Department of Aboriginal Affairs	Child care regulation
Department of Families, Housing, Community Services and Indigenous Affairs	Department of Ageing, Disability and Homecare	Environmental, including refuse removal, water supply, and upkeep of public facilities, such as libraries, parks, gardens, recreational facilities, and sports grounds
Department of Health and Ageing	Department of Community Services	
Department of Human Services	Department of Education and Training	
	Department of Housing	
	Department of Health	

State and territory government: Powers not specified in the constitution, referred to as residual powers, remain the province of the six states – New South Wales, Victoria, Queensland, South Australia, Western Australia, and Tasmania – and two territories – Northern and Australian capital territories, each of which is headed by a premier. State and territory governments assume the responsibility for transport, roads, health, education, public housing, law enforcement, family and community services, and local government. Each state also has a constitution.

Local government: There are over 650 local governments across Australia, headed by mayors. These are established and funded by state governments and take the responsibility for social planning, infrastructure development, and maintenance, refuse removal, water supply, upkeep of public facilities, such as libraries, parks, gardens, sports grounds, and recreational facilities, and child care regulation. Historically, they have not played a large part in welfare provision (see Table 15.1). Occasionally, the federal government has allocated special purpose funding to local governments.

This is the structural political context within which government policies come to be debated, created, and played out, and within which Australia's unique system of social provision emerged.

The Wage-Earner's Welfare State

As noted above, the "wage-earner's welfare state" emerged almost with the federation at the start of the twentieth century and was dismantled early in the 1980s. For most of that time, it formed a distinctive set of institutional arrangements centered on a state-regulated labor market as an alternate system of social protection to the British welfare state model. The wage-earner's welfare state was built on four pillars:

> ... arbitrated minimum employment conditions to protect workers; selective inward migration, perceived as a means to avoid migrants who would accept lower than Australasian-standard wages and working conditions; industry protection as the main economic incentive for employers to maintain labour conditions; and a market-oriented, 'residual' state welfare system designed as a last-resort safety-net for those (mainly males) whose living standards were not otherwise protected (Ramia & Wailes, 2006, p. 50).

To fully understand this unique welfare system, one must grasp the interdependence between industrial relations and social policy and the way in which it incorporated the rewards of work and residual forms of social protection within a single policy framework. Industrial relations comprise the processes which establish the 'rules' governing the employment relationship, which form the basis of standards in workplaces and across workplaces and industries. These standards include labor rights and employment conditions designed to limit labor market inequalities. These protective functions are intermeshed with social policy measures relating to 'underpaid, exploited, underemployed, unemployed and poverty-stricken labour ... [and] Problems associated with casual, part-time and otherwise non-standard labour [including] the household sphere' (Ramia & Wailes, 2006, p. 51). Let us briefly examine the four pillars of the wage-earner's welfare state, since they remain central to contemporary debates on welfare and feelings of loss following better times:

Compulsory arbitration: The system of compulsory arbitration was set in place soon after the federation by the establishment of the Commonwealth Court of Arbitration in 1907. As well as fixing the minimum or 'living wage' – referred to as the Harvest Judgment – the compulsory arbitration system concerned itself centrally with wage fixing, making a welfare state system unnecessary, at least for wage earners or breadwinning males (Castles & Uhr, 2007; Murphy, 2006). Hence, social protection depended crucially on the role of the arbitration system in dealing with those in work and who flowed in and out of paid work. It relied centrally on labor market or industry – or work sector – protections. As Murphy (2006) notes, the union movement had vested interests in maintaining gender distinctions in work and wages and in a system of social protection primarily delivered through men's work, thus favoring a residual system of income support crucially determined by work tests, in terms of which unemployment benefits were introduced in 1945.

Industry protection: Industry protection rested heavily on the regulation of employment conditions, the unity and relative power bases of employers and employers' associations and strong trade unions within the broader labor movement (Ramia & Wailes, 2006). The Harvest decision established the idea of a minimum wage and linked it to protection for relevant manufacturing industries.

Selective immigration: Given that Australian nation building rested heavily on successive waves of immigration, the skills of migrants were an important factor in developing the wage-earner's welfare state. Immigration policies attempted to address skill shortages in the labor market and rested heavily on people's ability to work and contribute to economic growth and development (Gray & Agllias, 2009).

Residual state welfare: The residual safety net for those unable to work and not expected to work, such as women raising children and disabled people, comprised tax-financed, residual, means-tested income support or social security benefits and a range of state welfare services. The wage-earner's welfare state was strongly opposed to universal benefits – and a welfare state system – believing strongly in a fair wage with residual welfare benefits only available to those with no labor market connections (Castles & Shirley, 1996).

Public and Private Sector Welfare Delivery: The Mixed Economy of Welfare

The work-related social protection mechanisms described above, together with residual welfare payments and services provided by the government and community-based voluntary welfare services formed the mixed economy of welfare, the second key element of the wage-earner's welfare state. This mixed economy had a complex division of function between the public and private sectors, and the boundary between the government and nongovernment provision – referred to in industry classifications as the community services sector – has always been fluid and subject to negotiation. Hence, it is extremely difficult to get a handle on the 'structure' of this mix of state and private sector arrangements (Berman et al., 2006; Murphy, 2006).

A crucial feature of welfare provision – both government and private – was the rise of professional social work, which was heavily influenced by the feminist movement and leftist welfare sentiments. Critiques of the wage-earner's welfare state as based largely on the male breadwinner supporting a nuclear family drew attention to the interrelationship between welfare, the family and breadwinning, 'to the welfare role of the family, and to the gender of the providers and recipients of welfare services' (Murphy, 2006, p. 44.02). For the most part, those receiving welfare and those caring for welfare recipients were women. Feminists, especially, highlighted the value of this unpaid domestic – caring and parenting – *work*, and subsequent policies began to take on the 'family first' ethos (Dalton et al., 1996; Weeks, 1994, 1995).

According to Murphy (2006), the nongovernment community services sector in Australia has been dominated by faith-based organizations and religious charities 'distinctly concerned with discriminating between the deserving and the undeserving' (p. 44.3). Already established during the colonial settlement period, voluntary, largely church-based organizations had, in the wage-earner's welfare state, to deal with those without access to a living wage. Having developed in an unsystematic, uncoordinated, fragmented, and disorganized way in a welfare culture where state provision through fixed wages was the dominant idea and philanthropy and mutual aid remained undeveloped, the nongovernment welfare sector has proved unequal to the demands of those falling through the cracks of formal welfare provision. Thus, the nongovernment sector has to contend with deeply embedded egalitarian values, in which everyone must have a 'fair go' (*see* Saunders, 2003, for a discussion on this) while seeking moral upliftment of those who, for some reason or other, have been unable to earn their living through paid work (Murphy, 2006; Reeves, 2006). Moral judgments as to who was deserving or not thus rested heavily on an individual's capacity for self-reliance. Able-bodied individuals, who shirked their responsibility by engaging in undesirable behavior, were clearly undeserving in this context.

Post-industrialism and the Australian Nation-State: The 1980s and Beyond

The theory of post-industrialism argues that the technological revolution and the coming of the information age has led to changes in the relationship between work and welfare, which, as we have argued, has always been a major factor in understanding Australia's welfare system. As we shall see, neoliberal ideology is said to lead to deeper inequalities, new ideas about citizenship, and accompanying responses to welfare entitlements. Applied to Australia, some would subtitle this section 'From social laboratory to welfare laggard' (Murphy, 2006), and this would be true if the focus of the analysis were the core pillars of the wage-earner's welfare state and the interplay between state welfare and protective labor mechanisms in Australia since the early 1980s. However, our focus is on the way in which welfare reform has reconfigured arrangements such that areas of provision which were not part of the welfare in the wage-earner's welfare state, pivotally unemployment and work-related family benefits, which some might see as new sites of vulnerabilities, have become the central core of the discourse on welfare under neoliberalism and a new priority for state welfare provision. Notably, the *Australian Institute of Health and Welfare Act 1987*, which outlines the core areas of welfare provision in Australia in terms of which data is collected and reported, focused on five primary areas of welfare: aged care, child care, disability, housing, and child welfare (Australian Institute of Health and Welfare [AIHW], 2007a). It did not mention unemployment benefits, nor did it include health and education as part of welfare. It thus reflects the narrow residual view of welfare characteristic of the wage-earner's welfare state, which from its inception made provision for the elderly, disabled, and single mothers. What we want to look at, then, is the way in which this focus has broadened to encompass unemployment and family policy under neoliberal welfare reform.

Changes to Australia's Wage-Earner's Welfare State Under Neoliberal Welfare Reform

Changing Ideologies

The beginnings of neoliberal welfare reform arise in several interrelated critiques relating to the huge role the government came to play in welfare provision during the twentieth century. While this played out differently in various international contexts, there were similarities in the arguments which began to steer welfare in the direction it subsequently took in most developed Western countries. These revolved inter alia around the level of government spending on welfare, the culture of dependency created by welfare provision, the role of the private sector, the inefficiencies of the vast government bureaucracy, and its failure to adequately address the problem of poverty. The changes which came about were influenced by several interweaving strands of thinking emanating from Third Way reconfigurations of the enterprising state (Considine, 2001), outcome-based New Public Management, workfare programs, and the conservatism of the New Right. The seeds of these changes were already evident in the marketization or contracting out of services previously provided by the government, which began in the late seventies. They flowered into the 'new' philosophy, values, and rules guiding welfare provision, most significantly cutbacks in welfare, increasing conditionality in welfare benefits and the further entrenchment of unemployment programs as part of welfare. Welfare payments of all stripes came to be seen as 'unemployment' payments, since all were received by recipients not in work and these recipients were forced to prove that they could not work and, therefore, were rightly entitled to welfare benefits. The essential target of active welfare, however, is those of the working age who claim income cash benefits:

> Thus it is not limited to people who may claim unemployment insurance but also includes people who are claiming social assistance, disability or lone-parent benefits. This means that we see the generalisation of the work ethic to all segments of the adult population. Yet the enforcement of obligations and use of sanctions tend to be punitive for some segments of the population, such as the poor, long-term unemployed and/or homeless people (Johansson & Hvinden, in Newman, 2005, p. 107).

What neoliberalism does is push the onus of risk firmly onto the individual, removing any concept of state responsibility, for the social protection of citizens. For example, individuals are expected to bear the financial risk of providing for their retirement through retirement planning and superannuation contributions. It reconstitutes citizenship through the language of responsibilities and obligations, rather than rights and entitlements. Those of the working age entitled to benefits have the reciprocal obligation and responsibility to actively seek to become a full participant in the labor market. It emphasizes active citizenship in which the citizen becomes a rational consumer or user of public goods, who exercises choice between providers or suppliers of welfare services in a mixed or pluralist welfare economy (Johansson & Hvinden in, Newman, 2005).

While neoliberalism appears to attack welfare, Hartman (2005) argues that its antiwelfare rhetoric masks the importance of welfare to the very existence of the neoliberal regime. What the neoliberal welfare regime does is to create a category of low-paid workers, whose incomes are supplemented by minimal benefits which are made contingent on the need to work for a minimal number of hours per week. It creates a casual workforce – with minimal work requirements – which suits employers who can then employ these largely untrained people who are obliged to the state on low wages and casual work arrangements. Employers seem to be doing the right thing by supporting this work-based welfare system while benefiting from the flexible – unregulated – arrangements which the government has created. In this way, welfare maintains peripheral, low-wage workers in a flexible labor market that supports employers' profit margins (Hartman, 2005). Those most affected by these new work-based welfare arrangements are women caring for children on parenting payments and disabled people in receipt of the disability support pension, which, as we shall see below, prior to the advent of work-based welfare, were not classified as unemployed.

Most significantly in relation to Australia, neoliberalism strikes at the very heart of the residual welfare system set in place by the wage-earner's welfare state and its integrated social protection mechanisms. But the changes were supported by the 'Australian union movement . . . which . . . helped to facilitate bargaining decentralisation from the Federal and industry levels to the enterprise level' (Ramia & Wailes, 2006, p. 61). The Workplace Regulations Act of 1997 built social protection into 'neo-corporatist industrial relations arrangements' (Ramia & Wailes, 2006, p. 58).

Changes to industrial relations policy – or workplace reforms (Castles & Uhr, 2007) – have been the most unpopular area of change in the intensification of the neoliberal welfare agenda, especially under the Liberal-Coalition Howard government from 1996 to 2007. In 2005, the Howard Coalition government introduced the Work Choices program, which sought, among other things, to maintain a minimum safety net, such as annual, sick, and unpaid parenting leave, while introducing a *national* industrial relations system responsive to 'changes in the structure of work, [and] increasing levels of unemployment' (Cox, 2006, p. 119). It sought, among others, to: (i) introduce Individual

Workplace Agreements to replace the collective enterprise bargaining system; (ii) relieve small companies with less than 100 employees of restrictive policies, such as unfair dismissal laws (which the government believed discouraged employers from taking on new workers) and the minimum award wage (which the government and others claimed hindered job generation); and (iii) limit trade union power. Unlike, New Zealand and other Western nations, however, the Howard Coalition government followed a pragmatic, poll-driven approach, in which the introduction of these legislative changes did not reach full force until the government 'won control of both houses of the Commonwealth Parliament' (Cox, 2006, p. 112).

On the welfare reform front, 'active' welfare recommendations coming through the OECD guidelines suggested a restructuring of services and greater conditionality of benefits to accompany the workplace reforms discussed above, ostensibly in the interests of greater *economic* efficiency (Castles & Uhr, 2007). They required that citizens played a more active role 'in handling risks and promoting their own welfare'(Johansson & Hvinden, in Newman, 2005, p. 101). However, these 'activation reforms tend to rest on a fairly narrow understanding of relevant and socially useful activity as they mainly recognise paid work and participation in the mainstream labour market' (Johansson & Hvinden, in Newman, 2005, p. 108). For many within the welfare sector, reform amounted to a program of retrenchment or rolling back of welfare, as governments everywhere sought to find ways to avoid blame for social 'expenditure cutbacks made necessary by changing economic conditions and, in particular by pressures emanating from the global economy … to control expenditure growth … recalibrate the relationship between federal and state governments, [and] … rationalise the process of intergovernmental relations' (Castles & Uhr, 2007, p. 111). As part of the rationalisation process, the Australian government commissioned a Welfare Reform Reference Group in 1999 to review the Australian welfare system. The outcome was the McClure Report (Welfare Reform Reference Group, 2000), which devised a 'framework of reciprocity' or mutual obligation 'matching responsibilities and duties with social rights and benefits' (Braithwaite et al., 2002), the best example of which is the Job Network, discussed below.

Increased Marketization of Services

An offshoot of criticisms of big government and excessive public spending was the marketization of welfare programs, which made services tradeable commodities delivered in quasi-markets (Considine, 2001). Through privatization, the government sought to dismantle the vast welfare bureaucracy it had created by contracting out services it had previously delivered and transferring them to the private – nongovernment – welfare sector via a tendering process. In other words, the government entered into contracts with nongovernment agencies to deliver services on its behalf. This marketization of services was accompanied by appeals for nongovernment welfare managers to run the sector more like a business following the influence of outcome-based New Public Management (Hood, 1995), where continued funding is contingent on the proven delivery of concrete outcomes (Western et al., 2007). Cox (2006) refers to Australia's approach as a 'gradualist corporatist inspired model' (p. 112), in which the state and territory governments are responsible for state-based social *services*, which they increasingly purchased from nongovernment organizations. This gave the nongovernment services a new and important role in service delivery, which would change its ethos from one of charity, social justice, and compassionate care, to one of business-like efficiency. Many faith-based organizations who joined the Job Network in its early days later withdrew for this very reason.

Emergence of the Job Network

Two concerns motivated the emergence of the Job Network: the increasing number of people on welfare payments – over 2.5 million people, an increase from 10 percent of workforce-aged beneficiaries in 1978 to 18 percent in 1998 (Newman, 1999), and the problem of the long-term unemployed, that is, those out of work for a year or more, which applied to over 21 percent of unemployed people in 2003 (Saunders, 2003). The Job Network replaced the Commonwealth Employment Services in 1998. It comprises about 360 contracted commercial – for profit – and not-for-profit community welfare organizations, including big charities, like the Salvation Army and Mission Australia, which provide federally funded employment services. The emergence of work-based welfare is the single most important event that signalled changes in thinking relating to work and welfare in the contemporary neoliberal society. Most significantly, the critiques of welfare outlined above had led to a reconstructed discourse on welfare dependency as a kind of addiction signalled in the notion of 'passive welfare.' To correct this wrong, what was needed was 'active welfare' and a policy in which there were reciprocal rights and responsibilities. These became enshrined in the notion of 'mutual obligation,' which introduced the requirement that some categories of unemployed people were required to work for a certain number of mandated hours to receive benefits – the jobseeker's allowance. This was already a part of the US workfare phenomenon, and work-for-the-dole programs, which tied welfare to work or work-like activities. Australia followed with the introduction of the Job Network as a series of measures to deal with the problem of long-term unemployment, which would assist those who demonstrated attempts at self-reliance, that is, who tried to 'help themselves,' such as 'the working poor, the casualised workforce, and those whose family responsibilities pose[d] especially difficult challenges for their work lives' (Ramia & Wailes, 2006, p. 60) (see also Cass & Smyth, 1998; Considine, 2001; Edwards et al., 2001; Johnson Tonkiss, 2002; Productivity Commission, 2002).

Most importantly, what the Job Network did was to create a category of unemployed people from groups where there was previously no expectation that they needed to work and were, therefore, not seen as unemployed, such as mothers at home looking after children and disabled people. Thus, unemployment statistics in 1999 reported that the number of people on unemployment benefits exceeded the number unemployed in labor force surveys by 19 percent (Whiteford, 2006). In other words, by forcing people 'to seek gainful employment as a pre-condition of benefit' (Castles & Uhr, 2007, p. 116), the Job Network created and enlarged the number of people classified as unemployed. At the same time, it made labor market activity a marker of good social citizenship and the principle pathway out of poverty or social exclusion (Marston & McDonald, 2003).

Job Network members were assessed on their degree of employability and allocated basic service or intensive case management on this basis (McDonald & Chenoweth, 2006). There was also the belief that many people, labelled dole bludgers, did not want to work so incentives had to be provided, including punitive, disciplinary mechanisms if this were necessary, to get people off welfare into work, if they were able. Many argued that the Poor Laws had once again reared their ugly head, with the division or separation made between the deserving in need of social care and the nondeserving in need of discipline out of a sometimes generational culture of welfare dependency (see Marston & McDonald, 2003; McDonald & Marston, 2005; McDonald et al., 2003; Productivity Commission, 2002 for an examination of the social relations embodied in the Job Network process).

Continued Growth in Welfare Spending

Australia has a positive international reputation in terms of quality of life indicators, ranking third on the United Nations Human Development Index, which provides a composite measure of life expectancy, educational attainment, and standard of living (United Nations Development Program, 2008). Further, Australian wages are among the highest in the OECD countries and work remains the most effective means of social protection in Australia (OECD, 2008a; Whiteford, 2006). While the Australian government currently spends less on cash benefits than most OECD countries, it targets this spending on the poorest 20 percent of the population (OECD, 2008a). The average OECD social expenditure, which includes cash, in-kind service provision, and tax breaks with a social purpose, as a percentage of the GDP was 21 percent in 2003, as compared with Australian spending of 18 percent (OECD, 2008b). While relative income poverty has risen slightly in the last 10 years, income inequality in Australia is less than in many OECD countries due to publicly provided services and a lower tax burden on low incomes (OECD, 2008a).

Despite neoliberal welfare reform, welfare spending in Australia has continued to grow (AIHW, 2007b; Castles, 2001; Castles & Uhr, 2007; Mendes, 2008; Saunders, 2003; Saunders, 2007b). The OECD Social Expenditure database shows that public social expenditure rose from 14 percent in 1990 to 18 percent of the GDP in 2003 (OECD, 2008b). If we examine the Commonwealth budget, social security and welfare spending has increased more than any other area of expenditure, from around 20 percent in 1972–1973 to around 41 percent in 2007–2008 (Laurie & McDonald, 2008).

If we are to provide a more comprehensive picture of welfare expenditure, including the government and nongovernment sectors, we must turn to Australian Institute of Health and Welfare (2007b) data from 2005 to 2006. This data, which excludes unemployment benefits but includes benefits and allowances to families, people with a disability and the aging, records total welfare expenditure of $90 billion (or 9 percent of the GDP) in 2005–2006. This figure would be larger if tax expenditure in the form of concessions and rebates were included (AIHW, 2007a). Cash benefits, which were solely provided by governments, accounted for 68 percent and welfare services accounted for 32 percent of this expenditure. Total expenditure on services and benefits for older people was $34 billion, families and children $27 billion, and people with disabilities $17 billion. The total spent on welfare services by the government and nongovernment agencies was $29 billion. The net value of services delivered by nongovernment organizations was $20 billion or 10 percent of the total investment in welfare services (AIHW, 2007b) (see Tables 15.2 and 15.3).

Table 15.2 Funding for welfare services 2005–2006 (totalling $28.8 billion)

Federal Government	State and Territory Governments	Individuals (through fee for service)	Nongovernment organizations	Local Government
40%	29%	20%	9%	2 %
$11. 4 billion	$8.4 billion	$5.8 billion	$2.6 billion	$0.6 billion

Source: AIHW (2007b)

Table 15.3 Government spending on welfare (2005–2006)

	Older people (billion)	Families and children (billion)	Disability (billion)	Other welfare (billion)
Benefits	$25.2	$22.0	$12.1	$2.1
Services	$ 9.0	$ 4.6	$ 4.7	$1.2
Total expenditure	$34.2	$26.6	$16.8	$3.2

Note: In 2005–2006 $80.8 billion of the total welfare expenditure ($90.2 billion) could be allocated by category
Source: AIHW (2007b)

In the mid-1960s, only 11 percent of working age adults received welfare benefits. By 2003, the proportion had grown to 27 percent , with almost 14 percent totally dependent on welfare compared to 3 percent in the mid-sixties, that is, 1:33 to 1:7 of working age people on welfare during a period when living standards had doubled (Saunders, 2003). Of all the OECD countries, Australia has the highest level of households where no one is working, while data shows that, in Australia, work is the most effective shield against poverty (Whiteford, 2006). Those concerned about the sustainability of these levels of unemployment and welfare spending point out that there were five workers for every working age adult on welfare in 2003 as compared to 22 in the mid-sixties (Saunders, 2003). This is especially worrying if one considers that spending on cash transfers rose from 3 percent of the GDP in the 1960s to 8 percent in 2000 (Whiteford & Angenent, 2002) and 18 percent by 2007 (Castles & Uhr, 2007).

More than one in five Australians currently receives some form of income support or welfare payment (ABS, 2008). The main areas of income support, apart from unemployment benefits, are the aged pension, family payments, followed by disability support and parenting payments. While changes to categories and data sets make comparisons difficult, social security payments to the aged, those with a disability, and families with dependent children have risen and unemployment payments have declined slightly since the 1999–2000 budget (AIHW, 2007a; Laurie & McDonald, 2008). The impact of welfare-to-work policies may have recently reduced the percentage of people receiving parenting payments and disability support pensions, as some recipients who would previously have received these have been transferred to, or commenced income support payments, such as the Newstart or Youth Allowance.

Aged Pensions: Aged (and invalid) pensions were the first form of income support to be legislated after federation. With Australia's aging population around two-thirds of the current retirees rely on a government benefit or pension as their main source of income (AIHW, 2007a). Aged pensions are means tested, but they are not linked to previous contributions or earnings. The aged pension constitutes the largest portion of the welfare budget at $22.6 billion in 2006–2007 (Australian Bureau of Statistics [ABS], 2008). These payments continue to have a high degree of public support, and public debate often includes calls for increase in the level of the pension. However, the proportion of older people relying on the Aged Pension is expected to decline in coming years, as the government policy, which introduced compulsory superannuation and incentives to remain at work for longer periods of time, starts to take effect (AIHW, 2007a).

Family Payments: These constitute the second largest item in welfare spending. Until 1975, family assistance was provided through the tax system, but was thereafter paid mainly through regular cash benefits (Whiteford, 2006). Family payments rose significantly during the Howard era (Mendes, 2008), costing the government $17.2 billion in 2006–2007 (ABS, 2008). Payments are directed at low- and middle-income earners to assist with the costs of raising children. They include the Family Tax Benefit (Part A and B), maternity payments – currently $5,000 for the birth of each child – and child care benefits, including a tax rebate to subsidize child care for working families. Like aged pensions, these generally enjoy public support, with the exception of the maternity payment (previously called the Baby Bonus). There was some public debate about this payment when it was first introduced, with some suggesting that it encouraged young people to have babies for income. Mendes (2008) argues that family payments have been an effective means of redistributing income to poor families and to maintain the real income of the poor even though inequality has increased.

Parenting Payments: Perhaps the least popular of welfare measures, parenting payments were introduced in 1973 as the Supporting Mother's Pension, when older women and mothers were not expected to work or raise children alone. However, today, more than two-thirds of women between the ages of 15 and 64 are economically active (ABS, 2008). Nevertheless, the situation is somewhat different for single or sole parents who become primary care providers during their prime earning years. Australia is among the most generous of the OECD countries in its support for lone parents (Whiteford, 2006). Parenting Payments are directed at working age adults – single or partnered, male or female – who have a very low income and primary responsibility for the care of a child under the age of eight years. Those on single parenting payments totalled 395,495 in 2006–2007. Of these 369,818 or 93 percent were women (ABS, 2008). While most recipients move off payments and return to work voluntarily, some spend 12 years on benefits, moving from one benefit to another (Saunders, 2003).

Disability Support Pensions: Currently, 3.9 percent of Australia's population has a profound disability (ABS, 2008). The government provides a Disability Support Pension to work-aged people, who have a physical, intellectual, or psychiatric condition that prevents them from working 15 hours per week. The number of people receiving DSPs increased from 230,000 in 1980, which represents 2 percent of the population (Saunders, 2003), to 714,000 in 2006–2007, which represents about 3.5 percent of the population (ABS, 2008). The government allocated $8.6 billion to the Disability Support Pension in 2006–2007 (ABS, 2008). Saunders (2007a) suggests that there has been a lack of research into the real costs of disability, let alone adequate accommodation through income support.

Changes to Benefit Arrangements

Changes to benefit arrangements, especially imposition of time limits, were designed essentially to restrict welfare to those who really 'deserved' it and to encourage those who could do so to return to work for a minimum of 15 hours per week. This is the area of greatest change which has evoked the most ire from welfare activists, especially attempts to extend 'mutual obligation' or welfare-to-work to lone parents, mainly single mothers, and people with disabilities. Equally unpopular was the introduction of punitive penalties for noncompliance. Research shows that these populations are most likely to require additional assistance from welfare services, which are not adequately funded to meet the increase in need (Australian Council of Social Services [ACOSS], 2008). For example, those on parenting payments are required to look for work, while new applicants are transferred to the lower Newstart Allowance of fortnightly payments of about $50 when their youngest child turns six, at which time assessments are made of their ability to meet the requirement of 15-hour work per week. In sum, in the reformed system: 'Benefits are still available, and in some instances are more generous than in the past, but only where other resources are demonstrably exhausted, and where the good faith of recipients is demonstrated by compliance with stringent activity tests' (Castles & Uhr, 2007, p. 117). The new system has several weaknesses: first, it relies on after-school child care places, which are limited; second, the new rules do not con-sider education and training as an alternative to work, so many recipients must choose between study or employment (Gray & Collins, 2007); third, it intrudes on the family sphere, and encourages women to accept unsuitable forms of employment to meet income support requirements (Gray & Collins, 2007).

The most drastic change to benefit arrangements was the introduction of the punitive practice of 'breaching,' that is, taking welfare payments away from those who did not meet the minimal work requirements. Frederick and Goddard (2008) cite a growing body of evidence that breaching has created a huge increase in demand for emergency assistance from nongovernment 'charities.' Introduced in 1997, there were 120,000 breaches in the first year. This increased by 187 percent over a three-year period to 346,000 in 2001, falling to 112,000 by 2005 (ACOSS, 2001; Commonwealth Ombudsman, 2002). Research also highlighted inconsistencies in the decision-making and application of breaching between and within Job Network agencies (Bigby & Files, 2003). Pressure from welfare activists, including charities handling the fallout, as to the unfairness of breaching led to internal reviews of this practice (Bigby & Files, 2003). The McClure Report (2000), while reiterating the impor-tance of mutual obligation, suggested that penalty decisions were necessary in some instances, but could be reduced if beneficiaries received individualized treatment, accurate assessments, and clear guidelines. But concerns remain, not least relating to groups who are disproportionately affected by breaching, such as rural and remote indigenous populations (Siewert, 2008), who are 'nearly fourteen times more likely to use community services than their representation in the general community would suggest' (ACOSS, 2008, p. 3) and those with mental health problems who are no longer able to access the disability support pension. Additionally, the Greens political party suggests that 'no payment' breaches doubled from the 2006–2007 period to 2008, when 31,789 breaches were recorded, leaving many, including those with dependent children, without payment for eight weeks (Siewert, 2008).

Conclusion

Clearly, then, 'work-based' welfare, which emerged through the Job Network and its incremental tightening of benefits, alongside workplace reform is yet another extension of the relationship between welfare and work, which has long characterized the Australian welfare system. The first choice was and remains integrated social protection through frontline taxation and work-based contributions, such as superannuation. But this does not help where people are not in work, that is, about 6 percent of Australia's population. The most contentious debates in Australian welfare have arisen around the Job Network and more restrictive measures related to welfare-to-work schemes, especially their extension to sole parents and people with disabilities, that is, those not in a position to seek gainful employment. Some claim that schemes like the Job Network are not primarily aimed at reducing unemployment, rather at maintaining governmentality and engendering 'particular ethical predispositions, attributes and capacities in [participants]' (Considine, 2001; Walters, in McDonald et al., 2003). A major issue surrounds the capacity of the nongovernment sector to meet needs for emergency relief brought about especially by breaching policies. A recent survey of the welfare sector showed an increase in eligible people turned away from services, about 4 percent of clients or 80,000 people, due to the rationing of services (ACOSS, 2008). Also problematic has been the ability of Job Network providers to make a profit out of job placement services by prioritizing the most job ready or responsive clients, called 'creaming' (Productivity Commission, 2002). This means putting the long-term unemployed and those with complex issues or intensive needs in the too-hard basket, called 'parking' (Productivity Commission, 2002). However, recent reports suggest that government responses to performance-linked payments, 'parking' and 'creaming' have resulted in increased monitoring and compliance demands being placed on Job Network providers, reducing their ability to provide flexible services and tailored support (Thomas, 2007). Still a persistent problem is those hard to place due to mental illness, particularly homeless people, for whom the Job Network has not been beneficial. Welfare agencies are citing an increase in the complexity of presenting client issues as a growing concern (ACOSS, 2008). Rudd's Labor government has recognized this and is currently introducing measures to contract nongovernment agencies to provide services targeted at hard to reach clients.

It is likely, however, that, following developments in the United Kingdom and the United States (Gray et al., 2009), there will be an increasing trend toward evidence-based policy in Australia (Kinnear et al., 2003), that is, basing policy decisions on empirical research. Evidence is accumulating internationally on the effectiveness of welfare-to-work reform programs for certain categories of unemployed people (Bloom et al., 2002a,b; Bloom et al., 1997; Farrell et al., 2008; Hamilton, 2002). This is likely to lead to a hardening of 'work first' or 'work-based' initiatives, which will affect the bottom 20 percent of income earners that absorb 21 percent of welfare expenditure (Saunders, 2007b). Still of concern, inequality is increasing, with poverty intensifying for at least 10 percent, possibly 20 percent of, Australians. However, Australia directs more of its spending to the poor than any other OECD country, achieving some redistributory effect through its targeted welfare system (OECD, 2008a). The richest 20 percent of the population receives only 3 percent of all transfer spending, while the middle 60 percent of households receive 56 percent, and just over 40 percent goes to the bottom 20 percent:

Even though Australia spends less than the OECD average on social security benefits, the formula for distributing benefits is so progressive – and the level of taxes paid by the poor is so low – that Australia appears to redistribute more to the poorest 20% of the population than any other OECD country (Whiteford, 2006, p. 29).

While Australia is the most generous OECD country when it comes to benefits for the poor, this is still not good enough for those who value Australia's 'fair go' culture, where everyone should be able to earn a decent living wage and enjoy a healthy quality of life. In this context:

> Adequacy of benefits can only be defined by reference to the living standards that Australian benefits afford in Australia, and political and social judgments about what is an acceptable living standard for Australians. The fact that benefits for the Australian poor are higher than benefits for the Italian poor does not help anyone in Australia pay the rent or any other bills. But it does mean that it isn't valid to argue for increasing benefits in Australia because Australia spends less on welfare than Italy and many other countries (Whiteford, 2006, pp. 27–28).

The fact is that the poor remain poor because of their low share of private income and the failure of income support to bring them up to a decent living wage. Problems are intensifying for those on low income and the unemployed who are increasingly being turned away from services unable to help them. More progressive welfare reforms with concrete programs for those in need of social care or caring for others are required. From where will the help come? Who is responsible for those pushed to the margins of the Australian society? Is this the government's responsibility or is the private sector better placed to provide needed services? This seems to be the central question facing welfare policy analysts at this juncture.

References

Australian Bureau of Statistics [ABS]. (2008). 1301.0- Year book Australia, 2008. Retrieved November 19, 2008, from http://www.abs.gov.au/AUSSTATS/abs@.nsf/DetailsPage/1301.02008?OpenDocument

Australian Council of Social Services [ACOSS]. (2001). Ending the hardship: Submission to the independent review of breaches and penalties in the social security system. Retrieved November 22, 2008, from http://www.acoss.org.au/upload/publications/papers/info%203316_breaches.pdf

Australian Council of Social Services [ACOSS]. (2008). Australian community sector survey, Report 2008. Retrieved November 22, 2008, from http://www.acoss.org.au/upload/publications/papers/4420__Paper%20154%20ACSS%202008.pdf

Australian Institute of Health and Welfare [AIHW]. (2007a). Australia's welfare 2007. Canberra: AIHW.

Australian Institute of Health and Welfare [AIHW]. (2007b). Welfare expenditure Australia 2005–06. Retrieved November 10, 2008, from http://www.aihw.gov.au/publications/index.cfm/title/10530

Berman, G., Murphy, J., & Brooks, R. (2006). Funding the non-profit welfare sector: Explaining changing funding sources 1960–1999. Economic Papers, 25(1), 83–89.

Bigby, C., & Files, W. (2003). Street level leniency or unjust inconsistency? An examination of breach recommendation decision making in a for profit job network agency [Electronic version]. *Australian Journal of Labour Economics, 6*(2), 277–291.

Bloom, D., Andersen, J., Wavelet, M., Gardiner, K. N., & Fishman, M. E. (2002a). New strategies to promote stable employment and career progression: An introduction to the employment retention and advancement project, New York. Retrieved November 20, 2008, from http://www.mdrc.org/Reports2002/era_conferencerpt/era_2000_2001.pdf

Bloom, D., Scrivener, S., Michalopolous, C., Morris, P., Hendra, R., Adams-Ciardullo, D., et al. (2002b). 2002 Jobs first, final report on Connecticut's welfare reform initiative. Retrieved November, 14, 2008, from http://research.yale.edu/datainitiative/reports/MDRC_Jobs_First_Eval_Exec_Summ.pdf

Bloom, H., Fink, B., Lui-Gurr, S., Bancroft, W., & Tattrie, D. (1997). Implementing the earnings supplement project: A test of a re-employment incentive. Retrieved November 14, 2008, from http://www.srdc.org/uploads/implementing_esp.pdf

Braithwaite, V., Gatens, M., & Mitchell, D. (2002). If mutual obligation is the answer, what is the question? [Electronic version]. *Australian Journal of Social Issues, 37*(3), 225–245.

Brodkin, E. Z. (2003). Requiem for welfare [Electronic version]. *Dissent, 50*(1), 29–37.

Cass, B., & Smyth, P. (Eds.). (1998). *Contesting the Australian way: States, markets and civil society.* Cambridge: Cambridge University Press.

Castles, F. (2001). A farewell to Australia's welfare state [Electronic version]. *International Journal of Health Services, 31*(3), 537–544.

Castles, F., & Shirley, I. (1996). Labour and social policy: Gravediggers or refurbishers of the welfare state. In F. Castles, R. Gerritsen & J. Vowles (Eds.), *The great experiment: Labour parties and public policy transformation in Australia and New Zealand.* Sydney: Allen and Unwin.

Castles, F. G. (1985). *The working class and welfare: Reflections on the political development of the welfare state in Australia and New Zealand 1890–1980.* Sydney: Allen & Unwin.

Castles, F. G., & Uhr, J. (2007). The Australian welfare state: Has Federalism made a difference? [Electronic version]. *Australian Journal of Politics and History, 53*(1), 96–117.

Commonwealth Ombudsman. (2002). Social security breach penalties: Issues of administration. Retrieved November 22, 2008, from http://www.ombudsman.gov.au/commonwealth/publish.nsf/AttachmentsByTitle/reports_2002_clink_execsum.pdf/$FILE/execsummary-recomms.pdf

Considine, M. (2001). *Enterprising states: The public management of welfare-to-work.* Cambridge: Cambridge University Press.

Cox, L. (2006). The Antipodean social laboratory, labour and the transformation of the welfare state [Electronic version]. *Journal of Sociology, 42*(2), 107–124.

Dalton, T., Draper, M., Weeks, W., & Wiseman, J. (Eds.). (1996). *Making social policy in Australia.* Melbourne: Allen & Unwin.

Edwards, M., Howard, C., & Miller, R. (2001). *Social policy, public policy: From problem to practice.* Sydney: Allen & Unwin.

Farrell, M., Rich, S., Turner, L., Seith, D., & Bloom, D. (2008). Welfare time limits: An update on state policies, implementation, and effects on families. Retrieved November 20, 2008, from http://www.mdrc.org/publications/481/full.pdf

Frederick, J., & Goddard, C. (2008). Sweet and sour charity: Experiences of receiving emergency relief in Australia. *Australian Social Work, 61*(3), 269–284.

Gray, A., & Collins, P. (2007). The interplay of welfare to work and work choices [Electronic version]. *Hecate: An Interdisciplinary Journal of Women's Liberation, 33*(1), 126–140.

Gray, M., & Agllias, K. (2009). Australia: The world in one place. In U. A. Segal, N. S. Mayadas, & D. Elliott (Eds.), *Immigration around the world.* New York: Oxford University Press.

Gray, M., Plath, D., & Webb, S. A. (2009). *Evidence-based social work: A critical stance.* London: Routledge.

Hamilton, G. (2002). Moving people from welfare to work: Lessons from the National evaluation of welfare-to-work strategies. Retrieved November 20, 2008, from http://aspe.hhs.gov/hsp/NEWWS/synthesis02/index.htm

Hardy, J. (2007). Is global capitalism eroding the state? Retrieved December 1, 2008, from http://www.e-ir.info/?p = 569

Hartman, Y. (2005). In bed with the enemy: Some ideas on the connections between neoliberalism and the welfare state. *Current Sociology, 53*(1), 57–73.

Hood, C. (1995). The "New Public Management" in The 1980s: Variations on a theme [Electronic version]. *Accounting Organisation and Society, 20*(2/3), 93–109.

Johnson, C., & Tonkiss, F. (2002). The third influence: The Blair Government and Australian Labor. *Policy and Politics, 30*(1), 5–18.

Kinnear, P., Grant, G., & Oliver, K. (2003, July 9–11). *Welfare reform in Australia: An evidence-based approach.* Paper presented at the National Social Policy Conference, University of New South Wales.

Laurie, K., & McDonald, J. (2008). A perspective on trends in Australian Government spending. Retrieved November 10, 2008, from http://www.treasury.gov.au/documents/1352/PDF/03_spending_growth.pdf

Marston, G., & McDonald, C. (2003). The psychology, ethics and social relations of unemployment [Electronic version]. *Australian Journal of Labour Economics, 6*(2), 293–315.

McClure, P. (2000). Participation support for a more equitable society: Final report of the reference group on welfare reform. Retrieved November 20, 2008, from http://www.workplace.gov.au/NR/rdonlyres/97EF2B51-F393-4FCA-AD97-64CCCDFE5258/0/McClureReport2000_Final.pdf

McDonald, C., & Chenoweth, L. (2006). Workfare oz-style: Welfare reform and social work in Australia [Electronic version]. *Journal of Policy Practice, 5*(2/3), 109–128.

McDonald, C., & Marston, G. (2005). Workfare as welfare: Governing unemployment in the advanced liberal state [Electronic version]. *Critical Social Policy, 25*(3), 374–401.

McDonald, C., Marston, G., & Buckley, A. (2003). Risk technology in Australia: The role of the job seeker classification instrument in employment services [Electronic version]. *Critical Social Policy, 23*(4), 498–525.

Mendes, P. (2008). Retrenching or renovating the Australian welfare state: The paradox of the Howard government's neo-liberalism [Electronic version]. *International Journal of Social Welfare, 17*(1), 1–9.

Murphy, J. (2006). The other welfare state: Non-government agencies and the mixed economy of welfare in Australia [Electronic version]. *History Australia, 3*(2), 44.01–44.15.

Newman, J. (1999). *The challenge of welfare dependency in the 21st century.* Canberra: Department of Family and Community Services.

Newman, J. (2005). Welfare governance and the remaking of citizenship In J. Newman (Ed.), *Remaking governance: Peoples, politics and the public sphere.* Bristol: Policy Press.

OECD. (2008a). Growing unequal? : Income distribution and poverty in OECD countries. Retrieved November 18, 2008, from www.oecd.org/els/social/inequality

OECD. (2008b). *OECD factbook 2008: Economic, environmental and social statistics.* Paris: OECD.

Productivity Commission. (2002). Independent review of the Job Network, Inquiry report, Report No. 21. Retrieved November 22, 2008, from http://www.pc.gov.au/projects/inquiry/jobnetwork/docs/finalreport

Ramia, G., & Wailes, N. (2006). Putting wage-earners in wage-earner's welfare states: The relationship between social policy and industrial relations in Australia and New Zealand [Electronic version]. *Australian Journal of Social Issues, 41*(1), 49–68.

Reeves, S. (2006, September 25–27). *Hope, faith and charity in the post welfare era.* Paper presented at the Australasian Political Studies Association Conference, University of Newcastle. Retrieved November 18, 2008, from http://www.newcastle.

edu.au/Resources/Schools/Economics%20Politics%20and%20Tourism/APSA%202006/
PUBPOLICY/Reeves,%20Sandra.pdf.

Saunders, P. (2003, July 9–11). *Why reform welfare?* Paper presented at the Social Policy
Research Centre "Social Inclusion" Conference, University of New South Wales.

Saunders, P. (2007a). The costs of disability and the incidence of poverty [Electronic version].
Australian Journal of Social Issues, 42(4), 461–480.

Saunders, P. (2007b). A welfare state for those who want one, opt-outs for those who don't
[Electronic version]. *Issue Analysis, 17,* 1–16.

Schut, J. M. W., Vrooman, J. C., & de Beer, P. T. (2001). On worlds of welfare. Retrieved
November 26, 2008, from http://www.scp.nl/english/publications/books/9037700497.
shtml

Siewert, R. (2008). Centrelink breaches doubled, Aboriginals hit hardest. Retrieved November 22,
2008, from http://www.greensmps.org.au/content/media-release/centrelink-breaches-doubled-
aboriginals-hit-hardest

Thomas, M. (2007). A review of recent developments in the Job Network, Research Paper
no. 15 2007–08. Retrieved November 28, 2008, from http://www.aph.gov.au/library/Pubs/
RP/2007-08/08rp15.htm#exec

United Nations Development Program. (2008). Human development report 2007/2008.
Retrieved November 19, 2008, from http://hdr.undp.org/en/reports/global/hdr2007-2008/

Weeks, W. (1994). *Women working together: Lessons from feminist women's services.* Melbourne:
Longman Cheshire.

Weeks, W. (1995). *Issues facing Australian families: Human services respond.* Melbourne:
Longman Cheshire.

Welfare Reform Reference Group. (2000). *Participation support for a more equitable society.*
Canberra: Department of Family and Community Services.

Western, M., Baxter, J., Pakulski, J., Tranter, B., Western, J., van Egmond, M., et al. (2007).
Neoliberalism, inequality and politics: The changing face of Australia [Electronic version].
Australian Journal of Social Issues, 42(3), 401–418.

Whiteford, P. (2006). The welfare expenditure debate: Economic myths of the left and the
right revisited (draft). Retrieved November 26, 2008, from http://www.sprc.unsw.edu.au/
ASPC2005/papers/Paper7.pdf

Whiteford, P., & Angenent, G. (2002). *The Australian system of social protection: An overview,
Occasional Paper No. 7.* Canberra: Department of Family and Community Services.

Chapter 16
South Africa and Post-industrialism: Developmental Social Welfare – A Policy Framework for Social Services with Children

Antoinette Lombard

Introduction

In 1994, the first elected democratic government committed itself to rebuilding the deeply divided South African society. This was no easy task, given the post-apartheid government's inheritance of "one of the *most unequal societies in the world* upon ascending to office in 1994" (Binza, 2006: 491). The challenge for the new government was to rejuvenate the growth of the economy so that it could generate jobs and provide social relief for the poor, thereby uplifting socio-economic standards in the black communities (Binza, 2006).

It was acknowledged worldwide that South Africa made a smooth political transition, which allowed for the creation of the legal framework for a democracy that guaranteed human rights and dignity for all South Africans (Terreblanche, 2002: 30). However, the legal freedom from apartheid could not completely surmount "its deep social and economic divisions" (Harsch, 2004: 4). The 2006 Budget Review (Republic of South Africa [hereafter RSA], 2006a: 102) emphasized the sharp divisions between the modern economy and marginalized communities, between formal employment and the insecurity of the unemployed, between the rich and the poor.

In addressing the legacy of South Africa's colonial and apartheid history, the government has adopted a transformative, developmental framework and is progressively becoming a developmental state (Department of Social Development, 2006a). The government has committed to growing the economy, at the same time ensuring the redistribution of wealth to make significant inroads into poverty and inequality. This has created an ongoing challenge to government's aspiration of being a developmental rather than a welfare state. Socioeconomic development cannot be separated from the country's political economy, which "is the way in which the production, distribution, and consumption of wealth

A. Lombard (✉)
Department of Social Work and Criminology, University of Pretoria,
Pretoria, South Africa
e-mail: antoinette.lombard@up.ac.za

J. Powell, J. Hendricks, *The Welfare State in Post-Industrial Society*,
DOI 10.1007/978-1-4419-0066-1_16, © Springer Science+Business Media, LLC 2009

are organised within a society; in other words, *who gains and who loses, and how"* (Schoeman, 2001: 316).

The newly elected government was faced with the immediate imperative of making a difference to the lives of the poor in the swiftest and most tangible way possible. To this end, it embraced social security as its priority antipoverty strategy (RSA, 2007a). This led to criticism of government's policies on fighting poverty, and the warning that increased welfare would not *buy the poor out of their misery*. "We should not make a welfare state and call it a developmental state," were the words of former First Lady Zanele Mbeki (Boyle, 2005: 1). This criticism begs for clarity on the function of social assistance in a development state.

From the perspective of human rights, a developmental approach enshrines the right to social security. The constitution (Act 108 of 1996) indicates in the Bill of Rights that everyone is entitled to social security and appropriate social assistance, including those who are unable to support themselves and their dependants. Given the high levels of income poverty in South Africa, social assistance plays a critical role in supporting children and families. The results of a study on the social and economic impact of South Africa's social security system (Department of Social Development, 2004a) demonstrate that the effects of South Africa's social grants on households are developmental in nature. The study yielded positive impacts for reducing poverty, addressing the problem of hunger, providing greater household access to piped water, promoting job search, and increasing school attendance (Department of Social Development, 2004a).

Although social grants are affecting the survival of the poor positively, this alone does not bridge the gap between the rich and the poor, nor does it facilitate participation of the marginalized sections in the mainstream economy. The right to development will, however, accomplish this. Thin (2002: 15) concurs, "Present and future generations need, not just a given quality of life, but the opportunity to contribute to progress (the 'right to development')." This finds expression in access to antipoverty programs that address the structural issues underpinning poverty and inequality (Lombard, 2008a). It is the "demand for increasing skills and for a knowledgeable society to contribute rigorously to sustainable development [which] becomes imperative in a developmental state like South Africa" (Binza, 2006: 503).

The Constitutional Bill of Rights (Act 108 of 1996) laid a solid foundation for the creation of a developmental social welfare system with the recognition of a range of socioeconomic rights for everyone and additional protection for children. In particular, Section 28(1) recognizes children's rights to family care, basic nutrition, shelter, basic health care services, social services, and protection (Giese, 2008: 17). The White Paper for Social Welfare (RSA, 1997) envisioned a developmental approach to social welfare that included social security and social services. The right to both social assistance and development is captured succinctly in a statement by the minister of social development at the Children's Act Conference (Department of Social Development, 2008): "Our responses to poverty ... [are to]

empower people to access economic opportunities, while creating a comprehensive social safety net to protect the most vulnerable in our society."

The aim of this chapter is to place developmental social services within the broader context of development in South Africa and to discuss the relevance and challenges of the developmental social welfare policy more specifically as far as social services for children in South Africa are concerned. The initial discussion on post-industrialism and the nation-state will present an outline of the policy and legislative framework for development, to be followed by the socioeconomic and political context for social service delivery within the framework of globalization. The next section will conceptualize the state's investment in developmental social welfare and social services. As a new ideology for children welfare, the Children's Act (Act 38 of 2005) (RSA, 2005) will be discussed as the legal framework for developmental social services for children from the human rights perspective, first in relation to children's rights to social services and second to their right to social assistance. In summary, the challenges for developmental social services, as they affect the implementation of the Children's Act, will be outlined, followed by a final conclusion on promoting children's rights and social services.

Post-industrialism and the Nation-State

The cornerstone and the premises for all policies and legislation in the South African democracy are entrenched in the Bill of Rights of the South African Constitution, Act 108 of 1996, which enshrines the rights of all people in the country and affirms the democratic values of human dignity, equality, and freedom (Lombard, 2008a). Prior to assuming power, the African National Congress (ANC) adopted the Reconstruction and Development Programme (RDP) (ANC, 1994) as its manifesto. The RDP was the first integrated socioeconomic policy for the country. It was intended to mobilize the country's human and economic resources to strengthen its democracy (Binza, 2006: 493). Achieving this would have required extensive involvement of government and state resources.

When the elected ANC government formalized the RDP as the government policy in the form of the White Paper for Reconstruction and Development (RSA, 1994), it scaled down the role of government in the program. This decision was criticized as downgrading the role of government to the mere *management* of both transformation and subsequent policy proposals concerning the privatization of state assets and trade and financial liberalization (*The Star*, 1995, cited in *SA Human Development Report*, UNDP South Africa, 2003: 63). In line with this shift, the Growth, Employment and Redistribution (GEAR) strategy was promulgated as South Africa's macroeconomic policy in 1996 (UNDP, 2003). The government's approach to reconstruction and development was now entrenched in neoliberal capitalism, which relied on the market and economic growth to address poverty and inequality. The GEAR's aims were to achieve growth and development by promoting growth through exports and investments; addressing uneven development and unequal redistribution of resources by creating jobs; and reallocating resources through the budget system (Binza, 2006: 496). GEAR was criticized because the redistributive rhetoric of the RDP "rapidly sank below the surface, reappearing in diluted form in the austere (GEAR) macroeconomic policy" (Lund, 2008: 91).

On a more positive note, since 2003, the GEAR has contributed to a steady economic growth rate by an average of 5 percent per annum (RSA, 2008a), maintaining the inflation rate between 3 and 6 percent per annum and servicing the budget deficit of the previous government, which, it was argued, would bring adequate funds for the government to spend on social development (Binza, 2006: 496). It is, however, well documented that economic growth does not in itself guarantee economic development (Midgley, 1996; Schoeman, 2001). Despite the steady economic growth, the GEAR has not succeeded in creating the required jobs, which Hosking (2003) (cited by Binza, 2006: 496) described as "... economic growth [that] was jobless." Fourteen years into democracy, South Africa faces a widening gap between the rich and the poor, along with increasing levels of poverty and inequality (Sewpaul & Hölsher, 2004; Gray, 2006; Binza, 2006). Terreblanche (2002: 114) laments that the compilers of the GEAR lost contact with "the imperfect reality of and deep-seated inequalities in South Africa." In his State of the Nation Address on 4 February 2006, the then President of South Africa, Thabo Mbeki, justified the slow delivery of socioeconomic goals by saying that "it would take considerable time before we could say we have eradicated the legacy of the past" (RSA, 2006b).

Inequality, Work and Welfare

To speed up delivery on poverty and inequality, the government adopted the Accelerated and Shared Growth Initiative [AsgiSA](2006d). In government's commitment to deliver on socioeconomic goals, AsgiSA calls on its social partners to fast-track shared economic growth (RSA, 2007b). Lombard (2008b) argues that the social welfare sector is the social partner closest to the marginalized and the poor, therefore playing an important role in the national effort to reduce inequality and eliminate poverty.

In line with its developmental agenda and the United Nations World Declaration on Social Development (UNDP, 2003), South Africa adopted the White Paper for Social Welfare in 1997. The white paper embraces a developmental approach to social welfare, intending to address poverty and inequity and promote social development by integrating social interventions with economic development (Department of Social Development, 2006a). The shift of social welfare toward a developmental approach is based on a constitutional, policy, and legislative mandate (Patel, 2005). The focus of the RDP on people-centered development (Binza, 2006) and its principles and ethos was central to the processes for transforming social welfare (Gray, 2006). The reorientation of social welfare to "developmental social welfare" was aimed at providing people with ways out of poverty, while the cash transfers would remain in place as a last-resort support (Lund, 2008: 1).

To give effect to the White Paper for Social Welfare, the Policy on Financial Awards to Service Providers (Department of Social Development, 2005a) and the Integrated Social Service Delivery Model (ISDM) for improved social service delivery (Department of Social Development, 2006a) were launched. Despite limitations (Lombard, 2007; Dutschke, 2008), these policies paved the way for operationalizing developmental social welfare and social service delivery. These policies, however, have not fully succeeded in facilitating the conversion to a developmental social welfare system (Dutschke, 2008). A legal framework for legitimizing developmental social welfare was required. This is due to realize once the Children's Act (No 38 of 2005) as amended by the Children's Amendment Bill [B19D-2006] (RSA, 2006c) has been promulgated (expected in 2009). It will be the primary legal framework governing social services for children in South Africa (Dutschke, 2008). In the South African Constitution, socioeconomic rights are inextricably tied to civil and political rights (Pendlebury, 2008), hence the importance of understanding the socioeconomic and political context of the country within a broader global framework.

Socioeconomic and Political Context Within a Global Framework

South Africa is a middle-income country located somewhere between the north and the south (Lund, 2008). Patel (2005) describes the country as a society in transition, struggling with addressing the twin challenges of globalization and its colonial and apartheid past.

Barber and Vickers (2001: 338) describe South Africa in economic and social terms as a *chameleon*, with a dual identity as both developed and undeveloped. Terreblanche (2002) also refers to this duality, saying that, on the one hand, the new South African government inherited the most developed economy in Africa, with a modern physical and institutional infrastructure. On the other hand, it also inherited major socioeconomic problems, including high levels of unemployment, abject poverty, sharp inequalities in the distribution of income, property, and opportunities, and sharp levels of crime and violence (Terreblanche, 2002).

Terreblanche (2002: 425–426) accentuates the economy's "two worlds" character as follows: "One modern, smart, professional, efficient, and globally oriented; the other neglected, messy, unskilled, downtrodden, and thriving on crime and violence." Schoeman (2001: 329) says the South African economy "is classified as an open economy, meaning that it is deeply influenced by and dependent on changes and trends in the international economy." South Africa's major export commodity is gold (Binza, 2006), so foreign earnings are extensively influenced by the market. The most salient issues facing South Africa today are poverty, unemployment, uneven distribution of economic growth, lack of domestic savings for investment, and the consequent need for foreign investment (Schoeman, 2001).

The discovery of gold and diamonds during the late 19th century and the subsequent discovery of coal changed the face, history, economic structure, and political economy of the whole southern African region (Schoeman, 2001). Mining, which forms the basis of South African industrialization, created a demand for low-wage, unskilled labor in the mines, necessitating the implementation of labor migration from across southern Africa (Schoeman, 2001). Labor migration contributed to large-scale social dislocation and the disintegration of traditional family life and customs among the population of the region (Schoeman, 2001). It further contributed to the impoverishment of rural areas relative to the urban areas that developed around mining and exporting activities (Schoeman, 2001), resulting in children and families at risk.

Vulnerability of Children and Families

South African domestic life was consequently characterized by unstable families and settlements resulting from the colonial and apartheid policies. Under the migrant labor system, men in their economically active years went to work on the mines and in cities, while families were forced to remain behind. The responsibility for sustaining the rural population was borne almost entirely by family members in the rural areas. In the urban areas, particularly in the mines and harbors, men were denied the right to a family life (Lund, 2008: 2). In addition, millions of people were resettled in the pursuit of "separate development" (Lund, 2008: 2).

Complex social challenges, such as widespread poverty, social fragmentation, a culture of violence, high rates of unemployment, and the HIV/AIDS pandemic, means that there is a formidable increase in the number of vulnerable children and families in dire need of social services (Proudlock & Jamieson, 2008). These challenges affect families' capacity to care for their children. Moreover, historical inequalities in investment in education, health care, and basic infrastructure have contributed to poor-quality services and persistent backlogs in historically disadvantaged areas. Child vulnerability, particularly in these areas, is further compounded by high levels of illness and death associated with HIV/AIDS (Giese, 2008). The overall rate of life expectancy has decreased, and an increasing number of children are experiencing death of a parent or parents (Lund, 2008). The AIDS pandemic has left increasing numbers of child-headed households in its wake (Meintjies, John-Langba & Berry, 2008).

In July 2006, there were just over 18.2 million children in South Africa, so children constituted more than one-third (38 percent) of the country's population (Meintjies et al., 2008). The *General Household Survey* (GHS) indicates that, in 2006, there were approximately 3.8 million "orphan" children who were without a living biological mother, father, or both parents in South Africa (Meintjies et al., 2008). The majority of these children are not only struggling with historically determined structural causes of poverty and inequality due to the socioeconomic legacy impacting on their parents' lives, but they face a repetition of this history in the extreme marginalized position they find themselves.

Patel (2005) states that national governments are beginning to recognize that the welfare and development of their societies are inextricably linked to regional and global realities, which means that poverty, HIV/AIDS pandemic, and seemingly intractable social problems can no longer be addressed unilaterally in South Africa. To make an impact on a regional and global level, the social welfare sector had to reposition itself as a change agent for reconstruction and development on the national level. This was accomplished by the adoption of a developmental approach to social welfare.

South Africa is part of the Southern African Development Community (SADC) and the New Partnership for Africa's Development (NEPAD), which are attempting to address these challenges both regionally and continentally (Patel, 2005). The process of moving toward democracy included becoming integrated and being signatory to many of the international platforms and conventions on human rights, along with setting up the necessary machinery within the country to advocate for these rights (Lund, 2008). Regarding children, South Africa became a signatory to the United Nations Convention on the Rights of the Child (CRC), which accorded, with the personal commitment by the first president of the democracy, Nelson Mandela, to the welfare of children (Lund, 2008: 5). This translated, early in his term of office, into raising the profile of children on policy and poverty agendas (Lund, 2008: 5) and the African Charter on the Rights and Welfare of the Child (African Charter) (Dutschke & Monson, 2008). The South African government has clearly made a decision to prioritize and invest in social services for children. Developmental social welfare provided the vehicle toward achieving this goal.

Investment of the State in Developmental Social Welfare

South Africa is one of the few countries to have adopted a developmental approach to social welfare in line with the Declaration of the World Summit for Social Development held in Copenhagen in 1995 (UNDP, 2003). South Africa's developmental approach to social welfare evolved from its unique history of inequality and the violation of human rights as a result of colonialism and apartheid (Patel, 2005). The welfare services were racially discriminatory, as well as slanted toward curative and clinical interventions rather than preventive services (Lund, 2008).

One of the most important developments in postapartheid social welfare policy was thus the move away from an almost singular focus on the "treatment" of social ills (the residual model) to an approach that is developmental in nature (Giese, 2008: 17). The new *developmental social welfare*, as embodied in the White Paper for Social Welfare (RSA, 1997) embraces a system that is "more just, equitable, participatory and appropriate in meeting the needs of all South Africans" (Patel, 2005: 1).

South Africa's developmental social welfare policy recognizes that widespread poverty is a driver of social problems (Proudlock & Jamieson, 2008). The developmental approach is thus a pro-poor strategy (Patel, 2005), molded by the theory of social development (Gray, 2006). Developmental social welfare promotes social development by integrating social interventions with economic development (Department of Social Development, 2006a) and, within the context of economic development, "seeks to link the social services to economic development in a dynamic way" (Midgley, 1995: 25). The developmental approach thus provides the social welfare sector with the key to making a meaningful contribution to the alleviation of poverty and inequities in society and to establishing social service professionals, such as social workers, as important social partners in achieving social development in an approach and strategy that facilitate and achieve integrated human, social, and economic development (Lombard, 2007).

Changes to the Welfare State

Throughout the history of social welfare in South Africa, social security has had the lion's share of the social welfare budget, which has always been at the expense of delivery of social services. Although the developmental approach made provision in the White Paper for Social Welfare, social security and social services, the extent of expansion of social assistance post-1994 was not expected. This can be attributed to the new government's commitment to social security as their priority antipoverty program. The neglect of social service delivery, inter alia, has led to deepening poverty, poorly developed protection services, and an increase in social pathologies (Department of Social Development, 2006a). A positive step forward was the historic transfer, in April 2006, of the responsibility for the management and payment of social assistance grants to an independent agency with its budget, that is, the South African Social Security Agency (SASSA). Although this was a victory for the agenda and budget of social welfare services, it compounded the crisis in social welfare service delivery, because it exposed the neglect of social welfare service delivery and the failure to realize the aim of achieving social development goals through social services (Lombard, 2007). Jean Benjamin, deputy minister of social development, articulated this neglect as follows: "... the intensive social security focus has been to the detriment of other developmental social services" (Department of Social Development, 2005b: 1). The government publicly acknowledged that no exit levels had been planned for social grants (Department of Social Development, 2006b). An exit strategy is a proactive and deliberate strategy to link social grant beneficiaries to opportunities for economic activities (Department of Social Development, 2006b) and to improve their capabilities, which reduces their reliance on income support alone, and to facilitate the reduction of high levels of poverty (Lombard, 2008a).

Social services for children have been neglected over the past 10 years, because of both the disproportionate budget allocation for social security and social services and the absence of a legislative framework in line with the constitution (Jamieson, Proudlock & Waterhouse, 2008: 10). The Children's Act (Act 38 of 2005) provided the long overdue legal framework that could do justice to both social assistance and social services within a developmental policy framework and as such introduced a new ideology for social services to children.

Legal Framework for Children's Rights: New Ideology for Child Welfare

A new law was required if the developmental policy set out in the White Paper for Social Welfare was to take effect (Proudlock & Jamieson, 2008: 35). The Children's Act is the culmination of a 10-year-long consultative law reform process (Proudlock & Jamieson, 2008: 35). The new Children's Act will soon be completed with the incorporation of the Children's Amendment Bill and will replace the Child Care Act (No 74 of 1983). The promulgation of the Children's Act will bring South Africa's law in line with the Bill of Rights and the international law (Jamieson et al., 2008). Loffell (2008: 86) describes the Children's Act, despite the reduction in scope indicated in its initial drafting, as reflecting "a dramatic broadening and deepening of the nation's commitment toward children as expressed in law."

The Children's Act will reiterate that children's rights and other socioeconomic rights underpin a developmental social welfare system (Dutschke, 2008: 29) that supports the large numbers of vulnerable children and their families more effectively, by means of both social security (social grants) and social services (Giese, 2008).

Children's Right to Social Services

The ambit of the right to social services extends from family support services to protection services, particularly for vulnerable children and children in need of care outside the family environment (Dutschke & Monson, 2008). Social services are generally classified in terms of levels of intervention, and include prevention, early intervention, protection, and alternative state care. They are delivered by state and nongovernmental social service practitioners and volunteers to support individuals, families, and communities who are at risk (Giese, 2008).

Services that were regulated in the Child Care Act (No 74 of 1983) and which the Children's Act (No 38 of 2005) continues to reinforce include:

- protection services for children who have suffered abuse, neglect, or exploitation, including a system to report, refer, and support children;
- foster care (including cluster foster care);
- adoption; and
- child and youth care centers.

Services provided for in law by the Children's Act for the first time include:

- practical care (e.g. crèches);
- early childhood development (ECD) programs;
- primary prevention and early intervention services for vulnerable children;
- support programs for child-headed households;
- drop-in centers for vulnerable children to access basic services (Proudlock & Jamieson, 2008: 36).

The focus on the ECD is a unique challenge for social service delivery for children in South Africa within a developmental paradigm. In South Africa, ECD has been defined to include children from birth through their ninth year, which is a conscious move away from the earlier definition of "pre-school" as meaning "before six years old," followed by formal schooling years (Lund, 2008: 47). According to Lund (2008: 49), the "broader scope of ECD acknowledges that children's developmental processes – physical, cognitive, mental, emotional, and social – are continuous, regardless of when they are officially eligible [to attend] primary school." Another unique feature of the ECD in South Africa is that, in 2004, the Department of Social Development undertook to incorporate an expansion of the ECD sector in the Expanded Public Works Programme (Lund, 2008: 49). Public works programs traditionally focus on infrastructure, like road maintenance, dam building, and weed clearing. Lund (2008: 49) is of the opinion that it is possibly unique internationally for two programs conventionally perceived as "social" in nature, ECD and home-based care for sick people, to be integrated into public works interventions, and she calls for this experiment to be closely monitored.

Given the major shift of the Children's Act to prevention and early intervention, Section 144 of the Children's Act outlines the types of prevention and early intervention programs that the government will be funding. Proudlock and Jamieson (2008: 38) list these programs as follows:

- preserving a child's family structure (e.g. home-based care for families suffering from chronic illnesses, like AIDS);
- developing appropriate parenting skills;

- developing the parents' capacity to safeguard the well-being and best interests of children with disabilities and chronic illnesses (e.g. support groups for parents of children with disabilities);
- diverting children in trouble with the law from the criminal justice system into restorative justice programs;
- helping children and families to access other government services (e.g. health care, grants, school fee exemptions, water, and electricity); and
- providing psychological, rehabilitative, and therapeutic services for children who have suffered abuse, abandonment, or grief (e.g. child and family counselling services and phone crisis lines).

Not only do these community-based projects reach out to children but the funding also provides skill development and work for the women and youth who run them (Proudlock and Jamieson 2008). This initiative provides for the integration of social and economic development in accordance with a developmental social welfare system (Proudlock & Jamieson, 2008: 38).

Children's Right to Social Assistance

The aim of social assistance is to provide families with an income that caters to their basic needs, thereby promoting equality (Smith, 2008). The rolling out of grants and their many benefits to millions of children is a remarkable achievement for South Africa (Smith, 2008: 55). Three of the various grants available fall in the children's domain. The 2008 midyear estimation of the South African population was 48.7 million (Statistics South Africa, 2008), while the number of social grants distributed in the country, on 30 June 2008, came to 12, 553 390. Of this total, the Child Support Grant accounts for the highest proportion of grants, that is (65.91 percent), followed by the Old Age Grant (17.97 percent), the Disability Grant (11.29 percent), the Foster Care Grant (3.68 percent), the Care Dependency Grant (0.83 percent), Grant-in-aid (0.32 percent), and the War Veterans Grant (0.01 percent). Of the three children's grants, 93.60 percent is distributed to child support, 5.22 percent to foster care, and 1.17 percent to care dependency. It is clear that the Child Support Grant is making the highest impact on income poverty. Although the numbers qualifying for the Foster Care Grant are lower, it is the most time-consuming to administer on account of the court procedures, which negatively affects developmental social service delivery.

The three children's grants are all linked to a means test, for which new regulations were announced in August 2008 by the social development minister. This forms part of the "government's war on poverty campaign" (Department of Social Development, 2008: 1). Aimed at combating inflation, it will allow just over a million previously excluded people to apply for a social grant.

The child-targeted grants are as follows:

The Child Support Grant (CSG), effected on 1 April 1998, represents a radical shift from the former family-based benefit State Maintenance Grant (SMG) to one that is "child-focused" (Lund, 2008). This accommodates the mobility of children between different households and anticipates that HIV/AIDS brings with it the spectrum of hundreds of thousands of orphaned children (Lund, 2008). The motto of the CSG is: "Keep your eye on the child and find ways to support the child," rather than maintaining barriers like the marital status of the child's parents, as was the case with the SMG (Lund, 2008: 53).

The CSG is available to children under the age of 15 and is valued at R240 ($25) a month per child. It is available to the primary caregiver of a child who passes an income-based means test for a maximum of six children per adult. No court processes are involved in accessing the grant (Giese, 2008).

The CSG was designed for children living in poverty (Smith, 2008), specifically to shift racially biased welfare spending toward children in very poor households and toward rural areas (Lund, 2008). Although it is too early to measure with any confidence what the lasting impact of the CSG will be, Lund (2008: 79) indicates that early studies have found a relationship between the CSG receipt and school attendance rates.

The value of the CSG within a developmental approach is aptly described by Thandika Mkandawire, director of the UNRISD (in Lund, 2008: viii):

> The Child Support Grant in South Africa is about forging a social policy that is at the same time fiscally redistributive, compatible with economic growth and development, and with the primary goal of the enhancement of children's well-being. It speaks to social justice arguments, and also economic arguments. It makes a strong case for such state action as a low-cost measure of transferring resources to the poor. It is an important contribution to the growing body of knowledge on interest in global social policy.

The **Foster Care Grant** (FCG) is available to the children whom the court finds in need of state care and protection (Smith, 2008) following a social worker's enquiry into the child's circumstances. The FCG is a cash grant to the value of R680 ($72) per child per month (Meintjies et al., 2008). Because the FCG is substantially greater in value than the CSG, relatives caring for children are increasingly making attempts to "foster" children in their care so as to access the more lucrative foster grant. Social workers are thus swamped with foster care applications by families in need of poverty alleviation (Giese, 2008). The high demand for the FCG is creating an exponentially large caseload (Giese, 2008) and is impacting negatively on the child protection system's ability to respond timely and appropriately to the needs of children who have been abused, neglected, abandoned, exploited, or trafficked (Smith, 2008). However, a positive change effected in the Children's Act now allows courts to make permanent foster care orders in specified circumstances (Section 186), which will eliminate the need for two-yearly reviews by social workers in some cases (Giese, 2008).

The **Care Dependency Grant** (CDG), worth R1010 ($107) per child per month, targets children with severe disabilities or chronic illnesses (Smith, 2008). This grant makes provision for the care of children with AIDS.

Challenges for Developmental Social Services to Children

The Children's Act provides the necessary legal framework to support the delivery of the full spectrum of social services (Giese, 2008). It is, however, only on the implementation level that the impact of the Children's Act on children's lives will become evident. There are many challenges ahead as far as the delivery of developmental social services to children in South Africa is concerned. Jamieson et al. (2008: 1) provide a summary of these challenges:

> The Act and Amendment Bill together provide a foundation for the reform and development of children's social services. The challenge now is to make sure necessary budgets are allocated, provincial departments' capacity for delivery is improved, the human resources challenge is prioritized, and sustainable funding is provided to non-profit organizations which provide the bulk of social services to vulnerable children.

Key challenges include the following:

Social Service Practitioners

There is a shortage of social service practitioners in South Africa. This includes social workers, social auxiliary workers, and child and youth care workers. Social work is recognized as a scarce skill in South Africa, which is described as a national crisis (Giese, 2008). The costing report of the Children's Bill revealed that, at the lowest level of implementation, at least 16,504 social workers would be needed in 2010/2011 for children's social services (Giese, 2008: 19). Looking at the higher level for implementation (better service standards), 66,329 social workers will be needed in 2010/2011 (Giese, 2008). This figure stands in glaring contrast to the 14,072 social workers currently registered at the South African Council for Social Service Professions. In a desperate attempt to address the shortage of social workers, the government released a Recruitment and Retention Strategy (Department of Social Development, 2004b) that resulted in the recruitment of students to study social work, while social workers' salaries and working conditions were addressed in an attempt to keep them in the profession. The fiscal budget for scholarships for social work is so abundant that any candidate who meets the criteria is guaranteed of a scholarship. This, however, has severe implications for the capacity of the 17 South African training institutions offering social work programs.

In addition to the need for more professionals, different cadres of people with broad-based helping and training skills are required to meet the aim of developmental social welfare, that of less institutional care for children (Lund, 2008: 41).

Allocation of Budgets and Capacity Building

Government's commitment to fund prevention and early intervention services, especially in poor areas, means that the vision of the White Paper for Social Welfare can now be put into practice (Proudlock & Jamieson, 2008: 38). The National Treasury and the nine provinces of South Africa will have to prioritize the implementation of the Children's Act when making decisions on budgets and the allocation of resources (Proudlock & Jamieson, 2008: 36). The Children's Amendment Bill prescribes that provinces provide for prevention and early intervention services; protection services; and child and youth care centers (Budlender, Proudlock & Monson, 2008). Giese (2008: 21) adds that "to ensure that 10 years of investment in drafting the Children's Act bears fruit, significant budget growth and capacity development are urgently needed to support implementation." The government should take the responsibility for building the capacity of the social service sector to deliver.

Partnerships Between Government and Not-for-Profit Organizations (NPOs)

Although the state does not take full responsibility for the delivery of developmental social services in South Africa, it is obliged to ensure that the services are provided and that they are accessible to all vulnerable children. In accordance with the practices of a developmental state, the government sees one of its responsibilities to be that of facilitating the process of development through the various institutions of the government, its partners, and the civil society (Department of Social Development, 2006a). There is, however, a slanted perception of this partnership, and Loffell (2008) alludes to the fact that protective services to children have remained largely the responsibility of the NPOs. Thus a partnership is required in which the NPOs are paid in full by the government for services rendered on behalf of the state (Proudlock & Jamieson, 2008: 37). The key stumbling block as far as the partnership between the government and the NPOs is concerned has always been that of funding (cf. Lombard, 2007; Smit, 2006).

Funding of NPOs

Service delivery in South Africa is heavily dependent on a "motley and unevenly spread collection of civil society organisations with all manner of mandates from different sources" (Loffell, 2008: 85). The bulk of their funding has to be independent of the government, with the consequent effect on social service delivery. This means that, in the absence of sufficient state capacity to deliver prevention and early intervention services, the nonprofit and voluntary sectors currently provide the majority of these services to children and families (Giese, 2008: 21). Loffell (2008: 85) continues saying that while these organizations are performing a state function, very few have proper service-level agreements with the government and many of them struggle to access subsidies. Inadequate support for NPOs and community-based initiatives will clearly "[compromise] the quality and continuity of services for children and [stretch] community resources beyond capacity" (Giese, 2008: 21). Implementation challenges include reforming the funding of NPOs delivering social services on behalf of the government and the recognition and development of the full range of social service practitioners (Proudlock & Jamieson, 2008: 40).

Conclusion

At a Gauteng Welfare Summit (2006: 11–12), it was resolved that the social welfare sector should play a much stronger role in building the developmental state and that a prerequisite for successful development lies within *a strong developmental social welfare system*. The White Paper for Social Welfare (1997) marked a turning point in the history of social welfare in South Africa. Not only has it redressed decades of historical imbalance but it has also repositioned social welfare as a role player in social development in the new democracy (Lombard, 2008b). While the white paper's vision of a developmental approach to social welfare has been translated into practice in the area of social grants, there is still a substantial shortfall in the delivery of social services (Giese, 2008). The Children's Act is a major step forward in addressing this gap. Proudlock and Jamieson (2008) comment that the Children's Act shifts the country from being a charity model to one that recognizes that children have a constitutional right to social services and that the state bears the primary duty of ensuring delivery of these services.

The Children's Act is a *pioneering step* forward in the realization of a developmental approach to social welfare services for children, which Proudlock and Jamieson (2008: 40) feel justifies celebration. The Children's Act as a whole provides the strong legislative foundation that was so desperately needed if the country is to respond adequately to the needs of vulnerable children (Proudlock & Jamieson, 2008). However, critical to "turn[ing] legislation into lived reality for children and their families" is "strong political leadership and decision-makers that can guide the crucial processes of identifying and assessing needs, constructing new service delivery mechanisms, carefully integrating the clusters of programmes, coordinating their activities and appropriating adequate resources" (September & Dinbabo, 2008: 121).

Government's "... ability to capably intervene and shepherd society resources to achieve national development objectives" will bring South Africa closer to the essence of being a developmental state (Naidoo, 2006: 483). The ultimate evidence of successful delivery of the Children's Act will be in preventive and early intervention services, which will signify that the South African society has secured the future of the country's children and youth. This achievement will enable South Africa to facilitate new forms of solidarity in promoting children's rights and social services across borders.

References

African National Congress (ANC). (1994). *The reconstruction and development programme: A policy framework.* Johannesburg: Umanyano Publications.

Barber, J., & Vickers, B. (2001). South Africa's foreign policy. In Venter, A. (Ed). *Government and Politics in the new South Africa* (2nd ed.). Pretoria: Van Schaik Publishers.

Binza, M.S. (2006). Continuous democratisation in post-1994 South Africa: An analysis of selected policies for combating poverty. *Journal of Public Administration, 41*(3):491–505.

Boyle, B. (2005). First Lady: State has failed the poor. *Sunday Times*, 11 December: 1.

Budlender, D., Proudlock, P., & Monson, J. (2008). Budget allocations for implementing the Children's Act. In Proudlock, P., Dutschke, M., Jamieson, L., Monson, J., & Smith, C. (Eds), *South African child gauge:* (pp. 41–47). Cape Town: Children's Institute, University of Cape Town.

Department of Social Development. (2004a). Economic Policy Research Institute. *Summary Report. The Social and Economic Impact of South Africa's Social Security System.* 30 September.

Department of Social Development. (2004b). *Recruitment and Retention Strategy for Social Workers in South Africa.* (Second Draft).

Department of Social Development. (2005a). *Policy on financial awards to service providers.*

Department of Social Development. (2005b). *Speech by Dr Jean Benjamin, Deputy Minister of Social Development: Launch of the Integrated Service Delivery Model.* Media Release. Cape Town International Convention Centre, 28 November 2005.

Department of Social Development. (2006a). *Integrated service delivery model towards improved social services.* RP31. Pretoria: Government Printer.

Department of Social Development. (2006b). *Linking social grants beneficiaries to poverty alleviation and economic activity.* Discussion document, 1 November.

Department of Social Development. (2008). Minister Skweyiya announces changes to means test to allow more people to apply for social grants. Media Statement. Pretoria. http://www. dsd.gov.za/dynamic/dynamic/aspx?pageid = 461& id = 1167 [Accessed 25 September 2008.]

Dutschke, M. (2008). Developmental social welfare policies and children's rights to social services. In Proudlock, P., Dutschke, M., Jamieson, L., Monson, J., & Smith, C. (Eds), *South African child gauge:* (pp.29–34). Cape Town: Children's Institute, University of Cape Town.

Dutschke, M., & Monson, J. (2008). Children's constitutional right to social services. In Proudlock, P., Dutschke, M., Jamieson, L., Monson, J., & Smith, C. (Eds), *South African child gauge:* (pp. 23–28). Cape Town: Children's Institute, University of Cape Town.

Gauteng Welfare Summit. (2006). *The integrated service delivery model: A review of the Gauteng Department of Social Development's response, and an NPO perspective.* Prepared by: Frans Rammutla & Nono Yende, Gauteng Department of Social Development and Beena Chiba,

Maya Keel & Jackie Loffell, Gauteng Welfare, Social Service & Development Forum. 26–27 October.

Giese, S. (2008). Setting the scene for social services: The gap between service need and delivery. In Proudlock, P., Dutschke, M., Jamieson, L., Monson, J., & Smith, C. (Eds), *South African child gauge:* (pp.17–22). Cape Town: Children's Institute, University of Cape Town.

Gray, M. (2006). The progress of social development in South Africa. *International Journal of Social Welfare, 15*(Supplement 1):S53–S64.

Harsch. E. (2004). South Africa marks a decade of freedom. Progress in many areas, but legacy of inequality runs deep. *Africa Renewal, 18*(2), July.

Jamieson, L., Proudlock, P., & Waterhouse, S. (2008). Key lesislative developements affecting children in 2007. In Proudlock, P., Dutschke, M., Jamieson, L., Monson, J., & Smith, C. (Eds). *South African child gauge:* (pp. 10–14). Cape Town: Children's Institute, University of Cape Town.

Loffell, J. (2008). Developmental social welfare and the child protection challenge in South Africa. *Practice: Social Work in Action, 20*(2):83–91.

Lombard, A. (2007). The impact of social welfare policies on social development in South Africa: An NGO prespective. *Social Work/Maatshaplike Werk, 43*(4):295–316.

Lombard, A. (2008a). The implementation of the white paper for social welfare: A ten-year review. Themed Issue. Ten years on: Challenges and innovation in developmental social welfare. *The Social Work Practitioner-Researcher, 20*(2):154–173.

Lombard, A. (2008b). Social change through integrated and economic development in South Africa: A social welfare perspective. *Journal of Comparative Social Welfare, 24*(1):23–32.

Lund, F. (2008). *Changing social policy. The child support grant in South Africa.* Cape Town: Human Sciences Research Council.

Meintjies, H., John-Langba, J. & Berry, L. (2008). Demography of South Africa's children. In Proudlock, P., Dutschke, M., Jamieson, L., Monson, J., & Smith, C. (Eds), *South African Child Gauge:* (pp. 64–70). Cape Town: Children's Institute, University of Cape Town.

Midgley, J. (1995). *Social development: The developmental perspective in social welfare.* London: SAGE Publications.

Midgley, J. (1996). Involving social work in economic development. *International Social Work, 39*(3):13–25.

Naidoo, V. (2006). Observations on defining a developmental state administration in South Africa. *Journal of Public Administration, 41*(3):479–489.

Patel, L. (2005). *Social welfare & social development.* Cape Town, Oxford University Press: Southern Africa.

Pendlebury, S. (2008). Foreword. In Proudlock, P., Dutschke, M., Jamieson, L., Monson, J., & Smith, C. (Eds.), *South African child gauge:* 6. Cape Town: Children's Institute, University of Cape Town.

Proudlock, P., & Jamieson, L. (2008). The Children's Act: Providing a strong legislative foundation for a developmental approach to child care and protection. In Proudlock, P., Dutschke, M., Jamieson, L., Monson, J., & Smith, C. (Eds.), *South African child gauge:* (pp. 35–40). Cape Town: Children's Institute, University of Cape Town.

Republic of South Africa. (1983). The Child Care Act. Act 74 of 1983. *Government Gazette,* (8765). Pretoria: Government Printer.

Republic of South Africa. (1994). White Paper on Reconstruction and Development. 1994. Notice No. 1954 of 1994. *Government Gazette,* 353(16085.23), November. Pretoria: Government Printers.

Republic of South Africa. (1996). *Constitution of South Africa.* Act 108 of 1996.

Republic of South Africa. (1997). Ministry for Welfare and Population Development. 1997. White Paper for Social Welfare. Notice 1108 of 1997. *Government Gazette,* 386(18166). Pretoria: Government Printers.

Republic of South Africa. (2005). Children's Act. No 38 of 2005. *Government Gazette,* Vol. 492., No. 28944. Cape Town. 19 June 2006.

Republic of South Africa. National Treasury. (2006a). *Budget Review 2006.* 15 February.

Republic of South Africa. (2006b). *State of the Nation Address of the President of South Africa.* Thabo Mbeki: Joint Sitting of Parliament, 3 February. http://www.info.gov.za/ speeches/ 2006/06021515501001.htm [Accessed on 4 February 2006].

Repulic of South Africa. (2006c). Department of Social Developement. *Children's Amendment Bill.* B9B-2006. http://www.dsd.gov.za [Accessed 1 April 2009].

Republic of South Africa. (2006d). *Accelerated and Shared Growth Initiative for South Africa* (AsgiSA). http://www.info.gov.za/asgisa/asgisa.htm [Accessed 8 March 2008].

Republic of South Africa. (2007a). *Budget Speech.* Minister of Finance, Trevor A. Manuel, MP. 21 February.

Republic of South Africa. (2007b). *Accelerated and Shared Growth Initiative for South Africa* (AsgiSA). http://www.info.gov.za/asgisa/asgisa.htm [Accessed on 8 March 2008].

Republic of South Africa. (2008a). *Budget Speech.* Minister of Finance, Trevor A. Manuel, MP. 20 February.

Republic of South Africa. (2008b). *Address by the Minister of Social Development, Dr. Zolo Skweyiya,* at the 'Getting South Africa ready to implement the Children's Act' Conference. 27 May.

Schoeman, M. (2001). South Africa's political economy in a global context. In Venter, A. (Ed.). *Government and politics in the new South Africa.* (2nd edn). Pretoria: Van Schaik Publishers.

September, R., & Dinbabo, M. (2008). Gearing up for implementation: A new Children's Act for South Africa. *Practice: Social Work in Action, 20*(2):113-122.

Sewpaul, V., & Hölsher, D. (2004). *Social work in times of neoliberalism. A postmodern discourse.* Pretoria:Van Schaik.

Smit, A. (2006). Funding strategies: Surviving imperial intentions, protean policies and ruthless reality. *Social Work/Maatskaplike Werk, 41(4)*:485-360.

Smith, C. (2008). Making the link between social services and social assistance. In Proudlock, P., Dutschke, M., Jamieson, L., Monson, J., & Smith, C. (Eds.), *South African child gauge:* (pp. 55–59). Cape Town: Children's Institute, University of Cape Town.

Statistics South Africa. (2008). *Mid-year population estimates 2008.* Statistical release. P0302. South African Government. 31 July 2008. www.statssa.go.za

Terreblanche, S. (2002). *A history of inequality in South Africa 1652–2002.* Pietermaritzburg: University of Natal Press and KMM Review Publishing Company (Pty) Ltd.

Thin, N. (2002). *Social progress and sustainable development.* Bloomfield, N: Kumarian Press, Inc.

United Nations Development Programme (UNDP) of South Africa. (2003). *South Africa Human Development Report 2003. The Challenge of Sustainable Development in South Africa: Unlocking People's Creativity.* Cape Town: Oxford University Press Southern Africa.

Chapter 17
Privatization Trends in Welfare Services and Their Impact upon Israel as a Welfare State

Joseph Katan and Ariela Lowenstein

Introduction

The implementation of a policy of privatization of social services is one of the hallmarks of recent changes in the character of the welfare state and in its practice in many Western countries. One consequence of such policies is that many of the services that governments and local authorities are legally obliged or wish to provide to various sectors of society are in fact delivered by non-governmental organizations (NGOs), including voluntary organizations and commercial enterprises. The process of privatization has assumed a variety of forms in these countries and to varying extents in all aspects of the spectrum of social services, including health, income support, education, housing, employment, and personal welfare services.

This chapter focuses on describing and analyzing the policy of privatization in Israel in one particular domain – that of personal welfare services. These services deal with the provision for essential needs of vulnerable individuals, families, and groups, namely, those who are unable or struggle to deal successfully with various hardships that impair their function and quality of life and make it difficult for them to integrate into society. These include, among others, the children and youth at risk, families in crisis, battered women, the handicapped elderly, the physically disabled, the mentally challenged, people battling addiction to drugs or alcohol, new immigrants, and the homeless.

The organizations operating in this domain provide a wide range of community-based and institutional services to these groups – including counseling, treatment, providing information and help (such as essential equipment for the home, for individuals, and for families), children and youth centers, retirement homes, institutions for people with mental or physical disabilities, day care centers, preschools and emergency centers for children, clubs, day centers and supportive communities for the elderly, housing solutions for the mentally and physically challenged within the community, shelters for battered women, and

J. Katan (✉)
School of Social Work, Tel-Aviv University, Tel-Aviv, Israel
e-mail: joseph@post.tau.ac.il

J. Powell, J. Hendricks, *The Welfare State in Post-Industrial Society*,
DOI 10.1007/978-1-4419-0066-1_17, © Springer Science+Business Media, LLC 2009

rehabilitation centers for people recovering from drug or alcohol addiction. The personal welfare services cater, in other words, to the needs of the weakest and most vulnerable sectors of society.

In the personal welfare services area in Israel, there has been an accelerated and comprehensive process of privatization in recent years, as clearly evident in two main phenomena. One is that a large part of national and municipal welfare services that the government and local authorities are legally obliged or wish to provide those in need are funded by the public purse, but delivered by NGOs. The other is that the lion's share of the government expenditure on personal welfare services is now handed over to the NGOs delivering the services. This chapter aims at examining this trend and gauging its ramifications for the function of the welfare services as a whole. This in turn will serve as the basis for understanding and evaluating the changes that Israel has been undergoing as a welfare state and for examining their significance.

The chapter consists of five parts. The first is devoted to clarifying what the privatization process means in the context of personal welfare services and to describing and analyzing its main constituents. In the second part, the principal arguments for and against privatization are presented. Part three reviews the extent of privatization in the personal welfare services in Israel, while part four discusses the main factors that have brought about the adoption and implementation of privatization of Israeli welfare services. Finally, the last part raises major issues concerning the assessment of the results of partial privatization of welfare services and their impact on the character of the welfare state in Israel. Additionally, preliminary conclusions are presented, drawn from a number of studies that examined various aspects of implementation of this policy in Israel.

The Concept of Privatization in the Context of Personal Welfare Services

In most welfare states, including Israel, there are three distinct frameworks for the delivery of personal welfare services to those in need (Carey, 2008; Ejsenstadt, 1996; Katan 2001, 2005, 2007; Katan & Lowenstein, 1999; Korazim-Korosy, Leibovitz & Schmid, 2005; Kramer 1994, 2000; Le-Grand, 1991; Schmid 2003; Werczberger & Katan, 2005; Wistow et al., 1996).

The first framework consists of national and municipal services provided exclusively by government ministries or local authorities. These determine which services are to be offered to citizens, decide who is eligible to receive them, provide funding, set out the conditions for their supply, and oversee their delivery. This arrangement of service delivery is in line with the aims of the traditional welfare state that emerged in the aftermath of World War II.

The second framework consists of national and municipal services delivered by NGOs. In this scheme, while government bodies and local authorities define the composition of services to be provided, provide full or partial funding, and determine eligibility, the actual delivery of these services is carried out by

NGOs, which serve, in effect, as the executive branch of the government ministries or municipalities, which also provide supervision. This arrangement, therefore, entails the privatization of the delivery of welfare services.

The third configuration consists of services provided by NGOs with no intervention by government or municipal bodies. They include both services that replicate those provided by the government or municipal services, as well as services that are not available from them.

This article deals with the second framework, which will henceforth be referred to as partial privatization. It is a characteristic of the changes that have occurred in recent years in the personal welfare services of many welfare states. In this scheme, the relationship between the government or municipalities and the NGOs responsible for providing the services is usually founded on a mutual contract that sets out the obligations and rights of both parties, such as quantity and quality of the services to be provided and their cost (Kramer, 1995; Peat & Costley, 2001).

This pattern of welfare services provision is known by a variety of names in the welfare states where it is practiced — such as "mixed economy," "quasi-markets," "welfare market," "welfare pluralism," and "the Contract Culture" (Ben-Ner, 2002; Doron, 1989; Glennerster & Le-Grand, 1994; Le-Grand, 1991; Wistow et al, 1996).

These names imply two central features of partial privatization: the participation of a variety of entities (government ministries, local authorities, voluntary organizations, commercial enterprises) in distributing services and the adoption of a number of aspects of the "market economy" in service delivery – such as the existence of several service providers, competition between them, and the ability of consumers to choose a provider of their choice. A typical "division of labor" between the public sector (government and municipal) and NGOs in the partial privatization scheme in Israel is presented in Table 17.1.

Table 17.1 Division of labor between government and NGOs in the partial privatization scheme of welfare services

Task	Responsible body
Defining the basket of services	Government or municipal
Determining eligibility for receiving services	Government or municipal
Service funding	Government, municipal; occasionally with partial participation by the consumer
Manufacturing and provision of service	NGOs (under Government or municipal supervision)

Two additional forms of partial privatization of welfare services have emerged and expanded in recent years in Israel and in other Western countries. One is the creation of partnerships between municipalities and NGOs to expand existing services and/or to develop new services. The initiative for such partnerships comes from either the municipality or the NGO (usually a nonprofit organization) – or both; the funding of the service is shared between them (albeit not necessarily equally); and the service is usually provided by the NGO, with a shared steering committee governing the delivery (Katan, 2005). The other new form of partial privatization involves the contractual hiring of employees in government ministries – such as the Welfare Ministry and the municipal welfare departments through external organizations.

What brought about this change in the delivery of social services? Which factors were instrumental in resisting such change? These questions are examined in Part II.

The Pros and Cons of Implementing Privatization Policy in Welfare Services

Various arguments in many publications have been raised in favor of and against the adoption and implementation of the notion of partial privatization of social services, in general, and personal welfare services, in particular, in Israel and other Western countries (Cnaan, 1995; Dolev 2005; Doron, 1989; Ejsenstadt, 1996; Glennerster &Le-Grand, 1994; Gotwein, 2006; Grindheim & Selle, 1990; Katan, 2001; Korazim-Korosy, Leibovitz & Schmid, 2005; Kramer 1994; Marsland, 1996; Milward & Provan, 2003; Schmid 2001; Schmid, 2003; Statham, 1996; Taylor-Gooby, 1998; Wistow et al., 1996).

Advocates of privatization raise four main arguments in favor of such a policy:

1. **Dissatisfaction with the adverse outcomes of the delivery of social services exclusively by the public sector (i.e., government and local authorities).** Public-only delivery is associated with a number of failings and disadvantages: mismanagement; inefficiency; high expenditure leading to wasted resources; maintaining bloated and rigid bureaucratic systems bent only self-preservation; inability to adapt to environmental changes; intervention of political considerations in decision-making; low staff motivation; difficulty in dismissing inefficient employees due to excessive power of professional unions; lack of competition; and denial of choice from service consumers. The net outcome of all these factors is a reduced quality of services and excessive government control over the lives of citizens.

2. **Advantages of the "market economy."** Privatization injects elements of the market economy into the delivery of welfare services, thus allowing consumers to choose their service provider and conversely to leave a provider who does not meet their expectations. The awareness of service providers that consumers may choose motivates them into providing high-quality services to attract consumers. The competition between providers spurs them into demonstrating flexibility and innovation and achieving efficiency in using the public funds given to them. According to pro-privatization advocates, the efficiency of the NGOs is proven, among other things, by the fact that the

cost of providing national and municipal services through them is lower than through national or municipal bodies.

3. **Integration of voluntary organizations and commercial enterprises in the domain of welfare services, thereby extending the scope of their activity and maximizing their potential.** Voluntary organizations are the backbone of the "civil society" and boast of a number of distinctive features that set them apart from other types of organization: they are not motivated by profit; they have a low level of bureaucracy (thereby enhancing their flexibility and adaptability to change); they encourage the involvement of volunteers; are committed to providing services to the weaker sections of society; have a tradition of cultivating social capital; they have a democratic form of management and ability to recruit funds and resources.

Commercial enterprises are also distinctive, by virtue of their emphasis on efficiency, the adoption of innovative management techniques, and organizational flexibility.

Expanding the activities of voluntary and commercial organizations into the welfare services arena may, according to the advocates of privatization, allow these attributes to be expressed more fully and lead to a widening of the scope of social services to various sectors of the population and to an improvement of their quality.

4. **Focusing government at national and municipal level on the tasks of defining the policy, of coordination and regulation.** A wide-scale involvement of NGOs in delivering services at national and municipal levels may allow the government and municipalities to avoid the heavy and expensive burden involved in providing the wide range of services required by various sectors and to focus instead, at the national and local levels, on the tasks of defining the policy, coordinating and regulating.

As we see, proponents of privatization call for the acceleration of privatizing social services for a wide range of reasons, ranging from ideological arguments rooted in a neoliberal outlook that focuses on the risks involved in excessive involvement of the public sector in the lives of citizens to more practical arguments concerning the bureaucratic and political nature of government organizations which interferes with their ability to handle the wide range of issues efficiently and the high cost of social services and its adverse economic consequences for the taxpayer.

They believe in the unique contribution of the commercial sector to economic growth – which they regard as the principal driver in reducing poverty and gaps between the rich and the poor – therefore seeking to bring about a significant overhaul in the way in which the state operates in the field of social services.

Conversely, opponents of privatization cast doubt on its ability to achieve the benefits hailed by its proponents and point to a number of unfavorable phenomena that may accompany its implementation:

1. **Undesirable changes in the rights and duties of government institutions at both national and municipal levels.** Privatization may adversely affect the range of

obligations and rights of the public sector in the area of welfare services. As previously noted, some advocates of privatization favor the move of government organizations away from the role of service provider to that of the service *purchaser*, since in this way they may be liberated from the considerable burden of providing services and focus instead on formulating policy, providing guidelines, coordinating, and regulating. However, the opponents of privatization cast doubt on the chances of this goal being achieved and point to the risk that outsourcing responsibility for service provision to nongovernmental bodies will undermine the state's commitment to the more vulnerable classes in society and impair the social rights of its citizens.

Moreover, far from easing the administrative burden on the public sector, the entry of a large number of organizations into the welfare arena in the wake of privatization may in fact increase the burden on it, making it difficult for the government and municipalities to provide the necessary guidance and supervision over service providers. This burden will be felt in particular by the social workers in municipal welfare departments, who will be obliged as a result to limit their direct contact with individuals and families and focus instead on various administrative duties for which they were not trained. Privatization may thus bring about a weakening of the state's involvement in the social realm, accelerate the development of a "hollow state," and seriously compromise the state's ability to ensure the welfare of its citizens.

2. **Limited competition between service providers**. Limited competition may result from overt or covert pacts between the service providers or from the domination of the service field by one or a handful of organizations at the expense of others. Such developments may make it difficult to maintain true competition between the organizations and to limit the actual choice offered to consumers.

3. **The refusal of NGOs to provide certain services.** Such a refusal may result from the unwillingness of voluntary organizations to relinquish their independent status vis-à-vis municipal authorities, or from the reluctance of private/commercial enterprises to work under the government direction.

4. **Termination of service by nongovernmental service providers.** Such an eventuality may come about when a given organization has failed to compete successfully with other providers, is unwilling to continue to abide by the conditions of contract with the "service buyers" (i.e. the government and/or municipalities), or has had its contract with the service buyers discontinued. Those most affected by such a termination will be the former consumers of said organizations, as in the case of the residents of a retirement home that is closed down.

5. **Difficulty of consumers in switching service providers.**The choice of providers trumpeted by the advocates of privatization may in practice be hampered by factors relating to the consumers themselves, such as lack of education or experience, lack of information about the activities of the service providers,

or difficulty in understanding professional information. Under these circumstances, consumers may find it difficult to act rationally and choose an organization that best meets their needs. The challenge facing consumers in choosing a suitable provider is compounded when the information provided is of a professional nature, requiring a high level of knowledge and comprehension. This highlights the inherent asymmetry in the encounter between a disparate group of individual consumers, on the one hand, and well-organized, sophisticated providers, on the other, who are equipped with a wide range of ways and means to win over the individual consumer. In such an encounter, many consumers may find themselves at a disadvantage and an easy prey for service providers out to market their products.

6. **Low cost of services achieved mainly by employing underpaid staff.** Even allowing for the argument that some national and municipal services cost less when provided by NGOs compared with public offerings, this is often the result of low wages, inferior working conditions, and exploitation of many of the staff at these organizations. This adverse impact on the conditions of workers is largely due to the fact that many of them are not unionized and due to the cap set by the government or municipal authorities on the rates of services provided.

7. **Privatization does not guarantee a lower cost of services.** Some researchers point out that partial privatization does not necessarily reduce the cost of services and may even lead to its increase, for two main reasons: first, the need of government and municipal bodies to manage the many NGOs operating as service providers entails carrying out a wide range of duties, such as negotiations, contract signing, oversight, etc. To perform these duties adequately may require the hiring of extra staff as well as an increased budget. And second, the NGOs, which in many cases have become the de facto providers of many welfare services, may band together and bring pressure to bear upon the "service buyers" (i.e., the governmental authorities) to increase the fiscal resources allocated to funding the service provision. The ability of governmental authorities to resist such pressures is not assured, given their reliance on the service providers. In the long term, therefore, privatization of service provisions may actually bring about an increase in costs.

8. **Erosion of the distinctive attributes of voluntary organizations and private/ commercial enterprise.** There is a distinct risk that partial privatization may affect the structure and operation of organizations providing national and municipal services, due to their dependence on public funding, and to the nature of the contractual basis of the relationship between the "service buyers" and the service providers, which commits them to a given activity. As a consequence, some of the distinctive characteristics of voluntary organizations – such as operational independence, structural flexibility, proactive development of new services, democratic management, and representing the interests of consumers toward local authorities – may be compromised.

The dependence on public funding and the obligation to maintain contractual undertakings with the "service buyers" may lead to a similar erosion of distinctive organizational attributes of private/commercial enterprises involved in the provision of national or municipal services.

9. **Diminished territorial equality.** The proliferation of organizations in the arena of welfare services may adversely impact the degree of equality in the scope and quality of services provided to the populations of different communities. The champions of privatization assume that the more NGOs are involved in providing services, the more likely the social potential in the communities they serve will be fulfilled. Detractors of privatization, however, warn of the dangers in adopting such a position, given the great variations between the respective social potential of various towns and villages and their ability to deal with various social problems without significant help from the government. An overreliance on "community potential" and subsequent reduction in state involvement may, therefore, bring about an increased disparity between communities favored with a rich network of voluntary organizations and members of high social potential and less fortunate communities where such resources are lacking.

Table 17.2 summarizes the arguments raised for and against partial privatization of welfare services.

Table 17.2 Arguments for and against privatization of welfare services

For	Against
Reduction of incidence of failures associated with government organizations	May ultimately lead to the retreat of government entirely from the arena of welfare services and from its commitment to the welfare of its citizens
Empowering of consumers by providing them with greater choice of service provider	Risk of limited competition – or conversely unrestrained competition between providers, thereby harming consumers
Improvement in quality of services due to competition between providers	Limited de facto choice for consumers
Increased efficiency of services in terms of costs and benefits	Lower quality of services due to commercial enterprises' greater concern for profit-making
Reduced cost of service delivery	
Broader scope of services, thanks to the entry of more organizations into the welfare arena	Proliferation of providers creates fragmented and over-complex system, marked by service duplication and lack of coordination
Maximizing the potential inherent in voluntary organizations and commercial enterprises	Difficulties in maintaining adequate regulatory oversight over nongovernmental operations
Frees public institutions from the burden of direct services in favor of formulating policy, regulation, and coordination	Lower pay and inferior working conditions for employees of service providers
Fund-raising and investment by NGOs yields more resources for services provision	Possible increase in cost of services due to the need to recruit more staff in the public sector dealing with regulation and coordination and due to pressure by service providers
	Risk of refusal by NGOs to provide services

To what extent were these arguments taken into account when the proposal to privatize welfare services in Israel was being considered? Does implementation of this policy reflect a certain bias in favor of the warnings about the inherent risks involved, or was it swayed more by its purported advantages? Does the fact that privatization has been only partial represent an attempt to obtain the best of both worlds, namely, to extract its benefits while minimizing its possible disadvantages by stressing the roles of government and municipalities in providing guidance and regulation? Does privatization in fact diminish the state's influence in social services and thus contribute to the formation of a "hollow state" that divests itself of its commitment to its citizens?

An examination of the scope of partial privatization of personal welfare services in Israel suggests that its proponents won out during its conception.

The Scope of Privatization of Personal Welfare Services

The responsibility for providing personal welfare services in Israel lies mainly with the welfare departments of the local authorities, although most fiscal resources funding such services are controlled by the national government. The municipal welfare departments provide a broad range of community-based and institutional services for the elderly, children, youth, the mentally challenged, the physically disabled, families, people suffering from drug or alcohol addiction, ex-convicts and their families, new immigrants, and the homeless. In the following section, we shall illustrate the extent of privatization of service delivery by presenting its scope in some of these areas (Ben-Zvi, 2001; Dolev, 2005; Ejsenstadt, 1996; Katan, 1996, 2001, 2005; Korazim, 2001; Korazim-Korosy, Leibovitz, & Schmid, 2005; Keinan & Lachman, 1997; Schmid, 2001; Werczberger & Katan, 2005).

Services for the Elderly

All institutional services for the elderly (retirement homes and sheltered housing) are provided by NGOs – be they nonprofit associations or private/commercial enterprises. These organizations also provide most community-based services for the elderly – including home care services, day centers, supportive communities, social clubs, hot meals, respite centers, home-based occupational programs, appliances supply centers, repair patrols, information centers, and programs for promoting healthy living.

The municipal welfare services departments, nevertheless, continue to fulfill a number of roles in the area of services to the elderly: steering the operations of the local home-care committees which determine the basket of services provided to those eligible; personal counseling for the elderly on various issues; initiating and running programs and services (delivered usually by other organizations), providing professional guidance, and helping in the placement of individuals in institutions.

Services for Children

In all municipal authorities, with the exception of Tel-Aviv, services for children outside the home (such as boarding schools and foster homes) are provided by NGOs. These also provide the greater part of community-based services, such as play centers, afternoon child-care facilities, preschools, day care centers, emergency centers for children at risk, supervised visitation centers, day-schools, and summer camps.

The welfare departments continue to fulfill the following roles: the activities of welfare officials responsible by law to ensure adequate protection for children at risk through various types of intervention, initiating various community-based programs for children and parents (whose operation is then typically handed over to NGOs); individual and group-based treatments for children and their parents; providing guidance to the organizations providing services to children; and preparing reports for the courts.

Services for the Mentally Challenged

Most institutional services (day-care centers) for the mentally challenged are run by NGOs. They also provide most community-based services for this sector – such as hostels and housing within the community, sheltered employment enterprises, social clubs, children day centers, diagnostic services, respite centers, and personal tuition.

For their part, municipal welfare services focus mainly on providing the following services: counselling and individual treatment of the mentally challenged and their families; placement in institutions; initiating and developing community-based services (delivered in the main by NGOs); counseling the NGOs delivering the community-based services and monitoring them.

The services that remain in the hands of municipal welfare departments: counseling and individual treatment of the physically disabled and their families and professional guidance to the NGOs providing the community-based services.

In all three service areas surveyed above, NGOs play a central part, but in other sectors – such as families and youth, people with addiction problems, ex-convicts, and the homeless – they also play a prominent role.

The wide scope of privatization of personal welfare services in Israel demonstrates clearly and unequivocally the impact that implementation of this social policy has had on the structure of welfare services and the welfare state's methods of operation. This impact is evident in several ways:

1. Most citizens in need of personal welfare services receive them from NGOs.
2. Most government expenditure on welfare services is channeled through NGOs.
3. The role of welfare services and many of their staff has profoundly changed, as it now centers on the tasks of an administrative nature, such as negotiating with other organizations, overseeing their operations, and writing reports.

4. Hundreds of voluntary and commercial organizations have entered into the system of welfare services. This trend is turning the welfare system into a crowded arena.
5. Privatization has led to a large-scale entry of commercial enterprises into the welfare arena as providers of national and municipal services, whose values and norms may also impact these services.

A survey of welfare services in Israel clearly shows, therefore, that in the debate over privatization, its proponents have had the upper hand. What has brought about such a large-scale enactment of privatization policy in Israel?

Factors Influencing the Implementation of Privatization Policy

The policy of privatization in Israel was instigated by the Ministry of Finance and formed a central plank of a wide-ranging strategy by the government to promote privatization in various spheres of its activity. This approach stemmed from the belief of most Israeli finance ministers in the principles of the market economy and was heavily influenced by Israel's conforming with worldwide globalization trends, such as joining international treaties like the General Agreement on Trade in Services (GATS) which encourage privatization. However, this policy has also been supported by ministers of welfare and most senior officials of that ministry, as well as by many directors of municipal welfare services. This support is largely due to the fact that the policy of partial privatization ensures that a number of key roles (such as financing, determining the basket of services and its eligibility, regulation, etc.) remain in the hands of national and municipal authorities and allow them to continue to be a dominant player in the services system, and because certain services (such as boarding schools and children day centers) have traditionally been provided by NGOs and therefore privatizing their delivery is not seen as either particularly problematic or radical per se, but merely an extension of an existing framework.

Of course, the policy is also supported by the NGOs themselves, since it has led to a considerable expansion of their operations and made them the beneficiaries of extensive financing from national and municipal sources.

The consensus between the government and most local authorities and NGOs over the privatization of welfare services in Israel is reflected in a range of operations, initiatives, and resolutions, some of which are presented below (Dolev, 2005; Iecovich & Katan, 2005; Katan, 2001, 2005; Korazim, 2001; Korazim-Korosy, Leibovitz & Schmid, 2005; Schmid, 2001).

The involvement of the Ministry of Welfare and of local authorities in establishing voluntary organizations to deal with planning and provision of welfare services for the elderly, for children, for youth, and for other sectors such as the physically disabled and the mentally challenged.

- Transfer of management of foster families from local authorities to NGOs
- Placing the provision of home care for the elderly in the hands of NGOs
- Privatizing government day-care centers for youth, for the mentally challenged, and for the physically disabled
- Making the transfer of government budgets to local authorities conditional upon outsourcing certain programs to NGOs
- Hiring staff at the Ministry of Welfare and in the municipal welfare departments on a contractual basis through voluntary organizations and commercial enterprises, rather than as standard employees.

Surprisingly, the wholesale implementation of privatization of welfare services has taken place without any significant public debate, where the various arguments for and against it could be systematically scrutinized. Even after the policy had begun to be implemented, resistance to it was only partial and stemmed from three main sources:

- Public sector staff, such as those at government institutions for the mentally challenged, who feared this would adversely affect their wages, their working conditions, and their right to organize. This fear is linked to the fact that one of the impacts of privatization is a change in the patterns of employment, such as the use of individual employment contracts as opposed to collective agreements, and the transition from direct employment to work on contract via an employment agency.
- Serviced client families, who objected to the privatization of government day centers for the mentally challenged, for fear that this would result in a deterioration in the quality of service provided.
- Several prominent researchers in the welfare field in Israel, who pointed out that the policy of privatization is part of an effort to undermine the welfare state and the state's responsibility for the welfare of its citizens. This objection was expressed mainly in professional papers (Doron, 1989; Gal, 1994) and articles in the press and expressing opinions at professional conferences.

These objections did not prevent the comprehensive implementation of the privatization policy, and at most brought about a delay in privatizing certain services, such as government institutions for the mentally challenged.

The wide-scale implementation of the policy of partial privatization of personal welfare services in Israel is a sign, as we said, that its advocates prevailed, but it is also worth examining the question: has privatization delivered the benefits anticipated by its advocates, or have the negative consequences that its opponents warned about been realized? Has privatization indeed hastened the collapse of the welfare state and the state's abandonment of its commitment to protect the social rights of its citizens – or is it merely a sign that the welfare state may be evolving but nevertheless alive and well and continues to govern the welfare of its citizens?

In part three, we shall attempt to answer these questions.

Implementation of Partial Privatization in Welfare Services – Preliminary Conclusions

The arguments put forward by advocates and opponents to privatization of welfare services highlight a series of questions and issues, the examination of which should serve as the basis for evaluating the outcomes of this policy. These are as follows:

- **The status and role of the government and local authorities**. How does privatization affect the ability of the government and local authorities to control the delivery of services to the population when this is in the hands of NGOs, and thereby implement its policy and aims in the area of welfare? Is partial privatization merely a prelude to full privatization? Does it reflect the decline of the welfare state and the emergence of the toothless "hollow state" – or does it allow the state to retain its ability to leave its stamp on how welfare services are delivered?
- **The ability of NGOs to provide a wide range of national and municipal services – and to continue to do so in the long run**. The privatization policy is based on the government's assumption that NGOs are capable of taking on the task of delivering a wide range of national and municipal services to a large number of consumers. Have these organizations picked up the gauntlet and met this challenge? If so, are they continuing to fulfill their mission over the long run?
- **Service delivery to the disadvantaged and to remote communities**. Has the outsourcing of service delivery to NGOs – some of which are profit-oriented – brought about preferential service to the privileged sections of society at the expense of weaker sections and remote communities?
- **Staff wages and working conditions.** How has partial privatization affected the levels of pay and working conditions of staff – both in the public sector and in the NGOs? Has it indeed brought about a significant decline in both?
- **The quality of staff providing the services.** Do the staff of the nongovernmental service providers share the same standard, quality, and commitment as their counterparts in the public sector?
- **Status and roles of professional staff in government and in local authorities.** How has privatization affected the functions of professional social services staff in the public sector and their ability to fulfill their values and professional expectations? Has it indeed significantly reduced the scope of their professional work and led many of them to focus on administrative tasks?
- **Governmental and public regulation.** One of the cornerstones of the partial privatization policy is the existence of a governmental/public regulatory mechanism to examine the extent to which the operations of the service providers meet the standards set out in their contractual undertakings. Does such regulation indeed exist? Is it achieving its aims?
- **Effect on voluntary organizations.** How does the participation of voluntary organizations in delivering national and municipal services impact upon their adherence to their founding principles – such as social commitment,

democratic management, and independence of public authorities – and the fact that they are part of the civil society?

- **Effect on commercial enterprises.** What effect has involvement in delivering national and municipal services had on commercial providers?
- **Competition between service providers.**Is there in fact true and fair competition between the organizations providing the services, and do consumers benefit from this competition?
- **Choice available to consumers.**Does privatization indeed empower consumers by enabling them to choose between service providers and to leave those who do not adequately meet their needs?
- **Cost of services.**Has service provision by NGOs brought about the anticipated reduction in the cost of delivery, compared to government or municipal institutions? If so, how has this been achieved?
- **Additional resources.**Are the NGOs investing in the delivery of national and municipal services' resources over and above what they receive from government or local authorities?
- **Use of profits/surpluses.**Has the participation of NGOs in the provision of national and municipal services been profitable for them? If so, how are these profits (in the case of commercial organizations) or surpluses (in the case of voluntary organizations) invested? Are they channeled, in full or in part, to developing and maintaining services, or to other purposes?
- **Initiative and innovation.** Are the NGOs showing initiative or innovation in their delivery of national and municipal services, beyond their contractual obligations with government and local authorities?
- **Proliferation of organizations.** Privatization has brought about a proliferation of organizations involved in the arena of welfare services. How has this affected the various players in this arena – including service consumers, government ministries, and voluntary or commercial organizations?

To date, few studies have been carried out on the privatization of delivery of national and municipal welfare services in Israel. Those that have covered only some of the services detailed above and provide only preliminary answers to some of the issues and questions raised. It is also worth noting that these studies examined the privatization of service provision mainly from the viewpoint of the service providers and only to a limited degree from the standpoint of service consumers. These studies, therefore, provide only a very partial picture of the outcomes of privatization.

The picture from all these studies as to the central issues arising from the implementation of privatization and its outcomes, as cited by its advocates and detractors, is as follows:

- **The status and role of government and local authorities.** One of the fundamental principles of the partial privatization policy is to preserve the status of the government and local authorities in shaping the welfare policy and in steering the operation of the organizations which have assumed the responsibility of providing services. In other words, the government at national and local levels is supposed to continue to function as the central and predominant player in the arena of welfare services.

Several studies indicate while national government and local authorities do still prescribe which services are to be provided to various sectors of society, the supervision that they maintain over the operation of many service providers is patchy and, in quite a few instances, ineffective (Schmid & Sabagh, 1990, 1991; State Comptroller, 2005). This weakness is due to both the sheer number of organizations operating in the services arena and the limited number of staff engaged in regulation and the considerable burden placed on them. Moreover, the ability of the government and the authorities to play the role of the "main player" guiding the operation of the service sector has been undermined by the fact that the NGOs are now the de facto dominant players in many of the services and are thus acquiring expertise and experience that are often no longer available to the public institutions, at national or local levels.

While the NGOs are dependent on public funding, the government and local authorities are equally dependent on these organizations, inasmuch as without them these services could no longer be provided. In many services, the non-governmental service providers have ceased to play the supporting role operating in accordance with guidelines prescribed by the "main player" and have begun to attempt – at times successfully – to constrain the government's ability to shape and implement policy as demonstrated by the success of companies providing home care services for the elderly in delaying publication of a new tender for services for a long time. However, in other areas, such as foster services for children, the government is still the "main player" and continues fairly successfully to steer the operations of NGOs handling foster families (Korazim-Korosy, Leibovitz & Schmid, 2005).

- **The state's commitment to the welfare of its citizens.** Partial privatization has indeed weakened the ability of the state and local authorities in determining the character of welfare services. However, the argument that this policy is nothing more than creeping privatization and represents "the thin edge of the wedge" that will ultimately lead to full privatization and the complete withdrawal of government and local authorities from the responsibility to ensure welfare services to those in need has not been borne out by the evidence. In none of the aforementioned areas has partial privatization led to full-scale privatization.
- **The willingness of NGOs to deliver national and municipal services.** The NGOs have risen to the challenge put to them by government and local authorities and have willingly assumed the role of delivering welfare services. There has not been a single instance where the Ministry of Welfare and/or local authorities have encountered difficulties in "recruiting" service providers. In fact, the policy of privatization has encouraged the establishment of many new organizations eager to enter the domain of social services. This has been clearly demonstrated by dozens of new organizations set up in the area of home care services for the elderly (Schmid & Borowski, 2000).

- **Continuity and persistence in service provision.** The Israeli experience, to date, demonstrates that the overwhelming majority of NGOs that have begun to operate as providers of national and municipal services have continued to do so over a long term. Only a handful of instances have been recorded where organizations have ceased operations, and in these cases, it was at the instigation of the government and/or the local authority which chose to discontinue the contractual agreement. It is also worth noting that termination of operations in these instances did not present a problem, given the many organizations available to take over.
- **Territorial equality.** The fear that outsourcing responsibility for providing services to NGOs may adversely affect the right of weaker sectors of society and residents of remote or disadvantaged communities to receive adequate services has not borne out. In fact, the implementation of the Long Term Care Insurance Law indicates that the privatization of home care services has created a competition between the service providers in a bid to "capture" every possible consumer, which in turn has maximized utilization for this service in communities throughout the country (Katan & Lowenstein, 1999).
- **Quality of services.** Studies that have examined this issue suggest that the quality of services provided by NGOs is good (Korazim-Korosy, Leibovitz & Schmid, 2005; Luski & Givon, 2005; Schmid, 2001; Schmid & Sabagh, 1990, 1991) and indeed equal in this respect to services provided by the public sector. This is apparent in services such as institutions for the mentally challenged, which are catered for by both public and private organizations (Keinan & Lachman, 1997; Levi, 2007) Some studies even point to a high level of satisfaction among clients of the NGOs. That said, there have been reports in the media of instances of low-quality services by NGOs, such as serious deficiencies in hostels maintained by a nonprofit association to replace conventional detention centers for youth detained for interrogation by police (Sinai, 2008).
- **Consumer choice.** This issue has been investigated in several studies, which indicate that privatization of service provision has indeed led to the simultaneous entry of several organizations into the arena in most service areas, thereby providing consumers with a true choice of service providers. However, in practice, this option has been exploited only to a limited degree, for two reasons: insufficient information about the organizations to enable an informed choice; and aggressive marketing by the service providers in an effort to "capture" as many consumers as possible before they had the chance to evaluate their options properly. "Capturing" of this sort has been particularly prevalent in the area of home care services for the elderly (Abbou, 2007). It is also worth noting that, in some service areas, such as day centers for children, many communities had no choice whatsoever, as only one service venue was on offer. The expectation, therefore, that privatizing service provision would empower consumers has been only partially proven.
- **Reduced costs.** Evidence from several sources indicates that privatization has indeed brought about a reduction in the costs involved in service delivery. For example, the per capita cost in government-run homes for the elderly

and institutions for the mentally challenged is higher than in nongovernmental ones (Levi, 2007) – due mainly to the differences in the number of
staff employed, their remuneration, and working conditions. However, it is
also worth noting that the wages of NGO staff are often a function of the
level of income their employers receive from the government for providing
these services.

- **Differences between public organizations, voluntary organizations, and commercial organizations.** One of the most interesting questions regarding privatization is whether there are differences between the various types of organization engaged in delivering welfare services. Studies that have examined this issue have looked at three principal aspects: the quality of services provided by the various organizations; their structural and functional attributes; and the skills of their staff and their attitudes toward their work and organizations.

Schmid (2001, 2002), who compared the quality of home care services for the
elderly provided by voluntary organizations and commercial enterprises, found
no substantial differences between them with regard to adapting the service to
their clients' needs, in the number of complaints made by their clients and in the
general level of satisfaction. However, Luski and Givon (2005) found that retirement homes run by voluntary organizations provide a higher quality service
compared to those belonging to commercial enterprises. Keinan and Lachman
(1997), comparing between private (mostly commercial) and government-run
institutions for the mentally challenged, found the quality of services to be higher
at the private institutions. Similarly, Korazim-Korosy, Leibovitz and Schmid
(2005), who studied the outcomes of outsourcing management of foster families
by local authorities to voluntary organizations, report a great improvement in the
quality of services as a result.

With regard to the effect of privatization on the attributes of voluntary
organizations engaged in providing national and municipal services, several
studies (Bar-Almog & Schmid, 2008; Iecovich & Katan, 2005; Koresh, 2003;
Schmid 2001; Zichlinsky, 2007) point to a blurring of many of the differences
between them and commercial enterprises and to an erosion of many of their
unique attributes that used to make them distinctive – such as the creation of
new services to meet the needs of consumers who are not catered for by the
government, local authorities, or commercial enterprises; representing the
interests of various sectors of society toward national and local authorities
and initiating changes in their policies; emphasizing the importance of volunteers; and democratic management. Moreover, many of these organizations
have adopted a commercial orientation, as evident in their recruitment of
managers of a business background and professional staff, thereby undermining the status of their volunteers. Although these changes stem from the
voluntary organizations' desire to improve their ability to compete against
commercial enterprises engaged in providing similar services, they have nevertheless obscured the differences between the guiding values and organizational

attributes of these two types of organization and to a gradual disappearance of the distinctiveness of the voluntary organizations.

Another issue examined in several studies is the difference in the attributes and attitudes of the staff employed in various types of organizations. The most comprehensive study in this area in Israel, to date, has been that of Freund (2005), who surveyed the attributes and views of some 500 social workers employed by 43 public organizations, 18 voluntary ones, and 15 commercial enterprises, all providing identical services. The study's findings indicate that while the absolute majority of staff in public organizations (approximately 70 percent) have tenure and are employed on a full-time basis, just over half of the workers in commercial firms (51 percent) are employed on personal contract, and only 44 percent of them have tenure. In voluntary organizations, approximately 58 percent of staff have tenure and 35 percent are employed on personal contract. With regard to qualifications, the highest percentage of staff with a master's degree is to be found in voluntary organizations (38 percent), while in both public and commercial firms, the percentage is around 31 percent.

The attitudes of social workers in the three types of organizations toward various aspects of their work and toward their organizations are generally similar and positive. However, in certain aspects, such as emotional commitment to the organization, commitment to the profession, and job satisfaction, the voluntary organizations appear to have the edge over other types, with commercial firms in second place and public sector coming last. Ben-Zvi (2006), comparing between instructors at publicly run youth centers and those owned by voluntary organizations, also found a higher level of organizational commitment within voluntary organizations.

Ronen-Yipargan (2006), however, reported different findings in her comparison between the attitudes of social workers toward their place of work and their employers at 13 organizations providing community-based services for the elderly (three municipal social services departments, four voluntary organizations, and six commercial organizations). Her study found a clear advantage for the departments of social services over other types of organization with regard to organizational and professional commitment, satisfaction with the organization and with work, and the perception of organizational environment. In second place came the voluntary organizations, with commercial enterprises coming last. Notably, the staff at the commercial organizations also testified that their employers placed a strong emphasis on profit-making and felt a high degree of incongruity between their professional values and the tasks they were asked to carry out, with the staff in voluntary organizations coming in second place in this regard. The staff of all three types of organizations, however, stated that their organizations placed a strong emphasis on the quality of service.

A preliminary look at how social worker employees of welfare departments in Israel view privatization is provided by Werczberger and Katan (2005). This study interviewed the staff of various ranks belonging to seven departments undergoing privatization. It found a wide variety in workers' views toward the partial privatization and its impact. Most support privatization and in

continuing to implement it, but with many the support is qualified and somewhat ambivalent. Most workers single out the contribution privatization has
made to the increase in innovation and variety of services offered to consumers
and the reduction in the cost of delivery. Nearly half of those interviewed
estimate that privatization has led to an improvement of the quality of services
and only few thought that they have deteriorated as a result. The remainder
have not formed a definite opinion on the matter.

Privatization has been most problematic, in the view of most of those
interviewed, in two areas: the confidence in continued delivery of services and
in their consistency across different communities. Most believe that privatization guarantees neither, and indeed may lead to a decline in services to certain
parts of the population. Most of the workers also reported that the regulatory
system of the service providers is patchy and inadequate and that since the
advent of privatization, their roles have changed. The picture that arises, therefore, from this partial and preliminary evaluation of the results of privatization
of welfare services in Israel, is a complex and contradictory one, which makes it
difficult to draw unequivocal conclusions for a clear-cut policy in this area.

Summary

The policy of privatizing of social services is perceived in recent years as one of
the major transformations of the welfare state and is thus at the center of public
debate in Israel, as in many other countries. This chapter has focused on one of
the main components of these services – personal welfare services – and has
sought to review and examine the privatization trends that have taken place in
them in recent years, in terms of their scope and their impact on the nature of the
welfare state in Israel. The central question examined in this chapter is whether
partial privatization has indeed brought about a substantive change in Israel's
commitment to its citizens.

The various attempts at gauging the results of the policy of partial privatization of welfare services, as described in this chapter, present an incomplete
picture that may provide ammunition to both supporters of privatization and
its opponents. Those in favor of privatization will undoubtedly emphasize the
fact that many of the arguments of those who objected to it have been dis-
proved. It appears that partial privatization has not led to the departure of the
state or of local authorities from the welfare arena and that NGOs have not
hesitated to assume the responsibility for a wide range of national and municipal services to the needy populations in both central and remote communities,
based on contractual and binding undertakings with national and local governments. The overwhelming majority of these have also maintained this service in
the long term. Moreover, the services provided by these organizations cost less
and are of equal or superior quality to those provided directly by government
and local authorities. Conversely, opponents of privatization will call attention

to its failings: the patchy and inadequate regulation by the state and local authorities over the delivery of welfare services and their diminished ability to direct the operations of the NGOs; the often restricted choice of options offered to consumers; the aggressive marketing by service providers; the low levels of pay and unfavorable working conditions of many NGO staff; the reported instances from time to time of serious deficiencies in the function of some of these organizations; and the erosion of the distinctive attributes of voluntary organizations.

In summary, therefore, it appears that, while partial privatization of welfare services reflects certain changes in the Israeli welfare state, it cannot be seen as a symptom of its decline.

References

Abbou, I. (2007). Attitudes and decision making in the elderly home care mixed market in Israel. *Civil Society and the Third Sector in Israel, 1*(2): 75–96 [in Hebrew].

Bar-Almog, M., & Schmid, H. (2008). *Political representation of third sector organizations providing social services*. Synopsis presented at the fifth annual conference for the study of social policy. Sapir Academic College [in Hebrew].

Ben-Ner, A. (2002). The shift in boundaries of the mixed economy and the future of the non-profit sector. *Annals of Public and Comparative Economics, 73*(1), 5–40.

Ben-Zvi, A. (2006). Differences in satisfaction and effective and continuous organizational commitment of instructors at occupational rehabilitation centers in the public and third sectors. Masters dissertation, Haifa University, Faculty of Welfare & Health Services, School of Social Work [in Hebrew].

Ben-Zvi, B. (2001). Long Term Care Insurance Law – reflections and implications for the future. *Social Security, 60*, 31–45 [in Hebrew].

Carey, M. (2008). What difference does it make? Contrasting organization and converging outcomes regarding the privatization of state social work in England and Canada. *International Social Work, 51*(1), 83–94.

Cnaan, R. (1995). Purchase of services contracting: A symbiosis of voluntary organizations, government and clients. *Journal of Health and Human Services Administration, 18*(1), 104–128.

Dolev, E. (2005). Partial privatization: The case of residences for the mentally retarded. *Mifgash, 22*, 9–31 [in Hebrew].

Doron, A. (1989). Privatization of social welfare services: A new area of conflict affecting the future of Israeli society. *Social Security, 24*: 18–34 [in Hebrew].

Ejsenstadt, M. (1996). Issues in the privatization of social services in Israel: Home care and correction and prevention of juvenile delinquency. J. Katan (Ed.), *Personal welfare services – trends and developments*. Joint publication. Jerusalem: The Center for the Study of Social Policy in Israel; Tel-Aviv: Tel-Aviv University, 189–210 [in Hebrew].

Freund, A. (2005). Work attitude of social workers across three sectors of welfare organizations: Public, for-profit and third sector. *Journal of Social Service Research, 31*(3), 69–92.

Gal, J. (1994). Privatization of services in the welfare state: The Israeli case. *Society & Welfare, 15*(1): 7–24 [in Hebrew].

Glennerster, H., & Le-Grand, J. (1994). *The development of quasi-markets in welfare provision*. London: London School of Economics.

Gotwein, D. (2006). Convicts and soccer players: Capital comes out of the closet. *Eretz Aheret 33*, 68–71 [in Hebrew].

Grindheim, J. E., & Selle, P. (1990). The role of voluntary social welfare organizations in Norway: A democratic alternative to a bureaucratic welfare state. *Voluntas, 1*(1), 62–76.

Iecovich, E., & Katan, J. (2005). Unique characteristics of voluntary organizations – do they exist in voluntary organizations providing welfare services to the elderly. *Social Security, 70*, 138–150 [in Hebrew].

Katan, J. (1996). The involvement of non-government organizations in personal welfare services. J. Katan (Ed.). *Personal welfare services – trends and developments* (pp. 137–160). Joint publication: Jerusalem: The Center for study of Social Policy in Israel. Tel Aviv: Tel Aviv University [in Hebrew].

Katan, J. (2001). Implementation of a privatization policy in the long-term care community services – preliminary conclusions. *Social Security, 60*, 129–155 [in Hebrew].

Katan, J. (2005). Privatization of welfare services in Tel-Aviv-Yafo: Principal features. D. Nahmias & G. Menahem (Eds.) Tel-Aviv-Yafo Studies, *Social trends and public policy* (pp. 75–96). Tel-Aviv: Dyonon [in Hebrew].

Katan, J. (2007). Partial privatization of personal welfare services. U. Aviram, J. Gal & J. Katan (Eds.). *Formulation of social policy in Israel: trends and issues.* (pp. 101–130) Jerusalem: The Taub Center for the Study of Social Services in Israel [in Hebrew].

Katan, J., & Lowenstein, A. (1999). Long-Term Care Insurance Law – ten years on: significance and implications. Jerusalem: The Center for the Study of Social Policy in Israel [in Hebrew].

Keinan, G., & Lachman, R. (1997). The relationship between type of ownership and functional emphasis in institutions for the mentally disadvantaged in Israel. *Megamot, 38*(3), 383–407 [in Hebrew].

Korazim, Y. (2001). *Committee report on the subject of the development of local associations for children at risk.* Jerusalem: Ministry of Labor and Welfare [in Hebrew].

Korazim-Korosy, Y., Leibovitz, S., & Schmid, H. (2005). The partial privatization of foster case services – issues and lessons after four years of implementation. *Social Security, 29*, 56–77 [in Hebrew].

Koresh, Y. (2003). Homes for the elderly owned by non-profit organizations and their desire to make profit. *Dorot, 68*, 17–19 [in Hebrew].

Kramer, R. (1994). Voluntary agencies and the contract culture: Dream or nightmare. *Social Services Review, 68*(1), 33–60.

Kramer, R. (1995) Nonprofits for hire: The welfare state in an age of contracting. *Voluntas, 6*, 105–112.

Kramer, R. (2000) A third sector in the third millennium. *Voluntas, 11*(1), 1–23.

Le-Grand, J. (1991). Quasi-markets and social policy in Britain. *Social Security, 37*, 32–45 [in Hebrew].

Levi, S. (2007). *Privatization of government residential institutions for the mentally challenged.* Jerusalem: Knesset, Research & Information Center [in Hebrew].

Luski, I., & Givon, J. (2005). *Efficiency and quality in nursing homes owned by non-profit organizations and business enterprises.* Jerualem: Taub Center for Social Policy Studies in Israel [in Hebrew].

Marsland, D. (1996). *Welfare or welfare state.* London: McMillan.

Milward, H. B., & Provan, K. G. (2003). Managing the hollow state. Collaboration and contracting. *Public Management Review, 5*(1), 1–18.

Peat, B., & Costley, D. L. (2001). Effective contracting of social services. *Nonprofit Management and Leadership, 12*(1), 55–74.

Ronen-Yipargan, K. (2006). Effect of union membership on professional ful-fillment, job satisfaction and organizational commitment of social workers in the sector of services to the elderly. Masters dissertation. Bob Shapell School of Social Work, Tel-Aviv University [in Hebrew].

Schmid, H. (2001). An assessment of the impact of the Long-Term Care Insurance Law on nonprofit and for-profit organizations providing home-care services. *Social Security, 60*, 90–112 [in Hebrew].

Schmid, H. (2002) Evaluating the impact of long-term care insurance law on non-profit organizations providing home-care services. *Social Security, 60,* 90–112 [in Hebrew].

Schmid, H. (2003). Rethinking the policy of contracting out social services to nongovernmental organization. *Public Management Review, 5*(3), 37–323.

Schmid, H., & Borowski, H. (2000) Selected issues in the delivery of home-care services to the elderly a decade after implementing Israel's Long-Term Care Insurance Law. *Social Security, 57,* 59–81 [in Hebrew].

Schmid, H., & Sabagh, K. (1990). *A study of the functioning of organizations providing home-care.* Jerusalem: The Paul Baerwald School of Social Work and Social Welfare, The Hebrew University and Myers-JDC-Brookdale Institute [in Hebrew].

Schmid, H., & Sabagh, K. (1991). *Efficiency and effectiveness of organizations providing home-care to the elderly.* Jerusalem: The Paul Baerwald School of So-cial Work and Social Welfare, The Hebrew University and Myers-JDC-Brookdale Institute [in Hebrew].

Sinai, R. (2008). Conditions in detention apartments: Ten youths to a room, spoiled food and warm water. *Haaretz,* 18 January, 2008 [in Hebrew].

State Comptroller Office (2005). *Annual Report No. 55-b.* Jerusalem: State Comptroller Office [in Hebrew].

Statham, D. (1996). *The future of social and personal care* (p. 43). London: National Institute for Social Work.

Taylor-Gooby, P. (1998). Markets and motives: Implications for welfare. *Journal of Social Policy, 28,* 97–114.

Werczberger, E., & Katan, J. (2005). *The effect of privatization upon personal social welfare services in local municipalities.* Tel-Aviv: Tel-Aviv University, The Pinhas Sapir Center for Development [in Hebrew].

Wistow, G., Knapp, M., Hardy, B., Forder, J. Kendall, J., & Manning, R. (1996). *Social care markets progress and prospects.* Buckingham: Open University Press.

Zichlinsky, E. (2007). Changes in Israeli third sector organizations and in their ability to produce social capital in light of processes of government involvement and commercialization (Doctoral dissertation). Ben-Gurion University, Beer-Sheba [in Hebrew].

Chapter 18
South Korea: Balancing Social Welfare in Post-industrial Society

Hyunsook Yoon

Introduction

Korean society is experiencing significant transformation as the country faces the challenges of global integration. The financial crisis of 1997 was a costly wake-up call, alarming in the astonishing extent of the interconnectedness of the global economy (Lee, 1999). It demonstrated that no country can pursue development without regarding intersocietal standards or the requirements of global capital (Gough, 2001). And, at the same time, its deleterious social consequences made a significant transformation in the welfare system in South Korea. While the Korean government faithfully followed the neoliberal suggestions, attached to the IMF's lending programs, it earnestly pursued an expansion and consolidation of social welfare programs as well. The crisis accelerated the process of transition from the precrisis 'developmental state' model to the 'democratic-welfare-capitalist state' (Lee, 2004) or 'to the inclusive developmental welfare state' (Kwon 2002; Kwon, 2007), in the context of the government's welfare reforms. These changes in themselves will shape social welfare in the country, as it traverses into the global century.

As general crisis in Korea deepened into an economic crisis of massive proportions, the high-growth orientation of Korea was dealt a large blow across a large number of sectors. Unemployment rates soared from 2.5 percent in 1997 to 8.6 percent in February 1999. The percentage of unemployed for six months or longer sharply increased from 7.8 percent in the first quarter of 1998 to 31.2 percent in the same period of 1999. Korea's Gini coefficient registered almost annual declines, slipping from 0.340 in 1986 to 0.282 in 1997. However, the onset of worldwide financial crisis saw Korea's Gini coefficient rising sharply to 0.316 in 1998 and 0.320 in 1999 – its highest point for more than a decade – before starting to decline again. At no point after the crisis did the Gini coefficient fall to levels recorded throughout the 1990–1997 period. Headcount poverty rates increased from 2.4 percent in the third quarter of 1997 to 7.8 percent in the same period of 1998. Rising unemployment and growing inequality and poverty were indeed a

H. Yoon (✉)
Department of Social Welfare, Hallym University, South Korea
e-mail: hyyoon@hallym.ac.kr

J. Powell, J. Hendricks, *The Welfare State in Post-Industrial Society*,
DOI 10.1007/978-1-4419-0066-1_18, © Springer Science+Business Media, LLC 2009

catastrophe throughout the Korean society. The ramifications of the financial turmoil eddied throughout the Korean society but settled no place more harshly than it did among lower income and elderly citizens.

For the first time in Korean history, welfare reforms came to be appreciated as an institutional means to keep the democracy and market economy sustainable. By incorporating welfare policies as an integral part of governance, the Korean government made clear its departure from the earlier precrisis 'development state' model, in which the authoritarian government was the single most significant actor, with a clear aim of promoting rapid economic growth for which it mobilizes resources and protects domestic firms from foreign competition. More importantly, in resolving social welfare questions, the government has come to rely heavily upon sustainable economic growth and the availability of family resources, not on the formal social safety net (Lee, 2004). The welfare reforms in Korea have strengthened state institutions and the welfare state in particular amid instability and flexibility in the global market (Kwon, 2007). In many respects South Korea has led the way in integrating policies supportive of economic growth and social welfare, recognizing that there is a significant overlap between what transpires in the two spheres (Peng, 2004; Song, 2003).

This chapter examines welfare reforms in Korea after the financial crisis of 1997 and explores the status of current welfare systems, including social assistance and social insurance programs (employment insurance, pension system, and health insurance). In the process, it discusses the difficult challenges facing Korea as it attempts to balance between social protection and economic growth in a burgeoning global marketplace. While new vulnerabilities have emerged from Korea's participation in global markets, Korea has also formulated a number of policies intended to promote social solidarity through state investments.

Social Assistance Program

The National Basic Livelihood Security (NBLS) system is often referred to as representative of the welfare reforms after the financial crisis of 1997. It clearly extends the social rights of the poor and constitutes the most distinctive change in South Korea's entire reform package. Regardless of reasons for being poor, those who were poor and could not maintain a minimal living standard, as defined by the Ministry of Health and Welfare each year, were able to resort to the NBLS as the last safety net for all. For this system, the calculation of the official poverty line and the delivery structure of public welfare, which qualified social workers for administered means testing and overseeing the provision of benefits, were institutionalized. The NBLS also stipulated a conditional provision of benefit for those who were poor but capable of work. They were required to participate in the Self-Reliance Support Programs, which were intended to help beneficiaries get out of poverty and to prevent unnecessary dependency of the employable poor on social assistance.

While the NBLS has been improved, there remain several concerns more than a decade later. First, in addition to an income test, eligibility depends on asset and family criteria. Combined income and assets must be less than the minimum cost of living, and only those needy persons without relatives capable of supporting them are eligible for assistance. According to one estimate, only about half of the persons with income below the minimum cost receive assistance. Second, the lack of transparency about income of the self-employed may divert benefits to those who are not eligible. Korea is a country where not all wages are recorded and cash income is common. Third, the NBLS itself discourages work once eligibility is determined, as there is no earning disregard.

In most OECD countries, social spending and tax systems significantly reduce relative poverty, defined as an income of less than half of the national median. Indeed, social spending and taxes reduced the poverty rate by more than half, from an average of 18.2 to 8.4 percent in the OECD area in 2000. Yet, the combined effect of government spending and tax measures have only a modest impact on the level of poverty in Korea, compared to other OECD countries, reflecting the still low level of social spending in Korea. However, the effectiveness of social spending on reducing poverty also depends on its composition and targeting of that spending. Part of the explanation is that, in Korea, 74 percent of public social outlay is spent on health and pensions and is thus concentrated on the elderly. In contrast, only 10 percent is spent on the working-age population, considerably below the OECD average of 17 percent. In particular, family benefits amount to only 0.1 percent of the GDP in Korea compared to an OECD average of 2.2 percent (Jones, 2008).

The limited impact of social assistance on relative poverty, which has risen since the 1997 crisis, is a concern. Indeed, the rate of relative poverty increased from 8.7 percent in the mid-1990s to 13 percent in 2000 – from below the OECD average to considerably above it. Furthermore, the upward trend continued, though at a slower pace, to 15.5 percent in 2003. As in other OECD countries, population ageing and changes in household structure – more single-person and female-headed households – have played a role in boosting poverty. However, increased poverty among families headed by a couple accounted for most of the rise in poverty, suggesting that higher income inequality was the key factor (Jones, 2008).

In 2008 the government is on the verge of introducing an Earned Income Tax Credit (EITC) to address rising income inequality through strengthening work incentives. The program will be introduced on a limited scale to salaried workers with two or more children, who do not own a home and have limited levels of assets. However, the problem of accurately determining the income of the self-employed makes the EITC inappropriate for the entire population. Despite the problems looming on the horizon, the EITC is a step in the right direction and one that recognizes individual autonomy in the process.

Employment Insurance System

As the unemployment rate soared, the government entered into a series of commitments to expand eligibility and coverage of the Employment Insurance System, which was initially introduced in 1995. Its coverage was expanded first to firms with five or more employees, later to those with one or more employees, and included provisions for mandatory contributions to training and wage subsidy schemes. This expansion increased the number of workplaces covered more than 17 fold, from 47,400 in 1997 to 800,000 in 2001. The same expansion of coverage was made with the Workmen's Compensation Insurance. In 2000, its mandatory coverage expanded to firms with fewer than five employees. Thus, the number of workers covered by the Workmen's Compensation Insurance increased from 8,237,000 in 1997 to 10,581,000 in 2001. Despite these expansions of coverage of social insurance for the employees, the majority of irregular workers are excluded, and, as of 2001, only 16.6 percent of the unemployed were receiving unemployment benefits (Hwang, 2003).

As Korea undergoes a rapid economic transformation reflecting its growing role on the world economic stage, the share of temporary workers is also increasing, from 16.6 percent in 2001 to 29.4 percent in 2005, the second highest in the OECD nations. Workers on fixed-term contracts of one year or less account for more than half of all temporary workers. Not surprisingly, there is a large wage gap: nonregular workers earned 62 percent as much as regular workers in 2005. A second factor explaining the upward trend in inequality is the increasing wage gap between large and small firms. The widening gap is also due in part to greater use of nonregular workers in smaller firms. In 2005, nonregular workers accounted for 54 percent of employees in small firms compared to 18 percent in large firms. Moreover, the wage gap is larger: nonregular workers in small firms earn only half as much as regular workers, while those in large firms earn two-thirds (Jones, 2008). Clearly, Korea will have to grapple with these emerging inequalities in the coming decades as their impact reaches well beyond mere income differentials to such areas as personal identity and the citizenship rights.

In addition to lower wages, nonregular workers also receive fewer benefits. The specter of ill-health and the inaccessibility of health care preoccupy many lower wage and nonregular workers during their working lives and certainly beyond. While 73 percent of regular workers receive a retirement allowance, overtime payments, regular bonuses, and paid holiday leave, alarmingly three-quarters of nonregular workers receive none of these benefits. Labor costs are further exacerbated by differences in social insurance coverage. More than four-fifths of regular workers are covered by all social insurance programs, while two-thirds of nonregular workers have no work-based social insurance. The low coverage of nonregular workers is not primarily due to differences mandated by the law, but instead reflects weak compliance and lack of enforcement (Ahn, 2006; Jones, 2008) (Table 18.1).

Table 18.1 Population indicators and projections for Korea[1]

	Population (in millions)	Growth rate (Percent)[2]	Fertility rate[3]	Life expectancy (in years)	Median age (in years)	Share of elderly[4](Per cent)
1960	25.0	2.3	6.0	55.3	19.9	2.9
1970	31.5	1.8	4.5	63.2	19.0	3.1
1980	37.4	1.5	2.7	65.8	22.2	3.8
1990	43.4	0.6	1.6	71.3	27.0	5.1
2000	46.1	0.6	1.5	75.9	31.8	7.3
2010	49.2	0.1	1.2	79.1	37.9	10.9
2020	50.0	-0.1	1.2	81.0	43.7	15.7
2030	49.3	-0.5	1.3	81.9	49.0	24.1
2040	46.7	-1.0	1.3	82.6	53.1	32.0
2050	42.3	–	1.3	83.3	56.2	37.3

[1] Projections by the Korea National Statistical Office for the period 2005–2050.
[2] The annual average growth rate for the decade. The figure in 1960, for example, shows the rate for the decade 1960–1970.
[3] The average number of children that a woman can expect to bear during her lifetime.
[4] The number of persons over the age of 65 as a percentage of the total population.
Source: Korea National Statistical Office.

It is important to improve the effective coverage of the Employment Insurance System (EIS) to reduce the differential in labor costs between regular and non-regular workers. In 2005, only 27 percent of unemployed persons received unemployment benefits, due in part to strict conditions to qualify for benefits as well as their relatively short duration. However, it was also because of the limited coverage of the EIS. Although nearly 80 percent of employees are eligible for the EIS, only 57 percent are actually insured, reflecting the difficulty of ensuring compliance. Increasing the effective coverage is complicated by the frequent turnover of nonregular employees and the large number of small firms. Indeed, 3 million of Korea's 3.2 million firms in 2005 had less than 10 employees. The recent initiatives of the National Tax Service to require firms to report the payroll of temporarily employed workers and contingent employees may be helpful in improving compliance. In addition, the collection of the four social insurance contributions (pension, health, employment, and industrial accident) will be consolidated in a single agency in 2009 (Jones, 2008).

Pension System

The National Pension System (NPS) expanded the population coverage to urban self-employed, to firms with fewer than five employees, temporary workers, and daily workers in 1999. Nine million individuals were added to bring the total to 16 million wage earners brought under the umbrella of universal coverage of pension insurance a reality by 2001. As the income of the self-employed is notoriously underreported in Korea, both public and expert opinions were against an integrated fund system as long as the pension scheme was structured with income-related contributions and vertically redistributive benefit formula. In the face of that opposition, the Korean government chose the integrated redistributive pension model, maintaining the solidarity principle, presumably addressing issues of equity and attempting to avoid any erosion of the rights of its citizens.

Despite efforts to ensure equity, the relative poverty rate – based on an income threshold of 40 percent of the national median – for households that include elderly persons has risen from 27 percent in 1991 to 38.8 percent in 2000, nearly five times higher than the 8.1 percent national average. In contrast, the average relative poverty rate for the elderly in the OECD countries, at 13 percent in 2000, was not far above the average of 10 percent for the total population of those countries. Since the advent of rapid industrialization and Korea's entry to the world stage as an economic power, there has been a weakening of the tradition of three-generation households in Korea. In 2005, elderly persons living alone or with a spouse accounted for 55 percent of households with an elderly person. In contrast, the share of elderly persons living with one of their children was only 39 percent. Still, three-quarters of the elderly receive financial support from their children, while one quarter earns income from their own and/or their spouse's employment. Pension still plays a minor role: only 14 percent of the elderly receive public pension, reflecting the relatively recent introduction of the NPS. In addition, 9 percent receive social assistance (Moon, 2006; Jones, 2008).

The maturation of the NPS in the coming decades will increase the income of the elderly. However, the number of contributors to the NPS leveled off at around a third of the working-age population in 2000. The proportion was significantly higher for men, at half of the male working-age population, compared to only a quarter for women. Adding the occupational pension schemes for the civil servants, military personnel, and private school teachers boosts the proportion of contributions to almost 40 percent of the working-age population. However, it remains low compared to the OECD average of 63.4 percent. The low level of coverage in Korea reflects the large number of self-employed persons and nonregular workers. The long-term projections of the NPS assume that less than half of the elderly will receive NPS pensions in 2030, suggesting that it does not expect a significant expansion in coverage. As the forces of industrialism make further inroads into Korea, the numbers of small firms and self-employed workers will continue to decline, so it is still possible that pension rates will improve as more workers are included in the ranks of regular works in big-sized firms . In the meanwhile, of course, lower incomes among older Koreans will remain problematic for the individuals living in poverty as well as the country as a whole. The relationship between work and welfare is painting in bold relief in Korea.

In addition to the low level of coverage, there is a risk that pension benefits will be relatively small. In its long-term projections, the NPS assumes that the average period of contributions of beneficiaries in 2030 will be 17.6 years and will increase only gradually to 20.7 years by 2050. With an annual accrual rate of 1.5 percent, the replacement rate for a worker, in 2030, who had earned an average income and had 40 years of contributions, would be 26 percent of their working life wages, less than half of the targeted replacement rate of 60 percent. Unfortunately, such an income is close to the minimum cost of living, which is set at 20 percent of the average wage. Moreover, there is likely to be a significant variation among beneficiaries, in particular between salaried workers and self-employed, in their periods and levels of contributions. In sum, the low level of coverage, short average contribution period, and small payments by those who are self-employed raise the risk that the NPS will not be adequate to reduce the rate of poverty among older persons. Despite its intent, Korea will have to grapple with a real erosion of the standard of living for its elderly population in the decades immediately ahead. Coupled with shifts in living arrangements and with other changes sweeping across the landscape, Korean elderly may face dire circumstances as they attempt to maintain their sense of identity and their viability.

Given the difficulty of substantially extending the coverage of the NPS, the Korean government recently introduced a means-tested universal pension, although at 5 percent of the average wage, it is well below the minimum cost of living, which, as noted above, is 20 percent of the average wage. Expanding the benefit to the minimum cost of living to prevent absolute poverty and extending its coverage to all persons over the age of 65 is estimated to boost its cost from 1.1 percent of the GDP in 2050 to around 6.8 percent. The OECD suggests that the Korean authorities have a choice between the current approach, which will provide a substantial public pension benefit to nearly half of the population, and systemic reform to create a two-part national system that includes a universal pension. There are advantages to each of these options. The current approach has the positive feature of requiring savings by the current working population in preparation for retirement, thus promoting intergenerational equity. The advantage of the two-part national pension is that it will prevent absolute poverty among the elderly. In terms of financing, the two-part system will rely more on tax revenue and less on social security contributions (Moon, 2006; Jones, 2008).

Health Insurance System

The National Health Insurance (NHI) system underwent dramatic changes after the financial crisis of the late 1990s. Before reform, the system was composed of about 420 health insurance societies with different contribution rates and independently managed funds for different workplaces and geographical areas. These societies were incorporated into a single health insurance plan operated by the public sector, which controls the administrative organizations of health insurance and hundreds of funds previously managed by financially independent agencies. A unified contribution standard across the nation was introduced, thereby increasing the equity of health insurance contributions. The 2000 Integration Reform combined the insurance societies into a single insurer and set a uniform contribution rate for all employees, thus improving equity. The reform also increased efficiency in management; administrative costs fell from 6.4 percent of the total expenditure in 2000 to 3.7 percent in 2004. In addition, the reform gave market power to the NHI as the sole purchaser of healthcare services. Without the consolidation of the many disparate plans into a comprehensive public-sector plan, the disparities in access to health care will be far greater than that of today. Of course, without further reform, the prospect of yet greater vulnerability among ageing Koreans is likely to become an even more pressing issue.

Clearly, the merger of social health insurance societies under NHI reforms has had little more than a limited impact on health coverage. Crucially, the merger has not fundamentally changed the benefit package previously offered by multiple insurance societies. This was characterized by low benefit coverage, with high out-of-pocket payment, problems of income assessment, notably for the self-employed, and still different contribution schedules for the self-employed and employees. The NHI and other public welfare programs find themselves competing with any number of other governmental priorities and even merger benefits are far from assured. To date, private sector health or social welfare organizations have made few inroads into Korea despite a strong trend toward privatization in other OCED countries and around the world.

The NHI achieved universal coverage in 1989, only 12 years after its introduction, providing coverage for 41 percent of the total health expenditure. The NHI is funded by employers, employees, and the self-employed, with the government paying about half of the premium for the latter group. The key private sector funding source for health care is out-of-pocket payments by patients, accounting for 37 percent of the total outlay. The high share, which includes co-payments on services covered by the NHI and full payment for services not covered, reflects the government's objective of achieving universal coverage of the NHI at low contribution rates, by keeping benefits low and excluding some diseases and diagnostic procedures. The co-payment rate is 20 percent for hospital care and 30–50 percent for outpatient care. Consequently, the NHI provides relatively comprehensive but shallow protection in case of illness. The system may also pose barriers to access for the poor since co-payments are unrelated to income and the cap on total co-payments is rather high (Jones, 2008).

Despite the shortfalls, public spending on healthcare, on a per capita basis, has expanded at a 10.1 percent annual rate (adjusted for inflation) since 1981, well above the OECD average of 3.6 percent. A cross-country analysis by the OECD projects that public spending on healthcare will rise by between 3 and 5 percentage points of the GDP in Korea over the period till 2050, the largest increase among member countries. First, given the tendency for medical expenses to increase with age, rapid population ageing in Korea is projected to raise public healthcare outlays by 1.6 percent of the GDP, double the 0.7 percent expected in the OECD. The elderly in Korea accounted for 23 percent of the total health expenditure in 2004, well above their 9 percent share of the population. Consequently, healthcare expenditure per capita was three times higher for those above 65 than for those below it. Second, relatively rapid growth in income, as living standard in Korea converges to the OECD average, will tend to push up the share of national income devoted to health care. Under this assumption, the level of health care spending in Korea in 2050 – at 6–8 percent of the GDP – would be comparable to the current level in some OECD countries, including Japan (Jones, 2008).

It is important to ensure that out-of-pocket payments do not limit access to health care. While out-of-pocket payments are useful in discouraging frivolous demands and in limiting costs, they may restrict access to care in the case of catastrophic or chronic illness and for those unable to afford even modest co-payments on services by the NHI. Given that the share of healthcare spending borne by the private sector is already high, there is little scope for controlling public outlay by shifting more of the burden to the private sector. Instead of increasing public health care financing, the OECD suggests several reforms to make the burden on employed persons somewhat less onerous. First, elderly persons, who are currently exempted from contributions to the NHI if they have working children, should be required to contribute. Given the maturation of the public pension system, elderly persons will be in a better financial position to shoulder more of the burden. Second, as with the NPS, it is essential to more accurately assess the income of the self-employed and reduce underreporting to achieve an equitable sharing of the financial burden among the labor force. The government currently pays about half of the contributions for the self-employed, resulting in transfers from low-income employees to high-income self-employed persons. In sum, it is important to ensure the fiscal sustainability of the NHI while trying to provide an appropriate level of healthcare services (Jones, 2008).

Challenges for Welfare System in Future

Although the Korean government put in place the structural foundations of a social welfare system, particularly of social insurance and public assistance in the economically difficult years after the financial crisis, the gross public social spending in Korea remained the lowest in the OECD at 6 percent of the GDP in 2003, well below the OECD average of 21 percent. As mentioned above, there is no shortage of priorities facing the national government, and perhaps the relatively low levels of public spending reflect the pressure of competing priorities.

The low level of spending is explained by a number of factors. First, the outlay on pensions, at only 1 percent of the GDP, is well below the OECD average, reflecting Korea's relatively young population and the immature pension system. The small proportion of elderly, combined with a per capita income level that is well below the OECD average, also limits public healthcare and long-term care expenditure. Second, a low unemployment rate, averaging less than 4 percent of the labor force since 2000, and the low incidence of long-term joblessness have limited spending on unemployment benefits and active labor market policies. Third, social welfare has traditionally been the responsibility of families, companies and nongovernmental institutions, and approach that appeared to support rapid economic growth (Jones, 2008; Shin & Shaw, 2003). Taken in combination, these factors reflect the confluence of issues that are part and parcel of industrialism that has altered the face of Korea in just a few decades.

Even so, three important factors will boost public social spending in the near future. First, population ageing in Korea is projected to be the most rapid in the OECD area between 2000 and 2050, increasing public expenditure on pensions, health care, and long-term nursing care. Increasing life expectancy and falling fertility are driving population ageing. Life expectancy increased 21 years, from 55 years in 1960 to 76 years in 2000, the largest in the OECD catchment area. During the same period, the fertility rate fell from six children in 1960 to below the replacement level in 1983 and further to 1.5 in 2000, 1.08 in 2005, reflecting long-term trends, such as rising labor force participation of women and changing social values. The median age of the Korean population, which was 20 years in 1960, reached 32 in 2000 and is likely to be nearly 50 in 2030, suggesting fundamental changes in the country's socioeconomic structure. Moreover, the share of Korea's total population over the age of 65 is expected to double from 7 percent in 2000 to 14 percent by 2018. In contrast, this transition is projected to take 71 years in the United States and took 115 years in France. The further increase in the share of the elderly from 14 to 20 percent in Korea is exceptionally rapid, at only eight years, compared with up to 30 years in major European countries (Table 18.2).

The second is the marked increase in income inequality and precarious employment patterns since the financial crisis. The ratio of decline in the top to bottom income has risen from 7.4 percent in 1990 to 9.3 percent in 2004. The decline in inequality recorded during the rapid growth in the fist half of the 1990s was reversed by the 1997 crisis and the severe recession in 1998. Since then, measures of inequality have fluctuated around the higher level, falling during the years of strong growth (2000–2002) and rising following the collapse of the household credit bubble and relatively weak growth since then. The Gini coefficient on a nationwide basis was 35.1 in 2006, the sixth highest in the OECD area and 13 percent above the OECD average. Nonregular employment is characterized by unstable jobs that pay low wages and provide limited coverage within the social safety net. The social polarization resulting from the increasing proportion of nonregular employees thus has negative implications for equity. In many respects, there has been an erosion of citizenship among the more needy sections of the Korean population and, of course, that also portends significant personal issues and challenges to the sense of well-being (Table 18.3).

Table 18.2 Indicators of income inequality in Korea (For urban salary and wage-earner households[1])

	Gini coefficient[2]	Quintile ratio[3]	Decile ratio[4]
1990	29.5	4.6	7.4
1991	28.7	4.5	7.0
1992	28.4	4.4	7.0
1993	28.1	4.4	6.8
1994	28.4	4.4	6.9
1995	28.4	4.4	6.8
1996	29.1	4.6	7.2
1997	28.3	4.5	7.0
1998	31.6	5.4	9.4
1999	32.0	5.5	9.3
2000	31.7	5.3	8.8
2001	31.9	5.4	8.8
2002	31.2	5.2	8.3
2003	30.6 (34.1)	5.2 (7.2)	8.9 (15.5)
2004	31.0 (34.4)	5.4 (7.4)	9.3 (15.7)
2005	31.0 (34.8)	5.4 (7.6)	9.1 (15.9)
2006	31.0 (35.1)	5.4 (7.6)	9.1 (15.9)

[1] Nation-wide data, available 2003, is shown in parentheses.
[2] The Gini coefficient is defined as the area between the Lorenz curve (which plots cumulative shares of the population, from richest to poorest, against the cumulative share of income that they receive) and the 45-degree line, taken as a ratio of the whole triangle. The values, which range from 0 in the case of perfect equality and 1 in the case of perfect inequality, are multiplied by 100 to give a range of 0–100.
[3] The ratio of the top quintile to the bottom quintile.
[4] The ratio of the top decile to the bottom decile.
Source: Korea National Statistical Office.

Table 18.3 The coverage of social insurance and benefits by type of employment

	Regular employees	Non-regular employees[1]
Benefits[2]		
All	73.0	9.5
Some	25.9	16.3
Nothing	1.1	74.2
Social insurance[3]		
All	81.2	29.4
Some	17.4	5.3
Nothing	1.4	65.3

[1] In the paper by Ahn, non-regular workers includes temporary and daily workers, as well as "non-standard workers". The latter category includes workers on fixed-term and part-time contracts, as well as alternative employment (dispatched workers, temporary agency workers, independent contractors, on-call workers and home-based workers).
[2] Includes the retirement allowance, over-time payments, regular bonuses and paid-holiday leave.
[3] Includes the National Pension Scheme, National Health Insurance and the Employment Insurance System.
Source: Ahn (2006).

Third, in the area of social services and social care, there has been little improvement compared to those of public assistance, pension, health care, and unemployment. Caring for chronically ill people, the bedridden elderly, and the disabled fell mostly to families, which in turn, meant women were most burdened by the requirements of care. The absence of improvement in social services and social care creates pressure for larger social outlays. For example, a National Long-Term Care Insurance system for the elderly was introduced in July 2008. Beneficiaries, who are chosen by the Health Insurance Corporation from among the elderly suffering from geriatric diseases, can receive public care at home or in institutions, or cash benefits to pay for private care. The challenge is to provide wider and more equitable access to long-term care services within the constraints of fiscal sustainability. The number of beneficiaries is initially limited to 80,000 (1.7 percent of the elderly population). However, 350,000 elderly persons (8.3 percent of the elderly) were already suffering from dementia in 2005. The number of beneficiaries is expected to double by 2010.

Korea now confronts difficult challenges in balancing social protection and economic growth (Cook & Kwon, 2007). The classic distinction between public good and growth in the for-profit sector is readily apparent as one looks across the options available within each sector. The experience of some OECD countries that are now trying to scale down public social spending in an attempt to promote efficiency and growth underlines the need to carefully design public social programs to achieve their intended objectives, while avoiding or limiting wasteful spending and negative externalities. Cross-country research by the OECD suggests that increasing the social protection spending accompanied by higher taxes can reduce growth, indicating a tradeoff between efficiency and social spending. As Korean cultural traditions and customs confront the burgeoning market economy that has brought so many positive changes, new uncertainties are being created.

References

Ahn, J. (2006). *Nonstandard work in Korea – the origin of wage differentials.* Seoul: Mimeo, Korea Labor Institute.

Cook, S., & Kwon, H. J. (2007). Social protection in East Asia. *Global Social Policy, 7*(2), 223–229.

Gough, I. (2001). Globalization and regional welfare regimes: The East Asian case. *Global Social Policy, 1*(2), 163–189.

Hwang, D. S. (2003). The coverage of employment insurance and national pension: The causes of the gap between the law and the actual coverage and policy alternatives. *Journal of Labor Policy (Korea Labor Institute), 3,* 87–109 [in Korean].

Jones, R. S. (2008). Public social spending in Korea in the context of rapid population ageing. OECD Economics Department Networking Papers No. 615.

Kwon, H. J. (2002). Welfare reform and future challenges in the Republic of Korea: Beyond the developmental welfare state? *International Social Security Review, 55,* 23–38.

Kwon, H. J. (2007). Transforming the developmental welfare states in East Asia. DESA Working Paper No. 40.

Lee, H. K. (1999). Neo-liberalism, social exclusion and welfare clients in a global economy. *International Journal of Social Welfare, 8*(1), 23–37.

Lee, H. K. (2004). Welfare reforms in post-crisis Korea: Dilemmas and choices. *Social Policy & Society, 3*(3), 291–299.

Moon, H. (2006). *Population Aging and Sustainability of the National Pension System.* Mimeo, Seoul: Korea Development Institute.

Peng, I. (2004). Postindustrial pressures, political regime shifts, and social policy reform in Japan and South Korea. *Journal of East Asian Studies, 4,* 389–425.

Shin, C. S., & Shaw, I. (2003). Social policy in South Korea: Cultural and structural factors in the emergence of welfare. *Social Policy & Administration, 37*(4), 328–341.

Song, H. K. (2003). The birth of a welfare state in Korea: The unfinished symphony of democratization and globalization. *Journal of East Asian Studies, 3,* 405–432.

Index

Lightning Source UK Ltd.
Milton Keynes UK
14 August 2009

142701UK00002B/17/P